A GOOD COUNTRY

A GOOD COUNTRY

MY LIFE IN TWELVE TOWNS
AND THE DEVASTATING BATTLE
FOR A WHITE AMERICA

SOFIA ALI-KHAN

RANDOM HOUSE
NEW YORK

Page ii photo credits from L to R: row 1: Adobe Stock/AardLumens, Adobe Stock/Branden, Adobe Stock/Wollwerth Imagery; row 2: Adobe Stock/marchello74, istock/stacey_newman; row 3: Adobe Stock/Luc Novovitch/Danita Delimont, Adobe Stock/SeanPavonePhoto; row 4: Adobe Stock/Vadim, Adobe Stock/Andriy Blokhin; row 5: Adobe Stock/Jin, Adobe Stock/SeanPavonePhoto, Adobe Stock/pixs:sell

Hardback ISBN 978-0-593-23703-8
Ebook ISBN 978-0-593-23704-5

Printed in Canada on acid-free paper

randomhousebooks.com

9 8 7 6 5 4 3 2 1

First Edition

For the loves of my life

Nadeem, Jahan, Isa

In the name of God,
Most Compassionate, Most Merciful

CONTENTS

PROLOGUE: AMERICAN

History is not the past; it is the present.

—Viola Davis

I used to imagine myself enormous, stretched into the sky, one foot planted in suburban Pennsylvania and another planted in the low cityscape of Hyderabad, Pakistan, somewhere between my grandmothers' houses. From on high, I could see both places in their entirety, and know them intimately. I could belong in both places without being constrained by either one; neither my sun-blackened knees nor my American accent would draw attention. Other times, I imagined ways to reverse the migration of my parents to America, thinking I could somehow fold myself back into the language and the culture in which I was named and from which my family came.

I was born in Tampa, Florida, and grew up speaking to my parents in English so that they could practice theirs. As a child, I was always navigating between a once-removed Pakistani identity and an America ostensibly built of many cultures in one. Much of my family still lived in Hyderabad, Pakistan, a city in the lower Indus Valley. So that's where we went every couple of summers while our neighbors and friends went to the Jersey Shore and Delaware beaches. My earliest memories are cut with passages beginning and ending with twenty-hour plane rides to the separate reality of my paternal grandparents' home. They lived, together with one of my aunts and one of my uncles and his wife and son, in a crumbling red clay house. It had three sheltered rooms, a tiny kitchen with a row of three simple metal grates used to hold small fuel canisters, like camp stoves lined up on the floor, and a spacious courtyard where we all slept on jute cots. In the evenings, when the intense heat abated, my older brother and I would put out our hands, circling around to my father and his several siblings gathered in the courtyard to visit. We were mimicking the beggars who trailed us, speaking in Sindhi, whenever we stepped into the street, "Aay, Allah, mukhay peysa day." Oh, dear God, give me some change.

I wanted to know why the children we saw on the streets often had missing limbs. When I was told that children were purposefully disfigured by adults, who then forced them to beg and then stole the proceeds, that knowledge was too brutal for me to fully integrate. So I carefully buried it in my young imagination, where it would drive my commitments and all of the work I would choose to do as an adult.

I could not yet see that the middle class to which our extended family in Pakistan belonged was small and precarious, not to be taken for granted. And the beggars, for their part, saw only that we were something other than themselves: people who ate regularly and wore clean clothes. Never mind that we were children without money of our own. Their hands reached out as much for the wealth we represented as for actual cash.

We took it all in, as children do. Neighborhood children in rags, a full tier of wealth above the beggars, squatted over open gutters to relieve themselves. Currency of coins light as paper, made of tin, and of no value at all compared to our dollars. Food heavily spiced or pickled to keep without refrigeration. Electricity that came and went throughout the day, powering small industrial steel ceiling fans in each room and bare fluorescent bulbs on the walls. One of my uncles, with his wife and eight children, lived in the smaller house next door, which shared a wall with my grandparents' home, so there was always a tribe of cousins nearby. There was no television, but we played endless card games and had piles of books from the free library back home. There were goats tied up outside in the alley and occasional chickens in the courtyard, which my cousins sometimes corralled to make room for a game of cricket. Rickety wooden ladders leaned against the courtyard wall so we could move between houses without stepping into the street and one auntie could pass a pot of milk or a plate of rice to another over it.

My father was the second son of his parents' thirteen children, born in 1942, five years before the British relinquished colonial domination of the Indian subcontinent and it split violently into India and Pakistan. (East Pakistan would win independence and become Bangladesh in 1971.) Hyderabad and nearby Karachi were all my father had known when he arrived in British Columbia in August of 1963 with a spare suit and some toiletries as a scholarship student. His ideas about Canadian culture were based entirely on old *Reader's Digest* magazines. One of two Pakistani graduate students enrolled at the university at the time, he arrived at the start of what would come to be known as the "brain drain." Over the next several decades, tens of thousands of Asian students just like him would be recruited to science and mathematics graduate programs in Canada.

Later, after he became a doctoral student at the University of Toronto, my father sent a pale blue aerogram home, asking that his parents arrange and plan his wedding to a woman of their choosing. He had bucked tradition in leaving home for school, but he intended to marry as his family had always done. Besides, he would likely know, or know of, whomever they chose. My family has inhabited Hyderabad for as long as anyone remembers, and the web of extended family and friends stretches far.

It would take at least a month for his message to arrive. He planned to travel home for two weeks at Christmas for the first time in five years in order to marry his bride and take her back with him to Toronto. When he applied for graduate student housing, the registrar, no doubt a Canadian of European descent and unfamiliar with how much of the rest of the world still got married, asked that my dad write his fiancée's name on the requisite form. Without knowing who his bride would be, and for no particular reason, he wrote the name Shahnaz.

When he arrived in Hyderabad a couple of months later, he expected to walk in a procession the very next day to the home of the woman his parents had chosen, where he would formally become engaged. No surprise, Shahnaz was not the young woman's name, and he wasn't sure how he'd square that with the registrar. Before he could give it much thought, a messenger arrived early in the day to cancel the procession. A rumor had spread that my dad was already married in Canada. Because the young woman's family could neither confirm nor disprove it, they had decided to call the whole thing off.

My grandparents arranged to visit the family of the second young woman on their list—she had a sister who was the wife of my uncle's classmate. She was nineteen and, having completed twelfth grade, had years more education than many in her generation. The second young woman's family had more reason to trust in my father, as her sister's husband could vouch for his situation in Canada.

The next day, my father would visit his brother's classmate and he would be able to see the potential bride, who would be asked to help her sister serve the midday meal. When she entered the room, she would not have met the men's gazes. Instead, looking down, she noticed my father's unfashionably wide pant legs, ascribing a comforting humility to this man from overseas. Later the same day, a cousin was dispatched to find her, calling her by an honorific meaning "elder sister": "Baji, you're going to be married!"

By some miracle, the second young woman's name was—is—Shahnaz, and she would be my mother. Within two weeks, she would travel to Toronto with my father, the first unrelated man with whom she had ever spent time alone. When they landed, my mother had two suitcases full of items that were fitting for a bride in southern Pakistan but fairly useless in the snow and ice of a Toronto winter. She had left behind so many of the things that made up her life to that point: her seven sisters and brothers; her father, a Sufi and dairy farmer; and her mother, who read the news in three languages each day but had little formal education. The suitcases held no novels written in Urdu, no strong black tea brewed with fresh buffalo milk, no kites for battles in the winter sky, no monsoon rains that steam off the pavement and rooftops.

Both of my parents describe those early years as a kind of bittersweet cloister. My mom, especially, describes the loneliness of being apart from her seven siblings and of realizing finally that no one would write back to her after she had sent swarms of aerograms. Their reticence was not for lack of love; none of them had experienced life outside of a settled extended family and community rich with connections and obligations and purpose. They had no way of understanding how isolated my mother was in her new life, separated from their world and also from the new world in which she had landed.

Until 1972, my parents had every intention of returning to Pakistan, out of loyalty and connection to family and country, as well as an abiding homesickness. My dad was offered a professorship at his alma mater, Sindh University, and he returned with my mother and my older brother, then a baby, to consider the position. But he arrived on campus to find that his mentor had been chased away and brutally beaten in sectarian violence that had become commonplace. Political parties that functioned like gangs had emerged in the gaps left by British occupation and partition. In a time when Pakistan desperately needed skilled and committed public servants, accomplished students and the children of privilege left in droves for countries that could offer more education and more stability. A military presence had become visible on the streets, corruption was rampant, and professors' salaries were generally supplemented by bribes for grades. In the postcolonial political landscape of Pakistan, power had vested among the northern elite, and ethnic Sindhis like my parents were increasingly shut out of opportunities for political power and professional advancement. This was not the future my parents imagined for themselves; they had been given, after all, the opportunity to raise their family in "a good country."

So my parents decided, against their parents' wishes and their own yearning, to make a life in North America even though they were outsiders there. Their skin color and accent, clothes, and culture made them targets of racism. When they had searched for a place to live that first winter while waiting for a dormitory room to become available, White landlords shook their heads in the doorways of run-down rooming houses and said, "Sorry, just let my last room." Curtains were pulled closed and For Rent signs turned over in the window as my parents made their way up the walks. They eventually found a Yugoslavian Muslim with a single room he was willing to rent them. My father's education and his talent in his field meant that he was given a measure of respect and status at the university, so he believed he could build a professional identity that would allow him, eventually, to live the dream of a middle-class Western life.

My dad took the first job he was offered, in Florida. The weather felt like home, with steamy afternoon rains, but my parents were lonely. No one looked like they did or talked like they did. There was no Muslim Students' Association to smooth their transition. They would stop in telephone booths to scan the white pages for common South Asian names, desperate to speak to someone in Urdu or Hindi. After I was born in November of 1974, they bought a one-story house on an island off St. Petersburg. But only days later, the small company for which my father worked collapsed and he was laid off without any notice. There were few other jobs for chemical engineers in that part of the country. My parents scrambled to sell the house they had just bought; they had enough money to survive for a single month. In that time, my father landed one job offer in Chicago, where they lived for several months in a cramped apartment in the distant suburbs, two mattresses their only furniture. But my father had his eye on the Northeast, where there were enough potential employers to settle and plan to stay. Within the year, he had moved us to an apartment in

Levittown, Pennsylvania, and taken a job at Rohm & Haas, where he invented and engineered plastics. My mother looked after my older brother and me while babysitting other children in the apartment block, and together they saved for a home.

That's how we ended up in a 1977 split-level house with green ceramic siding and hollow faux wood doors on the Delaware River. We'd landed in Fallsington, Pennsylvania, a stone's throw from where America began.

A GOOD COUNTRY

INTRODUCTION: EXTRA AMERICAN

O Liberty, white Goddess! is it well
To leave the gates unguarded?
—Thomas Bailey Aldrich, "Unguarded Gates" (1895)

On December 7, 2015, I sat on a rocker in my preschoolers' shared room, scrolling through the news while waiting for them to fall asleep, under a blanket to dim the light from my screen. Three days before, my husband, Nadeem, had left our house in Yardley, Pennsylvania, for business meetings in London. Five days before, there had been a mass shooting in San Bernardino, California, during which fourteen people were killed and twenty-two were injured. The shooters were a married Muslim couple, thought to have been politically radicalized by overseas organizations. It was the deadliest mass shooting since Sandy Hook Elementary School. The nation reeled and American Muslims took cover. In the post-9/11 politics of our country, an act of violence by any Muslim was broadly attributed to us all, and to Islam itself. We were expected to, and many of us did, respond by publicly condemning the attacks, seeing no way to reject collective culpability and still convey our horror at what had happened. We had no way of saying "We are *not them*—we should not be held accountable for their actions." Over the preceding fourteen years, the social space to assert this basic principle of human rights had all but disappeared for American Muslims.

The most we could hope for was to reduce the inevitable collective punishment, to minimize retaliation against Muslims and every person who might be mistaken for Muslim in our communities. In the days that followed the attack, a pig's head was lobbed at the Al-Aqsa Mosque just north of Girard Street in Philadelphia. I knew that mosque; my friends were community leaders there. I'd helped cover the exterior of the old factory building in which it was housed with a gorgeous geographic mural. My part had been to carve the ninety-nine names for God into ceramic tile that wrapped around the building just above eye level.

During the same period, a store owner in New York was beaten and hospitalized, a Somali restaurant torched in North Dakota, and several other mosques were vandalized or sent threatening messages. Employees at the American-Arab Anti-Discrimination Committee received death threats, several Muslim passengers were pulled off of flights, and Muslim organizations reported a broad escalation in threats and attacks across the country.

In suburban America, we opened our front doors more carefully, forgoing cultural or religious attire. More of us stopped going to the mosque. We kept our children home from school and said an extra prayer when we finally calmed our nerves enough to send them back. We kept our heads down at work and we volunteered at and donated to Muslim civil rights organizations, thinking that any day now it could be us at their doorstep. We tried to tighten the circles of our lives, make ourselves a little less exposed to the whims of the people around us. We still had to live, had to travel for and get along at work and school, had to shop and drive and be in public spaces. We pushed our worry aside and played with the kids. But we were terribly aware that in the American mind we had collapsed further into a monolith, each of us individually culpable for the misdeeds of any Muslim. There was little escape from our sense of precarity because we were all subject to the same limitation: We have no control over one another.

Muslims don't have a pope, or even a regulated clergy. And we are an incredibly diverse group of people from various parts of the world, speaking a variety of languages, adhering in different degrees to diverse cultural practices. The one thing we have in common is a personal declaration of faith, and even that is absent for those who consider themselves culturally Muslim, or Muslim by ancestry.

Eleven months earlier, on February 10, 2015, three Muslim students were shot, execution-style, by a neighbor who knocked on the door of their Chapel Hill, North Carolina, apartment. The apartment was actually home to two of them, Yusor and Deah, a strikingly beautiful, recently married couple who had grown up in North Carolina. Deah, who was twenty-three, had begun dentistry school; Yusor, who was twenty-one, was about to enter the same program; and Razan, Yusor's nineteen-year-old sister, was studying architecture and environmental design. All three were deeply engaged in their families, their schools, and their community, outstanding students who spent their time off preparing meals for local homeless people and planning a dental relief trip abroad for Syrian refugees. These three represented all of what I, as a Muslim, a mother, and a second-generation immigrant, hoped for my children: a vibrant dedication to meaningful pursuit, guided by a deep sense of social and environmental responsibility.

The three, and other neighbors in the complex, had been confronted by the angry and armed White neighbor named Craig Hicks several times before. Both Razan and her sister chose to wear hijab, scarves over their hair, as part of their daily faith practice. Hicks had approached Yusor and her mother on the day she moved in, telling them that he didn't like the way they looked.

Razan was visiting her sister and brother-in-law for dinner on the evening they were killed. The police immediately framed the killings as the result of a parking dispute, accepting the story that the killer, Hicks, told without question. Muslim Americans immediately understood the murders as hate crimes, absorbing the way Yusor and Razan were shot in the head while pleading to be spared, the eight separate bullets used to kill Deah—with a final shot through the mouth, on Hicks's way out—and Hicks's own numerous and emphatic anti-religious statements. Deah's sister, Suzanne Barakat, went to the media, asserting this for all of us in the weeks and months that followed, expressing how terrifying it had become to be identifiably Muslim in America.

And now the San Bernardino attack seemed to refuel an anti-Muslim rage that lived just beneath the surface of our neighborhoods, our police forces, our schools. Assaults against American Muslims were higher in 2015 than they had ever been—even higher than they had been in 2001 just after the 9/11 attacks; in 2016 they would climb higher still. In advance of the 2016 presidential election, Donald Trump signaled that he would support a registry for Muslims, an echo from the post-9/11 period that triggered another complex layer of collective trauma.

In the years that followed 9/11, many of us drank in the narrative that the men held at Guantanamo were there because they were guilty of something horrific, that therefore our own innocence would protect us. But those of us who took a sustained look learned that most of the 779 men (and boys as young as thirteen) at Guantanamo were held without charge or trial, and after living through hell were summarily released. We had seen photographs of torture at Abu Ghraib in Iraq, released in 2004. We'd seen the stress positions men had been held in, the unspeakable brutality and degradation they'd sustained. We feared the same thing was happening at Guantanamo (and we would ultimately find we'd been right in December 2019 when Abu Zubaydah, a man who had been misidentified as an al-Qaeda leader, held and tortured for four years at Guantanamo, drew images of his own torture). We learned that the vast majority of men and boys held at Guantanamo, 86 percent, were brought in without any intelligence by local people in Afghanistan or Pakistan in return for lavish bounties from the U.S. military, advertised on leaflets dropped from the air. Guantanamo had stretched our imaginations of what collective punishment against Muslims might look like, and how one could find oneself to be a target simply by being Muslim in the wrong place at the wrong time. It had the intended effect. American Muslims had grown to understand that our Muslimness would now be taken as compelling evidence of badness, even criminality or terrorism.

Under my blanket, my laptop pinged with a message from Cynthia, an old college friend living in Wisconsin. "How can I help?" she wanted to know. By then Trump was the leading contender for the Republican presidential nomination and had called for a "total and complete shutdown of Muslims entering the U.S." The message was clear that Muslims were the problem—not a lack of gun control, not extremism, not a society without proper mental health access.

My children, three and five years old, lay just across the room, their breath soft and even. My daughter had struggled over the previous two years with an undiagnosed illness featuring a myriad of symptoms that seemed unrelated. She was exhausted and furious, with unpredictable sensory issues and extreme food restrictions. She stopped growing and she developed urinary incontinence that followed no discernible pattern. Though she was once a toddler who could recite whole picture books from memory and took piano lessons from her beloved teacher, Mr. Pete, she had lost all interest in reading, writing, and music. We'd been struggling to make sense of her regression, and no one seemed to be able to help. We felt that each day we were losing her incrementally to an unnamable, invisible abyss. I had taken her to more than a dozen different doctors, switched pediatricians twice, sought help from five specialists at the top children's hospital in the region, and called every doctor in my extended social network, to no avail.

Working part-time from home, I was building the infrastructure for a multi-office legal services agency so it would be accessible to clients who couldn't speak English. But when I dropped the kids off at preschool every day, I wondered if I should be keeping my daughter home with me. I thought if I tried harder, maybe I could figure out what the doctors were missing. Increasingly, I wondered how my tiny girl, with mounting special needs and no diagnosis in sight, could possibly make her way as a Brown Muslim kid in American schools. Instead of the mostly plain ignorance I had dealt with, she'd have to face prejudice, harassment, or even violence.

There's a certain loneliness to having a child with a chronic illness. We were surrounded by loving family and friends, and they were kind, offering comfort and advice. But none of them was inside our struggle as parents, no one was staying up all night trying to make sense of blood tests and to chart new symptoms. No one, in the end, felt the weight of and responsibility for bringing our sweet girl back. Maybe that made me a little more aware of my responsibility as a parent to cut a path forward, not just in my daughter's treatment, but for the safety of our family. We had planned to live our lives in Yardley. We'd often said we'd retire on rocking chairs that overlooked the Delaware River. That future felt less and less certain.

Heart full, I walked down to the kitchen, composing a letter in my head: "Dear Non-Muslim allies," it began. "I am writing to you because it has gotten just that bad . . ." I posted that letter on a private Facebook page, aimed at the few hundred close friends and colleagues I had from school and more than fifteen years of social justice work. They knew that my commitments were based not only in patriotism, but deep love of country, a romance with folk music and progressive movements that made me feel a little extra American. Many of them knew me as a legal services lawyer working in low-income communities, who had also helped found the Philadelphia chapter of the Muslim civil rights organization, the Council on American-Islamic Relations (CAIR), and done many hours of outreach and interfaith work on its behalf. I knew that they, like the old college friend who'd pinged me asking how she could help, were stunned by the openness of Trump's anti-Muslim rhetoric. How do you respond to a presidential campaign that makes no effort to disguise its racial and religious animus? His transparent hatred and its popular appeal caught us all off guard. It allowed—it was designed to allow—only two responses: normalization and acceptance, or vocal rejection. I was inviting allies to swift vocal rejection because acceptance would mean that my family could never be safe again. The letter went immediately viral; and for several months I engaged the hopeful space that it created. I even began to think that America was my country still.

But as the months wore on, I found myself fielding repetitive vitriolic responses to what I'd written. I read Milton Mayer's *They Thought They Were Free: The Germans 1933–45*, a remarkable record of a series of interviews with ten Germans from a small town who had lived through the Nazi rise to power. Capturing plainly the priorities and considerations of those men during that horrifying period of history, Mayer demonstrated that ordinary people rarely feel themselves compelled to heroic tasks, even in extraordinary circumstances. Instead, we feel constrained and compelled by the most rudimentary of things: jobs, vacations, convenience, stability.

I thought of my work as an organizer, activist, and lawyer, and how, always, the struggle was getting people who did not see themselves as activists to take small steps, even ones in their own self-interest. I had been an optimist—I had asked people to vote, asked them to speak up about private, gendered violence, asked them to demand protections for social safety nets, and these requests were almost always met with apologetic refusals, for the most mundane of reasons. And I had always gone back to do it again, trying to be more persuasive, more effective. Despite my own activism, there were certainly causes that I felt were outside of my own interests, for which I could not be compelled to action. As I considered Trump's "total and complete shutdown" of people like me, I wondered, Which among my nice neighbors, not a single Muslim among them, would see us as a worthy cause? Which would use their own bodies to protect us, if it came to that? Which of them would come to the aid of the neighborhood's one Black family if it came to that? Would we, at least, come to each other's aid, friendly as we were? It was a sobering set of questions.

In the months that followed, my daughter's condition grew worse, as did the anti-Muslim rhetoric coming from Republican candidates in the 2016 presidential election. Every time Trump pushed the line on what could be said or proposed with regard to Muslims, he brought more of the Republican Party along with him. Muslims in several of my circles spoke casually about where they'd go if things "got bad." My apolitical sister-in-law asked me if we'd packed a "bug-out bag" in case we had to leave home quickly. Nadeem and I considered what we might do to help stem the rising tide. Should I run for political office? Go back to practicing law at a civil rights organization? But Nadeem had just begun a demanding job that, for the first time since we had children, allowed us to save something every month. Someone needed to make and keep medical appointments for our daughter and continue to balance her growing needs with those of our littlest one. That would have to be me. It was becoming increasingly evident that the most intense years of parenting were ahead of me, not behind me. We weighed leaving the Delaware Valley and giving up the dream of living near my parents, three generations all in the same place.

Everyone was panicked, me included, but that panic, particularly among immigrant Muslims, often lacked grounding in the history of how other racial and religious groups have fared in America. This should not have been so. About 20 percent of American Muslims are Black and another 40 percent identify as Asian, Hispanic, or mixed race. Many more are Middle Eastern or North African. Most of us had dealt with racism and xenophobia. But we weren't drawing the necessary connections between American history, our individual experiences, and our emerging collective reality as American Muslims. But not all of us understood the connections between those experiences and our emerging collective reality. I knew something about American history, the civil rights movement, and the evolution of immigration law, but I had never before found a way to situate myself within it. Muslims make up just over 1 percent of American society, South Asian Muslims a subset of that percentage. Previously that had made me feel invisible, but now it made me feel radically vulnerable.

I began to reconstruct my path through America, recalling my experiences in each place I'd lived, studied, worked, or worshipped, looking for the redemption of America in my memories. Surely there was a place where we could be safe, where even the most helpless among us, my daughter, could flourish. Instead, each set of memories contained a distinct, vehemently policed color line. Looking back, I began to see how I had been racially identified, or "racialized," differently by the people around me, depending on where I was and who those people were. Sometimes I passed for White, sometimes people or institutions demanded a detailed explanation of my racial identity, and sometimes I was imagined to be neither White nor South Asian but something else entirely. Because of these experiences, I was aware of the color lines, but I had never carefully considered how they had come to be drawn, and in whose blood.

The need to fully understand the segregated spaces I'd navigated and how that segregation is still enforced grew urgent. I wanted to hear the stories of the other people my country had tried to displace and erase, and to study how they fared. I wanted to see if I could possibly reconcile myself to—and more important, reconcile my children to—that truer picture of America. I learned that from the birth of our nation from a cluster of European colonies, its color lines have been wrought in a relentless series of brutal, forced migrations, sometimes across town, sometimes across or out of the country. Sometimes those migrations look like trafficking or frantic escape, sometimes like internment under armed guard, or incarceration, or decimation. I began to enumerate the several racist strategies that make and keep America segregated. From the myth of manifest destiny to racially restrictive covenants, the destruction of Maroon communities to so-called urban renewal, American history is one chapter upon another of dispossession, destruction, and dislocation.

Color lines, as well as the forced migrations through which they have been drawn, are the defining feature of America's topography. Today, they continue to determine where and whether Black and Brown Americans live, work, vote, and go to school; they determine where and whether they will have access to land or the ability to live in peace. They determine where supermarkets will be built, where the land and water will be sacrificed to resource extraction, industrial pollution and waste, and the courses of highways and fuel pipelines. These contours maintain the rules about which of us our society invests in and which of us is a target for persecution and violence. To be on the wrong side of the color line, to lack a claim to whiteness, is to become subject to every humiliation America can inflict; it is to become disposable.

Migration alone is staggering in its complexity—the loss of cohesive identity, culture, language, lineage—but forced migration is something else entirely. America is a case study in the forced migrations of Black and Brown people, often relentlessly enacted against the same group so that generations later, entire peoples are left to reconstruct who they are or might become from only the shards that remain. America is a place that habitually demands unimaginable sacrifice from its most vulnerable people: names, culture, faith, health, food, survival.

This book is my recollection of each place in America I've spent time in, and my investigations of America's forced migrations to and from those places *in the service of an ongoing colonial project.* I invite you to consider what it says about America's promise to those of us who land on the wrong side of its color lines, and to consider the euphemisms by which we are taught to accept and defend them.

We live not on the land that America occupies, but on the whisper-thin narrative that America is exceptionally good, that its premise is noble. Each time that narrative is pierced—as it has been again recently by Black Lives Matter protests against state violence and mass incarceration, and by Native-led and organized protests of pipelines and resource extraction that compromise access to clean air, water, and land—there is an immediate rush to patch the narrative, to maintain the pretense that America was and is for all of us. This book is my effort to tear that false narrative open, to tell you the story of how American Muslims have become, collectively, America's most recently racialized out-group, and to explain why my family had to leave.

ONE NATION UNDER GOD

Yardley, Pennsylvania

For if they take you in the morning, they will be coming for us that night.

—James Baldwin

In the summer of 2014, I landed in the Newark airport from Chicago's O'Hare International with my daughter, Jahan, three years old, and son, Isa, one year old, in tow. My husband, Nadeem, was driving the minivan across the country with the few boxes we wouldn't entrust to movers. My parents met me at the baggage claim carousel, happy to take over steering the stroller and holding Jahan's sticky hand while I collected our suitcase, exhausted.

Moving to Chicago had felt like an adventure, but coming home to the Delaware Valley was a sigh of relief. I felt as if we were a species of animal that had made an inexplicably hard trek to a remote and difficult environment only to give birth, and now we were returning to family and a sense of belonging. I had visited the Delaware Valley less frequently after Jahan's birth and not at all after Isa's. Traveling with infants is expensive and challenging, and Nadeem and I had not recovered from the loss of half of our income when Jahan arrived nine weeks early and I stopped working full-time as a legal aid lawyer. When I went back to working part-time, it only kept our heads above water. As I was mostly occupied with my very young children, my social circle shrank to a few other local moms.

So when in the summer of 2014 Nadeem landed a job within commuting distance of my parents' home, we jumped for joy. We actually held each other's forearms and jumped up and down like little kids. We could live in the same town, maybe even the same neighborhood as my parents. The children could grow up near their grandparents. I could work remotely at my part-time job. Nadeem's new job would mean more money, better healthcare, and proximity to an intimate community born of some of my oldest and closest relationships.

Living in Chicago with children had made Nadeem and me understand how untethered our own childhoods had felt without local extended families. Nadeem's parents were first-generation immigrants, too, in the UK. Each of our parents had been brittle with stress, unable to be vulnerable with anyone. Immigrants often recognize this stress in each other, and the children of immigrants often recognize the marks of it in each other. Nadeem and I had begun to dream of the comfort and stability of a few generations—or more—in one place.

Growing up in an America of suburban mobility, I'd always anticipated leaving home. Like many Americans, I did not always expect that my extended family would remain intact, sharing home and resources. Now, for the first time in my life, watching my parents with my children, allowing myself to be both a parent and still a child, I saw how important contact with extended family is in the modern world. I saw that it made all of us a bit better and less fragile. Having family and a personal history in a place brought a sense of ownership, a sense that my community had rights on me and that I could depend on it.

My parents had moved across the tracks from Fallsington, where I had grown up, to Yardley, just a bit farther north on the Delaware River and a two-minute drive door to door. So it was to Yardley we returned, renting one side of a modest duplex in a 1980s development, on its third or fourth round of families with young children. One day early in September, I picked up the kids at noon from their tiny Montessori school in the center of historic Fallsington.

Excited to share a chapter of my own childhood with them, I walked with them through the quiet streets of the colonial-era village, past the Moon-Williamson House. Tiny but significant, it is a house of squared logs, built as early as 1685 by Swedish settlers, and one of the first European settler houses in Pennsylvania that still stands on its original site. We stopped to see if we could join arms to get all the way around one of the majestic "bride and groom" Sycamore trees, said to have been planted by some of the home's earliest inhabitants. The old trunks were far too wide, so we went on to the penny candy store down the street. It was the same one I'd ridden my bike to dozens of times as a child. The kids and I ate our ice pops dripping in the September heat, legs swinging off the peeling porch.

Every day that autumn, a small group of parents with kids in half-day preschool gathered in the churchyard across the parking lot from the school, letting our children play in the falling leaves of towering oak trees, chase squirrels, and collect black walnut fruits before going home for naps. In these gatherings, I learned how the nearby towns had changed. While still noticeably segregated by race in most parts, this formerly conservative stretch between New York and Philadelphia had grown distinctly more cosmopolitan and politically liberal.

The parents in our preschool community were less likely to either work full-time on rigid schedules or to stay home full-time, and more likely to work from home or to have negotiated terms that allowed them to spend time with their young families. Many of them had moved to the suburbs after stints in Philadelphia or New York; they were still paying down their own student debt.

In these parents, I found a kind of immediate camaraderie that I had not experienced since college. I was, as I had always been in Fallsington, of a different race, religion, and cultural identity than everyone there, but we were all similarly middle-aged, dumbfounded and amused to find our worlds suddenly centered on the needs of late-born children. My former life as a Philadelphia legal aid lawyer, my faith as a Muslim, the way my children's skin settled into a dark brown over the summer, and my desire to be deeply engaged in my children's days were not surprising or alienating to any of them. It was one additional way in which the Delaware Valley felt more like coming home than I might have imagined.

Our rented house in Yardley backed onto Five Mile Woods Forest Preserve, or rather the woods that would be part of Five Mile Woods if it was actually five miles long. Five Mile Woods brought us songbirds and soaring hawks, deer and bucks with wide antler racks battling in the snow, foxes, and a groundhog the children named Sydney Clover Love, who lived under the shed and raided the vegetable garden. The children took their places in a small tribe of cousins, who now lived just an hour drive away, and spent holidays and school breaks playing hide-and-seek, building forts, painting their hands with henna. We were a walk of only several minutes from my parents' home, with one of the few remaining family farms in the area between us, and so the kids celebrated their birthdays in and generally commandeered Nani and Grandpa's backyard.

My parents were only a couple of blocks away from a new mosque, housed in what was once Bethel Christian Church, across from my old junior high school. On Friday afternoons, I often stopped with the kids to see my parents, catching my father as he left for his walk to weekly congregational prayers. Even in retirement, he dressed in slacks and a button-down shirt.

"Okay, I've got to go, khuda hafiz!" God protect you.

"Where are you going?"

"Got to do my penance," he'd say with a grin.

Things really had changed; in 1992, I was the sole Muslim student among eight hundred graduating seniors at Pennsbury High School. We didn't even *have* a local mosque then. By 2017, the local mosque was being expanded; the attendees had outgrown the original building, which they had occupied since 2005. Just one block beyond the mosque was a new Hindu temple, also in a renovated and repurposed church building, drawing congregants from nearby Bensalem, now a diverse community with many recent Asian and South and Central

American immigrants, as well as several families who had moved from Bensalem to the deeper suburbia of Yardley.

Despite these shifts, suburban Bucks County remains overwhelmingly White and conservative. Bensalem's population has been shifting, but its police department and township council are White, and the police department has taken a clearly anti-immigrant stance in coordinating arrests with Immigration and Customs Enforcement (ICE), the federal agency responsible for the deportation of the undocumented. In addition, all of Bucks County remains highly segregated, with a large majority of Black and Brown people pressed into neighborhoods like Bensalem, abutting Philadelphia, leaving affluent rural and suburban communities with well-funded schools still overwhelmingly White. Since the Covid-19 pandemic began, these more affluent neighborhoods have become embroiled in vitriolic debates over masks, quarantines, and inclusive curriculums for schoolchildren. Bucks County feels like a contested place, a battleground. I wanted to know how it got that way. Why was it so segregated in the first place?

Yardley and Fallsington are the kinds of towns that people around the world imagine all of America to be. Both have small town centers, old wooden libraries with pitched roofs and tall windows, and scattered centuries-old fieldstone farmhouses surrounded by newer suburban developments. Like every kid growing up in southeastern Pennsylvania, I was steeped in the mythology of their founding by benevolent Quakers, whose flight from English persecution gave rise to a tolerant colony premised on visionary pluralism. In an elementary school lesson on the early history of Pennsylvania, I was taught that William Penn marveled at the beauty and the bounty of the Delaware Valley, and at how the forest seemed to welcome him, clear of underbrush so that his horse could pass through easily. The image stuck, and as a child I was always on the lookout for these magical forests. All of the ones I saw had the same tangled understory. Much later, I would learn that Penn was unknowingly riding through forests shaped by the sophisticated land management of the Lenape, which included periodic controlled burns of the underbrush. The story I had been taught about Penn and the idyllic forest was *so incomplete as to be untrue.* I went looking for a more honest story, and found that it was barely obscured, as if someone had pulled the sparest of blankets over a thick historical record.

Yardley and Fallsington were some of the first towns in colonial Pennsylvania and America, with populations of Swedes, Finns, and Dutch even before William Penn, the English Quaker, arrived there. Penn and his descendants would dramatically accelerate European settlement in the area, eventually expanding westward to claim all of the land that King Charles II had "granted" to Penn in 1681 for a debt owed to his father.

On the land all along the lower Delaware River, Penn planned what he called his "holy experiment," a grand utopian scheme in which he imagined a new kind of personal freedom for himself, his fellow Quakers, and other marginalized European Protestant groups. Before immigrating to North America, Penn suffered years of hardship, persecution, and imprisonment in his native England for having joined the Religious Society of Friends. The Friends, later called Quakers, were seen as a threat to state authority in England during an era in which wars were fought to determine which particular Christian sects would be affiliated with which European states. With his land grant to Penn, the king aimed to rid himself of the vocal Quaker leader and simultaneously use Penn to stake a claim to land and resources across the Atlantic before they could be overtaken by Dutch, Swedish, or French colonists. This was the apex of the colonial period, when Europeans generally believed that whatever land outside of Europe upon which they set foot—either taking it by force, or more passively populating it—was theirs by right.

Penn really did imagine building a society premised on freedom of conscience and governance by representative democracy—that much is true. He recruited new European immigrants from splinter Protestant sects across northern Europe, thousands of whom hoped to escape a continent ravaged by constant battle between Catholic and Protestant powers. Eager to avoid this chaos and to avail themselves of generous land grants, large numbers of his fellow Quakers also moved, in spite of the hardship of transatlantic migration.

Penn wrote prolifically on liberty of conscience and moral governance. He believed that while the state had the right to require the civic allegiance of its subjects, and it had the right to compel moral conduct, it did not have the right, or even the ability, to compel the individual conscience. This conviction was derived from the core spiritual principle of the Quaker faith: that each individual has access to the divine truth or "inner light" without the mediating force of clergy. (Muslims share this theological principle, giving some of us a particular affinity for Quaker faith.) Quakers see themselves as pacifists; they reject the idea that faith can be coerced, believing that coercion makes a mockery of faith. So, Penn arrived without soldiers and maintained no militia. He provided work and education for both boys and girls, abolished capital punishment, and established a penal system in which prisoners had opportunities to learn a trade within his community.

Penn's idealism was barely tempered by the inconvenient reality that the land on which he planned to build his utopia was already fully inhabited by a people whose sustenance, faith, and culture were deeply tied to the land on which they lived. He resolved to purchase the land from Native people and to treat them equitably, and wrote them a letter to this effect, sent with his cousin and regent, who arrived ahead of him in the Delaware Valley:

I am very Sensible of the unkindness and Injustice that hath been too much exersised towards you by the People of thes Parts of the world, who have sought themselves, and to make great Advantages by you, rather then be examples of Good & Goodness unto you, which I hear, hath been matter of Trouble to you, and caused great Grudgings and Animosities, Sometimes to the Shedding of blood, which hath made the great God Angry. but I am not such a man, as is well known in my own Country: I have great love and regard towards you, and I desire to win and gain your Love & freindship by a kind, just and peaceable life; and the People I send are of the same mind, & Shall in all things behave themselvs accordingly.

The evidence suggests that the Lenape of the Delaware Valley found Penn's language persuasive, at least initially, perhaps viewing the growing European presence in North America as inevitable and seeing a peaceful fur trading partner as the best available alternative. But Penn's intentions were almost immediately compromised by the constraints of his colonial imagination. His project was paramount, and peace with the Lenape a means to that end. He did not adapt his broader vision to the already established society of the Lenape, and he certainly did not consider the assimilation of his community into their society. He may not have even been capable of such a vision; he could barely fathom a circumstance where his championed "freedom of conscience" could justify an individual's failure to observe the Sabbath.

On paper, and certainly from a seventeenth-century European perspective, Penn's Charter of Liberties and Frame of Government for Pennsylvania was an impressive attempt to separate personal and political identity, allowing leadership in his community to be conferred without regard to (western European) national origin, language, or even religious persuasion within the broad strokes of Christianity, requiring only "faith in Jesus Christ." Simple membership in the community was even more expansive, allowing that no one who "confess and acknowledge the one Almighty and eternal God to be the Creator, Upholder and ruler of the world . . . be molested or persecuted for their religious persuasion." Nearly a hundred years later, America's Bill of Rights was written to begin with an affirmation that "Congress shall make no law respecting an establishment of religion, or prohibiting the free exercise thereof," owing directly to Penn's notions of a free and good society.

But for many of the people in his new colony, the reality that Penn shaped with his wealth and authority was a dramatic departure from the ideals espoused in the Charter of Liberties, and from the rights he asserted at his own trial for publicly preaching Quakerism when he was still in England in 1670:

> I am arraigned a prisoner; my Liberty, which is next to Life itself, is now concerned . . . unless you shew me, and the People, the Law you ground your Indictment upon, I shall take it for granted, your Proceedings are meerly Arbitrary.

Penn went on to say that the law must be "indispensably maintained and observed"; otherwise, "Liberties are openly to be invaded; . . . Wives to be Ravished; . . . Children Slaved; our Families Ruined; and our Estates led away in Triumph by every Sturdy Beggar." He argued, he said, not for his own liberty, but for "many Ten Thousand families besides."

In spite of his condemnation of the excesses of those "Sturdy Beggar[s]" who would unlawfully deprive another of his liberty, enslaving his children and ruining his family, Penn was among the many English Quakers in Pennsylvania who enslaved Black people. He had purchased at least some of these people in 1684 from the *Isabella,* the first slave ship to arrive in Philadelphia, carrying people trafficked from the British West Indies and from West Africa, though there was no law allowing the permanent and generational enslavement of people in the colony at that time. Despite his courtroom protests fourteen years earlier, he was himself engaged in a practice of slavery that was "meerly Arbitrary." Eight of the people Penn enslaved are identifiable in surviving records, and there is evidence of others yet to be identified. These people were held captive at what Penn called his "plantation," now commonly referred to obscuratively as Pennsbury Manor. His letters gave instructions to his agent to acquire both adults and children as permanent slaves, noting a preference for enslaved Black people over indentured servants: "It were better they were blacks, for then a man has them while they live."

Once at Pennsbury Manor, the people Penn enslaved labored to clear land, build houses and outbuildings (in which they slept), supply household labor, and maintain the grounds, livestock, and crops, for decades. When one of the men whom Penn enslaved, Jack, found that his wife, enslaved by another man, was to be sold away to Barbados, Penn's wife, Hannah, refused to let him visit her. Instead, Hannah grudgingly conditioned a final visit at Pennsbury on Jack's wife doing the household's washing while she visited, a substantial payment in labor for the privilege of seeing her husband for the last time. Even so, Hannah also demanded references for the enslaved wife's character and capabilities before she would confirm the arrangement.

During the same years in which Penn wrote and expounded so prolifically on his ideals of liberty and religious pluralism, his worldview was explicitly racist, delineating entire peoples outside even his broadest, most tolerant ideals. Discussing the importance of morality for the success of a society in 1679, he ascribed blame for the final fall of Rome on "the Lewd Asiaticks [who] had this Revenge in their own Fall, that they ruin'd by their Vices, those they were no Ways able to resist by their Force." Penn's purpose here was to establish, in a polemical and abbreviated review of world history, that societies fall because they become corrupt themselves or are corrupted by other peoples. Unsurprisingly, all those Penn might have viewed as exotic, such as Jews and "the Vandals of Africk," the kingdom that ruled North Africa in the fifth and sixth centuries, he also viewed as "lewd" and given to "vice." This worldview allowed him to see Black people trafficked from Africa as having brought their suffering upon themselves, and to see himself as devoid of any particular responsibility to them.

Penn was aware of his contemporaries' arguments against slavery. In 1657, a decade before he departed England, his friend and mentor George Fox, who had *founded* the Society of Friends, addressed North American Quakers already in the colonies on the matter in a letter titled "To Friends Beyond the Sea, that Have Black and Indian Slaves." In it, Fox asserted that the Gospel must be available to all, even those who are enslaved, and then associated the Gospel with both liberty and freedom, writing,

> I was moved to write these things to you in all those plantations. God, that made the world, and all things therein, giveth life and breath to all, and they all have their life and moving, and their being in him, he is the God of the spirits of the flesh, and is no respecter of persons; but "whosoever fearth him and worketh righteousness, is accepted of him." And he hath made all nations of one blood to dwell upon the face of the earth, and his eyes are over all the works of his hands, and seeth every thing that is done under the whole of heaven.

Although he stopped short of arguing directly that Quakers free the enslaved, or even explicitly repudiating slavery as an evil, this letter would form the basis for Fox's continuing conflict with slavers in the Americas.

Within a year of Penn's arrival in the colony in 1682, fellow Quakers warned him of the potential for a rebellion of the enslaved, pointing out the particular problem of trying to maintain an enslaved workforce without also maintaining a militia among themselves. Some of them likely noted the contradiction between the pacifist ideals that prevented them from maintaining a militia and the practice of slavery itself. Penn's agent in Amsterdam, concerned about the pacifist and anti-slavery sensibilities of the people he was trying to recruit to Pennsylvania from Europe, wrote to advise Penn to limit the term of enslavement in the colony to eight years.

The first organized abolitionist protest from among the Pennsylvania colonists, in fact the first among all of the American colonists, was a 1688 letter written by a group of Dutch and German Mennonites living in Germantown, seven miles or so from the center of Philadelphia. This group, sometimes also referred to as Quaker, had been recruited by Penn himself, but had kept themselves apart from the main Quaker Meeting in Philadelphia. It was to that central meeting that they issued their letter. The Quakers had only grown out of the Mennonite tradition decades before, and the two Anabaptist faiths had much in common. So when the Mennonites delivered their letter, they appealed to what they presumed were shared values and experiences.

Angry, they did not address the letter to the English Quakers "Friends," as was customary. And they wrote with none of the political half measures of George Fox, or even later White abolitionists, who had become somewhat inured to the sheer depravity of slavery. Instead, they wrote impassionedly, insisting on the humanity of those who were enslaved, appealing to the rule of law, and demanding empathy and equity from the English Quakers whom they had crossed an ocean to join:

> Now tho' they are black, we cannot conceive there is more liberty to have them slaves, as it is to have other white ones. There is a saying, that we shall doe to all men, licke as we will be done our selves, macking no difference of what generation, descent, or Colour they are. And those who steal or robb men, and those who buy or purchase them, are they not alicke? Here is liberty of Conscience, wch is right & reasonable, here ought to be licke-wise liberty of ye body . . . In Europe there are many oppressed for Conscience sacke; and here there are those oppressed wch are of a black Colour. And we, who know that men must not comitt adultery, somedoe comitt adultery in others, separating wifes from housbands, and giving them to others and some sell the children of those poor Creatures to other men. . . . Pray! What thing in the world can be done worse twarts us then if men should robb or steal us away & sell us for slaves to strange Countries, separating housband from their wife & children. . . . And we who profess that it is not lawfull to steal, must lickewise avoid to purchase such things as are stolen . . . If once these slaves . . . fight for their freedom . . . will these masters and mastrisses tacke the sword at hand & warr against these poor slaves?

They threatened to inform their communities back in Europe that the Quakers of Pennsylvania were engaged in the horrors of slavery, which would turn back potential émigrés.

Penn, however, appears to have avoided these objections for as long as he was able. Although he did ultimately signal compliance with the decision taken at the Philadelphia Yearly Meeting in 1696 to curtail the further import of enslaved people and presented the Provincial Assembly with laws limiting the ability of slavers to sell enslaved people out of Pennsylvania, he never opposed or moved to abolish the institution of slavery itself.

Instead, in 1700, he introduced the earliest of Pennsylvania's Black Codes, An Act for the Trial of Negroes, which established an entirely separate set of penalties and restrictions on Black Pennsylvanians. In these, capital punishment of Black men was deemed permissible as a penalty for rape of White women, as was castration for attempted rape. The codes established a prohibition on Black Pennsylvanians carrying arms without a special license and made meetings of more than four Black people for reasons other than the business of those who enslaved them punishable by whipping.

After his final return to England in 1701, Penn continued to enslave people at Pennsbury. Though he spent time in an English debtor's prison after a dispute with the heirs of his agent, Philip Ford, his estate contained several enslaved people upon his death in 1718. They lived under the charge of a White man Penn hired as Pennsbury's overseer (who married the White maid), and a White gardener. Although one early will provided that one hundred acres be distributed to one Black man he had enslaved, for his own use and the use of his wife and his children, and another will would have freed all of the people he had enslaved, later wills did not make these provisions, so they did not come to pass. At the end, he seems to have forgotten about the people he had held captive, neither freeing them nor providing for them. In 1736, after his father's death, Thomas Penn wrote about a visit to the Pennsbury plantation during which he found "the kitchen house was very open, so that the servants [the enslaved], who look after the plantation could not live warm and dry. . . . No person had lived in the big house for near twenty years."

Just as certainly as Penn envisioned a utopia for the persecuted Protestants of Europe, he imagined himself the head of that utopia, enriched by a plantation worked and maintained by people enslaved because of the color of their skin. He died a slaver, with the children of those he enslaved bound in slavery as their parents had been. As the proprietor of the colony with the authority to have changed its course, Penn chose to maintain slavery, not to champion liberty. The Quakers of Pennsylvania would permit their members to traffic in other human beings for nearly one hundred years, until 1776.

Penn's deeply compromised, racially exclusive version of utopia foretells the story of America as it remains today, a story only partly told, premised on the theft and bondage of Black people, their labor, and their lives. Penn's own split consciousness—one made up of the grand ideals that he hoped would be his legacy, and another far more troubled and rarely acknowledged one—would become the modern consciousness of America.

Just as the broader demographics of Bucks County had shifted by the time I returned in 2014, the robust Muslim community in southeastern Pennsylvania looked and felt different from the limited web of family and family friends I had left in 1992. An old friend had started an Islamic Sunday school along the Main Line, a posh string of suburbs stretching west of Philadelphia. He created a space where older students could discuss and debate current events, including the twenty-first-century American doctrine of "preemptive warfare" in the Middle East and the challenges of being Muslim in America after 9/11, and younger students, girls as well as boys, could take turns leading prayers.

Several parents gathered upstairs in a second-floor loft during Sunday school to do zikr, a common Muslim meditation practice, focused on the ninety-nine names of God, among them The Compassionate, The Merciful, The Patient, The Truth. This group was civically engaged both inside and outside Muslim communities: Several of us were founding board members of CAIR-Philadelphia; one worked with a Quaker organization serving refugees; one would eventually win a seat on her local school board; another family ran an annual charity drive; several had done outreach to other faith or community organizations on behalf of American Muslims. All were likely to appear at anti-war events, participate in an annual drive to provide low-income Philadelphians with winter coats and other necessities, and organize the Sunday school's monthly service projects. We were all committed to a more inclusive, more compassionate America. And we all voted.

Engaged as we were, and aware of rising anti-Muslim sentiment as the 2016 election cycle began, we didn't often discuss politics at Sunday school. We were trying to preserve that time for zikr together. One warm fall Sunday, we held our congregational prayer outside on the playground, in an area that was visible to a regional commuter train. Our prayers are a bit of a spectacle for those unfamiliar with them—we move through several rounds of standing, bending, and prostrating in unison. This had never been a cause for concern before. Sunday train schedules are sparse and our congregational prayers were short because of the hundred impatient children in attendance. On this day, after prayers during which a train unexpectedly rumbled past behind us, my friend Iftekhar, who had started the Sunday school with his wife, looked worried.

"That's never happened before."

"What?"

"The train passing on a Sunday like that, behind our prayers. I wonder if someone would report a bunch of kids praying as a terrorist activity or something," he said with a nervous laugh. Then we both silently weighed the security risk to the children. What if someone angry and misguided came to the school with a gun?

Despite moments like these, I still felt mostly optimistic about the future, hopeful for my family. When I began work as a legal services lawyer in 2001, my profession and political engagement were an oddity in first- and second-generation immigrant Muslim communities. But in the years after 9/11, immigrant Muslim communities began to change focus so that they were less concerned with what was going on "back home." More of us wanted to better understand the rising anti-Muslim sentiment in America. Second-generation immigrants were inclined to break from the pressure to enter only STEM fields seeking financial security, and instead specialized in ways that would help them push back against stereotypes and discrimination. More of us became lawyers, appeared in or began to create our own media, and became community activists. I was relieved by these changes as a Muslim lawyer committed to social justice work. Increasingly, my religious community and my professional community overlapped—many of the people in both became dear friends, and our children ran together through each other's homes in a tribe ranging from four to fourteen years old.

I anticipated that the issues raised in the 2016 election season would reflect the interests of the people around me: a more diverse Bucks County, a more engaged immigrant community, an increasingly strapped middle class. The most recent Pennsylvania state elections suggested they would. Before my return to Bucks County, Democrats had largely been shut out of local and state politics. However, in the November 2014 general elections, the incumbent Republican governor Tom Corbett lost to the Democrat Tom Wolf, and in the November 2015 general elections, three open seats on the state supreme court were taken by Democrats, creating a five-to-two Democratic majority. These wins were by narrow margins, but my home county had long been considered a mix of rural and urban that was a reliable indicator of the politics of the country as a whole. Its transformation gave me reason to hope.

So I was stunned when Donald Trump became the clear front-runner among GOP candidates in the 2016 presidential election. The harder the line on immigration and on Muslims that he took, the more popular he became. His vitriol split the Republican field, and those who failed to fall in line with his proposed ban on Muslim immigration and special surveillance of mosques or "Muslim neighborhoods" also quickly fell out of the race. The sense of hope I had for newly engaged Muslim and immigrant communities faltered.

Many of my fellow parents and friends, whatever their race or religion, were upset by Trump, and dismissive of the crass reality TV star. Still, Trump yard signs and flags went up all around me. Nadeem and I suddenly felt the need to take stock of our neighborhood: just two South Asian families including us, one Jewish family, and one Black family, among almost a hundred houses. There were few other families who had been friendly. Our next-door neighbors, who hadn't spoken to us in the three years we'd lived there, not even to say thank you when I let them know their garden hose was left running or to share thoughts on our adjacent vegetable gardens, put a sign out. Then the neighbors diagonally across the street put one out, right next to the dead end where I'd been teaching my four- and six-year-olds to ride their bikes all summer.

Because of the virulence of Trump's rhetoric, we perceived each sign as a threat. A large brick house near the children's preschool and next to the Quaker Meeting House in Fallsington flew an enormous Trump flag, just under the American flag. Nothing about that juxtaposition felt right. Everything I thought I knew about the Quaker ideals of pacifism and pluralism was in deep contrast to what Trump espoused, although each purported to be the essence of America. The movement that Trump was rallying felt like a direct threat to my children, whom I left at school each day, just a few blocks from where the flag bearing his name waved.

In the Fallsington of my youth, the word *colonial* was used to mean "quaint" and was strangely dissociated from any suggestion of the people who were colonized or enslaved. William Penn and the Quakers were presented as heroes. In that version of history, Penn was a humble, benevolent leader who would not refer to the Lenape diminutively as his children, or even his brothers and sisters, but as "one body" with their Quaker neighbors. And in fact, Penn *was* different from other colonial governors of his time. In addition to paying the Lenape for land, he promised that the Lenape would retain the land that had not been purchased and could expect to live in peace alongside the Quakers. He ordered that crimes against the Lenape be treated and prosecuted the same way as crimes against Quakers to keep that peace. His promise ingratiated Penn to the Lenape, and several generations later, the Lenape would argue their land claims by referencing it.

Up until the arrival of Penn's recruits, the Lenape up and down the Delaware and Brandywine river valleys had proven to be shrewd negotiators and governors. Though organized without a defined hierarchy, these communities set the terms of trade with Europeans through decentralized, democratic self-governance and were remarkably successful at controlling engagements with and between early Swedish and Finnish settlers in the area. They agreed to lease portions of their land for periodic payment in goods, while retaining rights to hunt, fish, and cross over the land. These rights were essential; Lenape subsistence, at that time, depended entirely on the ability to hunt, fish, gather fruits and nuts, and cultivate their staple diet of maize, beans, and corn. The European practice of private ownership and conveyance was alien to the Lenape, whose concept of natural resources prioritized common use, diplomacy, and trade. Early settlers made their periodic lease payments while misrepresenting to their patrons in Europe that they had purchased rather than rented the land.

The Lenape rejected early colonial land use that suggested permanent, exclusive use and development. They permitted the building of trade posts in or near the Delaware Bay, at Kent Island, for example, but reacted with unusual and calculated violence to the Dutch attempt to build a plantation settlement at Swanendaelin in 1638, where the town of Lewes, Delaware, is today. Still, Lenape society was affected by the presence of early European settlers in dramatic and destructive ways. Four smallpox and measles epidemics were recorded between 1663 and 1677. The account of a German minister living in the Delaware Valley in the late seventeenth century suggests disease accounted for a 75 percent reduction of the Lenape population. Other written accounts from Dutch sources suggest a 90 percent loss of population. Such a loss would have been devastating, even apocalyptic. It would have radically changed families, orphaned countless children, and challenged cultural cohesion; it would have resulted in dramatic social and political instability. Similar losses among other Native peoples all along the East Coast drove the confederation of survivors and the creation of new social groupings and alliances.

Perhaps these losses emboldened Penn's promises to the Lenape; perhaps he believed that there was no need to fight if disease would ultimately deliver his community the land. Whatever his reasoning, Penn could not have intended to keep his promise of perpetual shared ownership to the Lenape of the Delaware Valley. We know this because at about the same time that Penn wrote flowery declarations of love for the Lenape, he had published pamphlets to recruit European immigrants to Pennsylvania on the promise of "five thousand acres, free of any Indian encumbrance [for] £100." Penn did not disclose this commitment in the letter to the Lenape that preceded his arrival.

Like many generations of settlers after him, he intended that his fortune would be made by taking control of Native land cheaply and selling it at a profit. In fact, before Penn ever set foot in Pennsylvania in 1682, he had already sold 300,000 acres to about 300 purchasers. By 1685, he had sold 600 tracts totaling 700,000 acres in what are still Bucks, Philadelphia, Montgomery, Delaware, and Chester counties in southeastern Pennsylvania. This represents most of the lower Delaware Valley, a vast stretch of land in and around Philadelphia reaching far back from the banks of the river. For Penn, the sale of land was as much a business venture as a holy experiment, yielding him nearly £9,000, or more than $2 million in today's dollars.

In the early years of Pennsylvania, Penn, his agents, and his descendants often paid multiple times for the same property, suggesting they were aware of the Lenape's intention to lease rather than sell land and were willing to comply with it. But over time, these payments ceased and the settlers' plots of land were fenced. Even the language of Penn's deeds grew more precise, emphasizing the permanent and complete transfer of land.

In the fall of 2018, I sat at the Pennsylvania Historical Society reading through decades of original colonial-era deeds in awe. Remarkably, many of them include the signature of an interpreter. But the language of the deeds was difficult for *me* to understand as a lawyer whose primary language is English. It is impossible to imagine that Penn was able, even through an interpreter, to convey to Lenape sachems, or leaders, who had no written language and no concept of deeds or private land ownership, the significance of a passage like this:

> For and in Consideration of the sums and particulars of Goods, merchandizes, and utensils hereinafter mentioned and expressed . . . at and before Sealing and delivery hereof in hand paid and delivered, whereof and wherewith the said Sachemakers doe hereby acknowledge themselves fully satisfied, Contented and paid. The said Indian Sachemakers . . . Have Granted, Bargained, sold and delivered, And by these presents doe fully, clearley and absolutely grant, bargayne, sell and deliver unto the sayd William Penn, his Heirs and Assignes forever.

Penn understood how alien the concepts in these documents were to the Lenape sachems from whom he required signatures and said as much in letters to associates back in England:

> They want or care for little no Bills of Exchange, nor Bills of Lading, no Chancery suits nor Exchequer Acct. have they to perplex themselves with, they are soon satisfied and their pleasure feeds them, I mean hunting and fishing.

He understood fully that it was not only the English language that was foreign to the Lenape but (of course) the actual transfer of land and the papers that effectuated it as established in British common law. He misunderstood, though, presumably because his aristocratic experience was limited in such things, the significance of the Lenape's ongoing use of and access to the land. Hunting and fishing were not merely pleasures; the land was integral to both Lenape subsistence and identity. The original documents themselves evidence, if anything, a complete lack of understanding between the parties. Some are signed by only the English parties, some have just a mark meant to designate the consent of the sachems, and one lists "as much as William Penn shall please to give unto me" for payment. The deeds read as tragically inadequate, even ridiculous.

Penn's celebrated utopia was, in fact, the death knell for a great majority of Lenape, as well as for traditional Lenape society and whatever it might have become in the Delaware Valley. When Penn returned to England for the first time in 1684, both his deputy governor, who was his cousin William Markham, and his surveyor general, Thomas Holme, wrote to him of the ever-increasing land disputes and demand for land in the colony, which far outstripped the land for which Penn had secured deeds from the Lenape. Disputes arose in Penn's absence, as Quakers proceeded to build fences and dams that would quickly destroy traditional Lenape subsistence and ways of life.

Ultimately, Penn was committed to his own plan for a "peaceable kingdom" but not to a peaceable future for the Lenape. That he pursued his aims with patience and diplomacy was as much due to pragmatism as to his Quaker pacifism; less than ten years before he arrived in Pennsylvania, King Philip's War was raging in New England, killing six hundred European colonizers in Massachusetts Bay, Plymouth, and Rhode Island and three thousand among the Narragansett and Wampanoag nations. Penn exercised caution to avoid a similar fate, which might have destroyed his community before it was even established.

His split intentions are clear in the contrast between how he spoke about the Lenape and how he spoke to them, urging would-be immigrants to his colony to view themselves as "moralizing the manners of the Nations they subjected; so that they may have been rather said to conquer their Barbarity than Them." His ideas about liberty, humanity, and freedom of conscience were tightly constrained by a deeply racist worldview, which allowed him to envision as utopia a community built by enslaved labor on stolen land.

Penn's ideas about religious freedom and pluralism within the constraints of European Christian identity would take on a certain momentum in America. They would eventually be codified in America's Constitution. Today, they are widely represented as broader and more progressive than they were. Penn's ideas were popular in colonial America *because* they were so limited to whiteness. European colonizers found themselves reliant upon their European neighbors. Though frequently foreign to one another in language, culture, custom, and belief, their ability to work and live with one another across their differences would be an essential foundation for survival and domination in this new place. Penn's novel concepts of tolerance and pluralism helped create a pan-European White unity. In this sense, Penn was one of the founding fathers of American whiteness.

Remarkably, three centuries later, his ideas would be stretched to form the basis upon which my own father, racially and religiously different from everyone around him, could settle and raise a family in Fallsington. But this cannot be attributed to Penn; instead, it can be attributed to the individuals and social movements who challenged the limitations of Penn's colonial imagination during the intervening three hundred years.

In 1776, thirty miles south of my childhood home, the United States Declaration of Independence was drafted to contain echoes of Penn's vision, proclaiming, "We hold these truths to be self-evident, that all men are created equal, that they are endowed by their Creator with certain unalienable Rights, that among these are Life, Liberty and the Pursuit of Happiness." Penn's inconsistencies were fully evident in the imaginations of the framers, who also understood "all men" quite narrowly. "All men" was a misstatement of intention, ultimately betrayed in that same Declaration, which refers to the Native inhabitants of America as "merciless Indian Savages, whose known rule of warfare, is an undistinguished destruction of all ages, sexes and conditions."

The framers of the Declaration of Independence were, as Penn was, entirely products of the colonial era, unable to conceive that warfare wrought by Native peoples might have been a reasonable attempt to secure their own ways of life, their lives, and their property from the diseases and overwhelming greed of European settlers. Many of their descendants retain the inability to perceive the humanity of Black and Brown people, so that our collective national history comes in waves of racial exploitation, persecution, and dispossession. Much of American history has been the story of conflict over who has a right to secure their lives, their property, and their ways of life, who among us has a soul, and who constitutes "all men."

America is the birthplace of a particular whiteness, that strange identity not quite based on skin color or on parentage, not quite on culture or on language. This novel identity is deeply American, meant to bind the vast array of European immigrants together and distinguish them from—save themselves from the horrors visited upon—Native and Black people in America. In a twenty-first-century America that is increasingly diverse, expected in census estimates to be less White than non-White by 2045, the purveyors of whiteness have emerged with renewed fervor.

Throughout 2016, more Trump signs sprang up in Bucks County. They were now outside houses on Stony Hill Road on the way to our favorite Korean restaurant and on the lawn of the one house on Big Oak Road between our home and my parents' place. That summer, I went to drop off our rent check at our landlord's house in the next development over, and sat for a moment, gobsmacked at a pickup truck across the street plastered with anti-Muslim, anti-government, and Trump bumper stickers. What was happening? Hadn't they heard what he had said about us? My family? Their neighbors?

Between 2002 and 2008, as vice president of CAIR-Philadelphia, I had spoken to dozens of groups—thousands of people—about my faith and what it means to me, offering a counternarrative to that of Muslim as terrorist or Muslim as collateral damage. But I had never spoken directly to my neighbors. So, for several weekends leading up to the 2016 election, I left the kids at home with Nadeem, collected my seventy-four-year-old father, who had never engaged in political activity beyond voting and a single anti-war demonstration in Washington, D.C., and went canvassing around our town. Our Democratic Party organizers, a local family who had opened their home up for training and distributing materials, told us that our list was vetted, so that we would only be encouraging already sympathetic voters to get out and vote. So we were conflicted when one house on our list had a Trump sign out front.

"Should we knock?"

"It could be that there's a Democrat in the family."

"Well, I've already rung the bell."

A woman about my age opened the door. It was a nice house, in a nice neighborhood, where houses go for half a million dollars. We did our spiel: "Is _____ at home? We have you listed as a registered Democratic voter. We're your neighbors and we're canvassing for Hillary Clinton and Katie McGinty." Katie McGinty was challenging the incumbent Pennsylvania Republican senator, Pat Toomey.

"I'm not interested."

"Okay, sorry to trouble you, have a nice day."

We turned to walk to the next house.

"How can you even do this?" said the woman through her screen door.

"Sorry?" I answered.

"How can you support her after all of the scandals, the emails, and Benghazi and all of that?"

We walked back up the drive to talk to her.

I started: "Well, I see the email issue as a breach of protocol, not a crime. We also don't know that her using a personal server actually compromised anything. As for Benghazi, I don't think any of us know enough about the attacks on the U.S. embassy there to say that anything could have prevented them. But I do know that I live in the neighborhood across the street. I'm Muslim, and Trump keeps saying that Muslims should be banned from entering the US and our mosques should be under surveillance."

"Did he say that?" she asked, clearly disinterested.

"Yes. He's said that several times. What is it that you find persuasive about his platform?"

"I'm a small business owner, and I can't afford to pay healthcare and taxes and all of that. I'm paying for my own kids to go to college, they're talking about 'free college.' Nothing is free; I shouldn't have to pay for everybody to go to college."

In response, my father launched into an uncharacteristically personal anecdote. "I immigrated to Canada in 1963," he told the woman. "I had no money. The Canadian government gave me a scholarship to study and I went on to get a PhD. And then I developed fifteen patented technologies that continue to drive millions of dollars in revenue for American businesses every year. You have to invest in education to have a growing economy. You might be contributing to someone's education, but others would be contributing to your children's educations, too."

She remained unreceptive, though our conversation lasted at least twenty minutes. She suggested, perhaps to be polite, that my father might be exceptional among immigrants, one of the good ones. We failed in our attempt at making her see herself in us, or at making her view Trump's racism as in any way a deterrent to her vote. And in some inexplicable way, the process of trying to convince her to care about us had been humiliating.

It was the only time in my life I can remember my father engaging a stranger at any great length, willingly. And it was certainly the only time I can remember him using his own story to persuade a stranger of a moral cause. He was uncomfortable allowing himself to be so vulnerable and did so only because he believed his country to be dangerously close to electing a terribly incompetent and even malevolent leader. Yet here was his neighbor of more than twenty years explaining that his humanity and security were not as compelling, politically, as her own marginal tax rate. This single encounter, in which my father and I felt we had to plead with our neighbor for our right to be safe in our country, to not be vilified and vetted, to enjoy life, liberty, and the pursuit of happiness, would change both my father and me, permanently.

Just a month before the election, Trump made a campaign stop close to home, in the neighboring town of Newtown, Pennsylvania, hosted at the Newtown Athletic Club (NAC) by its owner. I was determined to protest as a moral imperative, in order to demonstrate to a local business owner that his decision was unpopular and could hurt his business. But I still assumed that Yardley was home; I assumed that my neighbors would turn out in force to decry such a blatantly racist candidate. I was also preoccupied with my daughter's health, which had declined dramatically by then.

It was a great relief to learn that some of my new mom friends were already organizing a protest for the day of the campaign rally, outside the NAC's luxury complex. It sits near a highway but has vast parking lots on the other side of the building, and a substantial amount of land around it, partially occupied by pools, but also areas of unoccupied, landscaped, and fenced land. Handing the kids off to Nadeem and rushing out the door, I had not remembered to take the cellphone numbers of the mom friends I was meeting on the day of the protest, and the messenger app, which we had been communicating through, was not on my phone. The chain restaurant we had decided to meet in was closed, but I parked there anyway and walked into the protest site. The neighborhood was mobbed, though not with protestors. Trump supporters flying flags and sporting red hats were streaming in.

I was suddenly very conscious that I was alone, barely five foot two, and carrying a huge sign asking why NAC was hosting hate. I crossed the street away from several groups of people wearing Make America Great Again hats, and walked several blocks quickly, finding my friends among the scant hundred protestors. And then I stood absolutely stunned at the *thousands* of all-White Trump supporters spilling out into a large, fenced area outside after being unable to squeeze into the venue. There were so few of us there to protest that only a handful on the other side bothered to stop and jeer at us.

Overwhelmed at the size of their crowd, I stood silently. Kristen, whose son went to preschool with my kids, noticed, and asked if I was all right. I wasn't. It was plain in that moment that we were vastly outnumbered, that the people who felt most driven to shape the future of our national politics were on the other side of the fence, and that their vision for that future did not include people like me. But I felt far too in the right to be in the minority. Too much human capital, some of it my own, had already been expended fighting toward equality and justice for such a hateful candidate to still be drawing such a crowd. After years of social justice work in which I had remained optimistic, I felt unmoored.

We all did. The sun had set and we walked each other to our cars. As I drove out of the neighborhood, the magnitude of what we were up against became clear. Cars decorated with Trump paraphernalia lined the shoulders of Route 332 two deep, for a mile and a half, all the way back to Stony Hill Road, left by people who had hiked in to the venue to hear him speak.

It was election season, but it was also the season in which my daughter would enter kindergarten. One sunny morning in August, I pulled into the parking lot of a local public charter school. I had emailed my daughter's school over the summer, asking if I could sit down with her teachers. Because of Jahan's health issues, I wanted to make sure she would be able to take care of herself in the classroom. I also suspected that she'd be the only Muslim child in the school. I remembered how challenging that had been for me, even before 9/11. One of my dearest mom friends from the kids' preschool, a Jehovah's Witness, told me that she liked to go in and meet teachers, give them some information about the things her daughters could and couldn't participate in, and offer to answer any questions. So, I'd made up a little sheet about our holidays and food restrictions, including the things that we enjoy participating in, like the celebrations of our friends in different faiths, and an offer to come in with a treat and tell the children about Ramadan and Eid, celebrations in the Islamic calendar.

I was not nervous. The school had a reputation for being inclusive; it was unusually diverse for the school district we were in and taught in a method known for cross-cultural education and conflict resolution. I was meeting with the head kindergarten teacher and her assistant, both of whom I had first met at an orientation several weeks before. I had even graduated from the local high school in the same class as the assistant teacher in 1992.

"I also wanted to mention that we're Muslim," I told them, after talking through Jahan's medical situation. "Because of all the campaign rhetoric that targets Muslims, I wanted to offer myself as a resource, in case there are any questions, or in case anything comes up. We're a bit worried about how it might be, you know, if the election goes the wrong way."

After an uneasy glance at the head teacher, my old classmate said, "Well, things will be difficult either way." She was being conciliatory, I realized. She was trying to smooth the difference between my point of view and the Republican head teacher's, maybe even her own. I left wondering what my daughter's teachers thought of Muslims, and immigrants, and people of color; I was worried for Jahan.

So I was elated to find out that there was a Muslim teacher in the school. When I learned her name, which was identifiably Muslim, I told my daughter that she was probably about to celebrate Eid, just like us. I was happy to be able to offer my daughter a reflection of herself, and identify a potential support, in case she had to confront any of the anti-Muslim sentiment that was spreading through the media and culture around us.

The next day, Jahan came home and told me, "Mama, I told Mrs. Aziz that I was Muslim just like her!"

"That's great, baby. What did she say?"

She looked down at her toes and replied, "She said we don't talk about that at school."

That was around the time of the Townville school shooting in South Carolina, in which a fourteen-year-old boy shot and injured one teacher and two students and killed a six-year-old. There were thirty-one other school shootings that fall, at high schools and colleges around the country. I began to feel anxious about the beautiful plate-glass windows that flooded my daughter's school with light. Although I had to be buzzed in, the door itself was glass. I wondered if it was bulletproof. I wondered how much of the local support for Trump was linked to anti-Muslim sentiment and how its rise might make my own tiny, curly-headed six-year-old a target. Who would look out for her?

From the time my daughter was an infant I had sung her prayers and blessings; every night from the time she was a toddler, we would list together all of the many people who loved her and I would end by saying, "Most of all of everything, Allah saeen loves you, and God's love is the best love because that love comes from inside your own . . ." And she would gleefully shout, "Heart!" with the "r" sound missing so it sounded like "Hawt!" How would I now explain to her that our identity and our spiritual practice, the center of joy and comfort in our lives, was an object of loathing and fear for many of our fellow Americans, and that we had become a target for their hatred and their violence?

I learned that the Hindu temple I passed on the way to my son's school each morning now locked its doors before congregational prayers, and our local mosque had installed security cameras. These security measures were a response to the racially motivated shootings at the Mother Emanuel AME Church in Charleston, in which nine

Black congregants were killed in 2015, shootings and arson attacks on mosques around the United States, which occurred several times a month throughout 2016 and 2017, and a spate of attacks on Hindu temples in the United States (often because Hindus are mistaken for Muslims). Trump's candidacy, and his populist movement, had made all Black and Brown communities targets. In my peaceful suburban American hometown, we now had to be vigilant in our houses of worship because we had reason to fear violent, racially motivated attacks during our prayers.

After the November 2016 elections in which Trump won the presidency, we went to see my daughter's holiday concert at school. We listened to a couple of hundred children singing proudly about Christmas and Hanukkah for forty-five minutes. That spring, a group of Hindu moms visited the kindergarten class to teach the children about the celebration of Holi. Jahan was thrilled; she got to dance with colorful scarves and have her hands painted with henna, always a favorite. I offered, but was not ultimately invited, to come share about Ramadan in April. I had reconsidered, anyway. I had begun to worry that outing my daughter as a Muslim would put her in danger, something I had not ever considered until after Mrs. Aziz warned her not to mention that she was Muslim at school. Perhaps Mrs. Aziz was concerned for my daughter's safety, or her own; that kind of concern felt increasingly rational, even as it was heartbreaking. Still, her message and the contrast between how Muslims and other religious minorities were being treated was clear. In this relatively liberal space, where traditional color lines had otherwise grown a little more permeable and sometimes even solicitous of different kinds of people, new rules governed Islam and Muslims.

CHAPTER TWO

LIBERTY AND JUSTICE FOR ALL

Fallsington, Pennsylvania

Discovery [gives] an exclusive right to extinguish the Indian title of occupancy, either by purchase or by conquest. . . . If [this] principle has been asserted in the first instance, and afterwards sustained; if a country has been acquired and held under it; if the property of the great mass of the community originates in it, it becomes the law of the land, and cannot be questioned.

—John Marshall, fourth chief justice of the Supreme Court of the United States in *Johnson v. McIntosh*, 1823

Yardley was where we ended up, but Fallsington is where my family first really took root in America. That's where I lived from the age of three until the age of fifteen, and it's where my parents properly settled in. My mother decorated our split-level house with collectors' plates painted with Norman Rockwell–style images, a blond girl with a butterfly on her finger, a pale old man reading by candlelight.

My childhood in Fallsington had plenty of the kinds of moments portrayed in the paintings; it was a pretty magical place for a kid to grow up. The beautiful frame library in the historic section, which we called Old Fallsington, had nearly floor-to-ceiling windows where I could sit and read *Catcher in the Rye* cover to cover. Across the street, the elementary school parking lot sat empty most of the summer, and that's where my friend John learned to freestyle on his Haro Master bike. He had long hair, and he wore eyeliner and his sisters' jewel-colored shirts under a black leather jacket. Old Fallsington was the kind of place that could make you want to be exotic, because it was painful in its uniformity.

In the summer before we started fifth grade, my friend Allison and I had been riding our bikes over to Old Fallsington every week or so, trying to break into the small, historic Moon-Williamson House. We took turns being lookout and breaker-inner. The lookout was armed with lines of pretend poetry with coded meaning. "The grass is so green" meant no cops in sight. That was our main concern, as there always seemed to be a few bored police officers driving in circles through the quiet neighborhood. "The rocks are so hard" meant get on your bike and don't look back. We had tried every red-framed door, every red-framed window, in our determination to have a proper adventure.

I wasn't expecting the cellar window to give when I kicked it. But now it was open, and one of us had to go in. I went through the window on my belly, nearly scraping against the low ceiling until I made the short drop to the floor below. I found myself in a bare room with a packed dirt floor, a cool relief from the heat outside. I stepped up through a doorway and into the cobblestone kitchen with its traditional Bucks County whole-wall hearth set with period cooking implements: elevated pans designed for a small fire or hot coals underneath, hooks for hanging meat.

I opened the front door for Allison, who slipped in so that we could explore the rest of the house together. A short staircase led to a room with wide plank floors and another large hearth, set up as a rustic bedroom. Up a different short staircase there was another bedroom with a child-size rocking chair. Both rooms were blocked off by ribbons, and while it was a great rush to go beyond them, we were hesitant and well mannered in our criminality. We only left behind small notes, like calling cards, with our two-person secret club insignia and name, Infinity.

It was the early 1980s, and Allison and I had the same long bangs hanging over the same enormous plastic eyeglass frames, but we were otherwise as different as two little girls could be. Allison's assumptions about the world were different from mine and all new to me. Her dad wrote jingles for a living and her mother wrote novels, which I don't think were published. When she was driving us somewhere, she asked Allison and me for a word to describe the clouds that day, and she liked my answer: "Stretched." I was thrilled. When I visited for dinner, they made minimal preparations: They ate meat in the shape of the container in which it had been packaged, and vegetables out of a can. Her parents had been at Woodstock protesting the war in Vietnam, listened to rock-and-roll, and vacationed for a week in the summer "down the shore." Allison had a dog named Oreo, her own record player, and a purple shag rug for her bedroom, where she kept her pet goldfish, Iran and Iraq, which she pronounced "eye-ran" and "eye-rack." To my ten-year-old self, Allison represented all of America.

Meanwhile, my own household felt like a cultural island. My father carried a briefcase to work and was stressed by the effort of trying to fit into corporate America. He practiced any presentations he was required to make with a tape recorder in the bedroom, trying to find the places where his accent might obscure his meaning and also to smooth his anxiety, all the while churning out patents that pushed the limits of what plastic could do at a truly impressive rate. The work was creative for him; he sometimes dreamed about molecules and how they might fit together in innovative ways. In the end, though, he was driven by the need for financial security. The very thought of trying to support a family by writing jingles would have given him an ulcer. My mother bought rice and lentils in bulk; she caramelized onions and grated ginger. At night, she spread a plastic tablecloth on the family room floor and shaped potatoes, pulverized lentils, and spices into patties while we watched *Diff'rent Strokes* and *Silver Spoons*. By day, she taught herself to speak English fluently, worked in retail, and eventually got training as a medical technician. That's the job she held from 1982, after my younger brother was born, until she retired.

My parents saved relentlessly. They saved for the job loss or emergency my father always feared might be around the corner, and for trips back to Pakistan. They saved to help relatives back home and to pay the fees for their brothers' and sisters' immigrant visa applications, which wouldn't even be processed for another decade or more. Both of my parents came from homes where toys were made from empty cigarette packs, and when there was meat, you'd suck even the marrow out of the bones. In a country in which they were entirely on their own, they were terrified of being without, so were mostly oblivious to consumer goods like purple shag rugs. They saw animals as creatures that ought to be productive and were loath to take care of my preschool's hamster when it was our weekend. The ways in which they chose to assimilate were unpredictable: My mother weeded our strawberry patch in a pair of green shorts that were a long way from the full burqa, a black cloak she'd worn outdoors as a teenager back home. My father brought home copious amounts of Entenmann's baked goods from the grocery store and took up woodworking as a hobby. In many other ways, my parents remained stubbornly as they had been, continuing to pronounce Iran and Iraq the way that most Iranians and Iraqis, and most of the rest of the world, do: "ee-rohn" and "ee-rok." Their persistent accents did not serve them well in suburban America. Long after my mother was fluent, but while I was still an elementary student, salesclerks in department stores would impatiently direct the answers to her questions toward me, as if I were the designated interpreter.

Still, Allison and I were kids, so we could be the very best of friends and partners in the adventure of being ten. We were inseparable that summer that we broke into the log house. Allison came over from her house in neighboring Levittown to my house and we'd bicycle through my 1970s subdivision, with its six models in all different colors planted on hundreds of adjacent lots with clipped lawns.

We'd almost always end up in Old Fallsington, up the hill from the newer section in which I lived, which was formally known as the Village of Nottingham. We'd stop at the penny candy store, eat our treats on the porch, and then visit the log house before heading home, exhilarated to have been *somewhere* and done *something*.

On our final visit to the Moon-Williamson House, Allison and I invited two other friends to come with us. We needed witnesses to keep alive the thrill of our adventure. So, Rachel, who lived across the street, and Tracy, who was visiting from Levittown, rode their bikes behind us, up the long back road that connected newer Fallsington and Old Fallsington. We left our bikes and they all waited while I dropped into the basement.

I should have known everything had changed when I saw the big black box on a table with its knobs and little red glowing lights. But by then I had no choice. I couldn't reach the basement window to climb out, so I headed for the door. Maybe nothing would happen when I opened it? But a buzzing started right away, first barely audible and then louder and louder until it could be heard for several blocks. I yelled, "Run!" as I escaped out the door, and we all bicycled as fast as we possibly could, arriving back on Taylor Drive in a sweat. We stood together, discussing whether we should bike around the neighborhood to yard sales so that we would have "alibis." We never got caught, but we never got into the Moon-Williamson House again, either. By the time we worked up the nerve to go back the next week, the basement window was sealed shut with a newly installed lock.

As an adult, looking for the history of the town, I started there at the Moon-Williamson House, convincing the woman staffing the Fallsington Historical Society office to give me a tour of some of the original Quaker buildings: the fieldstone tavern, the schoolmaster's house, and the first village doctor's home and office. Then I paid a visit to Sam Snipes, a local legend and Quaker patriarch who traced his lineage back to the very first Quakers to arrive in William Penn's colonial settlement. I had known Sam when I was a child but only by reputation, and through his horses, who grazed in the cemetery across from the fieldstone Quaker Meetinghouse and beside the schoolmaster's cottage, and who I would visit when I rode my bike to the library. Later, I knew him as the owner of the local tree nursery. Sam, having spent nearly ninety of his ninety-nine and a half years in or near Fallsington, had lived through much of the history I was now looking for. He was five years old when the Ku Klux Klan met monthly at the local library in 1924. He could remember when Native children had been taken from their families to be forcibly assimilated and hired out to local farmers, and later, after he became a lawyer, he had fought for integration of local suburbs.

When the Moon-Williamson House was built in 1685, the Lenape might still have controlled much of the Delaware Valley, but their traditional social structures, including political and trade alliances, would already have been weakened by a dramatic loss of population. During Penn's lifetime, settlement along the Delaware River dramatically shifted the balance of power and authority. As the Lenape lost control and Penn's desire to sell land for profit grew, his benevolence wore thin. Earlier land arrangements that had kept European settlements to portions of the Delaware Valley and along tributaries, with the rest of the land presumed to be under Lenape control, fell apart. Settlers began to abandon the practice of periodic payments, asserting their right to permanent ownership of the land. By 1703, Penn created, through his agent, the precursor of modern "reservations." In that year, Penn designated a parcel of five hundred acres in what is now Chester County "for settlement" of a group of the Lenape called the Okehocking. The parcel was west of Philadelphia, cut off from access to the Delaware River valley, just south of the town in which our Sunday school zikr group would meet in 2014.

Penn began to see the land as his by default, only belonging to the Lenape if he explicitly provided for it. As the Lenape moved seasonally across their territory, the land they left was immediately claimed as part of Penn's territory and sold to European colonizers, who fenced it, forcing the Lenape to keep to the land they had traditionally occupied only in the summer months and to abandon much of the rest of their homeland. But this made their continued prosperity impossible. Their ability to hunt, fish, and gather wherever resources were plentiful was restricted, driving hunger and poverty; the Okehocking had accepted Penn's parcel only to preserve some sliver of their ancestral land, but it was not enough to sustain them.

Today, 180 acres of the parcel that was deeded to the Okehocking is maintained, undeveloped, by Willistown Township as the Okehocking Land Grant Historic District. It is dotted with the same sort of fieldstone buildings that are so common in Fallsington, including a meetinghouse, a school, and several farmhouses from when Quaker settlement overtook the parcel in the 1730s. Much of the rest of the original five hundred acres is now privately owned, cut into acre or half-acre lots just off the posh suburban corridor known as the Main Line, west of the leafy campuses of Villanova University, and Haverford, Swarthmore, and Bryn Mawr colleges.

As early as 1705, Lenape representatives filed grievances with the colonial courts and authorities to resist the increasingly aggressive encroachment and reclaim land which had been misappropriated in ways that restricted traditional uses. They were generally left without remedy when settlers refused to take down their fences and give up possession. Their pleas tell of the faith they had in Penn's early promise to them, their sense of betrayal, and the abuse they suffered at the hands of later migrants to the colony. These court actions are also a remarkable testament to the myriad ways in which Native peoples employed European colonial language, law, and culture in order to name the hypocrisy in which settlers engaged, and to fight for their lives and livelihoods. In 1725, the Lenape sachem, or leader, Checochinican, who spoke fluent English, made this plea at the Provincial Assembly in Philadelphia for his people's land along the Brandywine River:

When William Penn came to this country, he settled in permanent friendship with us, and after we sold him our country, he reconveyed back a certain tract along the Brandywine. . . . William Penn promised we should not be molested whilst one Indian lived, grew old and blind, and died,—so another to the third generation; that is the way of expressing it—from generation to generation; and now it is half the age of an old man since, and we are molested, and our lands surveyed out and settled before we can reap our corn off; and to our great injury, Brandywine creek is so obstructed with dams, that the fish cannot come up to our habitants. We desire you to take notice that we are a poor people, and want the benefit of the fish, for when we are out hunting, our children with their bows and arrows used to get fish for their sustenance.

Asked by the administrator of the proceeding if he had "expected to enjoy the land forever," Checochinican responded, "Not only we, but all the Indians understood it to be theirs as long as the water ran down that creek." Another sachem, Sasoonan, appeared before the Philadelphia council in June of 1728 to say "he was grown old and was troubled to see the Christians settle on lands that the Indians had never been paid for."

After Penn's death in 1718, his three surviving sons became the colony's proprietors. They claimed land in violation of Penn's treaty, selling it to Scots-Irish and German settlers without first purchasing it from the Lenape. They continued to assert that when Lenape families left any part of their land for temporary or seasonal pursuits, they had permanently abandoned it, making it available for the taking. The newer immigrants, not bound by the pacifism of the Quaker community, were encouraged to settle on the western outskirts of land claimed by Quakers and beyond, as squatters along the Susquehanna River, parceling and fencing as they went. On the frontier, aggressive appropriation of Native land sparked violent conflict. Rape, murder, and assault prevailed in the absence of colonial government regulation and in direct contradiction to Quaker pacifism and Penn's original promise of peaceful coexistence.

Penn's adult sons would renounce their Quaker faith and abandon all of the more redeeming aspects of their father's dealings with the Lenape. In their quest to acquire more land along the Delaware River, they would cheat their way to a vast land acquisition in an infamous 1737 transaction known as the Walking Purchase. They produced a copy of a deed they said had been executed between Penn and the Lenape, but for which land had yet to be measured off. By the terms of the deed, the land was supposed to include whatever could be walked by a man in a day and a half, northwest in a diagonal toward the interior of Pennsylvania, starting in Wrightstown on the lower Delaware River. The Lenape anticipated that Penn's sons would send someone to walk the distance through the woods, and from that spot, measure directly across to the Delaware River. That right triangle of land, pointing into Pennsylvania and bounded by the river on the other, would belong to the Penn brothers.

Instead, the Penn brothers cleared a path and sent trained runners, covering double the distance intended. Then, instead of marking that distance straight over to the river, they measured a wider angle, capturing a larger triangle of land for themselves, including most of the upper Delaware Valley. The Walking Purchase would be remembered as a great betrayal, ending all hope for Lenape security in their homeland.

In the 1740s, the Pennsylvania government began to prioritize its trade dealings with the Iroquois, a large confederacy of five nations whose territory stretched across the Great Lakes region, from Lake Ontario deep into the Midwest, leaving the Lenape without the primary benefit of their trade relationship with settlers in the Delaware Valley. Frustrated by the bad faith of the English in land ownership, land use, and trade, the Western Lenape took the side of the French against the settlers in the French and Indian War, beginning in 1754, and executed several attacks in their ancestral home on the Delaware, killing and scalping men, women, and children in targeted settler communities. By 1755, the Quakers had lost credibility as effective peacekeepers and negotiators on behalf of the colonies, and a three-year period of state-sanctioned violence ensued. In 1756, the Pennsylvania governor Robert Morris issued a bounty for the scalps of Lenape people: 130 Spanish dollars for men and boys over the age of twelve, and 50 Spanish dollars for women. This action played a significant role in the widespread use of scalp bounties to fuel European settlers' civilian attacks on Native peoples throughout America.

Two years into the Revolutionary War, the newly born United States prepared to battle British forces in the Ohio Valley, where the displaced Lenape had begun to carve a new home. In advance of the battle, the U.S. government offered the Lenape a deal, known as the Treaty of Fort Pitt (named for the U.S. military base situated in what is now downtown Pittsburgh), which would be its first official treaty with a Native nation. Most of the brief document binds the parties to reciprocal loyalty during warfare, specifying the needs of the United States in its immediate conflict with the British. The first five of six articles establish peace between the parties. They also permit the U.S. military free passage through Lenape territory, access to Lenape soldiers, and provisions of corn, meat, horses, and accommodation for payment, as well as provide that the United States will trade in weapons and clothing for Lenape soldiers.

The final article purports to guarantee "all [Lenape] territorial rights in the fullest and most ample manner, as it hath been bounded by former treaties," referring to substantial land in the westernmost strip of Pennsylvania and eastern Ohio, as well as a limit on European settlement in the Allegheny Mountains. Article 6 also, remarkably, suggests that the Lenape organize a confederation of peaceful Native people in the region to be considered for *statehood* by the Continental Congress. This was the last, best hope for Lenape and perhaps Native cohesion in the Northeast, but obviously was never effectuated by the nascent United States. The failure of our nation to make good on

Lenape territorial security and statehood cemented its colonial vision as one exclusive of Native peoples.

The new government's bad faith was almost immediately apparent to the Lenape, who protested at the following Continental Congress to no avail. Near the end of the war, in 1782, ninety-six Lenape men, women, and children who had been displaced by British soldiers a year earlier were killed by Pennsylvania soldiers while trying to recover their crops in eastern Ohio, ending any pretense of peace or security under the Treaty of Fort Pitt.

The scattered few Lenape who managed to survive the eighteenth century in the Delaware Valley by integrating themselves among the Quakers were both isolated from their displaced kin and held at arm's length by even the most benevolent and devout of their Quaker neighbors, among whom they were frequently known by an English first name attached to the designation "Indian." Dawn Marsh, a modern scholar of the Lenape, recently wrote the story of "Indian Hannah," who died in 1802, designated the last Lenape in the Brandywine Valley in the Quaker historical record. Marsh argues convincingly that this dubious claim was made in order to mark the fulfillment of Penn's promise that the land would belong to the Lenape until the last one had abandoned it, after which settlers would be free from Lenape claims to the land.

In 1811, the same year the last of Penn's sons died, the modern county map of Pennsylvania would be drawn. Pennsylvania had been taken from its Native inhabitants over the preceding century, and most had been driven to present-day Ohio. Almost all would be driven again in successive generations to Indiana, Missouri, Kansas, and then Oklahoma. Today, the majority of the Lenape from the western shores of the Delaware River live far removed from their ancestral homes, in Oklahoma, Wisconsin, and Ontario. Penn's utopian community in Pennsylvania splintered, with some descendants engaging in the broader campaign of violence against Native peoples, and others slowly evolving into the modern Quaker community, which would come to be known for its commitment to contemporary campaigns for racial justice and reconciliation.

Immersion in this history confused what I thought I'd known about the verdant patch of America along the Delaware where I had grown up. Of course, I knew that the Lenape who had inhabited that place were no longer present, but I had been raised on a series of fairy tales in which they first shared their land graciously and later "drifted away" from the area, as one contemporary website for the Okehocking Land Grant Historic District still claims. I had believed the lessons I'd been taught based on early biographies of Penn, which denied that he enslaved people at Pennsbury. Despite the frequent mention of enslaved people in the many letters between William Penn, his wife, Hannah, and their agents, those stories of the enslaved remain only partially excavated, the object of ongoing study by the historians at Pennsbury Manor today. In light of this history, I began to view the crowds at the Trump rally in Newtown differently, as the descendants of those early European settlers in the state. Perhaps some of them had actually understood the history of Pennsylvania better than I had, understood it and embraced it as an ongoing project to preserve a European American colony. Perhaps they thought of the project as one that they might be called upon to defend at any moment from people like my family; perhaps they believed as their English and Scots-Irish and German ancestors had that the very presence of Brown or free Black people in their midst threatened their wealth in and entitlement to the land.

When my parents arrived in Fallsington more than three hundred years after William Penn, no obvious evidence that the Lenape had ever inhabited that place remained. There were no community organizations, no reservations, no plaques, and no memorials. Pennsylvania is one of the few states without a single federally recognized Native tribe, although the Lenape have been recognized as a sovereign tribe on the other side of the Delaware River valley, in the neighboring state of New Jersey, since the 1980s. That group, the Nanticoke Lenni-Lenape, number about three thousand, but my father encountered only one Lenape woman in forty-three years of living in the lower Delaware Valley; she worked in the cafeteria of Rohm & Haas, the company at which he spent most of his career. In the absence of Lenape people, my parents, like most of their neighbors, thought little about who and what had come before them on the Delaware.

Had they been aware of the history of Fallsington, they might have reflected on their strange circumstance: They had left a newly postcolonial Pakistan, where they were among the Indigenous people recently liberated from British rule. They had landed in America, which, though also liberated from British rule, was still very much engaged in the colonial project of occupying the land and exploiting the resources of Native peoples. In America, there had been no handoff of power back to the original inhabitants as there had been in Pakistan (though that had been with much bloodshed and suffering). My parents had, unwittingly, chosen a path on which their children would benefit from the colonization of one country while their own parents had been among the colonized in another.

All of this was obscured to them as they found themselves in a world of vast new suburban plans with neighborhood schools, sidewalks, and strip malls. They were preoccupied with supporting their young family, with supporting their newly immigrated siblings, and with raising children who would not be so entirely assimilated to American culture that they became foreign to their own hearts. This was a real challenge. In the new 1970s development, we were the sole Muslim family and the sole South Asian family. In fact, only a handful of visible minorities lived in the sprawling development, and we were handily clustered together on one block: the Pierces, a Black family, lived on one side of us, and the Smiths, a Jewish family, lived on the other. Directly behind us were the Tylers. Dave Tyler was White, and his wife, Meija, was from the Philippines. A few doors down from the Tylers was a family that had moved from China, and elsewhere within the development was a single Hispanic family, the Ramirezes, whose accents and persistent tans weighed against their European origins in claims to whiteness. It was 1976, just past the height of racial segregation in American housing. Our families had no language or culture in common, but I remember each of them some forty years later because we were strangers in a sea of English, Irish, and Italian faces.

I knew our isolation felt strange, but I didn't know it was by design. In 1967, President Lyndon Johnson had convened the Kerner Commission, a panel charged with identifying the causes of protests and violent conflict that had erupted in poor Black neighborhoods in twenty-five cities across the country. In the spring of the following year, the commission released the Kerner Report, identifying various forms of institutional White racism as the combined causes of the unrest. Among the dozen areas of institutional racism identified in the report, the top four were police violence in Black neighborhoods, unemployment or underemployment, poor housing or lack of available housing, and inadequate education. Many Black and Brown home buyers had both the desire and the capital to own homes but remained pressed into urban ghettos. Civil rights advocacy had yet to dismantle the myriad laws and practices that barred them from most desirable urban and suburban housing. In response to the findings in the Kerner Report, Congress passed the Fair Housing Act in 1968, which prohibited all sale, rental, and financing practices that were discriminatory on the basis of race, religion, national origin, or sex. Without passage of the Fair Housing Act, it's unlikely that my parents would have been able to buy a suburban home in 1974 St. Petersburg, Florida, or three years later in suburban Fallsington. And yet, the arrangement of a handful of diverse families on a single block of Fallsington, buried deep within the development, smacked of tokenism. Our mostly White suburb included just enough carefully placed Black and Brown families to pretend at legal compliance, creating only superficial integration.

Despite the diversity of our particular block, we swam, unthinking, in the deeply racist culture around us: In games of cowboys and Indians, cowboys were heroes and Indians were ridiculous, antiquated, and exaggerated parodies meant to mythologize and marginalize the very real, living Native peoples who had by then survived four hundred years of colonization. Phrases like "Indian summer" and "Indian giver" were the unquestioned stuff of my Fallsington childhood, both ironically implying that Native peoples were tricksters and thieves, first giving and then snatching away what was valuable or desirable. And although we played among colonial Quaker fieldstone houses and were neighbors to several descendants of those early Quaker families, we never thought to question who had done the taking. The twin story lines of the antiquated and untrustworthy Native man and the mild and humble Quaker patriarch pictured on our oatmeal box made for a cohesive American narrative. There was the villain and the hero, the unworthy and the worthy, the darkness and the light.

In Fallsington in the 1980s, a middle-class suburban family could expect their children to come home from public school classrooms knowing only that the original inhabitants of the land were "Indians." At school, I never heard the words "Native American," "First Nations," or "Indigenous." And we continued for decades to use the misnomer "Indian," accepting the European designation even though it was based on a great mistake.

So much of what—and who—came before the Quaker settlement of Fallsington was established has been painstakingly destroyed and willfully forgotten. Sam Snipes, the local Quaker patriarch who would have been a boy in 1920s Fallsington, recalled encountering Native children only when they were sent by facilities, euphemistically called Indian boarding or Indian residential schools, to provide cheap child laborers for local farmers who requested them over the summer. The children he met were likely from as far west as South Dakota and Arizona, taken from their families by agents from the Bureau of Indian Affairs and interned at a nearby residential facility. The first such facility, the Carlisle Indian Industrial School, would have closed just a few years before.

The town of Carlisle is about two hours' drive directly west of Fallsington, in the Susquehanna River valley, named for the Iroquoian Susquehannock people who once lived there. It was partly because the elimination of Native people from Pennsylvania was so complete by 1879 that Captain Richard Henry Pratt chose the town of Carlisle, Pennsylvania, as the site for the first off-reservation residential Indian facility in which he intended to intern Native children. Its remoteness from the western reservations to which Native people had by then been driven and confined was strategic, as children would be unable to make their way back to their homes and families.

The explicit purpose of Pratt's so-called school was not actually to provide academic instruction; instead, he intended to "kill the Indian, but save the man." In other words, Pratt designed Carlisle Indian Industrial School to eliminate by cultural genocide the children of those Native people who had survived physical genocide. The movement of settlers and their railroads westward to the Pacific Ocean was then encumbered by the large Native nations of the Southwest and Midwestern plains. Having recovered from and built immunity centuries earlier to diseases brought by Spanish colonists, these nations were better prepared to mount a resistance to American expansionism than perhaps the U.S. government had anticipated. This posed a problem: What would be done with all of these people who stood in the way of westward expansion? Pratt believed that they ought to be assimilated, by force if necessary. Just as William Penn had done more than two hundred years before, Pratt rhetorically asserted the "equality" of Native Americans with White people. Then, he designed an institution intended to strip Native children of their languages, cultures, spirituality, and family bonds on the premise that those things were inferior, contemptible, and expendable, and that saving the children meant assimilating them into White American society.

Pratt's early assimilationist experiments were on seventeen Kiowa and Comanche prisoners of war whom he arranged to hold at the Hampton Institute, a school for free Black people founded after the Civil War, in 1868. Ten of the first forty-nine Native students enrolled died there. Nonetheless, Pratt pressed on, securing permission from the Department of the Interior to create a permanent school in the town of Carlisle, where the government already owned agricultural land with military barracks on it.

His plans for an off-reservation boarding school were approved by the Bureau of Indian Affairs of the Department of the Interior, on the condition that more than half of Pratt's students would come from the "most troublesome of the tribes." The bureau first sent Pratt to engage an aggrieved group of Lakota whom the government had recently displaced from their home along the Missouri River. He was instantly rebuffed by the leader Spotted Tail, who said, "The white people are thieves and liars. We do not want our children to learn such things. The white man is very smart. He knew there was gold in the Black Hills and he made us give up all that country and now a great many white people are there getting out the gold."

By the time Pratt was soliciting Native children from western nations, Native people had been largely forced out of the United States east of the Mississippi, and the devastating western campaigns to herd Native nations onto desolate reservations were well under way. Dozens of Native societies had already lost their traditional homelands and traditional economies, only to face starvation when rations and payments promised by treaty failed to appear. In this context, Pratt argued back to Spotted Tail that had the children of their people been educated in English, able to read and write and negotiate, perhaps the Lakota would have been able to retain their rights to the Black Hills and all of its riches. In desperation, Spotted Tail and the other leaders of his group relented, sending seventy-two children to Carlisle. Meanwhile, Pratt struggled to create a habitable facility for his project; the government provided sparse food rations, little in the way of clothing, and no beds at all at first, causing Pratt to plead that for his venture to be a success, the children couldn't be given a "starvation supply of food."

Pratt opened Carlisle with 138 Native children, at times relying upon persuasion and the increasing duress of western nations, as with Spotted Tail, and in other cases preying upon those who could not protest, as with the children of political prisoners. Photos of the first group to arrive at Carlisle Indian Industrial School show several dozen children from the Western Plains. Some were very young, dressed in traditional clothing, with long hair and stunned expressions. Photos of some of the same children, after being forced to cut their hair and adopt Western dress, were distributed to government officials as evidence of Carlisle's success at assimilating the children to secure funding and support. The children in that first group who arrived in 1879 were all given English names and stripped of their own. That practice persisted at Carlisle until it closed in 1918, and at hundreds of similar facilities modeled on it for several decades more.

Jim Thorpe of the Sac and Fox Nation, who was taken to Carlisle as a child and went on to famously win Olympic gold as a runner in 1912, was actually born Wa-Tho-Huk, meaning "bright path." While Thorpe's successes are often noted, less is said about the ongoing racism he faced even as he was at the pinnacle of his long athletic career, sleeping in steerage, separated from his teammates on the way to Stockholm, and digging through the trash to replace the shoes missing from his bag on the day of the race. Even his remains were embattled, auctioned off by his third wife to a Pennsylvania town, and then the subject of a 2015 Supreme Court case in which his sons and other relatives sought his remains for traditional burial. They were unsuccessful.

In 1886, Pratt acquired Apache children and young adults ages twelve through twenty-two who had been incarcerated in Florida as prisoners of war when their parents resisted the encroachments of settlers and miners on their land in Arizona. A photograph of the group suggests it included forty-three boys and girls, although there may have been other Apache children that arrived separately. Their parents resisted having their children taken away, but they were themselves powerless prisoners, held at Fort Marion, divided by gender, subject to minimal rations, rampant disease, rat-infested quarters, and contaminated water. The Apache children taken from their parents at Fort Marion later wrote about their experiences at Carlisle. Upon arrival, their hair was cut short and they were lined up by height to be assigned birth dates and names in alphabetical order. Thirty of them would die there of tuberculosis.

After passage of an 1893 congressional appropriations act allowing the secretary of the interior to "withhold rations, clothing, or other annuities from Indian parents who refuse[d] or neglect[ed]" to send their children aged eight through twenty-one to school for "a reasonable portion of the year," Pratt no longer needed to persuade parents to part with their children. The government took them by force, conditioning the survival of parents, and of entire societies, on the forfeiture of their children. By 1906, Congress had also passed legislation permitting the "placement" of Native children in "Indian Reform Schools" by the commissioner of Indian Affairs without the consent of parents, guardians, or next of kin. The Bureau of Indian Affairs established quotas, authorizing officials to take a certain number of children from each of the hundreds of federally recognized tribes. Government officials had come to see the children themselves as useful hostages whose vulnerability in confinement could be used to secure the cooperation of Native leaders.

Many Native parents and children protested the internment of children at Carlisle and the facilities that came after it. The historical records include an 1891 photograph of Oglala parents camped outside of one such facility in Pine Ridge, South Dakota; administrative notes on children who ran away from these facilities; oral histories of children being taught to hide when Bureau of Indian Affairs agents came to collect children; and countless parents' letters written to school administrators, begging for their children's return. Parents learned that they had reason to fear they'd never see their children again. Native children confined to residential facilities were often denied access to their homes and families for years at a time, if they made it home at all. When instruction ended for the summer, children at Carlisle and similar facilities were often sent on "outings," the common euphemism for hiring children out to labor in area farms and homes over the summer rather than sending them home. They were paid little for their labor, with half of the payment sent to school accounts, inaccessible to the students themselves.

Children who died of disease, malnutrition, or abuse in residential facilities or on outings were frequently unaccounted for in school records, and their deaths were not reported to their families, leaving descendants to hunt for their remains several generations later. There are more than 186 children, from more than three dozen federally recognized tribes, known to be buried on the grounds of Carlisle today. Excavations have unearthed several more unmarked or misidentified graves. Hundreds more children are now believed to have died at Carlisle than was previously recorded, and even more are believed to have died shortly after they left, having been sent home when they appeared too sick to survive.

Annual enrollment at Carlisle would expand to one thousand students by 1905. It closed after thirty-nine years of operation, having destroyed the childhoods of an estimated ten thousand children, over at least two generations. Native people are just now becoming successful in their campaigns to identify and repatriate the remains of their relatives from its burial ground. In 2017, the first three children's remains were reclaimed from Carlisle with quiet ceremony by the Northern Arapaho and reburied on the Wind River Reservation in Wyoming. Little Chief arrived at Carlisle on March 11, 1881, as a fourteen-year-old boy, along with Horse, who was eleven, and Little Plume, who was only nine. All three died within two years of their arrival.

According to the National Native American Boarding School Healing Coalition (NABS), the only organization in the country collecting data on the history of institutions like Carlisle, 376 similar residential facilities were eventually in operation across the United States, managed by the federal government, Christian missions, or the Catholic Church. By 1926 nearly 83 percent of Native children were being taken to live in them. Native people would not win the legal right to keep their children out of such internment until the passage of the Indian Child Welfare Act in 1978, five generations after the practice of abducting Native children was institutionalized. The Ojibwe scholar Brenda Child relied on thousands of heartbreaking letters from Native children and their parents, intercepted and filed away by the facilities in which they were interned, to reconstruct the practices and perspectives of facility administrators as well as the experiences of Native children and their parents. The letters demonstrate that Native children were incarcerated indefinitely, despite having parents who begged for their return, as in this 1925 letter from a mother to the superintendent of the Flandreau facility in South Dakota, where her daughter Margaret had been held for four years:

> So please be so kind Mr. House and let her come home for this summer the poor girl has not been home for [a] long time and I know she will feel more like going to school next fall if she sees her folks once more. I am willing to let her go as long as she wants . . . Dear Sir if you please let her come home I am begging you Mr. House so I will be looking for her . . . Hopeing you will be kind.

After three such letters from Margaret's mother, the superintendent replied curtly that there was nothing "that would justify me sending her home."

A milestone 1928 federal report, "The Problem of Indian Administration," found that Native children were frequently malnourished, overworked, physically abused, poorly educated, and overcrowded, resulting in epidemic illness within residential facilities. The same report found that the mortality rate of Native children at residential facilities was *six and a half times higher* than that of other children in the United States during the same period.

The impacts of Carlisle and the hundreds of facilities modeled on it were, and still are, devastating to Native communities. In addition to loss of family, community, language, culture, and even their own names, children in them were also forced to give up their spiritual traditions and practice Christianity, and they were subjected to extreme physical and emotional abuse for arbitrary reasons, including "acting Indian" or speaking in their primary languages. Numerous survivor accounts recorded and reported by scholars and journalists as well as a Special Committee on Investigations of the Select Committee on Indian Affairs report, presented before the Senate of the 101st Congress in 1989, evidenced widespread sexual abuse of the children within Bureau of Indian Affairs schools at the hands of the same teachers and administrators who, with horrifying irony, were charged with "civilizing" them. That report found that "BIA administrators repeatedly failed to report child sexual abuse allegations to law enforcement authorities and even threatened persons making allegations with slander suits. BIA's negligence led to needless cases of child molestation, yet many of the negligent officials were actually promoted to higher positions."

The U.S. government has never formally addressed 150 years of forced internment of Native children, or the horrors visited upon their bodies and spirits so that settlers might "kill the Indian." In spite of this, modern, global Indigenous alliances and Native representation in American politics appears to be growing stronger. In 2018, while the protests of the Dakota Access Pipeline at the Standing Rock Reservation made international headlines, a Lenape and Chippewa activist from New York City, George Stonefish, organized a powwow in Manhattan, the first to be held there since the Lenape were displaced in the early 1700s. When asked the significance of holding the powwow on ancestral land that is now also one of the largest modern megacities on Earth, he said without pause, "The Lenape are back." His sentiment confused me, because the Lenape are as visible in Manhattan today as they are in Bucks County, which is to say barely at all, while the land their ancestors inhabited is unrecognizable under concrete and skyscrapers. But Mr. Stonefish was asserting his continuing presence and claim in the modern urban world. His is the unyielding determination to return to or to remain in his home, a focus that the American colonial project has failed to destroy.

I'd gone looking for why my family and I had come to feel like outsiders in the Delaware Valley. What I'd found was that the Delaware Valley as I'd known it was constructed through a persistent campaign of genocide, in waves of dispossession and violent assimilation. Though I'd understood the broad outlines of this history, intellectually, for some time, the accounts I had learned were fictionalized to emphasize the virtue and entitlement of European settlers, and to elide or erase the degradation of the Native and Black people in their midst. The history as recorded in the original deeds and documents of European settlers of the time is clear. The premise and central principle of colonialism was the same in Penn's utopia as it was in all the colonies. White European settlers meant to take the land and derive its wealth, all of it, in perpetuity.

CHAPTER THREE

DEVELOPMENT

Levittown, Pennsylvania

It comes as a great shock to discover . . . that the country to which you have pledged your allegiance along with everyone else has not pledged allegiance to you.

—James Baldwin

My parents had chosen to live in Fallsington over neighboring Bristol, where my father worked, specifically because it was part of Pennsbury School District, which his colleagues considered better. Fallsington was many of the things that most people in the world only dream of. The streets were clean, the lawns mowed, trash collected and mail delivered reliably. Neighbors were generally friendly and helpful, children played together across age, gender, and race, up and down my block until the streetlights came on. We celebrated each other's birthdays and swam in each other's pools.

Fallsington was almost entirely White, but those of us who had managed to wrangle one of the six homes in the development sold to non-White families were accepted with kindness. It was our one Jewish neighbor, Mrs. Smith, who first invited my mother to the ladies' Tuesday-morning tea, which rotated between the homes of a dozen or so women. Preschool children would be penned in somewhere safe to play and moms would all sit in some adjacent kitchen or living room for a cup of tea and yellow cake from a boxed mix.

Fallsington was separated from the adjacent development of Levittown by the four lanes of Tyburn Road, made up of just a dozen streets or so in the newer section and half that many in the historic section. It had its own small elementary school, but my parents opted to have my brother and me bused another mile and a half from that school to Village Park Elementary School in Levittown beginning in first grade, to join the larger school's "gifted" program. That program seemed to them another of the many strange and wonderful opportunities of living in a good country, and they wanted us to benefit from it.

I could only sometimes pass for White, but I was not White. My family members were not White and could *not* generally pass. Maybe because I had spent most of my preschool years in Fallsington on a street slightly more diverse than the other streets, it had not occurred to me to think about how the children or my teachers at Village Park might perceive my racial ambiguity. I had no real way of understanding that they'd see my black hair and eyes as alien, an intrusion on their space. Levittown had been built as a Whites-only suburb thirty years before Fallsington, and about twenty years before Congress passed the Fair Housing Act in 1968. The segregationist attitudes on which Levittown had been premised still permeated its social life and institutions.

It wasn't until the first day of third grade, when Ms. Cunningham seated me, dark from the summer in the sun, and one other girl, one of the few Black children in the entire school, at the very back of the classroom, that I came to better understand my isolation at Village Park. Ms. Cunningham remained inexplicably and permanently angry at the two of us that school year, refusing to call on us or help us with any assignment, withholding the praise and compliments she offered the other children. I began to quietly hate my name, my black hair and eyes.

There were things about each of us that made her face twist into a mean smirk. Like when Kia brought in homework and had used pan-cake syrup in place of the glue she didn't have. Or when Kia's desk, the kind with a single open shelf beneath its wooden top, became too full for Ms. Cunningham's liking and she dumped it right in the mid-dle of class so that Kia would have to sit in the mess, sorting through it during the lesson. Or when Eid-ul-Fitr, the Islamic celebration at the end of Ramadan, arrived and I came to school with hands painted orange with henna. Ms. Cunningham yelled at me: "Haven't your parents taught you not to draw all over your hands with marker?" so loud and so furious that I couldn't explain. When I returned from scrubbing them in the bathroom, knowing it would do nothing, I told her that it was henna, but she only seemed more enraged. I remember that year for the stress I carried in my body, and for the three weeks I spent home sick, more ill than I had ever been in my young life. And I remember the pile of schoolwork Ms. Cunningham sent home for me to complete before I returned.

It is profoundly difficult to communicate what it does to a child to be loathed by their teacher for what they are, to be casually degraded or humiliated daily, even when it doesn't involve physical or sexual violence. I was porous to my teachers, looking to them to help me understand not only academics, but how to behave and belong out-side of my home, socially. I was vulnerable, and so Ms. Cunningham left a precise imprint of her hatred inside of me, for me to carry and battle with over the next two decades of my life.

As a child, I had a really hard time connecting actions to conse-quences, a detached relationship to my body and a tendency to day-dream. It's difficult to know how much of that had to do with feeling like I could never quite anticipate the expectations of adults or peers around me. If I adapted to fit the expectations of my peers, it often resulted in behavior that created conflict at home, and if I adapted to fit those of my parents, it was nearly impossible to relate to my peers. The expectations of my parents also seemed to shift each time one of their siblings immigrated, injecting some new judgment of life in America, having never before lived outside of Hyderabad, Pakistan, themselves. Expressions of joy and modes of entertainment were especially tricky: Food, religious holidays, and weekend plans made me foreign to my peers; music, pool parties, and sleepovers caused battles at home. And then there were run-ins with adults like Ms. Cunningham, who would have preferred for me to not be present in her space at all. Whether my tendency toward escapism was born of these things or not, I know that they exacerbated it. I felt my primary responsibility was to manage these arbitrary expectations as best I could, rather than settling on a fixed sense of right and wrong and establishing a cohesive identity. I read compulsively, to live vicariously and also to erase myself from actual life, where there were so many contradictory values and priorities.

I came home from the first day of standardized testing at my Levittown school and asked my father which little oval I should fill in to tell my race. The choices might have been Black, White, or Hispanic, or they might have, by then, included Asian/Pacific Islander. I don't remember. But I remember trying to puzzle it out. I don't look East Asian, and I knew I wasn't White, Black, or Hispanic. I was something missing, something unanticipated. My father took a few minutes, trying to figure out what White people might have intended by these categories, and making a quick assessment of which identity, absent an accurate one, would afford me the best treatment and the best opportunity. He landed, of course, on "White." It was clear from who occupied the White House, who occupied seats in Congress, and who ran both his company and every other American company of which my father was aware that everything he aspired to and wanted for me in America, the stability, education, meritocratic advancement, wealth, were most readily accessible to the White majority.

By middle school, I had already internalized the language of American greatness and exceptionalism, allowing it to drown out the ways in which my parents remained outsiders, at work and at school, in shops and in our neighborhood. I certainly didn't understand that I was feeling the effects of a deliberate exclusion and a powerful animus that had defined Levittown and so very many American suburban communities like it since it was built. As my class was preparing to go on a trip to the Statue of Liberty, our teacher decided that the class would have an essay contest. Each student was asked to write an essay on what it meant to them to be an American, and one student would be asked to read hers aloud when we arrived on Liberty Island. My essay won, presumably because it was the only one having to do with an immigrant experience. I don't remember what the essay said, only that I wrote what I knew was expected of me—that America is a land of opportunity, that I was grateful, that it had fulfilled its promise to me and to my family.

Levittown is widely known as an iconic innovation in postwar suburban planning. William Levitt built his first namesake development in Long Island, New York, and his second in lower Bucks County, Pennsylvania, before going on to build several other large East Coast developments. Before Levittown, Pennsylvania, was built, that wide swath of land in lower Bucks County along the Delaware was a neat patchwork of woodland and farmland, cut by several creeks and a few main arteries.

In 1940s America, a thin line separated urban and rural environments. Urban density often abruptly gave way to farmland, and home ownership was out of reach for most Americans. By the time World War II ended, in 1945, there was a massive housing shortage. An estimated 3.6 million American families out of a total of about 35 million lacked any housing at all. In the years after the war, home ownership rates rose dramatically across the country, from 44 to 62 percent, owing to a variety of factors. Not the least of these was a concerted increase in suburban development of modest but modern mass-produced housing for young working- and middle-class home buyers. At the same time, the federal government set up a program to insure long-term mortgages to low- and moderate-income people, freeing banks from the financial risks of making fifteen- and thirty-year loans on homes that might depreciate over time as collateral.

Builders like Levitt, who had first designed individual houses and exclusive developments for wealthy customers, shifted gears, recognizing the untapped potential for profit in selling tens of thousands of units of low-cost housing, offering a quality of life previously unavailable to low- and moderate-income buyers. In 1951, Levitt broke ground on his Pennsylvania development, which would provide housing to families from the state's northeastern industrial towns, the Philadelphia metropolitan area, surrounding rural areas, and even to some new Americans. Almost 6,000 residents of Levittown worked at the newly built U.S. Steel plant in Fairless Hills, which began production in 1952, and thousands more worked at nearby 3M or Rohm & Haas, like my father.

A 1951–52 advertisement for the popular Levittowner model home listed its price as $10,990, with a payment of $67 per month and no down payment for veterans. A 1953 standard Rancher model was valued at $8,490. In the first several months after sample homes were built, cars stretched for miles down Routes 13 and 1, filled with potential buyers. William Levitt's vision was attractive to a lot of young families: The development was planned to provide residents with green space, including mature trees and natural creek beds, as well as access to new schools, swimming pools, and a shopping center. It included several churches and a synagogue. The homes had carports or garages, state-of-the-art appliances, vinyl tile floors, landscaping packages of fruit trees and shrubs, and often an unfinished space that could be converted to additional bedrooms for a growing family.

By 1957, the sprawling development of more than 17,000 homes was still under construction, each of its neighborhoods populated with only one of six models, with each one of these at a different price point. It hardly mattered that the homes in each neighborhood were the same model, rotated on the lot. Residents of Levittown might have known that their homes were the basis for some ridicule in popular culture, like the 1963 song "Little Boxes," which mocked the sub-urban houses made out of "ticky tacky" to look "just the same," but the benefits of Levittown were beyond anything that they had ever thought within their means.

As the development grew, Levitt and his sons, who had taken an increasingly active role in the business, studied the needs and desires of their customers, adapting floor plans and finishes to suit them. To keep costs as low as possible, they rejected union labor, and built each neighborhood as if it were on an assembly line. Workers with a spe-cific skill installed their small part of each house before moving along to the next. Home buyers saw the Levitts as solicitous and conscien-tious builders, funding new schools and the expansion of police de-partments to serve the blossoming community. Perhaps the Levitts saw themselves in this light, as well; William Levitt wrote advertising copy that boasted, "The Most Perfectly Planned Community in America!"

Daisy and Bill Myers moved into a Levittown, Pennsylvania, three-bedroom house from their two-bedroom townhome in nearby Bristol Township on an August day in 1957. They wanted a home that could accommodate their growing family; they had two sons and were expecting another baby. The Myerses' house at 43 Deepgreen Lane in the Dogwood section was a modest thousand-square-foot Levittowner model. Like many of his neighbors, Bill was a family man and a veteran, with a blue-collar job as a refrigerator technician for a company in nearby Trenton, New Jersey. Daisy, like many post-war American women, worked outside the home as a teacher. Still, dozens of their new neighbors were outraged by the one way in which the Myers family was not like them: They were Black. Black families in America faced a myriad of institutionalized barriers to buying a home in the mid-twentieth century, but local civil rights leaders and Quaker organizers had encouraged the Myers family to buy a home in Levittown, pledging protection and support for the family.

As one of the few Brown or Black children at Village Park Ele-mentary in the early 1980s, I had no idea that William Levitt had conceived and executed his massive suburbs as Whites-only neighborhoods, refusing to sell any of his homes to Black people. I also didn't know about the riots that met the Myers family when they moved into 43 Deepgreen Lane. Confronted with the needs of prospective Black home buyers, who were crowded into old and decaying metropolitan housing, Levitt had proclaimed, "We can solve a housing problem or we can solve a racial problem, but we cannot combine the two." In truth, the two were inextricably entwined. William Levitt failed to see how his own efforts helped construct and maintain the "racial problem." He argued that "90 to 95 percent of [his] white customers would not buy into the community" if it included a Black neighbor, and then he spent his career catering to, rather than challenging, a racist White majority.

Levitt acted in and was conditioned by a rich legal landscape of explicitly segregationist law and government policy. Prior to 1968, federal agencies, including the Federal Housing Administration (FHA), the Home Owners' Loan Corporation (HOLC), and the Veterans Administration (VA), which provided loans to large suburban developers like Levitt and insured or provided long-term mortgages for individual homeowners, all had policies that maintained racial segregation and the exclusion of Black Americans from home ownership. These agencies barred banks from providing loans to families in Black or racially mixed neighborhoods. As in Levittown, racially restrictive covenants were often inserted into deeds to prohibit homeowners from reselling homes in White neighborhoods to Black families. These covenants were common and completely legal prior to 1948, and even when they became illegal and unenforceable, they nonetheless remained written in the deeds of countless American homes.

State and local laws and practices were just as racist. In response to massive post–Civil War migrations of free Black people in the early twentieth century known as the Great Migration, municipalities across the country implemented race-based zoning laws or encouraged deed restrictions to enforce segregation and maintain Whites-only residential neighborhoods. In the first half of the twentieth century the National Association of Real Estate Brokers (NAREB) consistently counseled members to avoid the mixing of races in residential real estate, leading realtors to adopt practices of "steering" buyers into segregated housing on the basis of their skin color. A 1957 NAREB manual listed "colored m[e]n of means . . . giving [their] children a college education and [who] thought they were entitled to live among whites" among those one should avoid introducing into White residential areas.

Within the same period, the federal government planned and built segregated public housing in American cities in response to the Great Depression, consistently responding to the housing shortages that both Black and White Americans faced by providing higher construction standards and more housing units in segregated Whites-only developments. In 1933, the secretary of the interior, Harold Ickes, established a policy by which new federal housing projects were required to be single-race, reflecting the predominant racial makeup of a neighborhood prior to new construction, reinforcing already segregated neighborhoods or disrupting the stability of integrated environments by establishing single-race housing projects. During this time, the government sometimes tore down integrated neighborhoods and Black businesses and amenities to construct clear racial divides. The FHA not only upheld deed restrictions that prevented the resale of homes to Black prospective buyers but published model language for such restrictions in the 1935–37 period and then opposed anti-discrimination measures in federal housing legislation in the 1940s. Police and local housing authorities adopted parallel segregationist policies that barred integrated recreation and sports facilities and activities. When housing was not made available to meet the demand of Black prospective home buyers, they were frequently forced to crowd into fewer units or to establish communities of shantytowns or other substandard housing.

The federal government continued to follow a similar policy of segregation in the construction of housing for wartime workers during World War II, creating "one of the most acute areas of racial tension" in the country. Even after the war, Black servicemen could not obtain the same government-guaranteed mortgages as White veterans. Concurrently, the FHA officially conditioned the approval of new subdivisions, approval that could then be used by builders to secure low-interest loans, on the exclusion of Black home buyers. Until passage of the Fair Housing Act in 1968, it refused to insure mortgages for Black home buyers in White neighborhoods or for White home buyers in Black neighborhoods. Banks and other lenders followed suit, refusing to offer mortgages at all under these circumstances. In this broader context, Levitt was but one player in the private-public partnership to maintain a segregated America.

All of these practices meant that Black Americans were effectively locked out of the private housing market through most of the twentieth century; the supply available to them was far lower than the demand. Between 1946 and 1953, less than 1 percent of new postwar housing built in Philadelphia by private developers was open to Black buyers; at the same time, Black residents made up roughly 15 to 20 percent of the city's population. Because demand so exceeded the supply of housing available to them, successful Black buyers paid more for homes on average than White homeowners did. For that premium, they would also contend with widespread redlining. Originally understood to mean the practice of denying mortgages and insurance in Black or racially mixed neighborhoods (based on whether borrowers lived in areas on a map literally marked in red by the FHA, as well as lenders and insurers), redlining has also come to refer to the choices of private and public entities to limit access to libraries, transportation, healthcare, retail stores, and high-quality education in Black or racially mixed neighborhoods.

When he broke ground on his Pennsylvania development, Levitt may have been unaware that the nearby Fallsington and Philadelphia Quakers had become involved in the nascent civil rights movement and had developed a commitment to racial equality and justice. By the time he had bought the land for his Pennsylvania development, the Philadelphia-based Quaker organization American Friends Service

Committee (AFSC) had made the project of desegregation central to its mission. Although legal challenges of housing segregation met with several failures through the 1950s, activists believed that creating conditions in which White and Black families were neighbors and providing opportunities for them to know one another personally were critical to the success of the civil rights movement and the future of the county.

While the U.S. Supreme Court considered *Brown v. Board of Education,* overturning school segregation in 1954, and southern activists launched the Montgomery Bus Boycott in 1955, the AFSC had been patiently working to identify Levittown homeowners who would be willing to sell to Black families. They were also searching for a Black family willing to brave the inevitable backlash to move into the all-White development. Before identifying the Myers family, local Quakers and activists from the newly formed Bucks County Human Relations Council had also spent six years organizing a group of pro-integration neighbors within Levittown. They hoped that the early desegregation of this flagship suburb would ultimately cause a sea change in racist housing policies and practices, as well as in the hearts and minds of White Americans.

Meanwhile, the Myerses had outgrown their small home in a small Black neighborhood of nearby Bristol Township. In a market with few options for Black home buyers, Bill and Daisy decided they would be willing to pay a premium for the house on Deepgreen Lane. Bill had previously done service repair calls in Levittown without encountering any hostility, and so perhaps underestimated what they would be up against. Civil rights activists anticipated the pushback but felt the Myerses were an ideal family to desegregate Levittown, because they fit a respectability profile that might make them acceptable to White neighbors: Bill and Daisy were in their mid-thirties and both had skilled or professional jobs. Bill was a World War II veteran and a graduate of the Hampton Institute. In addition to being a teacher, Daisy was a member of the Bristol Township Recreation Board. The Myerses relied on the assurances of supportive neighbors, local clergy, and activists who promised to ease their transition into the neighborhood. Sam Snipes (who owned the horses I visited as a child in Fallsington and recalled Native children working for local farmers there in the 1920s) and Peter von Blum of the Fallsington Quaker Meeting would coordinate welcoming visits from neighbors for the two months after they moved in. Snipes also provided legal representation to the Myerses for the purchase of their new home.

But many other Levittown homeowners had relied on Levitt's assurances and the restrictions written into their deeds that kept Levittown White. So, on August 20, 1957, when Levittown's first Black home buyers moved in, with two young children and another on the way, hundreds of their neighbors gathered in an angry mob across the street. Daisy Myers would later recount a headline in the paper that week that read "Tourists Gawk at Negro Home." The racist protests lasted several weeks. Several neighbors threw stones, breaking most of the windows of the Myers home and knocking a police officer unconscious. The crowd called police who were protecting the Myers family from racist aggression the "Gestapo," then painted "KKK" on the Myerses' next-door neighbors' home and burned a cross on Peter von Blum's lawn, as punishment for his support of the Myers family. Anonymous telephone calls carried chilling threats: "You wanna die in that house?"

Many other neighbors who were not directly involved in the harassment, violence, and vandalism were nonetheless indifferent, and complained that having a Black neighbor would wreck their property values (although FHA data at the time was clear that Black home ownership *increased* property values). Irving Mandel, the White man who had sold his home to the Myers family, lost his job as a result of that decision. Some neighbors called for a boycott of the gas company that serviced the Myers home. When the local bread delivery truck was vandalized for stopping at their home, deliveries stopped. Milk deliveries, also common in the neighborhood, were refused to the Myers household.

A local Quaker activist lived with the Myers family during three weeks of the harassment to provide extra protection and support. After six weeks, the police stopped providing patrols near the Myers home, and Quaker activists and supportive neighbors responded by creating an unofficial "citizens guard" in their place. In addition, the activists made donations to help offset the expense the Myers family incurred in repairing their home and coordinating the efforts of their friends and allies. A hundred and fifty Levittown residents wrote to Bill and Daisy Myers expressing solidarity. All of these efforts made the Myerses' existence in Levittown possible—they could not have borne the stress and threats to their family otherwise.

The open hostility of several White Levittown residents was recorded in first-person statements in the documentary film *Crisis in Levittown,* and the effects of their racism on the Myers family were recorded in Daisy's 2005 memoir, *Reflections on Levittown.* These records evidence the complexities of achieving desegregation in an environment of persistent, casual White supremacy. When another Black family, the Mosbys, moved into Levittown in 1958, civil rights activists themselves thwarted another sale to a Black family on the same block as the Mosbys, concerned that anything but a single Black family in a section would ultimately lead to White neighbors moving out, "tipping" the neighborhood to an all-Black enclave rather than integrating it. For this reason, Levittown would never be more than nominally integrated, and the Myers family would leave Levittown only a few years after they moved in when Bill Myers took a job in Harrisburg.

Until the late 1960s, while Americans joined the movement for civil rights all across the country, Levitt's racist thinking and strategy continued to be supported by federal government programs and he enforced his anti-Black policies vehemently. In his original Long Island development, also called Levittown, Levitt's firm initiated eviction proceedings against two White tenants, arguing that they had violated a restriction against the "use of the premises" by anyone who was not White when they invited the Black children of some of their friends to play in the yard. Up until he sold his real estate company in

1967, despite opposition by the NAACP, the ACLU, the national civil rights movement (by then in full swing), and, belatedly, the Federal Housing Administration, Levitt had refused to sell homes in any of his developments to Black people.

Levitt's segregationist policies shaped my young world in the 1980s. Even in 2017, 90 percent of Levittown's residents were White, and fewer than 4 percent were Black. The ongoing whiteness of Levittown is remarkable considering the demographics of surrounding areas. The same year in neighboring Bristol, 85.5 percent of residents were White, while 10.4 percent were Black; in neighboring Morrisville, 78.6 percent of residents were White, while 14 percent were Black; in neighboring Falls Township, which includes some parts of Levittown as well as Fallsington and Fairless Hills, 82.9 percent of residents were White, while 9.5 percent were Black. In the closest major city, Philadelphia, 41.6 percent of residents were White, while 42.6 percent were Black, demonstrating the overall success of racist efforts to keep Black Americans out of suburbia.

As in Levitt's day, children in Levittown continue to receive taxpayer-funded public school education in the highly regarded Pennsbury School District, which has a graduation rate of 89 percent and a student to teacher ratio of 15:1. Pennsbury High and its elaborate annual prom were celebrated in the 2004 book *Wonderland: A Year in the Life of an American High School*. By contrast, the Philadelphia School District has a graduation rate of only 66 percent and a student to teacher ratio of 18:1. Philadelphia has for many years been in a funding battle with the state government in Harrisburg to ameliorate the crisis-level problems in the city's public schools—crumbling school buildings with leaking roofs, failing or nonexistent heat or air-conditioning, lack of basic supplies including textbooks and paper, and inadequate support services to address the challenges driven by poverty among students.

Levittown may have been built as America's quintessential suburb, and William Levitt may have risen to some fame as the visionary who built it. However, Levitt remains most notable for having laid the

blueprint for how the segregationist policies of government and powerful private institutions would be implemented in the postwar era of
suburban housing.

———

Allison was a lot like the other kids at Village Park Elementary School,
White and Catholic, with names like Mary Jane, Gerry, Michael, and
Kelly. They all lived in the Levittown neighborhood immediately
surrounding the school, with the same name, Village Park. Even after
being bused over from Fallsington for four years, I still didn't much fit
in. I was too quiet, too dark, and too small for my age. I had a funny
name and my family never had a Christmas tree.

All the kids in Mr. Beam's "gifted" class played together on the
playground; they called themselves the Mystery Gang. Their play
mostly involved Mary Jane making up mysteries and adventures that
required them to run back and forth across the playground with occasional breaks in the hot box, a sort of cube-shaped area around an
unused doorway of the low, modernist white-brick school building.
It didn't matter what they were playing; the Mystery Gang was the
cool subset of fifth-grade life.

One day it occurred to some members of the Mystery Gang that I
was the only kid in Mr. Beam's class not included. I don't know if
some adult had pointed this out or if I had advocates within the group.
But Mary Jane was not at all happy about having to provide me with
a three-day trial period in which I would be allowed to join in on their
adventures and after which my full membership would be considered
and voted on by the group.

By the second day of my probation, I was desperate to go back to
playing hopscotch with my neighborhood friends, Rachel and Chris,
who had come to Village Park a year or so after I did, when the public
school in Fallsington closed down. I was baffled at why the other eight
members of the Mystery Gang were so content to chase a figment of
Mary Jane's imagination all over the playground. During a break from

the chase, the group gathered around its meeting spot—a random metal bar farthest from the school but still on the playground, the kind you could hoist your belly up to and then fold and tumble over if you liked. In a moment like a scene from a movie, toward the end of that gathering, I interrupted the conversation.

I was a shy, unheroic kid who liked books and *The Sound of Music*. But for some reason, on that day, I decided I had something to say to the Mystery Gang, and it went like this: "I've decided that I don't want to finish the trial. I know it's supposed to be three days, but I'd really rather go play with my actual friends, who didn't ask me to pass any tests to get to play with them." And then I walked off. To my great surprise, Allison followed me, exclaiming, "No one's *ever* walked away from the Mystery Gang before!" That was the day Allison and I became best friends.

That moment led to visits in each other's homes and long adventures in each other's neighborhoods, expanding my experience of Levittown. Middle school, and the friends I made there, took me into still more pockets of Levittown, further south and east of the school. Levittown is enormous, big enough to have its own subculture, its own shops and parks and playgrounds. It's all adjacent to Fallsington, but my family never ventured there socially except to come to the school for a few events per year, or to drop my brother and me off at friends' houses. Although I entered it every day to go to school and my family had rented an apartment there when we first arrived, I knew I didn't belong there, even as a token.

At nearly the same time as William Levitt was watching his first houses go up in Pennsylvania, another builder by the name of Morris Milgram was laying plans for a development just eight miles away in Bensalem. Milgram and Levitt had a great deal in common. Both were middle-aged Jewish men of Russian descent who inherited family real estate businesses, and both had started out building homes for the wealthy. But their visions for suburban development in 1950s Pennsylvania could not have been more different.

Morris Milgram was a lifelong social justice and civil rights activist who had reluctantly agreed to join his father-in-law's real estate firm. For several years, Milgram had been on the staff of the Workers Defense League (WDL), a labor rights organization with branches in more than a dozen cities that advocated on behalf of both White and Black sharecroppers in the South. He became deeply involved in the defense of a Black Virginia sharecropper who had killed his White landlord, arguing that the killing had been in self-defense. In the course of his advocacy, he worked closely with the WDL board member Pauli Murray, who was a Black civil rights lawyer, poet, professor, and activist. Three lines of her 1943 poem "Dark Testament" would shape his future:

> *Traders still trade in double-talk*
> *Though they've swapped the selling block*
> *For ghetto and gun!*

Recognizing this as a true representation of the conditions faced by Black people in America, including his own friends and colleagues in the civil rights movement, Morris Milgram agreed to join his father-in-law's firm on the condition that he could build homes "for all of his friends," regardless of race.

In 1954, seven years after he signed on as a real estate developer, he began building Concord Park in Bensalem, Bucks County. Concord Park was a more modest project than Levittown (as were most developments in comparison to William Levitt's), with fewer than 150 homes, compared with Levittown's 17,311. Like Levitt, Milgram hoped to provide modern housing for the employees of the area's big industries, including the nearby U.S. Steel plant. But unlike Levitt, he also wanted to meet the needs of Black families in Philadelphia who, in the postwar period, increasingly had the resources to move into newer housing with suburban amenities but were frequently denied mortgages or barred from White neighborhoods. More than that, he wanted to build a successful, desirable suburb that would serve as proof and inspiration that racial segregation was not only unnecessary, but an inferior way to organize society. Concord Park would be one of the first intentionally racially integrated suburbs in America. Having discovered so much more about how the Delaware Valley came to exclude and exploit Native and Black communities, I wanted to learn what, if anything, had resulted from Milgram's efforts to reverse the course of segregation in suburban development. The former residents of Concord Park had formed a Facebook group of alumni to stay connected with each other and to maintain the record of Milgram's efforts. In 2018, I sent a message to the group, and Lauren Swann answered.

Lauren's parents, James and Alice Swann, were among the early buyers in Concord Park. In 1958, they purchased a three-bedroom ranch with a garage in a neatly kept neighborhood of about a half dozen tree-lined streets. Looking to move with their two children out of older and much more densely built housing near Girard Avenue in Philadelphia, they were attracted by the mortgages available to Black families in Concord Park, and by the quality and affordability of modern suburban homes in the neighborhood. In a marked departure from Levittown's example, the fact that the development would be open to home buyers of any race had been advertised in Concord Park's promotional materials.

It was a good move for the family. Alice and James had three more children after moving to Concord Park, the first of whom was Lauren, born in 1959. Lauren recalls her childhood in Concord Park as a world apart from the turmoil of racist backlash to the civil rights movement of the time. Her birthday parties and Girl Scout troop were full of both Black and White girls from her neighborhood, the same girls she and her sister rode bikes with down sunny summer streets and whose mothers worked with her mother to create the neighborhood's cooperative kindergarten. The kindergarten, the playground built by a group of Concord Park fathers, and the neighborhood library collection in one neighbor's home were all efforts to mitigate the lack of public and private amenities provided in their narrow section of Bensalem between Street Road and Old Lincoln Highway. Together, Concord Park residents would develop their own robust social networks and services.

The Swann family spent more than ten years deeply involved in their special community, where White and Black children and families socialized together, played together, and attended the local Methodist church or one of the many social activities housed under its roof together. Like other Concord Park kids, the Swann children played with children in neighboring Linconia, the first all-Black suburb in Bucks County, which was built in 1923 when a White farmer named Frank Brown sold plots of his land to Black families looking to build their own homes, and with children from Bryn Gweled, an interracial intentional community (what we might call a commune) in nearby Southampton.

In many ways, Concord Park was built in the right place at the right time. It was close enough to Philadelphia that homeowners could take advantage of bus routes into the city. Also, the new suburban model was blossoming along the East Coast, and demand for new housing was high. Nonetheless, Milgram had to overcome a great deal of opposition to build a racially integrated suburb. His ultimate success was due in large part to the careful planning and preparation he did with the same network of Quakers, civil rights activists, and community organizations that had supported the Myers family in Levittown.

Real estate developers typically rely on large loans from banks to finance their projects, going into substantial debt in the building period and then repaying lenders and taking their profit after the sale of homes. Milgram had hoped to work with the mortgage-financing lender who had financed his previous, all-White communities. In spite of his successful efforts to demonstrate the marketability of homes in Concord Park, including the sale of a small group of sample homes, that lender ultimately refused funding, leaving Milgram to scramble for other lenders to fill in the gaps. His plan for Concord Park attracted the interest of George Otto, a wealthy Quaker businessman from nearby Morrisville. Otto was an active leader in an extensive network of Quaker organizations that were all, by then, working to demonstrate their faith-based commitment to racial justice, and had formed the cohort to support the integration of Levittown. He became a dedicated partner in Milgram's project and engaged all of his established Quaker connections to raise $150,000 by the spring of 1954.

However, once financing for the development itself was secure, Milgram struggled over the next year and a half to identify lenders who were willing to offer mortgages to home buyers in a racially mixed development. Two dozen potential lenders—traditional mortgage companies, labor unions, and religious organizations—turned him down. Most seemed convinced, as William Levitt had been, that a successful housing development must be racially segregated, and that integration would mean struggling sales or unstable home values, or both. The FHA refused to provide insurance on mortgages in a mixed-race neighborhood. Ultimately, a New York–based lender agreed to fund the first thirty mortgages before two local lenders provided the remainder of the mortgages.

Finally, when Milgram managed to secure mortgage lenders, he found that Black home buyers, barred from so much of the new local suburban housing, were far more eager to buy than White home buyers, who had many other options. Black home buyers were still pressed into overcrowded, segregated Black areas of Philadelphia while White home buyers were taking advantage of the postwar suburban housing boom initiated by builders like Levitt. By the end of 1954, Milgram had taken deposits from only ten White home buyers, compared with forty Black home buyers. George Otto responded to this situation by prioritizing the desperate need among Black home buyers for affordable housing. Milgram, on the other hand, prioritized the successful creation of a truly integrated American suburb, believing this could pave the way for broad gains in civil rights and integration across the country, even if it meant turning desperate Black home buyers away.

Incredibly, the pressures of planning for integrated housing in a highly racist social context with little available housing for Black families meant that the well-intentioned Otto and Milgram would also, in the end, turn down Black home buyers simply because they were Black. Milgram initially argued that to preserve White home buyers' interest in Concord Park, Black-owned homes needed to be limited to four or five families for every thirty homes, and only later increased to a rate of 20 percent. This would have been a general reflection of the racial demographics of nearby Philadelphia at the time. Otto opposed racial quotas at first but became concerned when White buyers purchased only twelve of the first seventy-two homes sold. He finally agreed that no more than 50 percent of the remaining homes would be sold to Black homeowners. Milgram and Otto's machinations were initially successful, and during the fifteen years following its creation, Concord Park would largely achieve its aim of a neighborhood almost evenly split between White and Black homeowners.

The project could not transform the segregated national landscape, which was held firm by the concerted efforts of much bigger builders like Levitt, federal policy, and the practices of lenders and real estate brokers. Still, Concord Park undoubtably transformed the people within it. Lauren Swann's stories about her neighbors coming together to create community-based services, such as the neighborhood kindergarten and library, tell us something about how committed the neighbors were to one another. The residents of Concord Park were also broadly committed to the cause of integration. During the siege of the Myers home in Levittown, an integrated group of Swann's neighbors in Concord Park went regularly to provide security for the Myers family. An advertisement taken out by the executive committee of the Concord Park Civic Association implored Levittown residents to welcome the Myers family, and reassured them that property values had gone up in their own integrated neighborhood in the short time since it had been built: "On the basis of our own experience . . . there is only one thing to do and that is to welcome this family as you would any other family, and especially to refrain from action which undermines the good and democratic name of your community."

Several original Concord Park residents became active in civil rights struggles that were a natural extension of their own experiences of integration, such as integrating the local swimming pool, which had previously excluded non-Whites, and picketing a local five-and-dime store whose southern locations denied service to Black people. These residents of Concord Park were an example of the politically transformative potential of desegregation, and they were actively invested in supporting desegregation in the broader society.

Ultimately, though, the home that was so attractive to the Swanns as a family of four would be the reason they moved out of Concord Park in 1969. With five growing children, they needed more space, and restrictive covenants prevented additions to their home. The Swanns found a home that suited them in nearby Warminster and, in the year after passage of the Fair Housing Act, were able to secure a mortgage. The public school to which their children would go was highly ranked, even more highly ranked than their previous school in Concord Park. But Warminster was almost entirely White.

Before the Swanns were to move into their Warminster home, it was vandalized twice. Once, the plumbing was ripped out; the second time, racial epithets were spray-painted on the walls. As the family prepared to move, a contractor took James Swann aside to warn him that some of the men on the block had been holding angry meetings about the arrival of a Black family in their neighborhood. He thought there could be threats, or even violence. Not long after the family moved in, a man phoned the Swann residence threatening to burn down their home and rape the girls. James Swann answered tersely, "I have nine rounds in this gun and you might kill me, but nine of you will not be going home." There is no way of knowing the terror that James and Alice might have felt for themselves and their five children after that phone call, but they were determined to stay. They told only the older children about the threats, but Lauren and her younger siblings couldn't help but feel the difference between Warminster and Concord Park. They had stepped suddenly into a world where color lines were mercilessly drawn and defended, and where crossing them would draw violent threats from their new White neighbors.

Lauren Swann now lives a few minutes' drive from Concord Park, in Bensalem, where she regularly attends its alumni events. For her, Concord Park will always be a success, and more important, it was a place where she belonged, despite pressures that would eventually overcome Milgram's original vision.

Milgram continued to struggle against the racist landscape after Concord Park was completed. Adjacent landowners refused to sell him land on which to expand his development, believing that a Black "enclave" would negatively affect property values, development, and investment in the area. As the Swann family's experience reflects, there was still very little suburban housing available to Black home buyers by the time many first-generation Concord Park families had outgrown their small ranch homes. Suburban Pennsylvania was still overwhelmingly segregated and buying in White neighborhoods was still terrifyingly dangerous. When it came time for Concord Park residents to sell their homes, they found that an overwhelming number of potential buyers were Black, and that Black home buyers were often willing to pay a premium to secure a home. By 1968, when the Fair Housing Act was passed, Concord Park was almost 100 percent Black. While it remains a beautiful, tree-lined little pocket of Bensalem, having shaped the lives of its original inhabitants in profound ways, it would not overcome the odds against integration in quite the way Milgram had hoped.

Nonetheless, Milgram went on to create several more integrated housing developments in northeast Philadelphia, in Princeton, New Jersey, and in suburban Newtown, Pennsylvania. In each of these contexts he faced the problems presented by the broader racist landscape: an overwhelming number of Black home buyers in need of housing and a dearth of White home buyers committed to integrated communities. When his efforts to build an interracial development in Deerfield failed after a protracted legal battle, he left building and began purchasing and managing rental properties in eight states including California, New York, Massachusetts, Texas, Virginia, and Maryland, changing their policies to welcome Black residents. He never lost sight of his original vision of integrated residential housing and multiracial communities. In 1968, the U.S. Department of Housing and Urban Development awarded him their first National Human Rights Award.

Despite Milgram's remarkable efforts, several recent studies have found that America remains profoundly segregated, with the average White person living in a neighborhood that is about 80 percent White, and half of all Black people living in a neighborhood without a White presence. Black home ownership rates are at the bottom of census estimates for racial categories at just over 40 percent. This combination of factors means that Black Americans are persistently denied the opportunity to build wealth and resources through home ownership, and are often unable to access jobs, schools, and services built in or near White communities. A February 2019 study by the nonprofit EdBuild found that a majority of American students still attend what the report calls "racially concentrated" schools, and that predominantly White schools receive a total of $23 *billion* more in annual funding than predominantly non-White schools although they serve the same number of students.

Recently, I sent a message to half a dozen old friends who grew up in and around Levittown with me in the 1980s. Not one was aware that the area's persistent, overwhelming whiteness was by design. No one had ever heard that Levittown's builder had intended for it to be an all-White neighborhood, or that many of its residents formed a violent mob protesting housing integration in 1957. During five years of elementary school in Levittown and another seven years of middle and high school in neighboring Fairless Hills, which was also built as a Whites-only community, my peers and I had learned nothing of the key historical struggles that had shaped these places that had in turn

shaped us. We had learned nothing of the heroes who worked so dili-
gently to create something better, something closer to the ideals so
many Americans claim as their own: Sam Snipes and the Fallsington
Quakers, the Myers and Mosby families, the AFSC, NAACP, and
ACLU, Morris Milgram, and George Otto. We all left Village Park,
and eventually Pennsbury High School, with no greater understanding of the unspoken rules, some established in our own neighborhoods, that governed where Black and Brown people could live in
postwar America.

CHAPTER FOUR

IVY LEAGUE

Princeton, New Jersey

Already [by 1776] the American mind was accomplishing that indispensable intellectual activity of someone consumed with racist ideas: individualizing White negativity and generalizing Black negativity. Negative behavior by any Black person became proof of what was wrong with Black people, while negative behavior by any white person only proved what was wrong with that person.

—Ibram X. Kendi

A s I progressed through middle school, I grew more conscious of the way that the black hair on my legs stood out even against my deeply tanned summer legs. I did not anticipate the expression on my mother's face when I asked if it would be okay for me to shave my legs and armpits, as if I had asked for something untoward, sexual. I felt ashamed at her reaction, but I didn't understand it. Or rather, I understood it as a relic of a society in which I did not live. My mother argued, halfheartedly, that no young woman should need to shave her legs, and I reminded her that my school gym uniform included shorts. She gave in quickly, handing me a new disposable razor from my father's packet, and closed the bathroom door behind her. I looked at the razor, then at myself in the mirror. I had never used a razor before and didn't know how. Should I wet my skin? Lather it like in television commercials? Would it hurt? I called to my mother from the bathroom door, "Mom, can you come here? I need your help." And she came, soaping a part of my underarm before slowly, awkwardly trying to shave long hairs at the edges, then finally stopping to trim them before handing me back the razor to complete the job.

I had no confidante about things like this. There were no Brown girls in my classes at middle school, and the daughters of my parents' South Asian friends were much older or much younger, or subject to more restrictive environments in which shaving would have been an even stickier subject. When I went to visit family in Pakistan every couple of years for a month or more at a time, it was very true that nothing that needed shaving was ever on display, but my reality was entirely different. Though I was still filling in the oval marked "white" on all my standardized tests, I didn't even know, or have language for, what exactly I was.

Because I lacked a language for it, I had accepted racial identity as something that people decided about me and then also determined what significance it would have, rather than something I had the power to assert. While my black hair and dark eyes marked me in one way in my suburban neighborhood, my unusually light skin for a Pakistani girl marked me in another way during visits to extended family in Hyderabad, which despite its size was not at all cosmopolitan. Pakistani culture is rarely subtle, and the eagerness with which many Pakistanis covet and privilege white skin is no exception. That I was both pale and American made me a spectacle and subject to an inordinate amount of unwanted attention and assault, including being assessed as a marriage prospect from an early age, and being groped by men on streets and in open rickshaw taxis. Depending on where in the world, or where in America or even with whom I happened to be, I was sometimes too dark and sometimes too light to be secure, though in the very same body.

Perhaps in an effort to help me understand who and what we were, perhaps just out of desperation to experience something familiar to them, my parents would drive us from our house in Fallsington for half an hour toward New Jersey or Philadelphia each weekend to gather with the handful of other South Asian Muslim families we knew, or would prepare to host them at our house. The gatherings would last late into the night, with adults dressed in shalwar kameez chatting in Urdu as a tribe of ten or twelve kids raced around them. Even in these small groups, there was a good deal of diversity: Indian Muslims by way of Uganda, a blond Christian midwesterner married to a dark-skinned Bengali man, a family who migrated to Pakistan from India during partition. In retrospect, it seems clear that we were as drawn to each other for reasons of mutual respect as we were for cultural sameness. There were notable differences in our languages or dialects, diets, origins, but we shared the hardship of multiple migrations, and the experience of having neighbors who always seemed to want to know where we were *really* from, even if we had moved in years before they did. Some neighbors asked casually, or curiously, but others as if we were trespassing while they had, themselves, risen fully formed from the clay beside their suburban houses. We were all surviving those experiences separately, and to come together was a relief.

By 1984 or so, the Muslim families in our circle of friends, and many others, began congregating each Sunday at a new mosque called the Islamic Society of Central Jersey (ISCJ). ISCJ was built in phases, and when the first phase opened on October 9, 1983, we were there for the celebration. It was one of the first purpose-built mosques in the region and the first mosque my family attended regularly. Right on the Route 1 business corridor that runs from Philadelphia to New York City, it sits on a relatively quiet stretch between Princeton and New Brunswick. The mosque was like a lighthouse to our families; it was the first sign to my parents and their small group of friends that they would not have to find a way to articulate and transmit every bit of religious and cultural identity they wanted to preserve in their children. It was a balm on the isolation of Muslim American suburban existence.

That stretch of Route 1 would come to feature centrally in my life. It's where I would buy my prom dress, after begging to be allowed to go, and where I would get married the first time, to the wrong person. It's where I would shop for avocados and peanut sauce at my beloved Trader Joe's when I returned to live in Yardley with my own children. It's the road down which my husband, the right person, would drive an hour each way, very carefully, as biochemists with brown skin and Muslim names in post-9/11 America do, to and from work. And before all of that, it's where I had what I think of as my "Malcolm X in Mecca" moment.

I was just shy of nine years old when I walked into ISCJ for the first time, and it was euphoric, like walking into a kaleidoscope: In those early days, ISCJ's Sunday-morning programs drew people from a radius of an hour or more, a geographic circle that was and still is among the most culturally and racially diverse on Earth. Traditionally, we would have been congregating on Fridays, but since we were all at work and school on that day, Sunday mornings brought people from up and down and around Route 1 and from all around the globe to that place. When the call to prayer sounded, a West African lady in her turban and long, wide-necked, short-sleeved dress lined up next to an Egyptian lady in her knee-length polyester skirt suit and blouse, calves showing but hijab pinned snugly at her throat. Next to her would be a Pakistani woman in an almost transparent shalwar kameez and slippery scarf, never quite secured to her head. There were as many interpretations of modesty as there were languages among us. I had an English auntie there and a Filipina auntie, an auntie who spoke Swahili and an auntie who spoke Arabic, all sharing tea and doughnuts after prayers together. It was a scene that was as unimaginable to a little girl who lived in Fallsington and went to school in Levittown as perhaps the diversity of Muslims on hajj was to Malcolm X in Mecca. And while I was not entirely at home there, I was also not any more alien than anyone else.

In many ways, ISCJ in its early days was the first America that I was enamored of: the one I spoke about as a kid at the Statue of Liberty but had never actually experienced, one that could welcome me. Once I had seen diversity at ISCJ—actual diversity, and not just another segregated place for a different color of people—I assumed that I was witnessing America's aspiration for itself. That Americans, by and large, were trying to steer their ship in the direction of that vision, to create pluralism, or a society built on the dialogue between us, where we each would be free to inhabit our identities, our commitments, and our faiths.

I could tell that my parents were relieved to have a brick-and-mortar institution to which they could belong. At the mosque, they felt comfortable in their skins and their speech, even alongside people from entirely different places and cultures. We called ISCJ "the Princeton mosque." It had a sort of tony ring to it because of nearby Princeton University, one that matched my parents' sense of pride in the place, even before the late phases of construction in which they added the golden dome and towering minaret.

Princeton University has long been an important barometer of American culture and ideology, having educated generations of the nation's elite, including political and social leaders, from both the North and the South, for 270 years. Princeton, the town, was also briefly the capital of the nation, for a little over four months in 1783. Although it seems too far north to be thought so today, in the eighteenth and nineteenth centuries it was sort of a borderland, one that was neither fully northern nor southern in its political or cultural commitments.

In the late 1700s, after the Declaration of Independence had been signed and the U.S. Constitution ratified, Princeton University was still the College of New Jersey, and served as an elite boys' post-primary school. The town itself was small and would have fewer than three thousand residents for the next fifty years. From 1790 until 1830, the population of New Jersey and a few adjacent counties spilling into New York State had the highest concentration of enslaved

Black people north of the Mason-Dixon line. By 1800, the number of enslaved Black people in New Jersey had reached its peak of 12,422— 6 percent of the population, but a handful of central New Jersey counties, including Princeton, were home to 75 percent of those enslaved.

Given the dependence of wealthy New Jersey residents on enslaved labor, New Jersey was last among northern states to introduce legislation toward emancipation, called the Gradual Abolition Act. Under that first New Jersey law, passed in February 1804 under overwhelming pressure from abolitionist Quakers in the western part of the state, every child born after July 4, 1804, to an enslaved woman would remain a "servant" to their mother's captor (or to the "executors, administrators or assigns" of such a captor) until the age of twenty-five if a boy or twenty-one if a girl. At those ages, they would have spent half of their lives or more, in an era where the average life expectancy was forty years, in essentially the same circumstances as if they had been enslaved, regarded as "slaves for a term." The purpose of delaying emancipation was to mitigate the loss of wealth and labor to slavers by allowing them to retain some percentage of the enslaved in perpetuity, and several more generations for a fixed period. In addition, by failing to prohibit slavers from transporting their slaves out of state, the law afforded New Jersey slavers the opportunity to sell the people they enslaved, even those considered slaves for a term, into southern states to recover their losses. There were provisions of state law that theoretically required the consent of the enslaved to be transported, or the consent of enslaved parents for their children to be transported, but these laws were regularly flouted by slavers.

By contrast to New Jersey, Pennsylvania had passed a law for gradual emancipation in 1780, and the last record of an indentured person dates to 1847. At the time New Jersey passed its law, the three northern states of Massachusetts, Vermont, and New Hampshire had ended slavery entirely, and the transatlantic slave trade was only three years from being officially abolished.

After the passage of New Jersey's law, the free Black population of the state rose dramatically. From 1800 to 1810, the number of free Black people in New Jersey increased by more than 75 percent, and more than 50 percent in the next census year. By 1820, there were 12,460 free Black people in the state—more free Black people than there had ever been enslaved Black people—and the number of enslaved Black people had dropped by a third to eight thousand. This caused great alarm and hostility among many of the White people of the state, who were by and large still dependent on goods and services produced and prepared by enslaved people. At the same time, the abolitionist fervor that had always been most pronounced in the western part of the state had waned because several aging Quaker leaders of the movement there were no longer active and the practice of slavery, increasingly concentrated in the eastern part of the state, was less visible to them.

Slavery would be practiced within New Jersey for several more decades. In 1830, an estimated one-quarter of New Jersey's Black population continued as forced labor, and in 1846, New Jersey prolonged the system while pretending at abolition by simply reclassifying the formerly enslaved as "apprentices for life." New Jersey would not fully abolish the practice of slavery in the state until it ratified the Thirteenth Amendment to the Constitution, a year *after* its passage by three-fourths of the thirty-six states then in the nation, in January 1866.

It was in this context that Robert Finley, a primary school teacher and a preacher born to a Scottish immigrant yarn merchant in Princeton, had graduated from the College of New Jersey at the age of fifteen. He later studied theology and directed what became the Princeton Theological Seminary, becoming a zealous Presbyterian pastor to his Basking Ridge congregation in 1794, where he spent more than twenty years. Finley was not content to be a small-town pastor. Fishing about for something he could call his great legacy, he began to champion a plan for the deportation of free Black people, not just from the state of New Jersey, but from the country as a whole. The same idea was also being propounded by a member of the Vir-

ginia House of Delegates, Charles Fenton Mercer, an anti-slavery organization in Ohio called the Union Humane Society, and the
missionary founder of the American Bible Society, Samuel J. Mills, at
nearly the same time, causing some dispute as to the idea's origins. It
is unclear whether Finley was the author of the idea, or just its loud-
est, most effective proponent, but it was Finley who ultimately mar-
shaled the interests of men in a position to turn the idea into a national
initiative.

Finley's plan, as he wrote of it to an associate named John Mum-
ford in February of 1816, was for

> the rich and benevolent [to] devise a means to form a *colony* in some
> part of *Africa* similar to the one at *Sierra Leone,* which might gradu-
> ally induce many free Blacks to go and settle, devising for them the
> means of getting there, and of protection and support, till they were
> established. [emphasis in the original]

Finley would have described his interest in "colonization" as
rooted in his benevolence and faith: While he opposed slavery, he believed that White people would not allow free Black people to thrive
alongside them, writing, "On this subject the state of the *free blacks* has
very much oppressed my mind. Their number increases greatly, and
their wretchedness too. . . . Everything connected with their condition, including their color, is against them."

In his Christian missionary zeal, he also believed that non-
Christians were inferior and that the entire continent of Africa (on
which he had not set foot) was uncivilized. He imagined an African
continent saved from backwardness by the influence of free Black
Americans, who had been elevated by their proximity to White Christian slavers and returned after several generations to proselytize and
civilize the people of that continent. This construction allowed him
to assert the deportation of free Black people from America as a benefit to White Americans, a charitable endeavor toward the peoples of
Africa, and a relief for Black people themselves:

Our fathers brought them here, and we are bound, if possible to repair the injuries inflicted by our fathers. Could they be sent back to
Africa a threefold benefit would arise. We should be cleared of
them;—we should send to Africa a population partially civilized and
christianized for its benefit:—our blacks themselves would be put in
a better situation.

Finley's project appealed to White abolitionists and slavers alike.
Slavers saw the proximity of free Black people as a bad influence, encouraging those still enslaved to attempt escape. Even self-proclaimed
abolitionists like Finley struggled to imagine free Black neighbors and
countrymen. Finley's writings suggest an inability to consider that
those who had been enslaved for generations had little or no connection to West Africa and that neither they nor the more recently trafficked had an obvious stake in the project of colonization. They
suggest that he was oblivious to and disinterested in the priorities of
free Black people themselves in those first precious chapters of northern emancipation, including the urgency of family reunification and
paid work. His plans instead gave voice to northern White supremacy's yearning: that free Black people could be excised, discarded, and
the horrors visited upon them and their families simply forgotten.
Just as William Levitt—builder of American suburbs—would argue a
century and a half later, Finley believed that his contemporaries' intractable racial hatred was a valid reason to eliminate Black people
from their midst.

In an era before railroads, Finley traveled more than two hundred
miles from Basking Ridge to Washington, D.C., to promote his idea
in the halls of power, arriving in early December 1816. There, he met
with President James Madison; the secretary of the treasury, William
H. Crawford; and Henry Clay, Speaker of the House of Representatives, winning all of their support for his project of colonization.
Within a few weeks, on December 21, the formal national organization of the American Colonization Society (ACS) had been discussed
and formed, with a constitution drawn up and officers, including Fin-

ley, Crawford, and Clay, appointed. After some persuasion, the American Colonization Society also managed to obtain congressional funding of $100,000 in 1819 for the objective of repatriating people "seized in the prosecution of the slave trade" and for installing an agent on the west coast of Africa to receive them. It was upon receiving this funding that the ACS arranged its first shipment of nearly ninety free Black emigrants on board the *Elizabeth*.

James Madison would eventually serve as president of the ACS after completing his term as president of the United States, in the early 1830s. Finley's vision would be championed by several other notable national leaders, some of whom had already considered the idea of deporting free Black people themselves, among them the former president Thomas Jefferson, future presidents James Monroe (for whom the eventual capital of the colony in Africa would be named), and the infamously racist Andrew Jackson. Jefferson was also unabashedly racist, writing about the unchangeable inferiority and lesser humanity of Black people, and therefore the problem of their freedom in America, arguing, "When freed, [Black people] must be removed beyond the reach of mixture [with White people]."

In a letter included in the First ACS Annual Meeting Report, Jefferson wrote that colonization was "the most desirable measure which could be adopted for gradually drawing off this part of our population" and explained that he had already pursued the possibility of shipping free Black people to Sierra Leone. Ironically, Sierra Leone was established by the British in the aftermath of the Revolutionary War to give a home to Black soldiers promised freedom for their military service *against* the United States.

Sierra Leone was also home to some free Black people who had not fought on the side of the British but had instead escaped American slavers and slave catchers or were born in an American state that had abolished slavery. Finding freedom too limited and too fragile in an America still raging with violent racism and predatory slave economies, they had arranged passage for themselves to West Africa. A Quaker named Paul Cuffee, of Black and Native ancestry, had made a relatively secure life for himself with a home and fortune in New England, in part by running a shipping company. Late in his life, he had helped settle a small number of these free Black people in Sierra Leone, seeing this as a service to people free at last to choose their homes.

Cuffee had accomplished something the founders of the ACS hoped to do on a much larger scale (though with different considerations), and he was Black. For this reason, the ACS saw Cuffee's endorsement as valuable to the success of their scheme. However, Cuffee immediately discerned the gulf between his own motivations and the plans laid by Jefferson and the ACS. He saw the ACS as an effort by White men to once again steer the destinies of Black people for their own interests. In response to the ACS's overtures, Cuffee supported the Black leadership groups in Philadelphia and Richmond, who argued that colonization was a thinly disguised plan for deportation, a "circuitous route back to bondage," writing,

> Whereas our ancestors (not of choice) were the first successful cultivators of the wilds of America, we, their descendants, feel ourselves entitled to participate in the blessings of her luxuriant soil, which their blood and sweat enriched; and that any measure or system of measures having a tendency to banish us from her bosom, would not only be cruel, but in direct violation of those principles which have been the boast of this republic.

Cuffee and other free Black leaders argued that colonization would strengthen slavery in the United States, leaving those still enslaved without aid and allies. In 1827, the first Black newspaper in the country, *Freedom's Journal,* came out in opposition to colonization as well. Black leaders' concerns were well founded; Thomas Jefferson had made clear his disregard for the agency of free Black people when he argued that "neither the resistance of free Black people, nor the habits of slavery, which might get in the way of effective self-governance, should halt the 'experiment' of colonization." Jefferson supported the forced removal of the first generation of Black people in America to have autonomy and freedom, regardless of whether they were willing to leave or had yet obtained the skills and literacy to build a successful settlement. The British, however, would refuse his early requests to open Sierra Leone for colonization.

General Robert Goodloe Harper attended the College of New Jersey just as Finley left. After having served in the U.S. Senate in 1816, and as a leader of the Federalist Party, Harper was asked to weigh in on the project of the ACS. In response, he spelled out the bad faith and hypocrisy that would become the blueprint of White American racism during this early period of Black freedom. His letter was read into the First ACS Annual Meeting Report:

> These persons are condemned to a state of hopelessness inferiority and degradation by their color, which is an indelible mark of their origin and former condition, and . . . makes us recoil with horror from the idea of an intimate union with the free blacks, and precludes the possibility of such a state of equality, between them and us, as alone could make us one people. Whatever justice, humanity, and kindness we may feel towards them, we cannot help considering them and treating them as our inferiors . . . we could never consent, and they never could hope, to see the free blacks, or their descendants, visit in our house, form part of our circle of acquaintance, marry into our families, or participate in public honors and employments.

Harper went on to lay into Paul Cuffee: "I may safely assert that Paul Cuffee, respectable, intelligent, and wealthy as he is, has no expectation or chance of ever being invited to dine with any gentleman in Boston; of marrying his daughter, whatever may be her fortune or education, to one of their sons; or of seeing his son obtain a wife among their daughters." He argued that American slavery was distinct from any other institution, requiring a unique resolution because, while one could "manumit a slave" in America, one could not "make him a White man," because the "mark and recollection" of slavery sticks with the emancipated Black person and remains in the "minds of the Whites." He argued that the "debasement" to which he and his colleagues and their ancestors had subjected countless Black people in slavery had now become a "habitual and voluntary" part of the Black character.

Like many supporters of the ACS, Harper is widely reported to have been anti-slavery, but he maintained that it was a necessary part of the southern economy and didn't let his politics stand in the way of being a slaver himself. At his death in January of 1825, the "chattel" of his estate were considered "too valuable to be given their freedom." His arguments in favor of colonization were a reflection of both northern and southern White interests of his time; he argued that colonization might encourage manumission (the freeing of the enslaved) and so should entice abolitionist support. At the same time, he argued, free Black people were idle and given to vice absent *the moral restraints and authority of their slave masters,* and therefore were a corrupting influence on enslaved people, inciting disobedience and resistance, so their removal should win the support of slavers. Several of Harper's ACS colleagues also added to his arguments that the removal of free Black people was necessary to prevent the enslaved from being easily "concealed" among them.

Toward the end of his life, Harper had an idea that he thought would solve the lingering problem of financing efficient colonization efforts. Just about fifty years before Richard Henry Pratt would have a similar idea about abducting Native children, Harper began work on a scheme in which free and enslaved Black children would be collected (supposedly with the consent of parents or owners) at seminary schools, *where they would be re-enslaved* for the purposes of learning reading, writing, mathematics, and Christianity, as well as producing saleable goods. The profit from their labor would be used to pay for their expenses and, ultimately, the cost of deporting them to Liberia, on the west coast of Africa. There, Harper wrote, they would finally live in freedom, for which they would have ostensibly been prepared by confinement and enslavement at Harper's schools. Strikingly, the pathology of White supremacy made Harper and Pratt both unable to grasp their own malignancy. They would not consider familial love and attachment among Black and Native people, because they were unwilling to concede their humanity. They could not understand the monstrosity of their own thinking because they were the products, and sometimes producers, of a context in which all of the most criminal and pathological human behaviors were acceptable so long as they were visited upon Black or Brown people by White people and never the other way around. So the ACS would appeal to and engage some of the most powerful men in the country, and not a small number of state and federal resources, beginning in 1816. Although its numbers would dwindle after 1867, it would not formally dissolve until 1964, during the modern civil rights era.

My family learned about another, older New Jersey mosque nearer to our house in Fallsington around the time ISCJ opened, and we went for a visit one Sunday. It was housed in a cramped brick Trenton row house where it had been established by the local Black Muslim community, not by recent immigrants. We were welcomed there, and it felt like a neighborhood block party inside, with laughter and food and kids. But I also sensed that my parents couldn't easily understand what people were saying when they spoke too quickly or in a dialect with which they were not familiar. They couldn't intuit where it was appropriate to stand or sit, or how to segregate by sex for prayers. In spite of the hospitality and generosity with which they were received, they felt themselves to be in a space in which they were the odd ones out, the ones who couldn't read the cultural cues, the ones who didn't belong while everyone else did.

In retrospect, it is clear to me that we were a lot like other immigrant families in failing to learn and understand the causes of American segregation. Ultimately, we participated in that segregation. My parents were not particularly curious about why Black Americans

seemed so consistently and effectively relegated to marginal neighborhoods, workplaces, and schools. They experienced the narrow
row house on a cramped Trenton street as far from the America they
found in suburban Fallsington, and uncomfortably similar to the rubble of postcolonial mismanagement they saw in the streets of Hyderabad. But instead of provoking in them a sense of solidarity, that
experience provoked a tension, maybe even a vigilance, about maintaining their own marginal place in America.

They wondered aloud why there was such a disparity between the
wealth and education of White communities and Black communities
in America more than a century after slavery had ended. The answer
that prevailed in their White workplaces and neighborhood during
the Reagan years was the story of American meritocracy, which suggested that anyone who failed to be wealthy and successful had just
failed to work hard and be worthy. As a result, my parents, like so
many Black and Brown immigrants, came to see themselves as necessarily separate from Black American communities, even Muslim ones.
The question of whether America was indeed a meritocracy for everyone, and the plain persistence of segregation around them, caused
them overwhelming anxiety. Having bet it all in migrating to America, they adopted attitudes that allowed them to believe and to hope
that whatever kept other people down would not also compromise
their own aspirations. This persistent failure of my parents and of
many recent immigrants like them to understand the racial history of
America, and especially the great waves of postslavery violence inflicted on Black Americans, has kept us from forging important alliances to build racial equality today. It also maintains the segregation
of American mosques and American Muslim communities.

I wish we had stayed at the Trenton mosque for other reasons as
well. One Sunday when I was perhaps ten years old, my father, older
brother, and I had gone to ISCJ without my mother and baby brother.
We had arrived just in time for prayers, a time when I would usually
accompany my mother to the back of the hall, lining up among aunties and friends. With no time to find an auntie in the crowd, and with

me still too young and daydreamy to send off on my own, my father set me between himself and my brother in a line of the men's section, head and body covered, and we began to pray. In the middle of prayers, I felt a large hand grab me out of the line by my arm, pulling me to the side of the prayer area. I was panicked until I saw that my father had followed. Interrupting prayers is a serious matter, and so this was completely unexpected.

The strange man who had grabbed me shouted at my father, "She should not be with the men! This is not right!" My father looked at him in shock, responding, "She is just a child, standing between her father and her brother. Should I send her away from me in this crowd?" I was no longer panicked, but still shaken. I felt shamed and, though I may not have had the word to describe it then, sexualized. I also felt disgusted. Here he was protesting my immodesty for standing among men, but he had also grabbed me, an unrelated girl, without my consent.

My father approached the imam, the prayer leader and mosque administrator, to resolve the matter once prayers were over and the sermon had been delivered. It was a memorable conversation, even to my child's mind. My father explained what had happened, and then asked me if I had any questions for the imam. Without any of my usual shyness or reticence, I asked, "Why did that man grab me and pull me out of line?" He responded that the man was wrong to have grabbed me, but that he was correct in saying that I should not have been among the men. Then his cheeks flushed as he continued, in a deep Egyptian accent, "When the man stands behind the woman, he has certain feelings that distract from the prayers." I hadn't imagined it—I *was* being sexualized. To both my father's and my own astonishment, I immediately replied, "But women are always in the back. Don't you think women have the same feelings when they stand behind men?" The imam went purple and told me I would understand when I was older, and my father took my hand as we headed outside to find my brother.

"What did you think of his answers, *beta*?" he asked, with the term of endearment he used for all three of his children. "Were you satisfied?"

"No," I answered, quickly. "Were you satisfied?"

My father sighed and then paused. "No, *beta,* I was not satisfied."

Decades later, when I was in my forties, I'd moderate a panel about women in the mosque in Philadelphia, at which several of the Black women present made the influence of the civil rights movement on their institutions clear. "We are present in all leadership positions. We weren't going to sit at the back of the bus!" What important lessons immigrant Muslims could learn from the Black Muslim American experience, I thought, and how impoverished we were, and still often are, by our failure to see that.

Back in middle school, around the time I started shaving my armpits and legs, I also sprouted breasts. I was both fascinated by this and confused. My father no longer seemed to know how to interact with me, whether because of my mood or my body, I don't know. All physical contact from anyone in my family besides my younger brother, who was still little enough to cuddle, stopped abruptly, aside from a hug after Eid prayers twice a year. This may not have had the same effect if I had grown up in a large, intact extended family, with cousins and aunties and grandmothers all around. But in the isolation of American suburbia, it was a profound loss. Though I didn't identify lack of affection as the cause, I felt intensely alone at home, and that feeling only abated when I was with friends. There were things I needed to be parented through during this time, but for reasons I don't think even my parents quite understood, they weren't available.

So, breasts. I had them and by the time I was twelve they were no longer tiny breast buds but entire C-cup entities of their own. Yet no one mentioned them. Not my mother, not my aunties from the mosque, not my father or brothers (although I'm glad for that bit, because it would have been humiliating). It's not that I wanted anyone to discuss them, but I was pretty sure I was supposed to contain them and obscure them under my shirts. I began choosing dark, oversized tops to wear, even in the summer, but that got old pretty quickly. I wasn't sure how to broach the subject, given how my mother had responded to armpit hair. Was I wrong? Was I not yet ready for a bra? I snuck into my mother's dresser and pulled out a blue satin one, quickly trying it on over my clothes. It was hard to tell with fabric in the way, but it fit snugly, and was maybe even too small. That did it. I told my mother that we needed to go bra shopping, not allowing myself to even observe her reaction.

It was an ordinary department store we went to, like a Target, and there was no one to do a fitting, so it was up to me to assert that the bras my mother had chosen for me were too small, which they plainly were. Then I really got brazen and asked if I could have the emerald-colored satin one I'd seen, in addition to the more practical white ones my mother selected. I felt guilty, as I often did when I saw the pinched reluctance with which my parents spent money, but I shoved that feeling aside. I was on a roll of uncharacteristic assertiveness, and it was one that had plenty of frustration behind it. I was angry at my parents, at the man who had pulled me out of the prayers, at the mosque, and at the imam. I didn't want to belong to any culture or tradition that was ashamed of me. I didn't choose to grow pubic hair or breasts. I didn't get a choice about being a girl and not a boy. I didn't think I should have to be punished for it, over and over again.

We would continue to attend ISCJ until I was in high school, with me standing at the back next to my mother for prayers, not wanting to be there. Despite my moment of euphoria at the threshold of ISCJ that first day, relishing the beauty of true human diversity, I had almost nothing in common with Malcolm X. Malcolm X was on the verge of self-realization when he stood in Mecca. I was a prepubescent girl at a suburban mosque, and I would stumble through life for several more years before finding my way home.

⸻

By 1824, the ACS had sent four ships with emigrants to West Africa to begin to populate land the organization had acquired in what was then called Upper Guinea. This land would eventually become the nation of Liberia. Several states, including New Jersey, had begun to set up their own colonization societies, the central role of which would be to continue to gather funds to pay for ships, provisions, and resettlement of free Black people. The founding members of the New Jersey Colonization Society (NJCS), at least half of whom were affiliated with the College of New Jersey, enumerated the purposes of the NJCS at their first meeting, in 1825: 1) abolition, because freeing slaves would be more palatable to slavers if they could be sure that free Black people would be removed from their proximity, 2) to "reclaim the inhabitants of Africa from savageness and brutality" through exposure to the Christianity, industry, and civilization of White people, for which free Black colonists would be a conduit, and 3) suppression of the "wickedness and barbarity" of the slave trade.

By the second meeting, held two years later, the objectives of the NJCS had changed: 1) to "remov[e] to the coast of Africa" free Black people in the United States, 2) to end the traffic in slaves "upon the coast of Africa," and 3) to "redeem the inhabitants of that vast territory [of Africa], said to contain 50 millions of inhabitants from the sin and sufferings of the bloodiest superstition." Abolition of American slavery had quickly disappeared as a purpose, reflecting the power and authority of New Jersey's slavers more than twenty years after the state's gradual manumission law was passed.

The president of the College of New Jersey, speaking at the second meeting of the NJCS, "disclaim[ed] in the strongest terms any intention of interfering on the one hand with the legal right to, and obligations of Slavery, and on the other, still more absurd . . . of perpetuating its existence within the limits of our own country." This is the unfortunate line that New Jersey and Princeton University would strive to walk for the rest of the nineteenth century: neither for nor against slavery. The members of the ACS and the NJCS, often in the administration and orbit of Princeton, would argue ardently against the slave trade in Africa, which they believed proved the "sinfulness and barbarity" of Africans, but continue to engage, placate, and ally with slavers within America.

The NJCS leadership asserted that colonization would handily do everything good, all at once: It would make America substantially whiter, it would save the souls of savage Africans (who they said lacked the civilizing influence of White Christian masters), and, incredibly, it would be a sort of reparation for the sins of the transatlantic slave trade. As had Finley, Jefferson, and several other founders of the American Colonization Society before them, the founders of the NJCS remarked with alarm on the growing numbers of free Black people among them:

> We find by the Census of 1810, that [New Jersey's] slaves are numbered at more than ten thousand, and her free blacks at more than seven thousand. . . . What a mass of ignorance, misery and depravity, is here mingled with every portion of our population, and threatening the whole with a moral and political pestilence.

For the advocates of deporting free Black people to Africa, the possibility that the group of people once subjected to the horrors of slavery would be free among those who had once enslaved them created sheer terror:

> We have a more dangerous foe, a foe admitted under the guise of slave or servant; one who is admitted without reserve into the bosom of our families . . . and yet one who secretly and cordially hates and despises the hand that feeds and maintains him.

This terror was perhaps the truest motivation of the elite men of New Jersey who continued to pour money into the project of eradicating free Black people in the state by persuading and paying them to leave. Over the next several decades, groups of White men from Massachusetts, Vermont, Connecticut, New York, Ohio, Maryland, Pennsylvania, Mississippi, Virginia, Indiana, Illinois, Alabama, North Carolina, and Missouri would do the same. Despite their efforts, the ACS was only ever able to send about 6,000 total passengers to Liberia, all before the end of the U.S. Civil War. The organization kept meticulous population records, including numbers of passengers and survivors, numbers of children born in the new colony, and numbers of those who left it. These records showed *nearly 42 percent* of the first 4,571 emigrants to Liberia, arriving between 1820 and 1842, *were dead by the end of that period*. Most died of various poorly diagnosed illness and disease, although just over 100 deaths were attributed to drowning, childbirth, and old age. A quarter died *within the first two years of arrival*.

The leadership of the ACS were undaunted by overwhelming evidence that they were sending innocent people to premature deaths. They adjusted their plans only slightly, to allow for the arrival of emigrants in the dry season, which they hoped would reduce the incidence of disease. At the same time, they mounted a "propaganda campaign" to allay the fears of free Black people they hoped to entice.

Liberia has had a tumultuous history since the ACS's "colonization" scheme. Initial conflicts and ethnic tensions between colonists and Indigenous people have persisted in modern Liberian society, and they have been a significant factor in its two civil wars. The two groups are distinguishable, tragically, by the color of their skin. Indigenous Liberians are typically much darker skinned, while those descended from the original deportees from America are generally lighter skinned, evidence of the long history of White American slavers raping the women they enslaved and then enslaving the children born of those assaults. Many of those originally resettled by the ACS arrived anticipating themselves in the roles prescribed for them by White men: missionaries from a superior White Christian culture. Attempts by the colonizing minority to govern not only themselves but the much larger Indigenous population have, unsurprisingly, resulted in broad resentment, continual power struggles, and violence.

In 1989, when I was in tenth grade, my family moved a mile or so from Fallsington to the next town up the river, Yardley. Yardley is the wealthiest part of Pennsbury School District, with the most highly ranked schools. My friends there were the children of solidly middle-class and upper-middle-class professionals, and when I went to their houses, I flipped through copies of *The Economist* and *The Nation* on their coffee tables, ogled the bookshelves and music collections in their bedrooms, and ate cheese and olives.

Almost immediately, I was absorbed into a group of mostly Jewish kids and felt suddenly that a narrowly and tenaciously White Irish and Italian Catholic identity did not define the social world in which I had to survive. My teachers were all still White and Christian, and my education still mostly lacked any mention of other people, cultures, or realities. But some of the kids on this new side of the tracks had a precocious level of self-awareness and sense of social justice that had been absent in the Levittown schools. When my out-of-shape gym teacher at Charles Boehm Junior High, Mr. Cochran, took our class out to "run the mile" around a track in searing summer heat and I explained that I was fasting for Ramadan, he insisted that I had to run with everyone else. I cursed at him and stomped off to the office for the inevitable suspension, but then several other kids gathered around him in protest to explain that Ramadan is a legitimate religious requirement for Muslims. He shrugged and said, "She's in America now," but the social messaging from my friends was unanimous: I did the right thing, and our teacher was a bigot.

The message from my parents was different: The fast was meant to teach restraint not just from food, but from anger and aggression. That was the more important commitment, and I had allowed myself to be provoked by his ignorance when I should have made the same point with grace. I was still pissed. Who was *that guy,* anyway? What was his life experience that he felt able to claim America in that way, to say what it was or what it was not, and define what could be celebrated or observed or practiced within it? Why did he feel entitled to decide what it meant for me to be "in America now"?

There were two classes available at Pennsbury in which Brown and Black people were discussed, and I took both of them. One, which was mandatory, was called Afro-Asian and the other, which was an elective, was called International Studies. Afro-Asian was the social studies course for tenth grade, meant to introduce us to the societies and cultures of Africa and Asia. Though the idea that a single class would propose to cover such a diverse set of nations, people, and cultures was absurd, it was nonetheless my favorite class, because we studied apartheid South Africa, including both the domestic and global struggles against it. There was something unusually honest and incisive about our discussion of racism in the context of South Africa. It didn't yet occur to me quite how much of what we were learning could be applied to the American context, but I felt the importance and the urgency of the issues at play.

Unfortunately, the class often introduced societies and cultures without reference to time, so that it was unclear how the people we were studying were related to one another, affected by modernity, or engaged with urbanism. Instead, our subjects, like the Mbuti of the Congo or the Bushmen of Botswana, were presented as ahistorical, two-dimensional caricatures of Brown and Black people hunting with spears or wearing loincloths, and sometimes both, without references to how cosmopolitan people might differ from rural people. It also failed to distinguish between anthropology and politics, or history and current events. The only Asian person we studied, for example, was Gandhi (pictured in a loincloth), in the context of his 1940s struggle for Indian independence. We did not then study, for example, the subsequent partition of India, or the persistent effects of colonialism, resource extraction, and cold war politics on it, but only the life and struggle of a single man who had been dead for more than forty years.

While it was helpful to have a course that acknowledged the larger world, the way in which it was taught distorted our perceptions of reality. For example, a large minority of people in Africa and a majority of people in Asia lived in cosmopolitan, industrialized contexts in 1990, but it would have been hard to reach that conclusion from our syllabus. The class hinted at the existence of Indigenous people and liberation struggles but failed to describe the global breadth of European colonization or its effects on them.

It was weird to be Asian in that class, to be handed a narrow and exoticized version of myself and the place my family came from, one designed to make it seem that those places and cultures were frozen in the past. It was also odd, in retrospect, to have conversations about the realities of apartheid South Africa in a starkly White classroom, set in a starkly White town, without any comment on America's own racial segregation, or America's own Native peoples.

In International Studies class, we studied the conflict in Israel and Palestine. I adored my teacher, and she adored exotic artifacts from around the world, which decorated her classroom. This was an elective class, in which there was another South Asian Muslim girl from the grade below mine. She was the only other Muslim I encountered in high school, and one of maybe a couple of dozen students of color I saw in all twelve years of my public education. Her name was Kiran, and I had never met or spoken to her before. She was smart, and generally completed assignments, but refused to do any of the work in the Israel-Palestine unit. She left all of that work, including tests and assignments, blank. Our teacher took me aside to ask me to explain why Kiran wouldn't do her work. I guess she thought that our Muslimness or our South Asianness meant I would know, but I didn't.

Around the same time, I approached my choir teacher, the popular, energetic Ms. Abelshauser, to shyly suggest that I help research a song from a Muslim tradition for the choir to sing. I thought this might be well received. Ms. Abelshauser had us singing several overtly religious songs from the Christian tradition, Bach's "Jesu, Joy of Man's Desiring," another song with the repeating refrain "*kyrie eléison*" (Latin for "Lord, have mercy"), and more popular Christmas music like "Carol of the Bells." I didn't mind at all. I loved singing these songs, and their beauty also made me wonder about Urdu devotional songs. Although my parents had passing familiarity with Urdu ghazels and qawwalis, they did not come from households in which these were sung, or households where there was reliable electricity, much less recorded music playing. I thought maybe Ms. Abelshauser could help me excavate this part of my own tradition. Instead, she was infuriated. I still recall almost thirty years later the way that she turned red in the face, the veins in her neck popping. Her voice raised combatively, she made clear that my suggestion was an unwelcome affront. She said she felt she had done plenty to ensure diversity, as we already had the song "Zum Gali" to represent minority faiths. The irony is that "Zum Gali" is a folk song about the settlement of Israel by hardworking pioneers. Not only is it not from any Muslim tradition, but from a Palestinian Muslim and Christian perspective, would seem to celebrate a chapter of devastating dispossession. "Zum Gali" was not related to my own tradition or where I was from; it was just part of a landscape in which I was expected to arrive empty and fill myself with whatever was offered. Art and music, even, were something not meant to be an expression of anything in me, just something I ought to be grateful to participate in, no matter how foreign. I backed away apologetically from Ms. Abelshauser, too anxious and confused to pursue it further.

My high school classes, when they related to Brown and Black people at all, were not designed for people who were themselves Brown or Black. We were meant to be, very occasionally, the topic of study, but we were never meant to be the students. Unlike the classes on literature, history, art, and economics that celebrated White subjects, protagonists, and pursuits as heroic, exemplary, and foundational, the two available classes on Brown and Black people portrayed us as universally antiquated, impoverished, exotic, and embattled. There was no discussion of Brown and Black people within contemporary America or American history, of American colonialism or of migration, despite the central roles we have played in all of those.

My education and my life in suburban Pennsylvania taught me that it was better to be White. The world, as it was being introduced to us in the classroom, revolved around White achievements and accomplishments. By contrast, we had been taught to imagine Africa and Asia as dusty deserts, as *wastelands,* inhabited by people with little relevance in the modern world. When my aunts and my uncles, whom my parents had sponsored for immigration, began to arrive in the mid-1980s and my cousins began to attend school in the neighboring school district of Bensalem, I saw that their classmates had little patience for their accents, for their shyness, for their difference. Their process of acculturation was painful to watch, mired as it was in ridicule and rejection.

By the end of high school, I was spending a lot of time with a small group of kids, some of whom were from Levittown and some of whom were from Yardley. They were all White and mostly Catholic, but they were a little edgy for suburbia: a little bookish, idealistic, given to going on hikes and reading Thoreau, happy to skip school and perform Shakespeare in the park for one another. Some had reason to feel displaced like me; two had lost parents tragically early. We were a little in love with each other, and with the new kinds of freedom that come with a driver's license in suburban Bucks County. None of this made any sense to my parents, who understood the natural order of things to include more restrictions for a young unmarried woman, and more concentration on a career-oriented plan for college. But *that* didn't make sense to *me:* I didn't have any of the fear I would have had in a Pakistani environment. I wasn't worried what the neighbors would think, didn't care what my marriage prospects were, and already understood that the luxury of a diversified economy meant that I didn't have to go to medical school or be an engineer to support myself.

I was feeling my way through adolescence in the traditionally confused and conflicted American way, but this was exaggerated because of the cultural distance between the society in which my parents were raised and the one in which I had to function. I had learned to not discuss much of anything at all at home: My idealism crashed directly into my parents' loving but anxious pragmatism, and everything from how I spent the money I earned at a pizza shop to my crush on a young Johnny Depp could create apocalyptic conflicts. My circle of friends, who had few of the social constraints of my family or faith community, included Jim, who became my first, and necessarily secret, boyfriend. He was one of the kindest people I've ever met, full of wonder, always on the edge of glee, weirdly obsessed with physics, and despite all of that still managed to come off as chill. He was also the first person in my life to ever call me beautiful. I had always felt myself too "other" to be beautiful, so his attention felt like the sun shining on me.

There's only one time that I remember Jim being curt with me. Having lost his mother to cancer, and then his father to complications of diabetes, all before he had graduated from high school, he was explaining to me how he felt God was a sort of invisible father, a confidant, present and real to him. Having never had this intimate experience of God myself, having instead been introduced to religion as an intellectual exercise and a cultural identity, I fell back on the central dogma of Islamic Sunday school. Anthropomorphizing God wasn't right, God was not like a person in any way, I told him. It pained him, I could see, in a way I hadn't intended, and he drew a hard boundary: "Both of my parents are dead, and I'm going to imagine God in any way I want to." The reminder that his faith was forged in loss I couldn't possibly begin to fathom stunned me into silence. The moment stuck with me because I had wondered, from the time I stumbled into books about Joan of Arc and the Spanish Inquisition in the school library, what it was that motivated real faith, the kind of deep loyalty to the Divine that could not ever be sacrificed, for which a person would risk their life. I saw something like it in my mother's sisters, who kept the entire extended family running by marshaling and carefully stewarding every narrow resource available, binding their own desires and ambitions to a guiding sense of faith and duty, without a trace of bitterness. But I'd had fleeting time with them, on trips to Pakistan, and I'd had no other, nearer models of this kind of faith characterized by love and certainty of the Divine. It would be another decade before I would begin to understand that kind of relationship to God, forged in plain need and entirely without dogma.

By my senior year in high school, the first Gulf War had ended but the popular justifications for that war lingered. Iraq had invaded Kuwait and America had intervened. With little public consciousness of how the United States had encouraged the conflict, Iraqis and Kuwaitis, and by extension Muslims, were painted as anachronistic desert patriarchs, unable to respect modern notions of the nation-state or resolve their own problems. In the broader context of the Iran hostage crisis, the Lebanese civil war, and the Israeli occupation of Palestine, the media machine had begun to pair the words *Muslim* and *terrorist* with increasing regularity. My ethnic identity was suddenly one that could land me on the "bad guy" side of NATO-drawn global alliances, and so also of high school alliances.

I had no real connection to the Gulf States or the Middle East and hadn't fully realized the ways in which "Muslim" had become a broadly pejorative word until one day when I was talking to Brent, who was in our tight circle of friends, about current events. He had asserted that the increasingly common phrase "Muslim terrorist" was appropriate, because "most terrorists are Muslim." Our argument quickly made the four others in our group uncomfortable. But I couldn't let it go.

I couldn't figure out how he could generalize so egregiously about—well, about me and people with whom I shared a faith. Also, Brent was a history buff. I was both outraged and hurt that he was willing to associate my entire religious group, and the ethnic identities to which he assumed most of us belonged, with violence. Americans had not yet transcended Italian mobster references, and he was Italian! Others in our group were Irish, English, German. We had, all of us, been born in the era of IRA bombings and Holocaust education. We lived in a country where the Native population is frequently spoken about in the past tense, as if its annihilation were not only complete, but unremarkable. All of us were of peoples who were somehow implicated in significant terrorism within living history. But no one said a word in my defense, and I was alien again.

Princeton University had a much more direct connection to the forced migrations and exploitation of Black people than through the ACS and the NJCS. Sixteen of the original twenty-three trustees of the College of New Jersey (which remained Princeton University's name until 1896) bought, sold, inherited, or traded people as property. An average of 40 percent of the college's all-White students were drawn from the southern slave states between its founding in 1746 and 1865, and the college actively recruited students and solicited donations from among the slavers of the South, Jamaica, and the West Indies. Although there is no remaining evidence of whether the iconic Nassau Hall was built by enslaved people in the 1750s, five of the six main donors to the project amassed their wealth from the labor of the enslaved. The celebrated northern Ivy League institution owes its wealth and standing to the traffic in enslaved Africans.

The brick house beside Nassau Hall was "the center of slavery at Princeton." At least five of the college's presidents lived there with their enslaved servants, some of whom were sold in an auction alongside other property on the front steps on August 17, 1766. This institutional reliance on enslaved labor and the profits of slavery meant that Princeton, like New Jersey as a whole, would drag its feet toward abolition. Afterward, the College of New Jersey would continue to support and enrich itself with the proceeds of slavery for many more decades. Key benefactors like Moses Taylor Pyne, who graduated more than ten years after the Civil War, funded dormitories, teaching endowments, and a library with proceeds his family derived from the sugar industry, which was reliant on the labor of enslaved people.

It is perhaps unsurprising then that during this same period, the lives of ostensibly free Black people in the North, particularly in New Jersey and several adjacent counties of New York, were relegated to the economic and social margins of society. The town of Princeton was rigorously segregated by race well into the 1900s, with free Black people living along Witherspoon Street on the north side of Nassau Hall and working as servants to the students, faculty, or college for very little money. Born in Princeton in 1898 to a father who had escaped slavery, and writing in the early twentieth century, the musician, actor, and activist Paul Robeson described it this way:

> Almost every Negro in Princeton lived off the college and accepted the social status that went with it. We lived for all intents and purposes on a Southern plantation. And with no more dignity than that suggests—all the bowing and scraping to the drunken rich, all the vile names, all the Uncle Tomming to earn enough to lead miserable lives.

There are several surviving accounts of individuals who lived this experience in the College of New Jersey's orbit. James Collins Johnson fled slavery in 1839, arriving and starting work at the College of New Jersey as a janitor that same year. He worked at Nassau Hall and then at a dorm and a classroom building, serving students in the most intimate of ways: bringing water, building fires, and emptying latrine buckets. Four years after his arrival, a student attending Princeton from Maryland recognized Johnson and alerted his owner, the son of a wealthy and well-known Maryland family, Severn Wallis. Wallis's father, Philip, had given Johnson to Severn in childhood as an enslaved "playmate" at their family's plantation near Easton, Maryland. It was from that plantation that Johnson had made his escape through Wilmington, Philadelphia, Trenton, and then finally to Princeton, which in 1839 had a large free Black population and an established African Methodist Episcopal Church (AME), an institution known for assisting those escaping slavery.

Severn Wallis, a lawyer himself, pursued the detailed procedures for claiming Johnson and re-enslaving him. In 1843, Johnson was tried and convicted under the Fugitive Slave Act of 1793, which Congress had passed to give local governments the power to capture and return to slavery those who had escaped. Johnson's return to slavery was forestalled, however, when a White woman in Princeton named Theodosia Prevost advanced Johnson the five hundred dollars (close to ten thousand dollars in 2020 currency) needed to buy his freedom.

Her motivations are unclear; she was from a wealthy and powerful family of slavers, the step-granddaughter of the third U.S. vice president, Aaron Burr, and the granddaughter of a president of the College of New Jersey. At the time that she provided the funds to keep Johnson out of slavery, she was economically independent, ran her own household, and was very well connected among the college's administrators.

James Collins Johnson is described in accounts by Princeton students of the time as a happy-go-lucky, "puckish mascot" of the campus. In her book on Johnson, *The Princeton Fugitive Slave: The Trials of James Collins Johnson,* Lolita Buckner Inniss, dean of the University of Colorado School of Law, demonstrates, through students' own accounts and records, how disparate this characterization of Johnson was from how he was actually treated: "He was caricatured by students for his stutter, called by a pejorative nickname, 'Jim Stink,' and treated with 'barely disguised disdain.'" Johnson's life, often recounted to focus on the gift of his freedom through the largess of a kindly stranger, is one that Johnson himself characterized quite differently, saying: "I never got no free papers. Princeton College bought me; Princeton college owns me; and Princeton College has got to give me my living." In fact, Johnson would take years to pay off the debt he owed to Prevost, continuing to work at the college as a janitor and a vendor of clothing and food until his death in 1902. Meanwhile, his childhood playmate and owner, Severn Wallis, would go on to become a provost at the University of Maryland.

The effects of the different levels of wealth and opportunity available to these two men would be generational. In trying to trace the descendants of each man, Innis found a "paucity of public and private documents recording the lives of Johnson's family," so that the record of Johnson's legacy ended with the death of his youngest daughter and two of her children. Meanwhile, she was able to easily reconstruct the history of the Wallis family, even finding three Princeton alumni among Philip Wallis's descendants.

In another example of Princeton's exploitation of marginal Black labor and the precariousness of Black freedom, Sam Parker, a Black man, served as an assistant to Joseph Henry, the college's chair of natural history in the 1840s. Henry was a noted scholar of electromagnetism and an active supporter of the ACS plan to send free Black people to West Africa. After Parker was hired by trustees of the college to assist Joseph Henry for the sum of forty-eight dollars per year (about one-fifth the average annual wage for White unskilled workers in 1840), he would work in Henry's laboratory as well as his household. Within a year, according to Joseph Henry's papers, Parker's assistance became critical to Henry's work. He supplied materials for the lab and fixed technical issues such that Henry noted his experiments could not go on when Parker fell ill. Yet Parker was treated like a piece of equipment himself, strapped to a chair while a current passed through him. Although Joseph Henry also allowed himself to be a conduit for the current, it is unlikely Parker had much choice, and when he was being experimented on, students assisting with the experiments, according to the records of the memoirist Edward Shippen, who was a student in 1845, "snapped sparks from his nose and chin." Shippen provides painful insight about how Parker fared outside of the classroom, writing, "We liked Sam, as an engine—and hated him as a ginger n*****, who owned 100 suits of clothes and put on airs."

Princeton University made the stories of Johnson and Parker public as part of a 2017 project to examine its long and troubling reliance on slavery and the subjugation of free Black people in the town. Still, with an endowment of $25.9 billion, the school has yet to announce monetary reparations to the descendants of those the institution had long exploited. In fact, very few American universities have made reparations for similar histories of profiting from slavery and maintaining institutional barriers to Black education.

In late 2019, Princeton Theological Seminary (separate from Princeton University) announced that it would set aside $27.6 million of its endowment to finance the payment of $1 million annually in reparations for its participation in the institution of slavery. The payment will fund thirty scholarships to the descendants of enslaved people, a full-time director for the Center for Black Church Studies, and the renaming of certain buildings for important Black figures. The Association of Black Seminarians took issue with the terms of the reparations, explaining that $27.6 million of the seminary's $1 *billion* endowment was not sufficient. Virginia Theological Seminary (VTS), which was built by enslaved people, is the only other educational institution to announce reparations to be paid from its endowment; it has set up a $1.7 million reparations fund, with estimated annual expenditures of $70,000. VTS has a total endowment of about $140 million.

In 2016, Georgetown University revealed that it had avoided closing its doors in 1838 by selling hundreds of enslaved laborers and their children, who had been enslaved, whipped, worked, and also forced to attend mass by the Jesuit priests who then ran the institution. Entire families were dragged onto ships and then sold apart to plantations in the Deep South, all of their names and ages recorded in university archives. Today, the university has yet to take action on a working group's recommendation to pay reparations to the descendants of those people. Instead, students voted to tax themselves about thirty dollars per semester, creating a fund meant to benefit the descendants.

Harvard, Columbia, and Brown have all published findings from studies similar to Princeton's and Georgetown's: Enslaved people were owned and their labor used by founders, trustees, and faculty—and sometimes the schools themselves. Yale, the University of Pennsylvania, and Dartmouth have announced similar projects. For more than two hundred years, the wealth associated with these schools was extracted from the trafficking in and marginalization of Black people, for White people. This is the story of nearly every elite institution of postsecondary education in the nation.

In retrospect, I think Brent wasn't trying to be a jerk. We used to say that we got along because we both had an overdeveloped sense of empathy that made us stormy teenagers. The difference between us was that in our shared context, my security and my success depended on empathy with people who were radically different from me. They did not look like me and their families did not look like my family, pray like my family, speak like my family, or eat and drink like my family. I crossed a social bridge each morning that stood directly outside my front door. In fact, it also stood between the family room sofa and the television. Sometimes, it stood on the dinner table between my parents and me. It's true that Brent and I shared an overdeveloped sense of empathy, but as a function of our overwhelmingly segregated environment, in which even the characters on television looked like him, his was exercised in a very narrow range. As a result, I believe it actually became *harder* for him to see people who were radically different from him, especially people with competing interests to his, as valid.

Brent's perspective, in which terrorism was ascribed only or wholly to Black or Brown people, was not anomalous; it is often the perspective of students of American history as it is generally written and taught. This is a theme that emerged repeatedly as I revisited how the color lines came to be in all the places I've lived: White culpability is frequently erased or excused, while Black and Brown resistance is frequently criminalized or pathologized.

I had limited knowledge of the Muslim world and the ways it had been shaped by European colonial and neocolonial interests with which to counter Brent's arguments. For example, I had experienced life in Hyderabad and Karachi, Pakistan, for summer months all the way through the cold war period. I knew that I encountered chaos and sectarian violence when I was there, especially during the late eighties and early nineties, with regular shootings and citywide all-day curfews so frequent that my cousins lost months or even years of school as a result. But I did not yet know that the port of Karachi had become the designated gateway for outrageous amounts of small arms and other resources flowing from the United States into the cold war battleground of Afghanistan, littering the path along the way with valuable foreign weapons, driving violence and corruption. All I felt confident about in that argument was that I had lived with and loved and met many more Muslims than he ever had, and felt that they were, on the whole, no better and no worse than the rest of humanity.

After the argument with Brent, I began to suspect that the Islamic pluralism on display when I first stepped into ISCJ might not, in fact, be America's vision for itself—at least not the only or the most widely embraced one. I had misread American history, or rather, American history had been misrepresented to me. In 2019, Nikhil Pal Singh wrote for the *Boston Review,* "Through the more than two centuries of frontier and counter-insurgency wars that the United States has fought (and continues to fight) the world over, the elimination and sequestration of 'savages' . . . has been represented as integral to the transit and development of American security, power, and prosperity." As Black people in the North became free, they were designated, just as Native peoples before them, "savages," that is, an uncontrolled threat to White power. Through the ACS, America's leaders spent substantial resources in the attempt to sequester them beyond its borders. Could it have been that when Brent defended the phrase "Muslim terrorist," he was just telling a truth about America's priorities and purpose? Could he have been explaining to me that American security was premised on identifying and putting down Black and Brown "savage" threats, and that "terrorist" was just a new variation on "savage"?

CHAPTER FIVE

FREE ENTERPRISE

Sarasota, Florida

You cannot separate peace from freedom, because no one can be at peace unless [they have their] freedom.
—Malcolm X

My family members are poster children for "chain migration," which is really just family reunification, where one family member sponsors and agrees to financially support other members of their family in the immigration process. In the early nineties, as I finished high school, my parents supported two of my father's brothers and two of my mother's sisters, along with their spouses and children, in their relocation to America. These were only the latest of several aunts, uncles, and cousins who lived with us for a month or more while they found jobs and housing. Our family is enormous; I have about seventy first cousins, many of whom have lived with me, or I with them, at one time or another. We like to declare that we're fully responsible for changing the demographics of the tri-state area, from White to "wheatish," as South Asians sometimes describe themselves. White America was and is still built the very same way, though the politically charged epithet "chain migration" is never used to describe White immigrants and their descendants.

In any case, with several extra mouths to feed, there were a lot of demands on our limited resources at home by the time I started think-ing about college. My parents' knowledge of American colleges and universities was not well developed; they only knew that I must go to college, ideally Harvard. I didn't have the grades, money, or really the self-esteem for Harvard. I didn't know about private school endow-ments that can mitigate the sticker price; I also didn't really have a language for what interested and engaged me. Socially and academi-cally lost, I was not like my older brother, who had headed for an elite polytechnic institute two years before with a full scholarship. I wanted to sort out what I thought and cared about without having to manage my parents' expectations, their newly arrived siblings' expec-tations, and the expectations of their broader South Asian commu-nity. For similar reasons, I was avoiding any campus with a Muslim Students' Association. I had come to associate Muslim identity with my parents' cultural presumptions, and both of these with an ongoing sense of conflict with the homogeneously White communities in which I'd been raised. I found my parents' expectations confusing and often irrelevant in American life, and the conflict painful. It never oc-curred to me that there were plenty of young Muslim Americans in exactly the same boat.

My top choice was a public, tiny, academically rigorous school only half an hour from where I was born, in Sarasota, Florida. The small faculty created the opportunity to craft one-on-one or small-group tutorials on subjects not offered in the standard curriculum, and long narrative evaluations instead of letter grades. I imagined an endless opportunity to explore my own interests, whatever they turned out to be. Ultimately, it was the student description that did it, which said something like "When you go out to dance barefoot in the rain at two A.M., you'll find there's someone already there." That sounded right; I decided I wanted to be there without ever having set foot on campus.

Our flight to Sarasota was the first time my mother had traveled alone to any place other than Pakistan, where a large extended family could gather her up on the other end. It was the first time she would fly into an airport and navigate on her own, rent a car, find our hotel room, take me to buy some essentials. My father wouldn't come. He seemed to have no recollection of how it all had happened: me going through puberty, developing interests foreign to his own, and now leaving home for a faraway college without a pre-med program. I had hidden my acceptance to a local direct entry medical program, one where you go straight from undergraduate school into medical school without having to apply, because I knew the pressure to accept would be overwhelming. In fairness, my father knew little about my development and interests because I kept them mostly secret. To avoid conflict, I kept my relationship to Jim secret, I'd refer to the boys in my circles of friends by girls' names, I hid books and music and clothes that were likely to be objectionable, and I even avoided conversations about school because my grades and interests seemed to be such a source of anxiety and disappointment for my parents. It would have physically pained my father to know I had rejected admission to an accelerated medical program and the security it promised. Even without knowing of the foregone option, he held his protest over the small liberal arts school that promised expensive airline tickets and no suitably marketable degree. My mother, stressed but grudgingly supportive, agreed to take me. I would have gone alone; I wanted nothing more than to see who I would become.

When we arrived that first day, we made our way from the student housing side of campus, with its triad of grungy modernist dorms around a central cluster of palm trees, to the pretty side of campus for a reception. There, at College Hall on the Sarasota Bay front, the sun shone against its pink marble, through the expansive windows onto cool tile floors. Time wrinkled and my mother was transported to the Florida she had left when I was an infant, the same sea of whiteness in which every connection to another woman who could speak Urdu or Hindi was unspeakably precious. My mother did what she knew how to do for me. Using some inborn radar, she began to identify every female South Asian student—Rachna, Ananya, Priya, and Joy that first day—stopping them for a chat and introducing me. At seventeen

I was, of course, horrified. She knew what she was doing; several of those women would become close, dear friends.

⸺

College Hall had been the mansion of Charles and Edith Ringling, now dressed down and modified to provide classrooms and offices on the upper floors, preserving a large downstairs common area and music room. The Ringlings built their pink marble home on the sparkling Sarasota Bay in the 1920s with wealth from the Ringling Brothers Circus, which Charles helped run with four of his six brothers. In 1919, the brothers merged Barnum & Bailey Circus, which they had purchased in 1907, with the Ringling Circus to create the iconic Ringling Bros. and Barnum & Bailey circus. The mansion of Charles's eldest brother, John, now part of the John and Mable Ringling Museum of Art, sprawls a hundred yards or so to the south, just beyond Charles's daughter's smaller but still very grand home, which serves now as the college's Cook Hall. Ca' d'Zan, as John's mansion is known, is a meticulously preserved example of the brothers' extreme wealth. In 1927, the 36,000-square-foot house cost $1.5 million to craft, the equivalent of $21 million today. And Ca' d'Zan was certainly more crafted than built; its roof is made from curved barrel tiles John imported from Barcelona, and the interior is laden with opulent art and artifacts, marble and tile, crystal chandeliers. When he was still alive, John kept his yacht, and his wife, Mable, kept her gondola, ready on the bay, where the sun sets spectacularly each evening, pelicans fishing in the foreground and dolphins leaping out by the keys.

Charles's son also had a smaller house a couple of hundred yards to the north, and beyond it, there is another massive neo-Mediterranean-style mansion, which sat crumbling behind an eight-foot-tall chain-link fence when I was a student. One of my roommates, Laura, led a small expedition of us over the fence to that estate one day, to harvest fruit from the trees. The entire place was to my Pennsylvania sensibilities a tangle of jungle, growing into and beginning to invade what had been a truly fantastic building, with heavy wooden arched doors and spectacular tile work. The trees on the estate had been grafted together, so that we were harvesting grapefruits and oranges and tangerines and other citrus fruits all off the same tree. We hadn't wanted to pay admission to Ca' d'Zan, but we'd seen enough of the neighbor's property to imagine the wealth and abundance the Ringlings had amassed nearly a hundred years before, at a time when Sarasota had little of its modern infrastructure. At the height of his fortune John Ringling was worth an estimated $200 million, the equivalent of $2.8 *billion* in 2019 dollars.

The traveling circus was, for several decades after the turn of the century, a lucrative industry and a grand institution. For most Americans, it was one of very few affordable opportunities for spectacle and entertainment, a living tabloid announcing the most bizarre and interesting facts and facets of the world outside their own. Radio didn't become widely available until after 1900, and television not until around 1950. The Ringling Brothers Circus was born in 1884, a few decades after Robert Finley's American Colonization Society stopped shipping free Black people to Liberia. And American circus culture began to lose steam right around the time Levitt's Whites-only suburban utopia was being built, although the Ringling Bros. and Barnum & Bailey circus held on far longer than most others, until 2017.

The circus's heyday overlapped the age of Jim Crow, when slavery was no longer the law of the land but White Americans wielded every other tool at their disposal to terrorize and humiliate Black Americans into servitude. Powerful elites in both the North and the South used the law to violently police segregation and protect exclusive White access to education and housing. In the North, they claimed exclusive access to well-paid jobs and unions, postsecondary education, and all the prime real estate. In the South, they claimed exclusive or overriding access to everything: public streets and accommodations, private shops, the most desirable wage labor, free movement and association in public spaces, and as much other liberty as they could get away with. This claim was enforced by widespread lynching, cross burning, bombing and arson, convict leasing, and spurious "vagrancy" laws enforced only against Black people.

In this context, the Ringling Brothers, like most large circus outfits, hunted for likely sideshow "freaks" among the strange and outrageous, the disfigured or exceptional, so that these could be transformed into evidence for whatever story might be told to sell tickets. In one such case, the Ringing Brothers Circus contracted with the White manager of Eko and Iko, two albino Black brothers who had a mass of distinctive snow-white hair and the ability to play any tune they heard on any instrument.

Eko and Iko were actually George and Willie Muse. By 1910, they had spent their early childhoods working as sharecroppers in tobacco fields in rural southwestern Virginia from dawn to dusk, wearing clothes their mother, Harriet Muse, had made of flour sacks, squinting to block out the sun that made their light-sensitive eyes stream tears. There was no school within walking distance for children of Black parents, no matter how pale their skin.

With limited options and opportunities to offer her sons, Harriet sent them temporarily to Charles Eastman and Robert Stokes with Morris Miller's Great American Shows when they were eleven and nine years old, in the hopes that they could earn money without laboring in the fields. Morris Miller's Shows would have been just one of hundreds of small carnivals and circuses in the country at the time, and the brothers would have performed locally, in some modest capacity, for a limited duration. But when Eastman and Stokes split in 1914, the boys were traded or perhaps just taken—trafficked, we would say today—for display in other shows and exhibits instead of being sent home. Willie Muse believed it was then that they were stolen by a self-appointed "manager" named Candy Shelton. During this period, they were marketed as racial and evolutionary anomalies, named variations of "Eastman's Monkey Men" and "Darwin's Missing Links" before being presented on the Worth Loos, Barnes, and, sometime around 1922, Ringling stages. There, they ultimately became "Eko and Iko, the Ecuadoran Savages."

Willie, who lived to be 108 years old, recalled in 2001 that early on in their time at Ringling, they were sent to bed every night with the story that their mother was dead, that there was no use pining for her cornbread and the ice cream she made them from snow mixed with milk and sugar. Harriet, it seems, never stopped looking for her sons, beginning with a 1914 ad pleading for their return that she placed in the Readers' Column of *Billboard Magazine,* the popular publication that today focuses on the music industry but then featured news, articles, and ads about fairs, circuses, and vaudeville shows.

Depending on the characters they were told to play, George and Willie were expected to stay silent or to grunt unintelligibly when performing, as if mentally deficient or alien. An effect of their albinism was progressive blindness. They were kept illiterate and were never paid for their labor, which in traveling circus life included breaking down and setting up the show every day or so in each new location, in addition to performing. Almost all of the money they brought in was profit for the men who traded and used them. By the time they were performing for the Ringling Brothers, their manager, Candy Shelton, was making $400 on them *each week,* about $6,200 in today's dollars. In turn, Shelton provided the brothers with their barest necessities and pocketed the rest, along with any extra he made from selling photos of the brothers. That was the deal until 1927, when their mother learned of a circus coming through Roanoke, the town to which she'd since moved. On the chance that this might be the outfit holding her sons, she rushed to the front of the sideshow tent on opening night, and the brothers remembered it this way:

Georgie spots her first and stops playing the moment he does. He elbows his brother. "There's our dear old mother," Georgie says. "Look, Willie, she is *not dead.*" The crowd is puzzled when the brothers drop their personas along with their instruments and rush from the stage. They greet their mother, folding themselves into her tall, sturdy frame.

Ingalls, the manager, struck up the band to distract from the brothers' falling so suddenly out of character into their tearful reunion, which ended in a confrontation between Candy Shelton and Harriet

Muse. Shelton insisted the brothers were his property, but Harriet stood her ground even as Roanoke police arrived. Unexpectedly, the police were compelled by her story that Shelton took her sons captive, without her or their consent, telling them that she was dead all the while that she had posted her ad in *Billboard* and sought help from social service organizations. The brothers were allowed to return with their mother to her home in Roanoke.

By then, the brothers had spent most of their lives in the circus and had created a place for themselves in it. They had become a big draw in the sideshow tent, which could bring in over $1,200 a day, and saw themselves as pulling one over on the kinds of people who lived in one town their whole lives and would come to such a show, calling them names like "lot lice" and "rubes." When George and Willie went home with Harriet, they found that their circumstances living in a small shack in Roanoke in the Jim Crow South were not necessarily better than the lives they had lived, exploited as they were, in the largest circus show in the country.

In southwestern Virginia where George and Willie Muse were born, a Black man was most likely to be a day laborer or a sharecropper. Black workers were generally excluded from factory jobs and the opportunity to learn higher-paid skills, like blacksmithing. In any line of work, they could be, and were, killed in the most brutal of ways for simple liberties like leaving one landowner's employ for another, or when accused of a petty crime. In cities like Roanoke, where there was greater competition for jobs, tensions were high and segregation brutally enforced, so that a majority of Black residents occupied the most menial positions, often washing, cleaning, and cooking for White people. When a Black person was mentioned in *The Roanoke Times,* reporters had to "put a 'comma colored' after [their] name," though nearly a third of the city's residents were Black at that time. By contrast, George and Willie had had worldly and unlikely experiences, like traveling by boat between Los Angeles and Hawaii to a sideshow gig in Honolulu, listed as "White" on the passenger manifest at the height of the Jim Crow era.

In spite of her years-long search for her sons, Harriet recognized that her sons' best opportunities might actually still lie in a circus sideshow, but she also recognized how they had been exploited by Shelton. Her next moves were remarkable. At a time and in a place where Black people were killed for far less, Harriet, who was illiterate, sought out a lawyer, who helped her to sue the Ringlings and renegotiate the terms of her sons' employment. For the rest of their working lives, she wanted to ensure that they would be paid for their labor, and that she would also be paid a portion and kept informed of their whereabouts. Eventually, she managed to secure a payment of $115 a month for the two of them, a rate just $7 shy of the median monthly wages for skilled Black male workers in the South Atlantic region in 1936. Shelton would cease to be paid on the brothers' behalf; $40 would be paid directly to her sons, $60 would be paid directly to Harriet, and $15 would be paid to the lawyer who helped make it stick by tracking the circus down every time the checks bounced or failed to appear. Harriet put aside her share of the brothers' income for decades and in 1939 used it to purchase 16.8 acres southeast of Roanoke in a village of small, wood-frame Black-owned homes, two Black churches, a "colored school," a Black cemetery, and a Black-owned store. That property and the five-room frame house with neither indoor plumbing nor electricity she built on it, both in the brothers' names, would place them among the mere 20 percent of Black Americans who owned a home in the 1930s. Harriet would live there for the next three years, and her sons would visit her there regularly until her death in 1942. Meanwhile, Harriet and her lawyer had set up another fund, which had grown to $23,000 by the time George and Willie used it to purchase a home in the Rugby section of Roanoke, newly opened to Black home buyers in 1961, for their retirement and convalescence.

The story of George and Willie Muse is a case study in the bizarre and insular imagination of postslavery White America. They were already living on the margins as sharecropping child laborers in the

Jim Crow South, but even that place, with the comfort of their mother, was insecure. As illiterate, poor Black children born to an illiterate, poor Black mother, they could be exploited mercilessly.

The brothers' story seems to end, if not well, certainly better than it could have, in large part because of their mother's tenacity and resourcefulness. But to be both Black and also singled out as a spectacle was often brutal. P. T. Barnum had launched his circus career in August 1835 on the literal body of another Black "exhibit." Twenty-five-year-old Barnum was working in a New York City dry-goods store when he decided to purchase Joice Heth, a Black woman, from a circus promoter. He created a fantastical story about the frail, toothless, blind woman, claiming that she had been born in Madagascar in 1679, had been the wet nurse and nanny of President George Washington, and was now an astonishing 161 years old.

When his claims to her age were challenged, Barnum announced that upon Heth's death he would provide a public autopsy of her naked body to prove his assertions, creating morbid anticipation of her demise. Less than a year later, he commissioned the New York City surgeon David L. Rogers to cut her open in an exhibition center before 1,500 spectators, who paid fifty cents each. Rogers refuted Barnum's claims as to Heth's age, saying that her relatively clear arteries suggested an age of no more than eighty years. Barnum responded by first suggesting that the autopsy had been not on Heth but on an old woman from Harlem he called Aunt Nelly, sparking an eighteen-month-long media controversy. Barnum eventually admitted that it had all been a scam, and that he had forced Heth into performance, sedating her with whiskey, saying,

> I . . . converted her into a most docile creature, as willing to do [his] bidding as the slave of the lamp was to obey Aladdin. I discovered her weak point . . . : WHISKEY. Her old master, of course, would indulge an old-bedridden creature no such luxury, and for a drop of it, I found I could mould [sic] her to anything.

Barnum also marketed William Henry Johnson, called Zip, for the narrowing of his head, exhibiting him in a cage, where he was to pretend to eat raw meat. Barnum's story was that he found Zip naked and walking on all fours in Gambia, and that he was a link between animals and humans. Zip was, in fact, from New Jersey, and according to his sister had been sold by his parents for exhibition in 1861 at the age of four, perhaps to help feed his five siblings. Johnson was paid only in room and board; he would perform until his death in 1926 at the age of sixty-five. Other people of color, sometimes actually from other countries, were similarly exoticized and commodified in ways that humiliated or destroyed them. In 1897, a boy from Greenland was displayed with his father in New York's American Museum of Natural History as "Eskimo Minik." When Minik's father ultimately died, his body was preserved in a glass case on display. Minik would lobby unsuccessfully for the return of his father's body until his own death.

In 1906, a twenty-three-year-old Mbuti man named Ota Benga was displayed holding a bow and arrow in a cage at the Bronx Zoo, along with a gorilla named Dinah and an orangutan named Dohung. Benga drew crowds of thousands, sometimes tens of thousands, and visitors were increasingly bold in their attempts to harass and provoke Benga, who ultimately retaliated by striking visitors, and attacking them with a knife and bow and arrow. The mayor of New York was unmoved by pressure from Black clergy who objected to Benga's degradation, refusing to meet with them and affirming the zoo director William Hornaday's characterization of Benga's captivity as "an ethnological exhibit." A *New York Times* editorial printed during Benga's captivity suggested that Benga benefited from his circumstance, asserting, "As for Benga himself, he is probably enjoying himself as well as he could anywhere in his country, and it is absurd to make moan over the imagined humiliation and degradation he is suffering." Benga was eventually released to a Black-run seminary but committed suicide in 1916 upon realizing he would not be able to earn his passage back to Congo.

There are many other examples of American circuses trafficking in Black people as objects of entertainment, often based on pseudo-medical ideas and the hypersexualization of Black and African women's bodies. Black people were also exploited for minstrelsy, a performance of skits and music made to caricature and ridicule Black people as happily enslaved, often done in blackface by both White and Black performers.

My college experience was made possible by the prosperity of the Ringling Brothers, itself built on the wild popularity of the Jim Crow–era circus. In the period after slavery, White America scrambled to reconfigure an economy nonetheless dependent on a Black underclass. As many Black Americans transitioned directly into sharecropping and other manual or service work performed for the comfort and maintenance of White households or property owners, White America also innovated new ways in which to profit from the bodies of Black people and Brown people, affirming, always, the idea of America as a nation *for* White people. The American circus did this by offering opportunities to laugh at and degrade Black performers, a release for racial anxiety in a national context where Black people were intimately engaged in the labor of maintaining White lives but barred from actual social intimacy.

Examining this history helped me to explore the depth of my own alienation at college. More than seventy years after Charles built the mansion that would become College Hall, my college continued to affirm a White American standard through its student body and faculty, which were overwhelmingly White. Its curriculum almost exclusively taught the works of White scholars, focused on the politics and histories of White societies, and examined literature and art produced by White people, though more than one in five people living in the country at the time (along with, of course, most people in the world) were not White. I took all of that for granted because as a student, it was all I had ever known.

My college was indeed a place where there was never a shortage of friends with whom to dance in the rain, sing under the stars, or skinny-dip in the Gulf of Mexico lit by phosphorescence. The student residence side felt more like a commune than a campus, punctuated with festivals, open mic nights, and town hall meetings. It was immediately a social fit for me, or who I'd begun to think I might be. It was a place where bookishness was cool, politics were progressive, and gender norms were bent. Even the town around campus drew activists, artists, and musicians with a similar vibe. I met a local activist, Aaron, at an off-campus event during orientation week. He had shaggy blond hair and brown eyes; he was tall and lanky, with a gentle tenor voice and features that verged on effeminate when he shaved his full beard. He wore cutoffs, Birkenstocks, and often a T-shirt that said something about beating swords into plowshares. Aaron spent a lot of time on our campus, sometimes partnered with campus activists on protests or education forums, and had a lot of friends there. He was on what he called a "sabbatical" from the University of Florida up in Gainesville.

He seemed to know everything about folk music and social movements, about environmental campaigns and liberation theology, and he used phrases like "ecofeminism" and "intentional community." Aaron was, for me, a sweeter America than I'd yet encountered, one that I imagined I could disappear into. These things that he talked about both fascinated me and revived my sense that there really was a possible, exceptional America, one with ideals that made sense to me and in which I could belong. I wasn't sure yet if I was trying to own or trying to avoid all of the complexities of being a second-generation immigrant, but it didn't matter. There was so much to learn and so much freedom to enjoy. One day, I left a potluck at someone's off-campus place early, homesick and exhausted from weeks of being always in the company of new people. I ran straight into Aaron on the way out. It was dark, so I had avoided the shortcut over a low wall and through a mown field, heading instead for the well-lit paths. "Hey, you're leaving early, are you okay?" he asked me.

"Yeah, I'm just . . . peopled out. I'm going to the library."

"How about tea and then the library?" Not long after that, we became inseparable. I made Aaron my home. And for many years after, I'd pursue activism and progressive culture as a more accessible substitute for the Muslim and Pakistani identity that had only ever been available to me in half measures.

There were, out of about eight hundred students at my entire college, maybe six South Asian women on campus; we were well represented compared to other students of color there. Four of us were assigned to live within one small area of campus, and two others across campus in a dorm of single rooms. Maybe it was an accident of fate, but we were living clustered together, and then found we had plenty in common. All of my professors for the next four years, except one, a visiting professor, would be White. It was Fallsington all over again. There was some security in our tiny cluster, a sense of shared origin that I didn't know would become so important to me away from home. Though we sometimes traveled in different circles, a few of us became close enough to be hennaing each other's hands, oiling each other's hair, visiting each other often, like family. South Asian students and, more broadly, Black and Brown students were not reflected in the curriculum. We were not the authors of the literature or the political theory that was taught, and we were not the subjects of history or sociology courses. We were generally not the producers of art or philosophy that was studied or critiqued. We were sometimes the subjects of anthropology classes, but not the authors of the frameworks employed to understand and investigate those cultures. Neither were we supported by the services of the college. And though none of us seemed to have the language to insist upon these things, we felt and sometimes spoke about their absence. We stuck together, quietly keeping each other from becoming invisible.

Oddly, this resistance was in tension with the desire to disappear, to assimilate, for all of us. We stuck together, but every one of us was dating a White man at the time. Shockingly, on that tiny campus where most students lived less than a five-minute walk from nearly every other enrolled student, I barely spoke to the one other Muslim student in my entering class (and perhaps in the entire school during the time I was there), an Iranian American man I'd befriend long after graduation. And because the sole dining hall closed before sunset and I didn't have a car, I gave up the Ramadan fast, which requires abstinence from food and drink from daybreak to sunset for thirty days, for the first time since I was ten.

In my second semester, I approached a professor of East Asian religions (there was no professor with a clearer expertise in Islam on the faculty at the time) and asked him to sponsor an independent tutorial on Islamic theology and the Qur'an. The tension between wanting to assimilate and wanting to understand where and from what I had come remained; I felt like I needed more information to resolve it. I wanted a systematic review of Islamic thought and theology. I wanted to know enough to distinguish between culture and religion. I wanted to understand the relationship between the pillars of practice and underlying doctrines, a historical understanding of how and where different sects and schools of thought developed. And though I did not yet know how to articulate it, I wanted to explore the relationship between religion and faith. What was it that drove real faith in the Divine?

At my professor's request, I patched together a motley set of readings. This was in 1993, the days before the internet, so my resources were limited to what was available through the state university library system. The English-language offerings on Islam were relatively scant, heavily weighted toward the esoteric on one hand and the vitriolic on the other. In the end, I collected enough material to build a syllabus. After a semester of reading and reporting to the professor's office for meandering biweekly discussions, I struggled to contextualize and synthesize what I was studying.

I asked my professor what he thought would be an appropriate final product from which he could evaluate my progress. He suggested a paper not on an area of Qur'an, theology, or faith, which had been the focus of my pursuits, but on the Muslim Brotherhood in Egypt and the rise of so-called political Islam. The suggestion caught me off guard. I hadn't studied modern theocratic movements, other than maybe a little bit of Christian liberation theology, and the topic bore no direct relationship to what I'd been reading. To understand political movements, one needs to understand the political systems and societies from which they emerge, and the political and social interests at stake for both supporters and opponents. Egypt was, for me, an entirely new subject; aside from a high school paper on its economy, I knew nothing about it. My professor was suggesting, in essence, that I write a paper for a different syllabus than the one we'd agreed on and discussed all semester—and one entirely different from the papers I'd been asked to write for his classes on Hinduism and Buddhism.

In retrospect, I realize that his suggestion followed a line of thought that was predictable in American politics of the time. The postcolonial landscape in several Muslim-majority countries included anti-colonial movements and groups seeking to reform or replace secular governments, which had been installed or supported by Western powers. In 1995, the Muslim Brotherhood in Egypt began to have some success in this decades-long project when it efficiently organized public aid and services in the aftermath of an earthquake. Both the Egyptian government and Western governments quickly moved to identify the Muslim Brotherhood as a suspect, or even terrorist, organization, rooted in what they called Islamism, a confusing term sometimes meant to imply extremism and other times used to describe any Islamic influence in politics at all. There are significant parallels between the Muslim Brotherhood and the Black Panther Party in civil-rights-era America, which was driven largely by the commitment to provide critical services where the government was failing to do so, such as breakfast programs and accompanying Black children to school in blighted and impoverished neighborhoods. Like the Muslim Brotherhood, the Black Panthers presented a political challenge to established state authority and were in return cast as militant and dangerous.

No doubt, the motivations and actions of each of these political movements are complicated and often controversial. The important piece for my story is that the American media in 1993 was spinning a powerful story about the danger of Islam in politics, which it did not extend to the Christian influence in American politics and the governments of nations with a White majority. This is because Islam was increasingly cast as an illegitimate moral basis for governance; or, more simply put, not a legitimate religion. So, when I went looking to understand who and what I was, that was the story my professor sent me to explore—the story of his own bias.

The census tells us that Sarasota County had a population of fifty-three at the turn of the twentieth century, but by 1930, that figure was a booming 8,498. Just before I started college in Sarasota, the 1990 census listed the population at 277,776. Of those residents, 262,836, or nearly 95 percent, were White. One wouldn't know it to drive through much of coastal Florida today, but before the Second Seminole War ended in 1842, coastal Florida had been a remarkably racially diverse, defiant contrast to the White supremacy of an expanding America for hundreds of years. Florida was a tenuous haven for many Native people of the southeastern United States who had confederated as the Seminoles, as well as for Maroons who had traveled the less well-known southern branch of the Underground Railroad. (Originally from the Spanish *cimarrón,* "Maroon" is now the broadly accepted term for those who escaped slavery and found a way to live freely in hidden communities.)

I returned to Sarasota in the fall of 2019 to meet Dr. Uzi Baram, a professor of anthropology who joined the faculty the year after I graduated. Dr. Baram, who encouraged me to use his first name, Uzi, has spent much of the past fifteen years developing the record of a historic Maroon community in the place now occupied by the modern city of Bradenton, Florida. His work not only resurrects the buried history of Black persistence and ingenuity during American slavery, but also fills out the record of Maroon relationships to, and identification with, the Seminole people living in Florida at the time.

Uzi picked me up at the airport, which is visible from campus, and took me a few miles up the road to Bradenton and also slowly back through time. Our first stop was a tidy, cheerful mobile home park near the meeting of the Manatee and Braden rivers. The wide Manatee River cuts into the west coast of Florida between Tampa Bay and Sarasota Bay. Its main tributary, the Braden River, flows north into the Manatee. The two together form a northern and eastern barrier around what are now the southwestern Florida cities of Bradenton and Sarasota, providing a clear view across the rivers northward toward Tampa Bay and eastward toward the center of the state, so that approaching enemies could be spotted quickly. Not far from their confluence, there is a critical natural resource, the freshwater Manatee Mineral Springs. In 1990, a historian named Dr. Canter Brown, Jr., identified the place where the two rivers meet as the site of the southernmost Maroon settlement in Florida, a place he called Angola, based on an early land claim made by two Cuban fishermen. The largest community of its kind in Florida, numbering at least seven hundred residents from 1812 to 1821, Angola was established as early as 1770. It swelled as other Maroon communities, from farther north in Florida, were raided or wiped out by U.S. military forces.

On the day I visited, the view across the Manatee River to the north and the Bradenton River to the east was spectacularly clear; it was easy for me to see why this was a prime defensive position, and a good spot for the Maroons to carve out homes for themselves. Uzi pointed out that while it felt like an ideal spot to search based on the historical record, every inch of land we could see was privately owned, leaving little room to go digging for the past.

Our next stop, 1.6 miles away down a straight stretch of road, was the place where Uzi elected to dig. The site was an empty suburban lot next to the then-capped Manatee Mineral Springs, within sight of the south bank of the Manatee River. Having been frustrated by private ownership of most of the promising archaeological sites that might be related to Angola, Uzi and a small team of scholars, educators, and community leaders began giving free, local public presentations on Angola and the importance of developing the archaeological record to discover the early history of free Black people during the era of slavery. After one of these presentations, Uzi was approached by a local couple who purchased and maintained vacant lots in suburban Bradenton as an investment. The couple happened to own the lot next to Manatee Mineral Springs, which had been featured in Uzi's presentation. They were willing to let him dig on their property to investigate whether the area near the spring had, in fact, been the site of a Maroon community in the early nineteenth century. In 2008, Uzi set up the dig, cordoning off one-by-two-meter excavation sites based on promising results from ground-penetrating radar tomography and then removing the soil in layers to unearth and accurately date evidence of Angola. On that first dig, he was able to identify and date post molds (where posts had previously been used to anchor structures) and other artifacts establishing the site as a part of Angola. Additional development of the site in 2009 and 2013 led to support by the City of Bradenton and the Florida Division of Historical Resources.

"With the help of the ancestors," he said, he was able to establish the area near the spring as one likely used by Angolans as a lookout to monitor movements across the river. For this practicing Jew, using his decades of skill and knowledge to record the exodus of people fleeing slavery, the invocation of ancestors was heartfelt. Over the next couple of hours, Uzi helped me piece together how Angola came to be. For much of early American colonial history, Florida was held by the Spanish, who in 1693 offered freedom and sanctuary to any who made their way to Florida and converted to Catholicism. Similarly, when the British fought the United States in the War of 1812, they enlisted soldiers from among the Florida Maroons, promising enduring freedom and protection in a British holding after the war. And so, while Canada was a northern beacon for those escaping American slavery, Florida was a southern beacon, especially for those who had been enslaved in Georgia and South Carolina. It was also a haven for the Seminoles, who had been pushed out of Alabama, Georgia, and South Carolina.

When I asked about the relationship between the Maroons and the Seminoles, Uzi reminded me how misguided it would be to think of either the Seminoles or the Maroons as a monolith, given the history. The reality, he suggested, is that each group was made up of individuals brought together by circumstance, but over many years and many routes, so that they would have likely retained different identities, interests, and even alliances. Individual Maroons, for example, might be descended from the enslaved brought by Spanish settlers in the 1500s, while others had been enslaved in the southeastern states of an expanding America, who were captured much later. Some individuals would have escaped in their first generation of bondage, others in their tenth, and so some might have retained an African identity or literacy in multiple languages, while still others might have had no connection to their African origins at all, with no opportunity for literacy or education. Some lived in relative freedom and isolation within independent Maroon settlements, others in communities of "Black Seminoles" paying tribute to nearby Seminoles for protection and adopting aspects of Seminole identity and culture. Some may have been scrambling for survival and alliances, having only recently freed themselves. All of these things might have changed for each person or community over time, as more of Florida was captured by the United States.

It's possible that some or all of the Maroons in a given settlement saw themselves not as one cultural community with a common destiny, but as small clusters and family groups linked together for economy and protection, so they would not have necessarily built alliances as one political unit. What makes the story of Angola so remarkable, and ultimately so painful, is that it *was* the culmination of hundreds of separate and heroic struggles toward freedom. It was the fallback position, a gathering place of individuals and small clusters of Maroons who had not only escaped slavery but then, over several decades, had been chased out of settlements they had carved out in northern Florida.

These were people using every reserve of strength and skill among them to build and defend a permanent and free home in the dry forest hammocks of the Florida wetlands, clearing land and planting corn, pumpkins, lima beans, tomatoes, and peas, all identified as "escape crops" by scholars who study the relationship between agriculture and state control. These crops could be hidden and stored and had staggered maturation times. The Maroons built cabins, raised families, and trained as soldiers; they were trying to live.

In 1815, when the War of 1812 had ended, the British withdrew from a fort they had established in the Panhandle of Florida, southwest of Tallahassee. They left the fort fully stocked with supplies to the armed Maroon soldiers who had fought alongside them, and those soldiers quickly offered sanctuary to Maroon families from the surrounding area. The more secure settlement at Angola had already been formed about three hundred miles to the south, away from the border with America. The move to create a southern Maroon outpost proved prescient when in 1816, the fort, by then known as Negro Fort, was destroyed in a naval attack while Andrew Jackson was commander of the southern military district.

Jackson, himself a slaver, was convinced that free Black people in Florida were a grave threat to the central institution of chattel slavery in the South. Two hundred and seventy Maroons were massacred when Jackson's troops fired a cannonball into the munitions store of the fort. That attack launched the First Seminole War, which drove Maroons from the Panhandle and dramatically constrained the movements of the Seminole people within Florida, barring them from the northern part of the state and confining them to a reservation in central Florida.

Jackson aimed to capture and re-enslave the Maroons of Florida during the First Seminole War. He pursued those who escaped as far south as Suwannee, on the Gulf Coast north of Tampa. Jackson's persistent attacks forced Spain's surrender in 1819, leaving Maroons who had fled to Tampa Bay and the settlement at Angola to their own devices. By 1821, lacking permission from the secretary of war to attack, Jackson nonetheless enlisted his allies among the Coweta Creek people to raid Maroon and Seminole settlements in southwestern coastal Florida. They destroyed Angola, capturing 250 to 300 Maroon men, women, and children, whom they delivered to Jackson's army in Georgia for re-enslavement. Others escaped overland to the Peace River, directly east of Bradenton, running along what is now Route 17, between the modern towns of Lakeland and Port Charlotte, Florida, and some oversea to the Florida Keys, while nearly 300 fled to the Bahamas, perhaps by enlisting the help of Cuban fishermen with whom they had regularly traded, or by using large canoes developed by the Seminoles for such travel.

Several years after ordering Angola to be destroyed, Andrew Jackson was elected president and immediately drove passage of the Indian Removal Act of 1830, providing for the removal of all Native people to land west of the Mississippi River. Jackson felt Florida, and the freedom it represented to Black and Native people, was a persistent threat to his ultimate goal: the consolidation of an all-White citizenry with a noncitizen, enslaved Black labor force. Determined to eliminate that threat, he demanded the removal of the Seminole people from even the central Florida reservation to which they had already been confined, and the "return" of the estimated four hundred Black Seminoles living among them, whom he saw as the stolen property of southern slavers.

By 1833, government officials had bribed, threatened, and cajoled representatives of the Seminoles into visiting and viewing land in present-day Oklahoma, beyond the westward border of America, in the "Indian territory" of the time, to consider the government's proposed removal of their people. Unsurprisingly, its foreign ecology and brutal wintertime weather did not appeal to them, nor did the prospect of being warehoused in a growing melee of dislocated Native peoples from east of the Mississippi. Despite their limited bargaining strength, most declined to move. The Seminoles who did move and the Black Seminoles among them faced an almost immediate outbreak of smallpox as well as conflict with the Creeks already settled there. Still, as pressure mounted in Florida, the Seminoles and the Black Seminoles continued to arrive in Oklahoma. Once there, the Seminoles found they lacked the authority to offer sufficient protection to the Black people among them.

In 1835, Jackson sent Quartermaster General Thomas Jesup to command the U.S. Army forces in Florida, ordering that the remainder of the Seminoles be removed by force to Oklahoma. When Jesup led 110 American troops to begin the task, they were ambushed and slaughtered by a group of Seminole and Maroon soldiers. Only three of those federal troops survived in what came to be known as the Dade Massacre, a significant battle in the fight for Native autonomy and the largest revolt of those formerly enslaved in American history. The battle started the Second Seminole War, during which twenty-one White-owned sugar plantations that had sprung up along the east coast were obliterated, with the enslaved Black people on them coordinating with and joining in the rebellion.

In the years that followed, U.S. military forces relentlessly pursued the remaining Seminoles, Black Seminoles, and Maroons of Florida, whose alliances deepened in the cause of defending themselves. Black people were only sometimes permitted to leave with the Seminoles to Oklahoma, and were often instead re-enslaved. Late in the conflict, they were promised freedom in exchange for their removal to Oklahoma. Removal itself entailed a journey by boat across the Gulf of Mexico, then a brutal walk of well over seven hundred miles along what became known as the Trail of Tears. The Seminole Wars created a great diaspora. Black Seminoles and Maroons were scattered to the Bahamas, deep into the Everglades, and west of the Mississippi, or taken back into bondage in the southeastern United States. The Seminoles, already a confederation of displaced Native peoples, were forced to flee deeper into the swamp or be removed to Oklahoma.

Over the ensuing decades, the diaspora would broaden. Some groups would flee Oklahoma because of rampant disease, and in the case of Black Seminoles, the constant threat of re-enslavement. These groups traveled through Texas, ultimately finding refuge in Coahuila, and then northwest of Santa Rosa, Mexico, where they traded military service defending the Mexican border for land and the privileges of Mexican citizenship. Some would return in 1870 at the invitation of the U.S. Army, forming the Black Seminole Scouts and settling in Brackettville, Texas.

In 1842, after the Second Seminole War ended, Congress passed the Armed Occupation Act, granting any single White man or White male head of household who could bear arms 160 acres in the territory of Florida, on the conditions that they apply for a permit, build a house and inhabit it for five years, and clear and enclose at least five acres. This had the intended effect of drawing European American settlers to the semitropics of southern Florida. Often, the same soldiers who had fought to destroy, re-enslave, and relocate Native and Maroon residents in earlier wars moved in, claiming expansive landholdings for themselves and their descendants.

A third and final Seminole War, fought from 1855 through 1858, targeted the remaining community of Seminoles, including an estimated three hundred warriors plus women and children. Maroon allies, by that time, were few enough that their presence itself was no longer considered a challenge to slavery, although Jackson remained concerned about the ongoing Seminole policy of offering sanctuary to Black people who escaped into Florida. The remaining Seminoles occupied the Everglades, using their reduced numbers and superior knowledge of the territory to evade U.S. military forces. Many of the Seminoles who took this final stand were ultimately removed to Oklahoma, but a smaller number continued to survive in the swamps of the Everglades and in Big Cypress Swamp.

During my second year at college, I moved off campus so that Aaron and I could share an apartment with our friend Laura. I had led my parents to believe that both Aaron and Laura were women to avoid conflict. But when I went home for winter break that year, I felt myself straining against the cultural constraints that always seemed to demand that I hide important parts of myself. While I was there, my parents hosted a gathering of family friends as they often did over holidays or on weekends throughout the year. The gathering was segregated by gender, with men at the front of the house in the living room, women in the family room, and children and young adults claiming parts of the kitchen, dining room, and basement. It was a relatively small gathering by their standards, maybe around thirty or forty people in all. At the time they regularly hosted my local aunts, uncles, and cousins along with family friends for gatherings of fifty people or more.

So I was mostly unaware of the new young man in the living room. There was nothing unusual about an uninvited guest, likely a visiting sibling or cousin or friend from abroad, tagging along at one of these occasions. The only unusual thing about this gathering was that my mother had asked beforehand what I would be wearing. Having been away in Sarasota, I had no shalwar kameez that fit. I had, however, brought a long dress I thought she'd approve of for its relative modesty, though it was a shapeless olive green tie-dye. When I showed it to her she looked mildly uncomfortable, but that was my mother's standard response to what I wore in those days. Perhaps she suggested I wear her clothes and gave up when I resisted, trying to keep the secret of the evening: The young man in the living room was a Sindhi Muslim student pursuing his master's degree in environmental engineering in America and keen to get married. He was there in our house because somehow it had been conceived among my parents or their friends or siblings that *I* might be an appropriate wife. In a profound miscalculation uncomplicated by any actual communication with me—*the maybe-wife*—my parents entertained this idea because I had, after all, expressed a grungy, hippie interest in environmentalism, the kind that propelled me to hike and camp in muddy Florida parks and eschew plastic and meat, though not the kind that propelled me into anything as practical as engineering.

At some point in the evening, I was pushed toward the front of the house, the men's section, where I had no business being, and told that I ought to speak to this young man, who must be bored among all of the "uncles" nearer my father's age. Similarly, he was pressed out of the living room and we stood there awkwardly in the foyer, him a recently migrated engineering student in pressed dress slacks and me an opinionated liberal arts student in a baggy, fraying tie-dye dress who had recently shorn off most of my hair in a fit of feminist exultation but hadn't shaved anything else in months. It was a brief, perplexing exchange. He asked what I was studying. I asked what environmental engineering *was* exactly. And then we parted ways. I'd just been interviewed and rejected for a role I hadn't been aware of, let alone expressed an interest in. I didn't even realize this until the next morning, when I awoke to find that my mother had placed his—I don't even remember his name—parting gift, a convex box carved from a piece of marble with a lid decorated in iridescent mother-of-pearl. My last best chance at a smooth transition into the life my parents imagined for me was lost. But lost to them, not to me. I was living with my activist boyfriend near my tiny hippie college, and happy there, as I explained to them on my final day at home.

Two weeks later, after I'd returned to college, my father called. "Sofi beta, I'm mailing you transfer applications to Bryn Mawr, Haverford, and Villanova." These private liberal arts colleges were all on the Main Line, the western suburbs of Philadelphia. I think he imagined this as a conciliatory move because they were, after all, "liberal" arts schools. I don't think he realized how beyond liberal my own college was. If the Ivy Leagues were penny loafers and the Main Line schools were sport sandals, my college was a pair of dirty bare feet. I told him I wasn't interested in transferring, to which he responded that he would not be helping to finance my education. I decided that if that was the cost of not ever telling a lie again, of relief from the constant anxiety of hiding things from my family, it was a price worth paying.

I continued my studies, very poor but untethered from the overwhelming weight of cultural and religious family expectations. I quickly ran headlong into an entirely different set of limitations. The absence of Black and Brown scholars in the faculty and curriculum meant that while my White peers in the humanities and social sciences were busy putting their own experiences and challenges in several hundred or even a couple of thousand years of European and American context, many of the other Brown and Black students and I were left to the process of maturation and coming-of-age without having a way to anchor ourselves in a larger story of the world or our own society.

A great failing of our campus culture of anti-institutionalism was that Brown and Black students had no ready place to caucus and no institutional record of how their needs had or had not been met by the college in the past. Thus, every new cohort had to reinvent the wheel. Brown and Black students already there would sometimes teach younger students of color what to read to supplement their learning and analysis. Painful and confusing racialized conflicts would repeat themselves and then be discussed publicly, if they were discussed at all, in town hall formats, where often the tiny minority of Brown and Black students were overwhelmed by the mostly White student body. The tools and networks that Brown and Black students on larger campuses use to fill in knowledge and resources they may not have been exposed to, or that might help them deal with discrimination in the curriculum or in the social life of campus, were missing at my college.

I did find tiny parts of myself and my experiences reflected in the classroom: reading Zora Neale Hurston's *Their Eyes Were Watching God* and a novel called *Nectar in a Sieve,* which describes a family in rural India. The latter was part of a course taught by a visiting South Asian professor in a class called Contemporary Asian Politics. I found myself profoundly engaged and successful in the class, but mistakenly thought this would transfer to other political science courses at the college, which focused entirely on American politics and political theory. In these other courses, I lacked the foundation that so many other students seemed to have in how American politics and government worked. Things that were reduced to footnotes in the texts and in the minds of other students, things like persistent racism and sexism, which showed up even in progressive politics, felt like the main topic of conversation to me. Black and Brown people, if they were considered at all, were not the subjects of sentences, but the objects of sentences that began with "except for . . ." I often felt like my priorities seemed naïve to everyone else in my all-White seminars.

Still, political categories, like the Right and the Left, or conservative and liberal, offered an organized way for thinking about the world around me that I found useful and compelling. Progressivism, or the pursuit of a more compassionate, pluralistic society premised on equality and human rights, was especially appealing to me as a way to orient myself personally. It allowed me to consider and pursue what I believed to be "goodness," to which I was actually committed, and gave me a way to talk about it outside of religion and culture, which I had for so long experienced as arbitrary and contradictory. It offered a comprehensive, or seemingly comprehensive, worldview, providing me a framework for intellectual and moral development.

I considered a major in political science, which required me to take classes with the senior faculty member in that department, who had a reputation for being abrasive and inappropriately attentive to his female students. I enrolled in one of his classes anyway with several friends, but after the second paper, I was asked into the professor's office. It was an isolated spot, in a corner of one of the Ringling buildings on the bay. His desk was placed awkwardly, blocking access to the door, facing into the room and out the windows. Maybe it was because of the spectacular view? Still, to enter or exit I had to squeeze past the professor. I sat in one of two chairs facing the front of his desk. I thought perhaps we would be going through my paper; I desperately needed help organizing my thoughts and editing.

My professor started by asking some questions about me. At first, the questions felt kind. He asked where I was from and followed up with questions about my family. But armed with this information, he then explained that I lacked the experience of my classmates (all of whom were White) and that he would be willing to "teach me how to walk the walk and talk the talk." I probably did lack political sophistication, I thought; I never seemed to understand the analytical frame of the discussion in class. But then he came around the desk so that he was only a foot or two away from me. Sitting on the edge of the desk, he was directly in front of me, with his crotch at my eye level. He continued to explain what would be required of me: more private meetings, one-on-one draft revisions. His proximity felt suffocating and I felt trapped. I felt like he was testing me, pushing my physical boundaries in sexually suggestive ways while telling me that I needed him to fix me in order to be successful. I believed that if I accepted, I would be in physical danger, that it would end in sexual assault.

I made an excuse to get out of the room and made an appointment with my advisor to see if I could possibly drop the class and still pursue a political science major. My advisor played down my fear and his colleague's suggestive behavior; he told me that the course requirement could not be relaxed for any reason if I planned a major in political science, so I continued with the course, avoiding contact with my professor outside of class, which earned me a derisive two-page evaluation that reads like a personal attack, ending "I hope and assume that she will do no further work with me because she is unable or unwilling to learn what I have to teach."

Crushed, I gave up on the idea of a political science major, and landed on anthropology and gender studies, still feeling not fully engaged in what I studied. Anthropology courses, like much of my high school Afro-Asian class, felt like they were built as a means for White students to study and mostly exoticize Black and Brown people, while gender studies classes seemed built of the complaints of mostly White women in Western contexts. I was fishing around for a way to make sense of my life and the experiences of people like me, but I didn't feel capable of constructing the syllabus for one of those small group or one-on-one tutorials that my college was known for—on migration, colonialism, race, or ethnicity—on my own.

Working in the media center, I discovered and then devoured the entire fourteen-part *Eyes on the Prize* PBS series on the American civil rights movement. In retrospect, the series, which was not taught in any class but was collecting dust on a shelf behind the counter in that sleepy out-of-the-way room in the library, offered me some of what had been missing from the curriculum, filling in some of the places where White American history is too entangled with Black and Brown American history, often marked with brutality and racism, for it to be neatly excised.

I took a class called Feminist Theology, which was much narrower than its name, focused on the struggles of Christian and Jewish women to find a place in patriarchal traditions. I loved the class and loved the professor, who reminded me a little of Aaron's mother. But I struggled to see how I would ever find my way in a Muslim community, much less find a sense of God and faith that felt personal to me. If these women, with their well-established churches and synagogues, many of which had split to create progressive congregations or sects where they prayed alongside rather than behind the men in their communities, still struggled to find their place, how would I ever be able to? Mosques in America, as I'd already seen, were very segregated. As a South Asian American *woman,* I felt I lacked a place in both Black mosques and the mosques established by recent immigrants. Without a community to learn in and push against and worship with, how could I address that thing inside that kept telling me I had unfinished business with faith?

Just as, in my second and third years, I began to use the flexibility of my college's program to seek out and focus on areas that seemed relevant to me, like race, gender, and colonialism, my academic advisor explained that these were marginal areas of academia and often had the word "studies" appended to them, as in "gender studies" and "race studies." A major in one of them would, he said, compromise my academic potential. Even at larger universities where these subjects were offered as standard courses, they were not seen as core academic pursuits, but as electives. I understood him to mean that all of the things that I was drawn to, all of the things that allowed me to root the study in my own, rather than a European or American, experience, was itself marginalized within the academy. I didn't feel I had a choice; I continued to pursue the themes that were central to me, wherever I could find them, and whatever they happened to be called. I constructed a combined major in social sciences and gender studies. It wasn't until the year after I graduated that a newly hired professor taught a class called Race and Ethnicity and several years later that the demographic profile of the faculty began to change.

Despite this struggle to find a place academically, I made my way into a peculiar but comfortable social nexus at college that reflected the tug-of-war between my desire to blend in and my desire to claim a truer, more complex identity and culture. I rode my beloved secondhand French racing bike to and from campus, where I took classes but also organized an activist coalition, hosted talks by local farmworker organizers, and created a campus chapter of the National Clothesline Project, an annual art installation made up of survivors' own responses to gendered and sexual violence. I was not as interested in speaking as in creating a platform for others to speak, not as interested in railing against our crappy campus meal service as in providing an alternative through the food co-op. I was drawn to service. Aaron was, by my third year, back up in Gainesville, finishing the final year of his own degree in environmental science. He made the trip down once in a while, especially when there was something going on. When I organized the women's Take Back the Night march across our tiny campus, Aaron dropped in to run the men's discussion group. Even though he was mostly in Gainesville, he was still a frequent visitor. I was sitting in a courtyard on campus with a group of girlfriends one time when Aaron's name came up. Maya said, "His mama raised him right." That was the consensus about Aaron.

That year, I lived in a wild, beautiful house built by an alum of the college out of wood that was slowly mildewing back into the South Florida landscape. The Tree House was a central hub of off-campus life. My housemates were a few Jewish students and a few peace church activists. None of their religious identities was incidental; at least three of them were actively engaged in the same sort of search I was on—my housemates marked Shabbat and focused their studies on

Jewish philosophers while others studied political movements that felt like extensions of Catholic liberation theology. I wish I could say that I was reflective enough to have understood my attraction to these friends at the time, that I saw my own desire to know myself in them.

Meanwhile, my housemates were having their own issues sorting out their identities. Several of them were in a band called Yeehaw Junction, playing a mix of bluegrass and funk, with a presentation that both glamorized and caricatured the South, and they hung a Confederate flag on at least one stage they played. One of them, Jewish himself and fairly progressive, would make a social media post much later, in 2020, wondering at his lack of awareness of its powerful racist symbolism, and at how we were all the confused products of too many *Dukes of Hazzard* reruns, which had glorified the Confederacy on prime-time television through most of the 1980s.

The broad history of racism in America had never been taught in any curriculum I had studied, even in the context of the American Civil War. Brief lessons about Martin Luther King, Jr., and the Underground Railroad were careful to elide the worst of the racist violence to which each responded. The Confederate flag could be flown at a campus open mic night because our college, like so many liberal arts colleges in the United States, was overwhelmingly White. So, the very whitest perception of the Confederate flag reigned, not explicitly, but culturally: as an old, comfortable anthem to which everyone knows the words but of which no one understands the meaning.

The curriculum I was taught, as a whole—not just at college but all the way through my public education—had been radically sanitized of White America's engagement with, and persistent obsession with ridding itself of, Brown and Black people. I would not have been able to articulate this then because I was swimming in that experience and had no other. What I might have said was that I didn't know if school was really for me. I felt like I was an imposter, like nothing there was really intended for my consumption. I was sitting on the sidelines wondering when I would be as moved as Brent had seemed by American history or Jim had seemed by physics or Aaron seemed by environmentalism and nonviolent movements. I knew that I couldn't get enough of stories written in English by South Asian authors; those books helped me reflect on my experiences and the factors that shaped my life, like immigration, brownness, colonialism, and the experience of coming from one culture into another. But those resources were mostly outside of my academic experience. I did not yet fully understand that the absence of Brown and Black people from the broader frames of an American humanities or social sciences curriculum suggested two things: a radical impoverishment and exclusion of those communities, so that their members were not allowed to produce their parts of those curriculums, and also that the curriculums as they existed were designed to disguise or deny the ways in which Brown and Black people have been economically, politically, and socially pressed to the margins throughout our nation's history. As a result, the education I was offered was like that early story about Penn and the idyllic Pennsylvania forest: so partial as to be simply untrue. It was no wonder I had no language for what interested me.

In the second semester of my third year at college, a visiting professor came from Syria to teach Arabic. A coordinator of the environmental studies department whom I liked, admired, and also worked for, suggested that the professor's wife, who wore a full-face veil, was very isolated in Sarasota, and that I could perhaps reach out to her. It came, I think, from a place of generosity and kindness for the professor's wife, but to me felt like a replay of my International Studies class in high school, where I was expected to relate to another Brown Muslim girl in ways prescribed by a White person. I actually found the suggestion alarming, because by then I had fully embraced the counterculture of the college and its inhabitants: I rarely wore shoes, was habitually in a sundress, bra optional. In fact, I think I probably would have been more alarming than comforting to the professor's wife. I had successfully orchestrated my escape from the expectations and pressures of my familial identity, and although I had found myself up against another set of racially and culturally constructed barriers at college, I wasn't sure how or whether I could find a third way.

The options for Maroons fleeing Angola in 1821 were limited. Some hoped to avail themselves of the British promise that they would have their freedom in exchange for the military service they had provided if they could arrive at a British holding. But previous Maroons fleeing to the Bahamas, then a British colony, had caused intense diplomatic tension between America and Britain over the institution of slavery. Angolans were afraid that they might be sent back, as other recent refugees had been.

To avoid capture, the Angolan refugees avoided Nassau, the capital, on a separate island of the archipelago that makes up the Bahamas. They instead landed at the town of Cedar Coppitt on Andros Island, traveling then by foot to the northwest corner of the island, where they founded the village of Red Bays. More groups of Maroons landed on Andros Island through 1837, rarely mixing with residents, and remaining mostly isolated from the rest of the island, and the other islands of the Bahamas, for more than a hundred years after that. There were no overland roads to the undeveloped northwest coast, and the muddy, shallow shoreline made it difficult to land boats. Among Bahamians, rumors spread of a village of people with "Indian blood" who hunted with bows and arrows on Andros Island. The group persisted despite its isolation, rebuilding when their original settlement was destroyed by repeated hurricanes, developing a method for sewing watertight baskets and for harvesting and preparing sea sponges for sale, and settling new locations along the northern shore of Andros Island. It was not until 1969 that a logging company built a paved road to Red Bays, finally making it more readily accessible to the rest of the island.

Dr. Rosalyn Howard, now a retired professor of anthropology at the University of Central Florida, established the connection between Angola, the Florida Maroon community destroyed in 1821, and the modern Red Bays community of Andros Island through the archival record and oral histories recorded in her ethnographic work on Andros Island. She discovered an attachment to an 1828 letter from the "Searcher of Customs," which lists the names of ninety-seven "foreign Negro slaves" whom the customs officer had captured and taken from Red Bays to Nassau, believing them to have been stolen by the Spanish. That list contained many of the same last names still prevalent among the endogamous Andros Island community: "Bowlegs," "Russell," "Lewis," "McQueen." In the same letter, it is mentioned that those captured had been on Andros Island for seven years, a timeline that coincides with their expulsion from Angola.

Two names that appear on that document from the Bahamas, Sipsa (or Scipio) Bowlegs and Peter McQueen, match names marked on a surviving log made by the Creek agent who had tried to capture them at Angola for General Andrew Jackson. On that log, Bowlegs and McQueen are marked "ran away." It appears they fled to Andros Island, and found sanctuary. Remarkably, their descendants live there even today, continuing to bear their names.

As we wandered the site near Manatee Mineral Springs, Uzi told me about Red Bays' recent reconnection to Angola. After he had completed the first series of excavations at the site in 2013, a woman named Daphne Towns happened to be walking by. She noticed the placards that described the archaeological discovery that evidenced the Maroon settlement of Angola there. The grassy suburban lot in a modest residential neighborhood of small one-story homes was nondescript except for its view of the Manatee River and the squat concrete cylinder that capped the spring. Without the placards, Towns, who had lived in Bradenton for twenty-five years, might have walked right by. In reading them, Towns made the connection between that site in Bradenton, Angola, and her ancestral home in Red Bays. She knew herself to be one of Angola's descendants. Towns herself was born on Andros Island, and recalled stories about how her ancestors were forced to flee Angola nearly two hundred years before. She contacted Reflections on Manatee, a museum in the historic district of Bradenton named on the placards, and museum staff directed her to Uzi and to Vickie Oldham, the director of the multidisciplinary research project "Looking for Angola," which had developed around the dig. Once connected to the scholars and activists involved in the rediscovery of Angola, Towns began hosting an annual "Back to Angola" festival in 2018, during which current residents of Red Bays reverse the path of their ancestors back to the site of Angola.

In January 2020, Uzi completed a much broader fifty-by-thirty-meter excavation to preserve the archaeological record of Angola that remained near Manatee Mineral Springs. The city helped fund a museum on the adjacent lot to house the artifacts and to guide visitors' experiences. It also extended plans for a walking path along the Manatee River to include the former site of Angola.

Learning about the wealth the Muse brothers generated for the Ringlings and the history of Angola's destruction a century before provided new context for my own liberal arts college experience. That I was a Brown student, disoriented on a mostly White campus, making my way through a curriculum with little reference to Brown and Black Americans was not accidental or unpredictable. Sarasota in 1992 was as White as one might expect after free Black and Native people were repeatedly chased beyond the borders of a young America by its military. It was also the experience one might expect in a nation that had, even after emancipation, relegated Black workers to the economic margins, to sharecropping, to menial and dangerous work, or to circus sideshows—foreclosing most economic and social opportunities. These histories helped ground my experience of the 2016 election, the "Muslim ban" and the suggestion that mosques ought to be surveilled. In studying these histories, I found that Brown or Black communities have often been cast as an existential threat to White America, and that this becomes the justification for relentless marginalization, degradation, exclusion, and even expulsion.

CHAPTER SIX

MANIFEST DESTINY

Leupp, Arizona

By following its own legal traditions, the arc of the Western moral universe never bends towards Indigenous justice. At best, it ignores it. At worst, it annihilates it.
—Nick Estes

While still a college student, I started following my friends home on weekends and some vacations, to see what those homes were like and to fill in some of what felt unresolved in myself and out of balance in the curriculum I was studying. I followed Joy home to her Indian immigrant parents' decadent house in Orlando, with a waterfall and pool in the lanai, built for entertaining. I followed Aaron home to his parents' house in Virginia, where we ate exceptionally well-balanced, simple, wholesome meals from the *More-with-Less Cookbook,* and everyone sang in four-part harmony without even trying. I followed Nora home to rural middle Tennessee—the hippie version—where the idea of family was wide open and included a tangle of organic farmers and Beat poets. And Aaron and I followed our friend Nathan to his father's modest frame home in upstate New York.

My sense of general uprootedness chased me into a lot of extraordinary and diverse pockets of America. I could not yet grasp that they were as strange as the corner from which I'd originated. At the time, I experienced each of them as somehow more representative of America than my own family. They introduced me to a complex, fascinating society, made up of the waves of immigrants that have come to this place. Each community I entered was trying to define or redefine themselves and their place in society; each had their own story—based on spiritual or ethnic identity, based on a particular kind of lifestyle or observance, on a shared experience of persecution, persistence, or achievement, or on some combination of these. All seemed to be reaching for a past identity from some time before their migration to America, something with which to understand and assert themselves in the present. Joy's parents held massive Indian parties, with only Indian faces and Indian food. They were the parties of first-generation immigrants who had "made it" and were now trying to re-create the social context that gave "making it" value.

Aaron's family walked a tightrope between the secular modern world, in which his mother's feminism and scholarly ambitions made sense, and the patriarchal, farming, missionary lifestyle to which previous generations had belonged. Though I did not know it then, they were descendants of William Penn's colonial community, and maintained their ancestors' devotion to pacifism in the service of God. Aaron's parents, deeply immersed in their religious community, still sang in four-part harmony at church every Sunday morning, still kept a kitchen garden, mending and spending modestly. These were more than habits; they were an identity and a claim to legitimacy. They implied the higher morality that made their original migration essential.

Nora's family moved to the country to join a commune, creating a rural counterculture that had as much to do with literacy and reflection as with soil and sustainability. This raised the ire of their closest Tennessean neighbors, who often saw them as transplants with high-minded ideas. As transplants, they learned to bend themselves around the extremes of racist southern culture at churches and potlucks and to accept a world that has kept itself almost entirely White and Protestant.

Nathan was raised by a single Jewish dad. It was clear where Nathan got his unusual sweetness when he talked about his dad, who called him by his middle name, Apple. He drew his identity from his father, taking a year to study Torah in Jerusalem, but said almost nothing about his mom. It was as if she didn't enter into his story.

My many forays into other people's homes and communities would eventually lead to an understanding that my own conflicted and broken sense of identity was not unique. It was not that other immigrant Americans, even White Americans, had whole, cohesive identities. It was only that some groups had a more distinct sense that, and were more likely to be treated as if, America was primarily and permanently their own. Some were more likely to refer to others as "minorities," implying that the most important way of counting and calculating social groups was by race and religion, and subtly asserting that the most significant outcome of this calculation was that the majority was White and Christian.

In 1994, the summer before my third year at college, I set out to find an America I hadn't yet seen. I was looking for internships that offered room and board because my work-study job wasn't available in the summer, and without it I had no grocery budget. My friend Jen and I answered an ad for summer interns placed by an alum, Kate Hawke, to work at the Gateway Ranch, near the southwestern corner of the Navajo reservation in Leupp, Arizona. Kate had built the ranch with her then-husband Mark Sorensen, an activist and school administrator, to be a sustainable center for cultural exchange between the town of Flagstaff and the reservation. Mark was committed to Native rights and had been invited to serve as principal of the Native-run Little Singer School in the mid-1970s.

Jen and I drove her Corolla eight hours up through to the Panhandle from South Florida, and then three days across the country, stopping at youth hostels and occasionally truck stops to sleep in the sedan along the way. I was in the middle of a vegan experiment, but on a budget, eating a gross mix of peanut butter, water, raisins, and oats for just about every meal. I hadn't planned very well for any other aspect of the journey, either. Casual research was different in the age before the internet and cellphones, and, regrettably, I hadn't made time between final papers of the semester and our trek for library research. We just got in the car one day with some food and clothes and set out for a place different from anywhere either of us had ever been.

I was about to encounter a population of people indigenous to America for the first time. On the Navajo reservation, I was surprised to find that I looked enough like I belonged to be asked if I was from there. I was a deer in strange headlights, a Brown person who had lived without a cohesive Brown context, encountering a somewhat alarming picture of how Brown people figure into the racial consciousness of America. Later, filling in the history of that place, I would learn that it had been the site of a late chapter in the European colonization of America, a place that evidences how America alternately views Brown people as a threat to be contained or a labor force to be harnessed.

Nearly two hundred years after William Penn arrived in the Delaware Valley and less than ten years after the destruction of Angola, the U.S. military established Fort Defiance on the grazing land of the Navajo, or as they call themselves, the Diné, in present-day Arizona. When New Mexico was annexed by the United States at the end of the Mexican-American War in 1848, some of its residents, who were a mix of Spanish and other European settlers, as well as Genizaros and Native people, were permitted to become U.S. citizens with voting rights. The Diné identified many of the new citizens still as Mexicans, with whom they shared a long, antagonistic relationship marked by raiding and kidnapping.

The Diné had navigated the complex political and military forces of rival groups in the area for centuries by then and maintained their homeland between four sacred mountains, in a varied landscape that stretches from northeastern Arizona to northwestern New Mexico, up into both the southeastern corner of Utah and the southwestern corner of Colorado. They migrated seasonally through this land, maintaining orchards and crops and shepherding livestock. Having survived the diseases spread by Spanish colonizers to the South more than two centuries earlier, they had rebuilt and recovered so that they were in a better position to defend themselves against White settlers than Native peoples along the East Coast had been. Still, the constellation of political alliances and interests of the 1860s were not in the Diné's favor.

Although White ranchers would eventually challenge the whiteness of former Mexicans, seeking more power and land for themselves as well as exclusive access to the vote, the U.S. military of that time protected the interests of all U.S. citizens in New Mexico against the Diné. This meant that the resources of the Diné's traditional enemies were now redoubled. The Union army promised White settlers and the earlier Mexican inhabitants of New Mexico, Arizona, Colorado, and Utah access to grazing lands and security from Diné raids, traditionally undertaken to defend against the abduction and enslavement of Diné women and children as well as incursions upon Diné land and resources.

In addition, the U.S. military was charged with creating and protecting a railroad through traditional Diné land that would connect the East and West coasts. The railroad served the interests of White speculators who wanted an access route to more land and to the promise of gold in California. These same speculators believed traditional Diné land held valuable mineral resources that might be extracted for profit. Finally, with the Civil War raging to the east, the military had an interest in consolidating control of the western frontier to keep it out of the hands of the Confederates. All of these factors drove the Union government's commitment to removing the Diné from their homeland between the four mountains.

In turn, these interests and the containment of the Diné in service of them were justified by manifest destiny, that uniquely American doctrine of colonial taking and genocide. A blend of racial and religious supremacy, manifest destiny is a euphemism for the assertion that White Americans have a God-given right to eliminate Native people and take their land. They did just that, from coast to coast, beyond the Mississippi River and across even what White settlers themselves had originally designated "Indian territory."

I knew the stripped-down version of manifest destiny, the one that 1980s public school education made every effort to present as compatible with modern ideals of equality and pluralism. But I had not been offered a competing ideology with which to compare manifest destiny; there was no Native voice, no study of colonization as a phenomenon. The account of manifest destiny that I learned in school felt hollow precisely because it was a gloss meant to obscure and justify colonial economic interests in the fur trade, land speculation, and resource extraction—in short, the greed—that drove American colonization. The history of the Diné filled the yawning gaps in my learning.

By 1860, the Diné and the Union military presence were in a contentious relationship. Soldiers wanted to limit Diné use of grazing land surrounding their outpost at Fort Defiance, and sometimes killed Diné livestock that wandered through. The Diné raided supplies and the military's livestock to make up for their losses. Periodic peace treaties made between the two groups could only be temporary, as the overriding aims of land speculators, the Union government, and the military negated the interests of the Diné.

Recognizing the precarity of their position, the Diné nonetheless continued to visit Fort Fauntleroy, another military outpost within their traditional territory, to trade and to race their horses against the soldiers'. In the fall of 1861, there was to be a horse race between a Diné chief named Manuelito and an army lieutenant. Bets were made and there was plenty of anticipation. After it became clear that the lieutenant won only because Manuelito's reins had been cut, the Diné protested and tried to prevent Union soldiers from taking the winnings. A Diné man was shot for trying to force his way into the fort where the goods that had been bet were being kept. A colonel ordered the use of cannons, and a slaughter of the Diné, including women and children, ensued.

Soon after these events, Union forces at Fort Fauntleroy were joined by additional troops from the west led by Brigadier General James Carleton, who loathed the Diné. Carleton had fought for Union control of the Southwest against Confederate forces, and was displeased that when Union troops withdrew, the Diné and Apache people reemerged. Carleton believed that the Diné should be removed in order to make room for White miners to exploit the resources rumored to lie beneath traditional Diné territory. To accomplish this, he developed a plan for the "pacification and subjugation" of the Diné. He proposed internment on a desolate, cramped piece of land adjacent to Fort Sumner in New Mexico called Bosque Redondo, arguing that it would be the most efficient means of eliminating the inconvenience of Diné existence, writing to his colleagues in Washington, "You can feed them cheaper than you can fight them." Having overcome the nearby Mescalero Apaches (a far smaller group on much less formidable terrain), Carleton was emboldened, and anticipated quick success. But when he tried to condition a new peace treaty with the Diné on their voluntary migration to Bosque Redondo, they refused.

In July of 1863, Carleton responded to the Diné resistance with a campaign of terror, enlisting Kit Carson, an outdoorsman and Union army officer at Fort Fauntleroy, who had a reputation for living among and having an intimate understanding of the Diné and other Native peoples in the region. On Carleton's orders, Carson headed military attacks on the lives and livelihood of the Diné, destroying their water sources, their villages, the cottonwood trees that provided shade overhead and drew water up from beneath the ground, the sheep and goat herds on which their economy was based, acres of crops, and the legendary, bountiful peach orchards in Canyon de Chelly. More than five thousand fruit-bearing trees were cut down, and the abundance of the land damaged for generations by the loss of vegetation.

By autumn of that year, Carleton had ordered that every Navajo male be killed on sight; offered bounties to be paid for each horse, mule, or sheep killed; and paid rewards to soldiers who returned with the knot Navajo men wore in their hair. Loss of critical resources and unrelenting violence forced the surrender of the Diné that winter. Over the next two years, large groups of Diné were marched on at least three routes of between 250 and 450 miles in "The Long Walk" to the desolate site at Bosque Redondo in New Mexico, where they were kept under armed guard.

A substantial number of Diné remained behind, hidden among the canyons, creek beds, and mesas as campaigns to destroy them continued, physically reducing the landscape to the barrenness we now imagine in the American Southwest, and cementing a characterization of the Diné as wandering, impoverished desert nomads, raiding to survive. The Long Walk itself is recalled by the Diné as degrading and devastating. Up to twelve thousand people, including the elderly and small children, infants, pregnant women, and the ill, traversed the rugged terrain to Bosque Redondo. Those who could not keep up were left to die; children were sometimes stolen along the route and sold by enemy groups into slavery. Those who survived and arrived at their destination were vulnerable to disease and malnutrition and subject to cramped conditions and despair from loss of identity and livelihood. Women were assaulted and sexually abused. The lakes and streams at Bosque Redondo were "black and brackish," part of the Pecos River floodplain, which is fed by saline groundwater, and the soil was poor. Crops that the Diné planted for themselves were attacked by corn worms two years in a row, causing malnutrition and starvation. Because of the lack of crops grown onsite and reliably potable water, both food and water had to be shipped in, making the cost of Diné incarceration outrageously expensive for the U.S. military. This drew attention from Washington and from New Mexicans who felt government rations for the prisoners were an extravagance.

Several Diné escaped Bosque Redondo, which was too large to be properly guarded, to take their relatives information about the widespread malnutrition, starvation, infection, and conflict that would ultimately kill a quarter of the people confined there. Unable to justify or sustain what was effectively a concentration camp, the government agreed in 1868 to instead confine the Diné to a portion of their homeland. During the period of the Diné's incarceration, President Lincoln and General Carleton, on behalf of the Union government, and numerous private contractors had been engaged in the exploitation of gold and silver deposits that had been identified in other parts of Arizona and New Mexico. However, explorations for such deposits on traditional Diné territory had been unsuccessful and military campaigns had left the land degraded, so the Diné's territory no longer seemed particularly valuable to either the government or private prospectors. General William T. Sherman concluded that the Diné's traditional homeland was a "waterless, worthless waste." This mischaracterization of their homeland is perhaps what saved the Diné from being moved further east to Oklahoma, which had become, in the decades prior, the territory onto which Native people from every corner of the expanding United States had been forced. Whatever the condition of their embattled homeland, the Diné were desperate to leave Bosque Redondo, or Hweeldi, as they called it—"the place of great suffering."

At Bosque Redondo, the 9,000 survivors retained only about 2,500 total head of livestock, whereas the majority of Diné families had previously owned "between 50 and several hundred head of sheep and goats" each. The Diné had been not only incarcerated but deeply impoverished, and were going back to the widespread destruction of their homes and agricultural land. In a cursory effort to prevent starvation, the U.S. government provided each family with a small amount of money to purchase livestock.

The boundaries of the new reservation, as set out by the Navajo Treaty of 1868, designated the Diné a fraction of their traditional homeland. On returning, the Diné spread out, as they were accustomed to doing, across their traditional territory, paying little attention to the official boundaries of the reservation, which had been drawn to save the best grazing land to the east for White and Mexican ranchers, and to avoid a southern railroad route. They believed the provisions of their agreement with the military allowed them to do so, partly because General Sherman had exaggerated the area to be included in the reservation, and also because the agreement contained a clause allowing them to use areas not settled by White people. The Diné were quick to replant orchards and to expand their stores of livestock.

Even with the Diné's confinement to a reservation, America could not conceive of a society with space for the Diné to engage their traditional culture and economy. The same treaty that allowed the Diné freedom from the confines of Bosque Redondo also mandated compulsory schooling of their children ages six through sixteen in government and missionary ("English") schools "in order to insure the civilization of the Indians entering into [that] treaty." That is, in exchange for their limited freedom, the Diné were forced to submit to the cultural and religious indoctrination of their children, sometimes for years at a time, in places like Pratt's Carlisle Indian Industrial School, where administrators violently punished expressions of Native identity, including names, languages, and faith traditions. Beginning in 1882, Diné children would be imprisoned at institutions both on and off the reservation. Eleven years later, Congress would pass a law requiring compulsory school attendance for all Native children. Having failed to contain the Diné at Bosque Redondo, the government's policy became to beat the Diné culture and identity from their children.

The Gateway Ranch, where I stayed with Jen for a month during the summer of 1994 between my second and third years at college, sat within sight of the Painted Desert, called that for the brilliance and variety of colors that mark geological time across its mesas. Mark and Kate had built the entire ranch off-grid, with wind and solar power, an attached greenhouse with a rainwater irrigation system, and several outbuildings that would host cultural exchange programs and events between the Diné and the surrounding non-Native community. The gardens at the ranch were still fledgling, and the outbuildings, including a large studio built from straw bales and a modern version of the traditional Diné hogan where the cultural exchange work of the ranch was to happen, were unfinished. Our job was to assist in the gardens and do some of the messy, hard work of getting the outbuildings ready.

Jen and I slept and ate in an old bus outfitted with a bathroom and a small kitchen, built into one side of the larger straw-bale building. During the day, we painted the interiors of the outbuildings, sealed the hogan's concrete roof, pulled weeds, worked at the school, and babysat. We did a fair amount of work, but we were the first of the ranch's interns; Mark and Kate had not yet created a system to organize our labor. There was plenty of waiting around to be directed toward the next project or provided the materials to complete it. During those times, Jen and I hiked, made friends with a nearby couple who had built their massive yurt, a one-room circular house, themselves, and followed our Diné friend and sometimes supervisor, Justin Willie, around the ranch and Little Singer School.

Justin lived on the reservation, working at both the ranch and the school. He had planned and put in the permaculture gardens at both locations and started fruit orchards on the reservation itself, often studying the slopes of the land on the reservation and building long, elegant, tapered retaining walls out of rocks he found scattered around. He built them to capture water, he said, so that the trees he planted would grow. He told me that the area had all been covered in cottonwood trees before the Diné were forced onto the reservation and its dense, less mobile population created too great a demand for lumber. Because the cottonwoods were no longer there to hold groundwater close to the surface, where it could support other plants, he was trying to create low spots between retaining walls for the water to pool, delaying the time before it dissipated into the sandy soil, and planting those spots with the seeds of fruit trees. He habitually planted the pit of each plum or peach or nectarine he ate, trying to re-create a landscape of abundance.

One night, Justin invited Jen and me to camp on the large, flat boulders near his place under the stars, and we did, though we were wary of snakes. He slept several dozen yards away in his family's home, a modern version of a traditional hogan, with a concrete roof but without running water or electricity. That night was the first and last time in my life when I was not at all afraid of a man twice or maybe three times my size. He must have been more than twice my age as well, but he was a real friend, the kind who shows you their treasures plainly and only hopes that you will see and appreciate them. We went for a walk to a mound made of broken Hopi pottery, and his sadness was quiet but evident. When I left, he gifted me with an abalone shell, which I carried with me through ten moves until it finally broke, and then I buried it.

Justin had traveled off the reservation for several years, fought in the Vietnam War, and then spent some time as a mushroom farmer in Japan. He had demons I had not imagined yet: the experience of combat, the generational loss and trauma of genocide and forced displacement, and a reservation home that would always be, at least partly, evidence of ongoing occupation. His father had been a code talker in World War II, using the Navajo language to send unbreakable coded messages and win the war for the Allies. Justin had followed in his father's footsteps to war, but while the code talkers were welcomed back as heroes, no one was allowed to return from Vietnam feeling that way. Justin had features that might easily be mistaken for East Asian. Writing now about him, I wonder how it must have felt to find himself engaged in a battle against people who looked so much like him, on behalf of a government that had so relentlessly persecuted the Diné.

There was fragility in Justin that I could relate to, a sense of trying very hard to learn what it was to be good without any reliable yardstick. During his time in the military, he had seen things that many people around him had not, just as I had seen things that were entirely foreign to the suburban whiteness around me—the stark and often brutal poverty of southern Pakistan. We both held on to some devastating realities that could never be integrated, or even really spoken. I went looking for Justin as I began to write about my time at Gateway but learned that he had passed away six years before, struggling still with his demons. When I knew Justin, I hadn't yet come to view myself as a settler, owing an enormous debt for the space that I occupy, since the original colonial taking is the platform for every subsequent sale and purchase, every resource extraction, and every land use. I hadn't yet reckoned with what indigeneity means, with what is lost when a person with a hundreds- or thousands-of-years-long ancestral connection to a particular ecology or landscape is displaced or erased. Modernity, in which we less intimately inhabit the ecology around us, makes this reckoning difficult, if not impossible. While I was struck by the plain beauty and goodness of Justin's constant planting and building, I didn't realize that he was engaged in a desperate effort to reconstitute, stone by stone, seed by seed, something that was both inside himself and outside of himself at once.

I didn't know enough of Diné history to understand the root of the reservation's poverty, its shoddy government housing, the minimal infrastructure and utility access, and the ubiquitous meals of white fry bread. The drive west had been my first encounter with the wide, sparse land that makes up so much of the middle of our country. It had felt far away from the bustling East Coast, but the reservation was even more distinct, like the land itself was trapped between cultures, neither stewarded by the American government nor allowed to be independently stewarded by the Diné.

At the same time, I was also trapped between cultures. My ties to family felt broken, and I had been trying to enjoy the space and freedom that college had promised. But I could not seem to shed my identity as a Muslim or the child of Pakistani immigrants. I wanted to rid myself of so many gendered rules my parents had for me: that I would dress modestly, avoid interest in or even awareness of romance, and be prepared to get married to someone who shared my parents' but not my own cultural identity. Without even planning to, I had blown up every one of those expectations. My rebellion wasn't studied—it wasn't even rebellion, exactly. I just *was* happy barefoot in a sundress. I just *was* always inclined to explore many of the activities and subjects and places that were off-limits. But I could not complete the escape. I carried with me strong cultural parameters about what was respectful and proper that I couldn't shake. Even at my college, where it was the rule, I couldn't seem to call my male professors by their first names. That kind of familiarity with an older man felt wildly inappropriate. And I carried a painful sense that in losing my family I had lost myself. This deepened my feeling that I was only drifting through the curriculum, searching for a protagonist who looked like me. At Gateway, and on the Diné reservation, I was still drifting, still absent from myself. I was not home the way that Justin was, ready to build and to plant. I was not even aware yet that I was trying to reconstitute anything. I was just uncomfortably silent, unsure how I was being identified or how I wanted to identify myself, willing myself to be brave, to try out places, words, and experiences to see if they might fit.

The U.S. government would break the treaty that returned the Diné to their homeland again and again. When coal and oil extraction became a national priority and then again when uranium extraction became a priority, the autonomy of the Diné would be bent to allow non-Native access to these resources.

In 1923, in response to pressure from private mining companies, the U.S. government unilaterally replaced the traditional Diné council of elders that had refused incursions by mining companies onto their land. The government selected Diné people educated in off-reservation schools to be the new "Grand Council" and declared that this new body alone would represent Diné interests. Although the Grand Council created the appearance of autonomous governance, it required the approval of the secretary of the interior to make any binding decisions and was expected to rubber-stamp business and government contracts. By maintaining the fiction of Native autonomy and a special government relationship with Native people, the U.S. government could better control the availability, price, and use of key energy resources. But as the demand for oil, coal, and uranium increased, so had the Diné successfully increased their population and their wealth in livestock, on what was, from a popular American perspective, a desert wasteland. Despite the machinations of the Grand Council, the Diné's presence and bounty remained inconvenient obstacles to the profitable mining of energy resources on reservation land, and the adjacent land on which they lived in substantial numbers. In addition, some of the most likely areas for resource extraction was grazing land that the Diné, by then, shared with the Hopi, so that the Grand Council alone could not provide the unfettered access that mining companies desired.

The Hopi Reservation was created by executive order of President Chester A. Arthur in 1882, more than a decade after the creation of the Navajo Nation, in order to force Hopi children into mission schools. Traditional Hopi territory was adjacent to traditional Diné territory, and both nations' traditional territories were substantially larger than the reservations allocated to them. The U.S. government drew Hopi Reservation boundaries in an area directly west of the Navajo Nation, already inhabited by hundreds of Diné people. The creation of a Hopi reservation on this land ultimately required the two nations to compete for key resources. Over the next several decades, the Navajo reservation was expanded in piecemeal legislation in response to population growth until, in 1934, it completely surrounded the Hopi reservation. The government's actions during this period pitted Diné and Hopi interests against each other, so that, as one U.S. Department of the Interior document reports, "relations between the two [nations] were often hostile."

In this contentious context, and in response to increasing demand for oil and coal, Congress passed the Indian Reorganization Act of 1934 (IRA) to replicate the Navajo Grand Council, replacing traditional Native governance with IRA councils on many reservations across the country, including the Hopi reservation. The Creek and Cherokee activist and writer Ward Churchill calls what followed "the disaster inflicted on Native North America by IRA colonialism." Although the vast majority of Hopi people on the reservation initially resisted the installation of an IRA council by abstaining from the referendum vote held by the U.S. government, the council was nonetheless established without their consent. The council immediately pursued a strategy of alignment with private mining corporations empowered by government contracts in order to extract the wealth that the reservation land had to offer, although perhaps without a clear understanding of the broad health and environmental implications of those contracts. By 1943, the Hopi IRA Council was able to secure exclusive rights to the land surrounding the main Hopi villages, previously held in common with the Diné, known as Grazing District 6, and to lease that territory for the extraction of oil.

Meanwhile, the growing Diné population had spilled over into other shared grazing lands with the Hopi. With increasing evidence of oil and coal deposits beneath the Colorodo Plateau, the U.S. government was no longer willing to expand Navajo reservation boundaries in response to population growth. By 1941, the U.S. Bureau of Indian Affairs commissioner John Collier had instead commissioned a report on the "Navajo problem." As the framing suggests, the report would find that within the government's constraints, Diné territory was overpopulated and overgrazed, leading to soil erosion. The proposed solution was no longer to make space to maintain an expanding human population, but to find a way to reduce and contain that population, eliminating people the government perceived as expendable.

In 1964, the Hopi IRA Council hired the lawyer John Boyden to negotiate a deal between the Hopi IRA Council, the Navajo IRA Council, and Peabody Coal Company to lease land to establish a 44,000-acre open-pit, or strip, mine at Kayenta, Arizona. That mine would produce eight million tons of coal a year for nearly fifty years. Looking to expand their profit from resource extraction, the Hopi

IRA Council further retained Boyden to argue for the division of the grazing land the Hopi held jointly with the Diné. They wanted all the land used in common with the Diné to be split, and Diné livestock limited to their half of the land's government-mandated "carrying capacity." In subsequent congressional actions, the Diné were ordered to reduce the livestock in the joint area by 90 percent, and when they could not comply, they were barred by the court from building new homes, corrals, or other necessary structures within the joint area.

Fully invested in resolving the "Navajo problem," or rather what they saw as the problem of Navajo existence, the government proposed the forced culling of more than half of the 1.2 million head of livestock that represented Diné wealth and subsistence. In some cases, the government took and slaughtered animals, returning only the meat they found useful, canned, and not all of the parts of the animal that could be used by a Diné family; in some cases animals were "sold off, shot, . . . [or] burned." The government also imposed excess grazing fees for those families who owned more than a designated number of animals.

By 1971, Boyden had helped the Hopi achieve a permanent division of the joint areas, requiring relocation of Hopi and Diné people to their separate sides of the new dividing line, though few Hopi lived in those areas. The relocation of 17,500 Diné people, without compensation, left the Hopi half of the joint land clear, opening it up for further mining endeavors. The demarcation line provided the Hopi IRA Council with control over the southernmost parts of already explored coal seams and allowed for the creation of a coal strip mine at Black Mesa; that mine would eventually make even the Diné side of the joint area uninhabitable due to overwhelming destruction and contamination.

In other words, the contamination from the Black Mesa mine itself conveniently cleared even more land seen as critical for mining efforts in a process that Traci Brynne Voyles, professor of women's and gender studies and director of the Center for Social Justice at the University of Oklahoma, has recently termed, in her 2015 book by the same name, "wastelanding." This process of soil and water contamination created a population of Diné people deprived of their traditional agrarian and pastoral livelihoods and made them dependent on wage labor. Local mines, the original source of the pollution, were often the only available jobs near their communities, where unemployment rates can reach 60 percent.

World War II established the military value of uranium and the government interest in locating a source of it within the United States, to establish uranium "self-sufficiency." The terrible irony is that the military quest for nuclear self-sufficiency would directly rob the Diné of their ability to maintain their own self-sufficiency. By 1948, uranium was being mined alongside coal and oil on Diné territory and continued to be mined until passage of the Diné Natural Resources Protection Act in 2005. Over the intervening five decades, half of America's domestic uranium reserves would be mined from more than 2,500 sites on the Navajo Nation, employing more than 3,000 Diné workers. In 2015, Voyles reported that Diné territory was littered with "upward of 2,000 abandoned uranium mines, mills and tailings piles." Abandoned mines were often left without any type of land restoration or reclamation attempted, and without even markings to warn the communities around them of the risks they pose. The tailings left from uranium mining consist of fine radioactive particles that are scattered by the wind so that they leach into surrounding land and water. Exposure has been documented to cause elevated rates of death from lung cancer, silicosis, tuberculosis, pneumonia, and emphysema, as well as an increase in birth defects. Uranium miners themselves are hardest hit, with lung cancer rates *fifty-six times* higher than the national average; astronomical rates of stomach, liver, bladder, pancreatic, and prostate cancer; and a staggeringly low average life expectancy of only *forty-six* years, compared to a national average life expectancy of nearly *seventy-nine* years in 2015. Radiation effects are multigenerational, sometimes causing abnormalities in the DNA of those exposed. Today, Diné children have vastly elevated levels of testicular and ovarian cancer, as well as novel illnesses related to exposure in utero.

While Native communities absorb the health and environmental costs of resource extraction, they do not share in commensurate profits. Leases for mining on the reservation are always issued to private mining companies by the U.S. Bureau of Indian Affairs, ostensibly on behalf of Native peoples; the agency routinely waives environmental protection standards and corporate land reclamation responsibilities, to the financial benefit of private companies and the environmental devastation of Native peoples. Although mining lease and royalty payments made up the overwhelming majority of Diné and Hopi revenues through 2019, the agreements on which these revenues were based were far less lucrative than the lease terms provided to non-Native landowners at sometimes barely half of the market rate.

Coal from the mines at Black Mesa, which operated from 1965 through 2005, was turned into slurry and pushed through a pipeline to the Mohave Generating Station in Nevada. This process demanded enormous water resources, causing "extreme desertification" of the surrounding land, so that it sometimes sank several feet, and leaving many Diné families without a local source of potable water. The Kayenta coal mine was in operation from 1973 through 2019. When both were running, the Kayenta and Black Mesa mines produced an average of 14 million tons of coal per year, powering Arizona, Nevada, and Southern California, and using 1.3 billion gallons of water a year from the Navajo aquifer to wash and transport the coal. Meanwhile, up to 10 percent of Diné homes on the reservation lacked electricity and up to 40 percent didn't have running water. The wealth of the land, as identified by non-Native people, was effectively transferred off the reservation, from the Diné to private, non-Native coal and uranium companies, leaving open-pit mines, contaminated water, and radioactive uranium tailings in their wake.

For decades, private mining exploits, driven by government interests in coal, oil, and nuclear energy, were disguised as land disputes between the Diné and Hopi, and as opportunities to make those peoples "self-sufficient" through wage labor. Instead, the government and private mining interests undercut both Diné and Hopi self-sufficiency and sacrificed both Diné and Hopi health and longevity for private profit. Their traditional homelands were taken, and the land they were left with slowly bored and blasted and piled with waste. However non-Native people may have devastated it, the Diné continue to call the land between the four mountains their sacred home. In early 2020 Navajo reservation leadership, in partnership with the Environmental Protection Agency, began cleanup of twenty-four abandoned uranium mines.

I would keep following friends home, trying on their lives, for the entire time I was at college, and even for some time afterward. In the middle of my final year, a year and a half after I spent that month at the Gateway Ranch, Aaron and I followed Nathan all the way to Israel during winter break, where he was taking a year to study Torah and sharing a house with another Torah student and an Orthodox rabbi, all American. The start of the journey was a moment of foreshadowing, a moment that foretold how suspect Muslims would become in America over the next decades. Aaron arrived first, and I arrived several minutes later at the ground-level check-in desk for our El-Al flight from JFK Airport in New York to Jerusalem. Having checked in quickly, Aaron sat in a row of seats under the window. I waved to him as I rushed up to the desk to complete my own check-in.

I expected my check-in to be perfunctory, but the airline staff kept asking questions. What was the purpose of my travel? What was the name of the friend I was visiting? How did I come to have a friend in Jerusalem? Had I ever traveled there before? I was perplexed. My name did not immediately give me away as Muslim. What I didn't immediately understand was that I was nonetheless being racially profiled as potentially Muslim or Arab, which to them meant *dangerous*. I was a solo traveler with little luggage, young, with dark hair and darker eyes, skin slightly tanned from the Florida winter sun, a little raggedy. Perhaps it was good I was confused about them trying to figure out if I was Muslim, because I was a terrible liar, not very good at obfuscating anything. Ultimately, they asked Nathan's address in Jerusalem, and I said, "I don't have it on me, let me go and ask my boyfriend." And that did it: The profile for a Muslim woman was broken. "You're traveling with him? Together?" the man asked, nodding to where Aaron sat, with his blond hair and solid German name making him, ironically in this situation, racially innocuous. "Yeah, he has the address. I'll just go and get it."

"No need," he said, finally smiling. "You're checking this?" he asked, indicating my hiking backpack, and then directing Aaron and me on to our gate. After a week ending in the observation of Shabbat at Nathan's house in West Jerusalem, we made our way into occupied Palestine, East Jerusalem and the West Bank. Then we made our way to Egypt, where I could hear the azaan, the Muslim call to prayer, ringing out as church bells might, from every minaret in every town. Aaron and I traveled through the Sinai Peninsula, stopping at Saint Catherine's Monastery to climb Mount Sinai, where both the prophets Moses and Muhammad (peace be upon them both) traveled. We stayed in Cairo, and then in Aswan, Luxor, and Alexandria, landing finally in the Siwa Oasis, where we met a family with five children who were curious about us. We'd bought a set of cheap matching rings, telling anyone who asked that we were married, which felt true. When the Siwan children asked, Aaron said he was Christian and I said I was Muslim, which also felt true, but confused them. They believed that such a union was impossible, that while a Muslim man could marry a Christian woman, the opposite relationship required that the man first convert to Islam. I knew that this was a widespread conviction, but I also knew from my college tutorial on Islamic theology and the Qur'an these two translated verses that contradict it: "There is no compulsion in religion," and "Those who have attained to faith in this Divine writ, as well as those who follow the Jewish faith, and the Sabians, and the Christians, all those who believe in God and the Last Day and do good will have their rewards with their Sustainer—no fear need they have, and neither shall they grieve."

When Ramadan began, Aaron and I were still in Siwa. We woke to the azaan and walked together to the single, tiny open-air restaurant where we could eat a pre-dawn meal, keeping the fast for the rest of the days we were there, and eating or drinking only after sunset. I was as far from any religious practice as I've ever been during my years at college, but the azaan is a powerful call. Muslims living outside Muslim-majority countries often remark that it is what they miss most about living in such a place. Those who travel to majority Muslim countries for the first time are often moved by the haunting recitation, which combines a declaration of belief with an urging to worship. It interrupts each day five times, or perhaps I should say, each day revolves around the five daily pronouncements, which compel people to complete a few-minute series of prescribed prostrations and prayers, sometimes in mosques, but often in shops, offices, and schools, even on street corners. Hearing the azaan in Egypt was jarring. I was not in Pakistan, my family's country of origin, but in one of the many other places that the world's (then) nearly 1.3 billion Muslims inhabited. This azaan was not calling to, was not associated with, my family. It was not an ornament of our culture. It was both much more expansive and much more personal. It was calling to *me:* It was intimately familiar in a completely new place, reminding me just how large the Muslim world is, how much diversity it might contain. There, the azaan inspired my first prayers in years and my outrageously unorthodox Ramadan fast, alongside my Protestant boyfriend, Aaron, in a tiny oasis town in Egypt.

After several days in Siwa, Aaron and I traveled back to Alexandria, into Cairo, and then across the Sinai Peninsula, and back to Jerusalem for a few more days before flying home to America. I asked Nathan about the mats in all the sinks and tubs. He explained that his roommate, the Orthodox rabbi, had installed them because non-Jews, Indigenous Palestinians, had built and lived in that home for decades before being chased out. He didn't want to touch what they had touched, which he considered unalterably unclean. Nathan laid out the rules for me so that I would not trespass in a way that his roommate would find unacceptable, so that I would not soil the space with my presence. Oddly, I was not offended, though maybe I should have been. Instead, I noticed how Nathan and I both were unformed enough at that time in our lives to take on the rules made by those around us, whatever they happened to be. Nathan was trying to imagine a Jewish and maybe even an orthodox identity for himself, and so was trying on those ideas. It was only a direct threat to his own humanity that returned him to himself: Months later, the rabbi roommate told Nathan that he did not consider Nathan to be a Jew, because only his father and not his mother had a Jewish lineage. It wasn't just the Palestinians who were unclean, not just Aaron and me, but Nathan as well. Nathan was clearly crushed by this revelation but found within himself the fortitude to reject it. He identified as Jewish, and that identification within himself was unshakable, essential to who and why he felt he was in this life. Hearing the azaan in occupied Palestine and Egypt had stirred a similar sentiment in me.

I had intended to return to the Navajo reservation in the spring of 2020, a plan that was forestalled when the world was rocked by the worst global pandemic in a hundred years. The Navajo reservation has been particularly hard hit by Covid-19, and the government's lack of support instructive about the modern state of its relationship with Diné people.

Early federal health services for Native people were established as a military function, aimed at stopping the spread of infectious disease to army posts. After World War II, Americans felt increasingly that the government ought to have a central role in providing for the healthcare of its people. And yet it was clear that the government had failed to establish the same standard of care for Native men, up to a quarter of whom were turned away from the draft when they were found to have tuberculosis. This led to the official transfer of BIA's Indian Health Service (IHS) to the civilian Department of the Interior, and eventually to the Department of Health, Education, and Welfare (now the Department of Health and Human Services). The rapid development of the IHS as a permanent function of civilian government in the late sixties was based on a climate of civil rights advocacy, and President Nixon's surprisingly principled view that Native peoples had, through two hundred years of treaty agreements, purchased a "a pre-paid health care plan in perpetuity."

Despite the profound advocacy that shifted the approach of the BIA and its services from assimilation and "termination" to some limited self-determination in 1934, the IHS has remained seriously underfunded. This has become starkly apparent because of the overwhelming burden of the Covid-19 pandemic. By May 2020, residents of the Navajo reservation were experiencing the highest concentration of Covid-19 transmission in the country at 2,500 cases per 100,000 people. For the 175,000 people living on the reservation, there are only forty-six ICU beds and four hundred hospital beds. The same number of Americans in other parts of the country can count on an average of sixty-three ICU beds among them. Clean water for sanitation and drinking is still lacking across the reservation, making basic hygiene difficult.

As the Covid-19 situation in Arizona became increasingly desperate in the spring and summer of 2020, Diné leadership took extraordinary and successful measures to "flatten the curve," or dramatically reduce transmission of the virus. They set up curfews to reduce movement within the reservation, as well as washing stations. They also set up checkpoints and restricted access onto the reservation, pushing back against a long history of invasion and forced relocation. The efficiency of the Diné's Covid-19 response underscores the work that the Diné have done since the 1923 creation of the Grand Council to reappropriate the leadership structures imposed by the government so long ago. Such leadership suggests a new era in Native rights, one that defies modern attempts to marginalize and "wasteland" their homes and bodies.

To the north, several reservations in South Dakota also set up checkpoints in April 2020 to limit the spread of Covid-19. The Cheyenne Sioux Indian Health Service facility has only eight inpatient beds and six ventilators to serve a population of ten thousand, making checkpoints to enter the reservation an essential element of an effective public health response to the pandemic. Nonetheless, the Republican governor, Kristi Noem, welcomed the Sturgis Motorcycle Rally, an annual August gathering of motorcyclists that brings an estimated 500,000 people to a small town in western South Dakota, accessible by arteries running through the Standing Rock, Cheyenne, Pine Ridge, and Rosebud Sioux reservations. While the governor failed to mandate masks, Native leaders were quick to close routes through their reservations to limit the spread of Covid-19. The Sturgis rally caused an estimated 250,000 new cases of the disease according to a study that used anonymous cellphone data to identify it as a super-spreader event. Although Noem dismissed the report, North Dakota and South Dakota led the national rankings of new Covid-19 cases in the country by September 2020.

Noem had already threatened legal action over the checkpoints in May. The Cheyenne Sioux Reservation refused to abandon them, arguing that they had effectively kept cases low. In response, federal officials have threatened to cut federal funding to the reservation, including coronavirus relief aid, prompting a lawsuit by the Cheyenne.

Reading and researching the history of the Diné left me feeling the utter relentlessness of the campaigns against them. If they were not hunted, they were interned; if they were not starved at Bosque Redondo, their land, livestock, and orchards were decimated; if they were not pressed into the mines to be irradiated themselves, their children were left to breathe the air and drink the water contaminated by mining waste. What my husband, Nadeem, said when I recounted these histories to him was always some version of the same perplexed grief: "*Why?* It's not as if America has a dearth of land. In the 1800s land speculators were still recruiting European settlers; vast stretches of America are minimally populated even today. It's not as if the federal budget isn't big enough to clean up the tailings or provide clean drinking water. *Why is the assault so relentless?*" Those questions usually launched a long conversation about competing budgetary and policy interests. But as I read and studied, another, fuller explanation came into focus.

Native populations pose a particular kind of challenge to the project of America. As an active colonial project, based on the replacement of a Native population with a European one, America is deeply threatened by the original claims of Native peoples to the land. In fact, America is threatened by its own origin story of genocide, land theft, environmental racism, and colonial resource extraction, because modern human rights standards have evolved to recognize these things as egregious violations. The persistent government assault on the Diné undercuts Native voices and power, so they are less able to bear witness to America's colonial taking and violence, less able to demand justice.

As the primary targets of America's modern military campaigns overseas to maintain control of energy and other natural resources, Muslims now pose a similar challenge to America's global claims to moral authority. It is no coincidence that at the same time, Muslims have become the targets of rhetorical assault by American political leaders. American Muslims who are themselves vocal or visible as political leaders or activists, or even those who are identifiably Muslim in their workplaces or schools, are increasingly the victims of discrimination, threats, and harassment. Muslim contributions, voices, and interests are as delineated from White American contributions, voices, and interests as those of other Black and Brown Americans before us have been. Like our Native brothers and sisters, we are now required to overcome the presumption that we are the enemy.

BEST INTERESTS OF THE CHILD

Sioux Falls, South Dakota

Once human beings are defined as the problem in the public consciousness, their elimination through deportation, incarceration, or even genocide becomes nearly inevitable. White nationalism at its core reflects a belief that our nation's problems would be solved if only people of color could be gotten rid of, or at least be better controlled.

—Michelle Alexander

Just after my month at the Gateway Ranch in the summer of 1994, I met up with Aaron at a place called the Social Justice Design Institute (SJDI), a month-long summer camp for progressive artists and musicians inclined toward political activism. SJDI was led by the music professor and composer Herbert Brün, some of his former students, and other people in the orbit of the campus on which he taught. It was meant to inspire student activists to "imagine and design a [society] they would prefer" and then to express those ideals through theater, art, and music.

Elizabeth, the student activist who would become my housemate at the Tree House that fall, had crossed paths with the founders of SJDI and arranged for them to come to our campus to host a series of discussions and performances in the spring of my second year. They raised issues I found compelling, including political engagement, poverty, and inequality, inspiring those of us who were involved in campus activism. They were real adults, shining with idealism; still building lives around political activism, music, and theater; and trying to get others to do the same. The way to learn more, they said, was to come to their summer camp, SJDI. Aaron planned to go, and I wanted to go, too, but wasn't sure I could afford it. I applied for a scholarship to cover tuition as well as room and board and got it. I just had to find a way to get to Sioux Falls, South Dakota, where that summer's camp was being held in a large Victorian house, on loan from a friend of one of the organizers.

When I boarded a Greyhound bus to travel more than a thousand miles from Flagstaff, Arizona, to SJDI in Sioux Falls, South Dakota, I was tan from the Arizona sun, with thick black hair falling straight to my chin. Dressed in simple cotton pants and T-shirt, and with a second-hand hiking pack, I was the kind of scrawny that comes from traveling on a shoestring budget, just over a hundred pounds and barely five foot two. I had very little cash, half of it in quarters for pay phones wherever I could find them.

During a six-hour stop at the bus depot in Jackson County, Missouri (named for President Andrew Jackson, the architect of "Indian removal"), on the border with Kansas, as the summer sun set, I was terrified. The passengers were mostly male and I felt suddenly like I couldn't make enough space around myself to avoid their attention. As the clock inched closer to our departure time for the last leg, 12:50 A.M., their leers became more suggestive, more pronounced. I avoided the bathrooms and dug a heavy steel pocketknife out of my bag to wear on a string around my neck.

I'd thought it was just because I was a young woman. I couldn't have avoided it: The bus was the cheapest way to get to my next destination; even today, a bus ticket from Flagstaff to Sioux Falls costs less than a hundred dollars. I didn't understand that I was experiencing the magnified danger of being a *Native-looking* woman traveling alone through what some people call "flyover country." I had not yet learned about the devastating numbers of Missing and Murdered Indigenous Women and Girls (MMIWG) in America. My two-day journey would take me through a triangle of land between three of the region's most densely populated Native communities. Within this triangle, I was not light enough to pass; I was raced as "Indian."

The irony is that I am, ethnically, the kind of Indian early European settlers in the Americas thought they were encountering—the kind from what they called India, before it also became Pakistan and Bangladesh. In an even further irony, the India of Asia before the British arrived was not a monolith at all. It was a place of tremendous regional diversity that persisted under the Mughal Empire, with distinct languages, politics, and cultures. In some sense, "Indian," whether in America or in Asia, is a figment of the colonial imagination; it is the name of a lens through which White colonizers see us, and, as a result, how we sometimes come to see ourselves. In both places, it is arguably a synonym for "savage." Maybe it stands for the savagery ascribed to us, or maybe it identifies us as the objects of savagery. The truth is that none of us is Indian. Importantly, we are diverse from one another, whether native to South Asia or to the Americas, with complex cultures and faiths that endured for thousands of years prior to European colonization. Our groups have names and ways of being that are often derived from, and tied intimately to, a specific ecology. These are obscured in a colonial context, where we are renamed by whatever colonial authority there is. The colonized everywhere are assessed only for whatever value, labor, or service we might provide, then assimilated or destroyed.

As I looked at the history of Sioux Falls, I began to better understand my experience on that bus from Flagstaff. My route that summer had taken me through five of the ten states identified by the Urban Indian Health Institute (UIHI) 2017 report as those with the most reported incidence of MMIWG. I'd traveled through Arizona,

New Mexico, Oklahoma, and along the border of Nebraska and Minnesota, the locations of 40 percent of cases cited.

The National Institute of Justice (NIJ) has found that Native women experience the highest rates of rape and sexual violence of all racial categories in the United States and, in some counties, are murdered at a rate more than *ten times* the national average. High rates of poverty and homelessness contribute to high rates of sexual exploitation and trafficking among Native women. All of these, the NIJ report suggests, are linked to the "torture and trauma" of colonization, including dislocation, dispossession, persecution, and abusive residential schools. On reservations, the issue of MMIWG intersects with issues of environmental justice. A growing body of reports, studies, and congressional testimony suggests that oil pipelines and the "man camps" that house their workers, often located on or near reservations, increase rates of violence against Native women and girls.

In January 2021, the U.S. Department of Justice dedicated an issue of the *Journal of Federal Law and Practice,* to missing and murdered Indigenous persons. It contains an article drawing on the National Crime Victimization Survey, the National Violence Against Women Survey, and the National Intimate Partner and Sexual Violence Survey to provide the most comprehensive data on violence against women and girls over age twelve identifying as American Indian or Alaska Native. These respondents had the highest lifetime prevalence rates of any racial category for physical assault at 61.4 percent, stalking at 17 percent, and rape at 34.1 percent. Combining rape and physical assault, two-thirds of respondents experienced at least one violent incident in their lifetime. Respondents also experienced much higher rates of intimate partner violence than their White counterparts, 38.2 percent compared to 29.3 percent. Combining rape, physical assault, stalking, and intimate partner violence, 39.8 percent of respondents experienced some form of these in the preceding year. Violence against Native respondents, particularly sexual violence, was broadly interracial; 94 percent of perpetrators of rape or sexual assault were identified as White or Black.

There was little hope of a comprehensive investigation of the problem of MMIWG in the United States until the recent appointment of the former congresswoman and member of the Laguna Pueblo nation Deb Haaland as U.S. Secretary of the Interior. Lacking a powerful champion of the issue, advocates previously encountered a persistent lack of governmental funding and support. In addition, jurisdictional rules and lack of proper race reporting in law enforcement have compromised prosecution and data collection on reservations and in urban settings. Native governments retain sole jurisdiction in crimes on reservation lands only when both the victim and the perpetrator are Native, which is only a small minority of cases involving MMIWG. The federal government retains jurisdiction over the rest and often declines to prosecute, leaving many crime victims in Native communities without recourse. In addition, the same UIHI study cited previously found that many municipal law enforcement agencies' computer data systems lack a way to accurately designate the race of Native victims, and that these agencies frequently fail to provide the information they do have to advocates.

In April 2021, after only two weeks in office, Secretary Haaland announced the new Missing and Murdered Unit (MMU) within the Bureau of Indian Affairs to investigate the extreme and ongoing violence against Native peoples in America, particularly violence against Native women and girls. After a federal inquiry into MMIWG in Canada, that government deemed the matter a genocide. The crisis of MMIWG in the United States is believed to be similar in nature and magnitude.

Like Native women, Native children have been taken from their communities at an alarming rate. In the era after their forced confinement in residential schools, Native children have continued to be disproportionately represented in many state child welfare systems, which then frequently place them with non-Native families. In the 1960s, the Association on American Indian Affairs (AAIA) found that between 25 and 35 percent of Native children "had been placed in foster care, adoptive homes, or other institutions—and 90 percent of those kids went to White families." This problem has a nefarious precedent. From 1958 through 1967, the federal government pursued the forced assimilation of poor Native children from the western part of the United States by placing them with non-Native East Coast families through the Indian Adoption Project. In 1978, as Native peoples developed incremental political power, and as the disastrous outcomes of such programs became clear, Congress passed the Indian Child Welfare Act (ICWA), legislation aimed at keeping Native children in Native communities.

But ICWA has not resolved the disproportionate representation of Native children in South Dakota's child welfare system. In 2015, the American Civil Liberties Union (ACLU) filed a case on behalf of the "Redbud and Oglala Sioux" in federal court, alleging that the defendants, all in their official capacities within the state child welfare system, had implemented policies and procedures in violation of ICWA and the due process clause of the Fourteenth Amendment. In the process of discovery, the ACLU found that Native parental rights in South Dakota were often terminated in hearings that lasted no more than sixty seconds, that parents were denied the ability to challenge the adequacy of those hearings, and that the state won *100 percent of hearings over four years*. Of the more than eight hundred children taken from Redbud and Oglala communities between 2010 and 2014, most were placed with non-Native families. The Redbud and Oglala won declaratory and injunctive relief in federal court, with the court ordering changes to state child welfare procedures.

Although the ACLU reported that some important changes had been implemented in accordance with the order, an appeals court later overturned the decision, ruling that the case should not have been heard in federal court at all. The Supreme Court declined review. In 2017, the ACLU cited South Dakota Department of Social Services statistics that showed an Indigenous child was still "11 times more likely to be placed in foster care than a White child in South Dakota." Similarly, a 2017 report by the National Indian Child Welfare Association found that while Native children account for 12.9 percent of the children in South Dakota, they are 47.9 percent of children in the state's child welfare system. Advocates argue that the disproportionate removal of Native children from their communities is driven by racist ideas about the capacity of Native families to care for their children and the misinterpretation of poverty as neglect or abuse. Opponents have argued that the child welfare standard of the "best interests of the child" should not be compromised by adherence to ICWA, and that removing children from Native communities is necessary where there are limited Native placements for at-risk children.

In early 2020, a Court of Appeals reheard an argument in the case of *Brackeen v. Bernhardt* alleging that ICWA, because of the preference it creates for keeping Native children with their Native communities, is unconstitutional. The plaintiffs include the states of Texas, Indiana, and Louisiana, along with seven non-Native people who wanted to adopt Native children. They argued that procedures for adoption under ICWA were unconstitutionally race-based, and that ICWA both exceeded permissible federal authority and also impermissibly delegated federal powers to tribes. In 2021, the Fifth Circuit Court of Appeals published a 325-page opinion in the case, affirming the overall constitutionality of ICWA but getting rid of protections in the law that require specific acts, testimony, and record-keeping before placing Native children with non-Native families. The judges deadlocked on a key provision of ICWA, which requires that preference be given to placing Native children with extended family, members of the same Native community, or foster homes approved by that Native community. All parties petitioned for a U.S. Supreme Court review of the appeals court decision on September 3, 2021.

When I finally arrived at SJDI, it was before eight o'clock in the morning on a Sunday. No one was around at that hour, so I walked through the sleepy business district near where the camp's activities would be held. By the time I made my way back, Aaron was already there.

"Sof!" he shouted as I walked through the door and dropped my backpack, crushing me in a bear hug. I was arriving at the closest thing to home for a couple thousand miles in any direction. I had been distant from my own family since leaving for college, and I was exhausted from two long days on a bus. I recognized some of the other people there, both students and teachers, but wasn't close to any of them.

Herbert Brün, the senior instructor at SJDI, was in his late seventies. He was the oldest of our summer school group, and my favorite for the way he listened carefully in discussions. Brün was a composer on the leading edge of electronic and computer music, exploring the purpose of music in society. He was also, as a German Jew, one of a small minority left on Earth. He fled Berlin in 1936 at the age of eighteen, to study in Jerusalem three years before World War II began. The family he left behind were killed in the Holocaust.

Herbert saw traditional music, with its steady and predictable beat, as reflective of commercialism and social conformity, which he wanted to disrupt. Both his musical and his social purpose was to challenge the routine by creating more thoughtful, more purposeful experiences. I had grown up in a household with little music, and no Western classical music. So I had no sense of the canon he was trying to challenge or of how his own music was new. Not only did I not understand Herbert's music, but I'd been raised in a culture in which elders are not a part of one's peer group, and so I found Herbert hard to approach. Nonetheless, Herbert and I sometimes ended up taking long walks through the neighborhood during breaks. Although I asked him to help me understand his music, he deflected, instead asking me about myself.

He was interested that I identified strongly as Muslim, if not religiously at that point, then perhaps culturally. And he always ended our walks by saying, in his still strong German accent, "Be sure that your passport is in order." The directive stuck with me, a memory right at the front of my thoughts for decades to come, although I could not say why. So sure was I of my Americanness then that I only remember thinking it an odd thing to say to a young woman. It certainly wasn't something he said to anyone else that I know of, or in any of the group discussions we had. For the next twenty-five years, his words stayed with me as the impression of a man who had survived the Holocaust, not as a warning about my own future. Now, as I excavate the history of the place in which Herbert and I found ourselves together that summer, I wonder if he knew about the relentless destruction and forced migration on which it had been built. I wonder whether he might have foreseen some of what was in store for American Muslims.

———

While military forts and settler incursions were eroding Navajo land and resources in Arizona, White settlers were also flooding into the northern plains. The region was inhabited by Dakota, Lakota, and Nakota communities, who speak dialects of the same language and know themselves as the Oceti Sakowin, or People of the Seven Council Fires. The name imposed upon them—*Sioux*—was taken from a French derivation of an Ojibwe word meaning "little snake." (I'll use their name for themselves, Oceti Sakowin, throughout this chapter, except for place names or quotes from legal pleadings.)

A small sliver of the vast Oceti Sakowin homeland, east of the Mississippi, was taken first in an 1837 land cession treaty. In the intervening years, the American doctrine of manifest destiny took hold and the Mississippi River was no longer seen as the western boundary of its colonial project. In 1851, under the Treaty of Traverse des Sioux and the Treaty of Mendota, the United States took a great swath of territory west of the river, across the southern half of present-day Minnesota, along with narrow strips in South Dakota and Iowa. This region, on both sides of the Mississippi River in Minnesota, had been home to four bands among the Oceti Sakowin, known collectively as the Eastern Dakota, or the Santee.

As had been the case in the deeds and then the Treaty of Fort Pitt with the Lenape two hundred years before, both the 1851 Treaty of Traverse des Sioux and Treaty of Mendota were drafted in a complicated language and signed with only a mark by several Santee representatives, indicating limited literacy and fluency in the language of the contract. Then, after signing, both treaties were unilaterally changed by the U.S. Senate to eliminate Article 3 of each, which had originally created a protected, permanent reservation for the Santee along the Minnesota River, in the southwest corner of the state. In place of Article 3, the Senate included a provision that allowed the government to purchase, for ten cents per acre paid into a trust, even that narrow strip of the river valley originally designated as a reservation. With this change, the treaties would give the U.S. government control of about twenty-five million acres in total.

The treaties, and the process by which they were made, were confusing and duplicitous in several other ways. The government was to pay more than $3 million to the Santee under the treaties, but in the form of annual annuities, or interest payments on sums held by the government in trust rather than payment of a lump sum. In addition, they required that future annuities also *be paid directly to European traders* instead of the Santee themselves, so that the traders could then take out the cost of items bought by the Santee on credit, according to their own accounting, before releasing the excess funds. The Santee had reason to mistrust both the traders and government negotiators; they were still owed annuities that the government had promised under the 1837 agreement. Also, traders were part of a conscious government plan to use debt to take more land. Thomas Jefferson had conceived this design more than half a century before, writing:

> to promote this disposition to exchange lands which they have to spare & we want, for necessaries, which we have to spare & they want, we shall push our trading houses, and be glad to see the good & influential individuals among them run in debt, because we observe that when these debts get beyond what the individuals can pay, they become willing to lop th[em off] by a cession of lands. at

our trading houses too we mean to sell so low as merely to repay us
cost and charges so as neither to lessen or enlarge our capital. this is
what private traders cannot do, for they must gain; they will conse-
quently retire from the competition, & we shall thus get clear of
this pest without giving offence or umbrage to the Indians. in this
way our settlements will gradually circumbscribe & approach the
Indians, & they will in time either incorporate with us as citizens of
the US. or remove beyond the Missisipi. the former is certainly the
termination of their history most happy for themselves.

It was, for the Santee, as if they had been forced to sell their homeland and livelihood as well as their physical, spiritual, and cultural
context. And then instead of payment, they were given a series of
convoluted and conditional promises. The Santee resisted, until Luke
Lea, one of the negotiators, reminded them that they had little choice,
when the government "could come with 100,000 men and drive
[them] off to the Rocky Mountains." Once the 1851 treaties were
signed, land speculators swarmed to buy this land cheaply from the
government, hoping to either hold it until its value grew or divide it
into lots for sale to immigrants recruited from Germany and Scandi-
navia. Some of these speculators had also been traders, looking for a
new source of profit with which to clear debts from the fur trade,
showing signs of failure after two hundred years of unsustainable
hunting practices in every successive region settled by Europeans.

By 1855, the rations and annuities promised in all the three previous U.S. treaties with the Santee were arriving late, in addition to
which the Santee had identified discrepancies in the funds being dispersed by traders. By 1858, they were informed that they no longer
owned even their twenty-mile-wide strip along the Minnesota River,
and that they had also unknowingly ceded hunting rights elsewhere.
As their ability to hunt diminished, their dependence on the annuities
and food rations promised under the 1851 treaty grew desperate. By
the summer of 1862, the United States was embroiled in the Civil
War and had been diverting resources to its own troops while abrogat-

ing its treaties with the Santee. By the end of this period, the Santee who remained along the river were starving.

Though the government now claimed that strip initially designated as a reservation along the river, it was the last vestige of familiar ecology preserved for the Santee in the original treaty language and many Santee remained there. Settlers had already bought up the land surrounding it, treating Santee who dared leave as enemies, so that the strip began to feel less like a protected entitlement and more like a forced and hungry containment, a tinderbox. In July 1862, Santee delegations went to the two federal administrative offices along the river, called "agencies," which remained to disperse rations and annuities. They asked for the release of food supplies to which they were entitled under the treaties. Staff at the Upper Agency dispersed enough pork and flour to hold the status quo there for a while longer. But at the Lower Agency, a federal employee named Galbraith refused to release food stores. Then, turning to the four traders whose goods filled the agency warehouse, Galbraith asked what they'd like to do. A local trader named Andrew Myrick insisted they wait for the government annuity before providing the Santee food, suggesting that the Santee eat grass and dirt, and in some versions of the story, their own waste.

In that hungry summer, Myrick's derision proved too much. Four young Santee men who were out hunting killed five settlers in angry retribution. This event, and none of what came before—the forced relocation, the land theft, the failure to provide food rations to replace the hunting rights and land that had been stripped away, and the subsequent loss of both lifeways and subsistence—would later be identified as the cause of the Dakota War on a marker outside the town of Mankato, Minnesota:

The Acton Incident. On a bright Sunday afternoon, August 17, 1862, four young Sioux hunters, on a spur-of-the-moment dare, decided to prove their bravery by shooting Robinson Jones. Stopping at his cabin, they requested liquor and were refused. Then

Jones, followed by the seemingly friendly Indians, went to the neighboring Howard Baker cabin, which stood on this site.

In truth, even after the young hunters' spontaneous attack, Santee leaders were divided on what should be done. One chief feared collective punishment for what the four hunters had done. Others felt that because the U.S. military was preoccupied with the Civil War, they might as well strike the first blow in a larger battle for their homeland. Little Crow, the war chief, counseled that U.S. military strength and the numbers of settlers were overwhelming, saying, "They fight among themselves, but if you strike at them, they will all turn on you and devour you and your women and your little children just as the locusts in their time fall on the trees and devour all the leaves in one day." Ultimately, the anger, hunger, and frustration from decades of increasing encroachments on their land and the loss of their sustenance won out. Under Little Crow's leadership, the Santee attacked the lower agency, where Andrew Myrick's dead body would ultimately be found, his mouth stuffed with grass. The fighting progressed, but one elder would later describe the Santee position:

> It was not the intention of the nation to kill any of the whites until after the four men returned from Acton and told what they had done. When they did this, all the young men became excited, and commenced the massacre. The older ones would have prevented it if they could, but since the treaties they have lost all their influence.

The increasingly vulnerable position of the Santee, without land or compensation for it, without even the ability to feed themselves, had caused fractures among them. Young raiders chose civilian targets in addition to the military ones counseled by chiefs, and chiefs themselves were divided. Between 400 and 850 settlers were killed in the ongoing attacks.

By September, Little Crow had sent a message to General Henry Sibley, a longtime trader who had married a Native woman and had then taken the military role of containing and ultimately removing the Santee from Minnesota, to negotiate a truce and was rebuffed. Meanwhile, the Santee chief Wabusha sent a message to Sibley bargaining prisoners for mercy and blaming Little Crow for the Santee attacks. Neither approach had any hope of success. The existence of the Santee had become, for the adherents of manifest destiny, an intolerable obstacle. Governor Ramsey of Minnesota proclaimed, "The Sioux Indians must be exterminated or driven forever beyond the borders of the state."

With little hope of a peaceful resolution left, Little Crow led a battle against General Sibley's troops and was roundly defeated. In the end, 400 Santee men were tried, with 303 sentenced to death. President Lincoln commuted all but 39 sentences over the objections of Governor Ramsey, who warned that Minnesota settlers would exact revenge if the penalty was not harsh enough. Those 39 men were hanged, publicly, in the largest mass execution in the United States. The remainder were imprisoned. In addition, more than 2,000 other Santee women, children, and elders were rounded up and imprisoned without charge at Fort Snelling. Many fled to Canada, to traditional hunting grounds in North Dakota, or westward to live among the Lakota in the aftermath of the war. For those who remained, deportation to the Crow Creek Reservation, just west of Sioux Falls in South Dakota, began in 1863.

Three years later, the Santee could be found scattered across South Dakota reservations along the border with Minnesota, at Lake Traverse Reservation and Devils Lake Reservation, and in Nebraska, at Santee Reservation. In the aftermath of the Dakota War, the U.S. government abrogated all its treaties with the Santee, spurious though they already were, and until 1868, the Minnesota state government offered bounties for "Sioux scalps," twenty-five dollars to members of the military and seventy-five to civilians. To exist as Santee in Minnesota had been criminalized and the state-sanctioned penalty was death.

Today, there are no Santee or "Sioux" reservations in the state of

Minnesota at all. On September 18, 2020, President Donald Trump campaigned for reelection in Bemidji, Minnesota, a town with, ironically, an Ojibwe name. He addressed the nearly all-White crowd, descendants of those early German and Scandinavian settlers who replaced the Santee, this way:

> From St. Paul to St. Cloud, from Rochester to Duluth, and from Minneapolis, thank God we still have Minneapolis, to right here, right here with all of you great people, this state was pioneered by men and women who braved the wilderness and the winters to build a better life for themselves and for their families. They were tough and they were strong. You have good genes. You know that, right? You have good genes. A lot of it's about the genes, isn't it? Don't you believe? The racehorse theory; you think was so different? You have good genes in Minnesota.

The racehorse theory Trump referenced is the idea that selective breeding, as applied to exceptional racehorses, preserves "good genes." In this case, Trump was lauding the German and Scandinavian gene pool and, as many critics were quick to deduce, the successful racist exclusion of "bad," or non-European, genes.

———————

The seven instructors at SJDI included five men and two women, all White except for one who was a South Asian American academic. Briefly, they were joined by Patch Adams, the healthcare advocate and doctor famously portrayed by Robin Williams in a film by the same name. The other students were also mostly White, except the two of us who were South Asian, and all of us were in college except for two high school students. There were ten or twelve students in all. All of us were at least passingly middle-class and many of us comfortably so. The first day, when we sat in a circle in the family room, we were asked to fill a page beginning with the phrase "I want . . ." And then we shared what we had written. Every one of the teachers began with a similar statement that included food, shelter, education, and healthcare for everyone. This exercise left an impression on me. I had not, until then, ever imagined that a personal expression of desire could or should be directed at basic human rights for everyone. Still deeply influenced by the extreme poverty I'd witnessed visiting Hyderabad as a child, this immediately struck me as the most ethical way to orient one's life, and from then on, it would be how I oriented mine.

SJDI's objective to use art and theater in the service of social justice activism was admirable, but it was otherwise a poorly run commune. Though our purported purpose was to imagine a society that *each of us* would prefer, our instructors had a well-developed template for what their own ideal society would look like, so there were right and wrong answers to almost every question they posed. As a group, the instructors lacked diversity of identity and experience; this allowed them to believe that there were few legitimate alternatives to their own ideals. Just after the "I want . . ." exercise, several of our instructors led a discussion about the revolutionary potential of the internet to make information and therefore education widely available, which they said would work eventually to eradicate poverty. But I had just come from the Navajo reservation, where both hogans and government housing frequently lacked reliable electricity—or electricity altogether—and indoor running water or sanitation. Six months before, I had completed an independent study project in rural Sindh, outside of Hyderabad, Pakistan, and learned that the government had been promising and failing for decades to provide reliable electricity to even major urban centers and had never provided any electricity at all in many rural areas.

"How does that work if the world's most vulnerable people don't have access to electricity?" I asked, leaning in from my spot on the floor, at the edge of a rough circle we'd made in the living room, spilling across a wide doorway into the dining area.

"Well, this is really a discussion about *our* society," Kyle explained.

"Okay, how does it work if America's most vulnerable people don't have access to electricity or to technology?"

"There are always public libraries, right? And most people, here, I think, have electricity. The cost of technology will be high at first, but then eventually it'll go down. We're talking about the potential of *universal* access to information." He turned away, signaling that the exchange was over.

In the discussion that followed, it was clear that I was the only one in the room who had been in environments where people lacked access to electricity and even clean drinking water, for whom access to computer-mediated education and information would likely remain a wild fantasy. It was an early lesson in how lack of diversity makes for ineffective priorities and politics, as well as policy. A feature of the teachers' echo chamber was that they were adamant that their own collective experiences were sufficient to inform choices that they hoped to make for others.

There were other issues with SJDI, behaviors that contradicted the group's stated ideals. One teacher was in a sexual relationship with a student who was still in high school, something he presented as a "youth rights" issue, and when the organizers ran out of money, they tried to collect the tuition they'd previously waived for me. The predatory nature of both of these challenged my belief that progressive communities could provide what I'd been searching for: a safe environment, a consistent, cohesive moral worldview, even a personal identity. I began to understand that progressive communities had the potential to get things wrong or even engage in abuse, despite their ideals. I was also frustrated because I'd been impressed by Kate and Mark's work at the school and ranch, and Justin's work on the landscape, all so deeply rooted in service to the communities and ecology around them. SJDI felt different, and not in a good way. I wanted *to be of use,* somehow, to *do something good,* and none of the discussion or performance of SJDI felt like it served anyone outside of that small group. This was no ready-made utopian community for me.

Aaron wasn't a particularly active participant while we were at SJDI. Outside of our usual circles, I could see that he was shy and socially awkward. He seemed both in awe of and also a little disdainful of the group's often brazen ideas and idealism. Aaron saw environmentalism as critical to any social criticism, and saw his approach as more grounded in the history of social movements. He leaned in to me while we were there, and though he was using me as a social crutch, I was deeply invested in the relationship. I wanted that role. But I'd also been intensely affected by my time at Gateway Ranch. I'd seen aspects of myself on the Navajo reservation, a colonized place like the colonized place from which my own family had emerged, to which I was still trying to make sense of my relationship. I felt a vague yearning for an indigeneity of my own, some sense of belonging to a place. I was missing whatever it was that Justin had been rebuilding for himself as he planted his peach pits. Although I had never experienced an active occupation of my homeland as Justin had, I was the child of a diaspora set in motion by colonialism. That new, still vague realization, not quite of what had been lost, but that something *had* been lost, shaped how I experienced SJDI and also how I experienced Aaron. I found myself arguing with Aaron about things that I knew seemed bizarre to him.

"I just think America is too big," I'd say, alone in our dorm room.

"What does that even mean?" he'd answer, frustrated.

"Just . . . we act like we all have something in common, but it's this enormous country, with really diverse ecosystems, and immigrants from everywhere, and we've built this commercial culture based on a mutual experience of fast food and prime-time TV. The cultures that are actually grounded in these places have been beaten down and warehoused on reservations."

"But America isn't going to split up. What's the end point of that argument?"

"I don't know. It's just hard to imagine that people all the way out here could be committed to national politics run from D.C. And it's hard to imagine that anyone could be invested in the places they live if the national culture is based on the idea that you can buy the same things from the same stores, from one coast to the other."

I was less well-grounded academically than Aaron. He hadn't been where I'd just been, and he didn't have much interest in my critiques, which he saw as irrelevant and impractical. That was my insecurity. I was out in the world without any other anchor, and when Aaron didn't value my experiences, it scared me. I needed Aaron to affirm what I thought or felt for it to be valid. Maybe even for me to be valid.

Each successive generation of European settlers for more than two hundred years after William Penn used the same formula he did for accumulating wealth and ensuring upward mobility: taking and selling land and taking and selling the products made from the labor of people they exploited or enslaved. The U.S. government acted in concert with and protected the interests of those settlers and their descendants, facilitating land speculation, resource extraction, and the unimpeded exploitation of other peoples. Such was the unquestioned entitlement of these men in the colonies, and in the states those colonies became. As late as 1834, in the Indian Intercourse Act, Congress still asserted that the domain of White settlers ended at a frontier along the Mississippi (apart from the already established states of Missouri, Louisiana, and Arkansas), preserving all land to the west for the Native peoples who lived there, citizens of their own territories. But within two decades, where—and often whether—Native peoples in the path of the ever-expanding United States were meant to survive was an open question.

Whiteness was, by the mid-1800s, an explicit and planned feature of America's early vision for its own future. The Naturalization Act of 1790 allowed only White people to naturalize. After the passage of the Fourteenth Amendment in 1866, everyone born in the United States, including people of African origin but "excluding Indians not taxed," was recognized as a citizen. By 1870, Black people were finally granted the right of naturalization in addition to birthright citizenship, though they would continue to be trapped by a web of law, policy, and private terror aimed at keeping them in servitude. Native peoples, Asian peoples, and anyone else deemed neither White under the law nor of African origin remained unable to naturalize. The particular humiliation for Native peoples in being barred from citizenship was, of course, that they were already living on—and not just that but subsisting on, and drawing identity, faith, and culture from—this land.

In the month after the Treaties of Traverse des Sioux and Mendota were signed in Minnesota, the commissioner of Indian Affairs held council with several Great Plains nations, including the Oceti Sakowin. There, they signed the Fort Laramie Treaty of 1851, under which Native peoples were promised the free and autonomous control of a large territory across Wyoming, South Dakota, and Nebraska, with smaller portions of Montana, North Dakota, and Kansas. This treaty was breached upon the discovery of gold in Montana in 1858.

Nonetheless, hoping to avoid open conflict with the formidable Oceti Sakowin, the U.S. government offered the designation of a smaller "Great Sioux Nation" exclusively in South Dakota west of the Missouri River in the second, 1868, Treaty of Fort Laramie. Large groups of the Oceti Sakowin had already been dispossessed by the westward advance of missionaries, the military, and other settlers. They knew that the government readily breached its own treaties but also hoped to retain a place in their traditional homeland while avoiding war. The treaty promised them "absolute and undisturbed use and occupation" of more than half of the land in South Dakota, west of and including the Missouri River, and including the Black Hills, all of which was primarily the traditional territory of a group among them called the Lakota. The treaty language guaranteed that "no [other] person . . . [would] be permitted to pass over, settle upon, or reside in" that land. It also designated an additional and larger tract of land in Nebraska and Wyoming "unceded Indian Territory."

In exchange, the Oceti Sakowin were forced to agree to "relinquish all claims or rights in and to any portion of the United States or Territories" except as those within the limits defined by the treaty, and to cease opposition to transcontinental railroads not on their designated land. In addition, the treaty was designed to encourage deep assimilation, providing financial incentives and private land ownership to those who would farm rather than hunt and requiring the Oceti Sakowin to send their children to settler-run schools:

> In order to insure the civilization of the Indians entering into this treaty, the necessity of education is admitted, especially of such of them as are or may be settled on said agricultural reservations, and they, therefore, pledge themselves to compel their children, male and female, between the ages of six and sixteen years, to attend school, and it is hereby made the duty of the agent for said Indians to see that this stipulation is strictly complied with.

Predictably, the American government would break this treaty as well. In 1872, amid rumors spread by private prospectors of gold in the Black Hills, President Ulysses S. Grant tried to purchase that land back for the United States. When he was unsuccessful, the secretary of the interior, Columbus Delano, signaled that he would not oppose a military breach of the 1868 Treaty of Fort Laramie. Lieutenant General Philip Sheridan, who commanded the Military Division of the Missouri, ordered Lieutenant Colonel George Armstrong Custer (who, after a 1871 court-martial, had been demoted from the rank of Major General) to conduct the Black Hills Expedition in 1874. President Grant's son and two of his brothers were among the dozens who traveled with Custer; thousands of private prospectors followed.

This incursion, and the subsequent loss of their land to a flood of prospectors, launched open conflict between the Oceti Sakowin and U.S. military forces. Congress halted all further appropriations and annuities payable to the Oceti Sakowin under all previous treaties until they ceded the Black Hills. With subsistence foreclosed through either their land base or the payments promised by the government in exchange for land, the Oceti Sakowin were fighting for their survival. Ultimately, the U.S. forces were defeated and Custer would die in the 1876 Battle of the Little Bighorn, the same year that the settler village of Sioux Falls was incorporated on the far eastern border of South Dakota.

In response to this military defeat, the U.S. government sent in Colonel Ranald Mackenzie, who, with reinforcements, pursued a brutal strategy of killing entire villages of Lakota and Cheyenne civilians. When the Oceti Sakowin finally surrendered in 1877, the U.S. government took 7.7 million acres in the Black Hills without providing compensation. It ostensibly reestablished subsistence rations to the Oceti Sakowin, though these had always been capricious and unreliable. The U.S. government proceeded to unilaterally change the terms that had been set out in the Treaty of Fort Laramie, replacing it with "The Sioux Agreement of 1889." Instead of a large continuous parcel of land including the Black Hills, the Oceti Sakowin would be divided onto 10 percent of the land promised by the 1868 treaty, on six scattered patches of land, including the Standing Rock Reservation.

Immediately after the surrender of the Oceti Sakowin, Homestake Mining Company began operation in Lead, South Dakota. Over the following 126 years it would extract 40 million ounces of gold, more than $18 billion worth, from the Black Hills, becoming the largest, deepest gold mine in North America. All of that wealth has been expropriated from the Oceti Sakowin. Gold prices climbed over $1,400 per ounce in 2019, spurring renewed exploration and interest in mining ventures, as well as concerns of critics that such ventures would compromise clean water access in the region.

Ten years after the Homestake Mine was established, Congress passed the Dawes Act of 1887, also known as the General Allotment Act. This legislation designated treaty or reservation land piecemeal to individual Native people, who could then, after a period of time, resell the land, even to non-Native buyers. This approach made it easier for the government and private speculators to access lucrative resources through private transactions with individual people without raising the specter of the overall loss of Native land. Since passage of the Dawes Act, Native peoples have suffered the loss of a combined 27 million acres, two-thirds of what was originally allotted.

The Oceti Sakowin have spent a century seeking legal redress for the theft of the Black Hills, starting within a legal infrastructure that offered no venue for treaty claims. In 1980, *fifty-seven years after the start of litigation,* the Supreme Court of the United States affirmed that the Black Hills had been taken by the government unconstitutionally, because it was a taking without compensation. The legality of the taking itself was not considered by the court, only the amounts owed in compensation for the entirety of the Black Hills. This amount, defined early in litigation as $17.5 million by the U.S. Claims Commission, has been earning interest since that time; it was estimated at $105 million in 1980, and at $1.3 billion in 2011.

The Oceti Sakowin have refused to accept a payout of any funds for the sale of the Black Hills, despite widespread and pronounced poverty among their people, maintaining that the Black Hills hold sacred, inestimable value central to their identity, faith, and culture and are not for sale. In 2011, responding to signals that President Obama hoped to resolve the Black Hills conflict, the Oceti Sakowin continued to negotiate for resolutions that would meet the needs of their people instead of a fleeting monetary award. One such proposal called for "the return of 1.3 million acres of the Black Hills," relabeling the trust money as back rent and then agreeing on the terms of future rent for the resources from the land to the tune of roughly $7 million a year.

No resolution was reached. Instead, ten years on in the battle to rehabilitate their land base, the Oceti Sakowin are not only recovering from more than a century of violent dispossession, but they face a new challenge. The privately owned, newly proposed Dewey-Burdock uranium mine would cover approximately 12,600 acres within the Black Hills region and use approximately 8,500 gallons of groundwater per minute.

This long history of persecution is the backdrop for the massive protests of the Dakota Access oil pipeline near the Standing Rock Reservation that began in 2016. These protests have acted as a sort of national public service announcement, making clear that Native peoples still live, struggle, and sometimes even thrive on their land against terrible odds. The Standing Rock Reservation lies between the Black Hills in the west and Sioux Falls to the east, on 2.3 million acres of rangeland at the border between North and South Dakota. It is one of the modest land remnants of the great nation of the Oceti Sakowin, who were first displaced, then interned, and finally scattered in the treaties of 1851 and 1868, and "The Sioux Agreement of 1889." The relentless dispossession did not end there.

The Standing Rock Reservation as it exists today is nearly 56,000 acres smaller than it was even in 1889, as a result of the Pick-Sloan Missouri Basin Program, in which the government took, and mostly flooded, land surrounding dams built along the Missouri River. From 1948 to 1962, the project would progressively flood the reservation's most fertile agricultural land, destroy habitat used for hunting and fishing, and eliminate sites with deep spiritual significance. It would force the relocation of 190 Native families on the Standing Rock Reservation and 900 Native families in total. As a result, according to 2007 congressional testimony given on the impact of the dam, "entire tribal infrastructures and economies were destroyed."

The project would create the Oahe Reservoir in 1962, located just half a mile upstream of the Standing Rock Reservation, and now the only supply of drinking water for its residents. The complex history of the place is encapsulated in the name of the reservoir, built on the site of the Oahe Mission and Industrial School, established in 1872 and run by Thomas Riggs and his wife, Nina. Riggs wrote that he named the mission after a Dakota council lodge that had previously stood on the site, the bottom portion of which was called "Ti tanka ohe," with "ohe," now Oahe, meaning "foundation."

In the tradition of Carlisle Indian Industrial School in Pennsylvania, the mission school's stated purpose was to "civilize" and "Christianize" Native children. Thomas Riggs left a well-developed record of his views and interaction with the Oceti Sakowin, whom he referred to interchangeably as "Dakota" or "Indian." He and his family occupied, maybe even exemplified, that middle ground of racism that the author, professor, and anti-racist activist Ibram X. Kendi calls "assimilationist," neither anti-racist nor segregationist. The Riggses did not loathe the Oceti Sakowin among whom they lived for generations. They often admired them, but were nonetheless wholly committed to converting them to Christianity and to their own ways of living. Their objectives were rooted in an explicit elevation of whiteness and a studied ignorance of how their own intrusive presence caused despair and destruction. Nina Riggs wrote:

> Some of these women are very attractive, modest in spite of their loose morals in living, and in their motherhood very beautiful. I am yearning for these souls. Will ever the day dawn and the daystar arise in their hearts?

And about her pregnancy and the birth of her son, Theodore, in 1874:

> I have been thinking . . . of the great shrinking from strange faces which I felt . . . of the yells wich were the last sounds in my ears at night and which awakened me at all hours as the Indians went by to their feasts; of the filth I saw all about me . . . of the bullet that went whistling through my room . . . I have been thinking of these things and how "God gave me" a little fair, white, healthy, merry, happy boy, as lovely as though I had not lived through such things. ,

Thomas wrote about how he brought the logs for the Riggses' house in from upriver, hoping that he "should be spared the opposition" of the Oceti Sakowin village near Oahe. He paid one individual for it, rejecting the claims of others who came to demand their payment for the cut trees. He was aware of the concept of shared ownership among the Oceti Sakowin; he had struggled with members of the surrounding community to obtain individual deeds in the foreign, settler way. But he seemed unable to grasp how these things came together, so that the cutting of trees was perceived as a loss to an entire village, and the loss of the wider landscape was the inevitable consequence of a settler occupation he helped to bring:

> Co-kan-tan-ka was really quite a man, and I well remember one day in 1881, when he and I climbed the southern end of Slim Butte. It was a wonderful view, looking down to the east . . . clear beyond the Missouri . . . not a bush, tree, or bare hilltop to break the expanse . . . After fully half an hour of silence, as the sun began to go down, Co-kan . . . turned to me, and rising from the stone (on which he was seated), said: "I have been crying and praying, for I shall never again see this country as I have seen it before."

The Riggses accepted and sometimes championed their roles in destroying the context and culture of the Oceti Sakowin, even while they understood—and depended on—the Oceti Sakowin's superior knowledge and adaptation to the environment in which they lived. Riggs often noted his need for and use of Native guides. He acknowledged both the already prominent elements of reverence and worship in their culture, as well as the skill and the strength of the Oceti Sakowin in their buffalo hunt, so that he found "the term 'lazy Indian' had no proper application."

Yet, as a missionary, Riggs had a central, unyielding aim that he and his family pursued with a deep sense of entitlement. His mission would provide an entry point for the broader military campaign to clear Native people from the land, or at least to make them so assimilated as to be unremarkable to settlers. For example, both Thomas Riggs and his father did much to develop a written Dakota language, perhaps allowing that language to be preserved for the Oceti Sakowin in the context of overwhelming colonial pressure. But they did so to provide translations of the Bible and ancillary texts for the central purpose of converting the Oceti Sakowin to Christianity.

Ultimately, in the Dakota War of 1862, Riggs gave little weight to the plight of the Oceti Sakowin who had been perilously deprived the rations for which they were forced to exchange their livelihoods, in violation of treaties they had made with the U.S. government. It is hard to imagine Riggs would have been unaware of this reality, inter-acting daily, as he did, with the Native community around him. In-stead, Riggs quickly retreated from his assimilationist position to a plainly segregationist one as the conflict escalated, *joining the settler military apparatus as chaplain and general advisor to General Sibley,* allowing his knowledge of the Oceti Sakowin to be used in battle against them, successfully. Then he went right back to preaching to them. Riggs and missionaries like him were the advance team in the military cam-paign to displace Native peoples, to make them dependent on and vul-nerable to the state so they could not resist colonial encroachment. By the nineteenth century, the Oceti Sakowin had already been made dependent on food rations; in the twentieth century, the Pick-Sloan Missouri Basin Program made the residents of the Standing Rock Reservation completely dependent on the Oahe Reservoir for drink-ing water.

That dependence would become a critical issue some fifty years later. In 2014, Energy Transfer Partners (ETP), operating as Dakota Access LLC, proposed a crude oil pipeline to run directly underneath the Oahe Reservoir. Construction on the 1,172-mile-long pipeline began in 2016 and it became operational in June 2017, transporting 570,000 barrels of crude oil a day. The problem is, crude oil contains a "cocktail of organic toxic compounds," including the known car-cinogen benzene.

Scientists like Dr. Jon Conway, lead researcher at the Lakota Peo-ple's Law Project, have helped detail the environmental hazards of the Dakota Access Pipeline (DAPL). When I spoke to him in October 2020, he characterized the Oahe Reservoir as "by far the most likely place for a catastrophic [oil] spill to occur." The nature of the pipeline itself, he said, poses a risk. It is a novel use of a relatively new pipeline technology, horizontal directional drilling (HDD), in which a borehole is drilled at an angle and then turned horizontally to run underneath an obstacle, after which the pipeline itself is pushed and dragged through the borehole. In this case, the borehole runs through gravel, which, unlike clay, is highly permeable to any leaked toxins. The total length of the reservoir crossing at 7,800 feet, with 5,420 feet under the actual lake, is one of the longest HDD sections in the world to pass under a body of water. It violates the standard practice of limiting use of HDD to under a mile and raises concerns about the condition of the welds holding the pipeline together.

The DAPL route underneath the Oahe Reservoir was only one of three possible routes examined in the Army Corps of Engineers' environmental assessment for the pipeline. One route avoided any crossing of the Missouri River, another would have crossed the river ten miles from the towns of Bismarck and Mandan, with overwhelmingly White populations, and for which the river is only one of several sources of drinking water. Although the Army Corps of Engineers ranked the Oahe Reservoir crossing as the route posing the greatest social and environmental risk, ETP was inexplicably allowed to proceed with construction on that route.

Published studies on the adverse health effects of exposure to crude oil contamination of water tend to be location specific. However, a review of several of these studies undertaken by a team of chemical, mechanical, and biomedical engineers at Worcester Polytechnical Institute indicates that health impacts include elevated rates of cancer (specifically of the stomach, rectum, skin, kidney, cervix, lymph nodes, and a class of cancers affecting stem cells, especially in children under ten), skin rashes and sores, malnutrition, and pregnancy complications including spontaneous abortion, as well as generally increased morbidity and mortality. The same review discussed increased death or devastation of several animal species who inhaled, ingested, or were coated with crude oil at the surface, which had a secondary effect on the economy of the people relying on fishing and wildlife for nutrition, and for underwater ecosystems.

DAPL's contaminant leak detection technology is no better than the industry standard, which has witheringly low detection rates of 20 to 30 percent of spills. It is incapable of detecting small leaks of less than 1 to 2 percent of capacity. So, leak detection depends heavily upon surface observation. That is, to avoid the ongoing contamination of their only source of drinking water, the residents of the Standing Rock Reservation rely on an oil company that proposes to use twice-monthly overhead drone observation to detect spills. Such spills would be difficult or impossible to observe when the surface water is frozen, or during the wet season, when the Oahe Reservoir tends to drain, through the sand and gravel soils, into underground aquifers that lie between the reservoir and the pipeline. There is no known plan to assess or address the contamination of the underground aquifers. Dr. Conway recorded a total of thirteen known leaks on the DAPL prior to October 20, 2020.

Legal and direct-action protests of the pipeline have been under way since 2016 to halt construction of the DAPL on the route that passes under the Oahe Reservoir. The Cheyenne River and Standing Rock Sioux nations have alleged that the Oahe Reservoir crossing has or will result in

> treaty rights violations, religious infringement, and environmental degradation in violation of the National Historic Preservation Act (NHPA); the Clean Water Act (CWA); and the National Environmental Preservation Act (NEPA). . . . They argue that an oil spill affecting Lake Oahe would pose an existential threat to the Tribe's rights, culture, and welfare, and would fundamentally undermine its Treaty-protected rights to the integrity of its homelands and the waters that sustain the Tribe.

The U.S. District Court for the District of Columbia denied plaintiffs' request to stop construction, but the Army Corps of Engineers simultaneously agreed to do a more thorough environmental assessment of the Oahe Reservoir crossing, and ultimately a comprehensive environmental impact statement (EIS).

The Trump administration reversed course immediately upon taking office in January 2017, pressing the Army Corps of Engineers to issue all required permits to allow completion and operation of the DAPL. Despite a federal court ruling in March 2020 striking down permits for the DAPL, and a subsequent ruling that pipeline operations must halt pending an EIS and the issuance of new permits, Energy Transfer Partners won the right to continue operating the DAPL on appeal. According to activists, ETP had continued to operate the DAPL illegally, without permits, while the pipeline itself was considered "an encroachment." The battle to halt operation of the DAPL pending a full EIS is ongoing in federal court as of this writing.

Meanwhile, direct-action protests have captured the imagination, interests, and widespread support of Americans in a new way. The Oceti Sakowin and allies, who describe themselves as Water Protectors, have employed a number of novel strategies that have transformed the nature of protest in important ways. The Water Protectors' camp itself was organized and governed by the Oceti Sakowin, with rules for both Native and non-Native allies who wanted to enter the camp and participate in the protest, including cultural and spiritual deference to the Oceti Sakowin's practices and priorities.

In a novel organizing strategy, footage of the camp, of protests, and of police brutalization of Water Protectors were uploaded to Facebook. This didn't just bring in non-Native awareness and support; it helped to create awareness among Native communities and funnel critical resources to the Protectors' camp. Even the accomplished lawyer, judge, and descendant of the San Felipe Pueblo who served as the civil ground coordinator of the Water Protector Legal Collective was first mobilized when she saw Facebook footage of dogs being deployed by police to attack people she sees as kin. Social media also created the opportunity for solidarity and organizing in other Black and Brown communities. For example, a new generation of Muslim activists were drawn to the camp, perhaps seeing recent struggles of the Arab Spring and protests of the Iraq and Afghanistan wars reflected in the images from Standing Rock. That non-Native and Native allies alike would rush to, and not away from, the site of struggle, often at significant personal risk to themselves, felt like a great shift in the American consciousness, opening new possibilities for anti-racist solidarity. Seemingly overnight, in the fall of 2016, defending human rights in Native communities moved from a marginal to a central space in progressive politics, against a backdrop of rising international Indigenous rights activism.

There are now 574 federally recognized tribes in the United States, and they remain more vulnerable than any other demographic in the country today, with the highest rates of chronic illness and suicide and the lowest rates of life expectancy, postsecondary education, and employment. They are still far more likely than other racial or ethnic groups to experience violence or be victims of a sexual assault or other violent crime. I went looking for the history of Sioux Falls and found a relentless story of colonial displacement and dispossession alongside a ruthless story of violence and forced assimilation. More than 150 years after those first treaties memorializing the dispossession of the Santee, the Oceti Sakowin still lack security on their ancestral land. Despite a rhetorical commitment to liberty and justice for all, American policy is *still* premised on the idea that the existence, health, and success of its own Native peoples are, at best, an inconvenient obstacle. What did that portend for my own twenty-first-century Muslim family?

Elizabeth, a year above me at college, had invited me to move in with her and a few other students at the Tree House beginning in my third year, just as I returned from my summer at the Gateway Ranch and SJDI. The Tree House was a hub of communal, sweet, musical off-campus life. It was home to several members of Yeehaw Junction, the popular campus band, and hosted Sunday evening "family dinners" for housemates and guests, by invitation. By the time I was invited to the Tree House, Aaron and I had been hosting similar off-campus potlucks at the place we shared with Laura. I probably seemed to Elizabeth a good fit for the house's culture. Still, I was surprised at the invitation. I thought of the Tree House as the home of the "big kids" and I still felt very much like a "little kid." Elizabeth made clear that Aaron wasn't included in the invitation. Couples wrecked the house vibe, she thought. I was planning to say no, but Aaron thought maybe it was a sign that it was time for him to head back up to Gainesville and finish his own coursework.

There was both a lot to love about living at the Tree House and a lot to hate. I was allergic to the mold growing on and in the house but had never before experienced allergies. So, I felt sick a lot and didn't know why. But evenings in the house were magical. Nathan, who I would visit in Israel the following year, lived there then, and would periodically take breaks from studying philosophy to walk into the center foyer, roaring, "Jah, Rastafari!" When asked what the heck he was shouting about, he'd give a complex and fascinating talk about the relationship between the Hebrew Yahweh and the Rastas' Jah or Yah, or summarize whatever else he'd been studying. I loved Sundays, when everyone in the house shared equally the task of cleaning the always-sandy house and then worked together to make dinner for the six of us and all our friends. But I hated the expectation that anyone who cooked, at any time, would make a meal large enough for a crowd. I'd come from a long line of women who spent much of their waking hours preparing every meal from scratch for a large family and had no interest then in joining them.

In my final year at college, I moved up to a room on the second floor of the Tree House, where Elizabeth had installed a bed that hung from the exposed rafters. It was a room befitting a tree house, and Nora, the Tennessean who would become one of my closest friends, had taken the room across the hall. By my final semester, Aaron had graduated and was back in town. I mostly made my own schedule as I worked on the senior thesis required for graduation, leaving time for long walks with Aaron on the bayfront. One evening, I asked Aaron what he planned to do next, after both of us had graduated. Having abandoned my applications to graduate school in favor of going to visit Nathan the previous winter, I hadn't given it much thought.

"I don't know. Maybe I'll go up to Illinois where the SJDI folks are."

"Really?" I was stunned. I'd thought we'd make plans together. I was pretty sure, though, based on my summer in Sioux Falls, I wasn't interested in a community centered on SJDI.

"I don't know. I was just thinking about it."

"I'm just a little surprised. It didn't even seem like you enjoyed being at SJDI."

"Maybe I could finally get paid for activism and organizing somewhere. What do you want to do?" Aaron backtracked quickly.

"I don't know. I might want to apply to graduate school next December. I was going to check out the career center listings. But I was thinking we'd go someplace together." Aaron seemed less sure, and I had a hard time containing my confusion. While he was in Gainesville, I'd sometimes felt like our relationship was a convenience for him, that he stuck around because I was his anchor on my campus and its crunchy, progressive social scene. That was too painful for me to reconcile. I knew he was not committed, but I didn't allow that to change anything at all. Not the trust I had in him, not the love I had for him, not the dependence I had on him. We continued to make plans together and I let myself believe that was enough.

The internet was still in its infancy, no help in searching for jobs, so I was limited to the photocopied job announcements in the career center's three-ring binder. I started applying to anything that involved social justice and Aaron sent out a few résumés, as well. Later that spring, I accepted a job with the Association of Community Organizations for Reform Now (ACORN) in Little Rock, which was a well-known community organizing network with offices across the country, and Aaron with a nonprofit in the same town. We were happy to know what was next, even if we had very little understanding of what we'd be doing there, beyond that both organizations would be working to get an initiative on the statewide ballot that fall.

Despite the distance that remained between my family and me, both my older brother and my mother flew down to Sarasota for graduation. My brother, who was in graduate school in Boston, had actually come to visit me in the wooden house the year before, laughing at its cracks and crevices and how it was, he said, "very granola." But he also admired the things I could do that he couldn't, for the first time in my memory. I could drive a stick shift, and I could hold my own in a conversation with him about his own major, economics. When they came for graduation, both my mother and my brother seemed to accept my life as it was. Aaron was there, and they were warm with him. We didn't all share any meals together, or have any extended discussions, but I'd started to wonder if my worlds could meet without being destroyed.

CHAPTER EIGHT

URBAN RENEWAL
Little Rock, Arkansas

*Nobody hates us as ourselves. . . . They don't hate us because we
did something or said something. They make us stand for an
evil they invent and then they want to kill it in us.*
—Marge Piercy

I t can be jarring for a kid from the Northeast to drive into a town like
Little Rock, Arkansas. I was used to the urban and suburban sprawl
in southeastern Pennsylvania or on the Gulf Coast of Florida, where
Tampa Bay tumbled into St. Petersburg, through Bradenton and Sarasota, all connected by the Tamiami Trail. But Little Rock emerged
suddenly, a disconnected mirage of a city in the Arkansas River valley
as we came over a hill on Highway 40.

After I graduated in 1996, Aaron and I packed a U-Haul with a
couple of mattresses, some bricks and boards we'd turn into a book-
case, a futon, and loads and loads of books—everything we owned at
the time. I showed up to work at a creaky, messy Victorian house that
had been converted into ACORN's office. After spending the summer petitioning for a campaign finance reform ballot initiative, I'd be
organizing low-income voters around issues like healthcare, housing,
and voting rights.

I was idealistic about Little Rock. I had read (and watched that

PBS series) about school desegregation there during the civil rights movement and believed that, while it had been violently opposed by the town's White population, it had also been largely successful. I had not yet learned how civil rights history is frequently told to focus on a sliver of a victory while in reality White America grows new strategies to maintain its primacy. In 1996, focused as I was on that sliver of a victory, I assumed that any progressive group in Little Rock would reflect the racial diversity of the town and that women as well as men would be in leadership positions.

That summer, all of us on staff at ACORN went out to Walmart parking lots and the summer festivals held in small towns across the state to collect signatures on petitions. We were trying to get an initiative on the state ballot that would limit campaign contributions for state and local political races. Each of us would roam, usually alone, for eight hours at a stretch, trying to engage strangers in conversations without getting tossed out for trespassing or loitering. Then we'd go back to the office for a few more hours of meetings, administrative tasks, and phone banking.

The script for petitioning was innocuous enough, even boring:

"Are you interested in trying to get big money out of Arkansas politics?"

"Would you like to get a law on the November ballot that would limit large campaign contributions?"

"Remember to vote yes on Act 1 in November!"

Many of the people I found myself addressing responded by ignoring me, but White women, in particular, often also found ways to suggest I was somewhere I didn't belong—that is, in front of them, speaking. "But . . . what *are* you?" one woman asked as she reached out and grasped at my hair. I swallowed my alarm. Another asked, "And what's your *last* name?" My first name and my appearance did just enough to reveal my foreignness in Arkansas. Many more made the observation, "You're not from 'round here, are you?" My first four weeks all over Arkansas, like that bus from Flagstaff to Sioux Falls, taught me that there were some places in America where race is policed more fastidiously than others. It taught me that if I did manage to pass, it was entirely at the discretion of the nearest White people, some of whom felt entitled to do a hands-on assessment of my person.

I had wanted to be out in the world, organizing, but the experience of doing that in Arkansas compounded the already difficult transition away from my tiny college campus, where I had substituted the approval and support of my peers, especially Aaron, for that of my family. In Little Rock, I had neither my friends nor my family, and strangers on the street felt free to question my humanity.

Then I got my first paycheck. Having worked the exact same hours, hired at the same meager salary as my cohort of young hires, my paycheck was still a couple of hundred dollars short of theirs. So I asked about it, and when my boss couldn't come up with a reasonable explanation for the difference, he agreed to fix it. I was already reeling at the overt racism I'd encountered while petitioning. It was humiliating, like the sexualized danger I'd felt on the bus from Flagstaff to Sioux Falls, being pulled out of prayers at the ISCJ mosque, and Ms. Cunningham's constant fury in third grade at my Levittown public school.

I was also confused by and uncomfortable with the internal politics of ACORN. I'd expected an organization that reflected and took its lead from the largely Black community for which it was advocating. Instead, the administrators and sometimes senior organizers, all but one of whom were White, set the organization's priorities and the same two volunteers, both Black women, were handed scripts at public events, expected to read out what had been written for them as the public faces of the organization. There was little room for criticism, especially coming from new field organizers, but also coming from the community we were supposedly serving. The expectation was that a good organizer would put their head down, work a lot of hours for little money, and then either, if they couldn't hack it, be churned out in the constant staff turnover, or, after several years, join the group of about five people who formed the core administrative team. The paycheck was really an excuse for me to leave. I didn't want to be there, and I didn't yet know anyone in town who'd understand why not, not even Aaron.

I hit a wall then, unsure of what I was doing in Little Rock, suddenly aware of how little held me there, but not sure where else I might want to be. I had no social network, no friends, no real sense of what I'd do there next. I was exhausted from the move, and anxious. I told Aaron I was going to take a couple of weeks to figure it all out and holed up in our apartment with a stack of Marge Piercy novels and some watercolors, reading and painting postcards to send to friends scattered across the country.

My move to Little Rock was entirely beyond my parents' comprehension. It felt so far away from the East Coast, a dozen small towns and lots of farmland from the state line in any direction. I had moved to the Deep South for a job that barely paid the minimum wage (even less if you took into account the long workdays). My parents' expectation was that I would go to graduate school, ideally professional school, and learn a skill with which I could support myself for the rest of my life. That is the expectation, with its emphasis on education, that first-generation immigrants and other Black and Brown people often have, knowing that the best possible chance we can give a child for success, and perhaps even survival, is education. Learning a skill, we hope, will allow our children to transcend some of the discrimination and hostility of their environment with status, or accomplishment, or the sheer value they create with their labors. Because education can confer knowledge, wealth, and power, many of us will surrender or withstand almost anything to obtain it and provide it for our children.

Forty years before I arrived in Little Rock, the city had, of course, been the epicenter of Black America's struggle for school desegregation, one of the defining moments of twentieth-century America.

The desegregation of Central High made famous the image of young Elizabeth Eckford walking determinedly toward the school with two angry White women just behind her, jeering menacingly, and behind them a mob of grown White men, women, and armed police officers. But, interested as I had always been in this history, most of what I knew about those events came from a snapshot in time provided by the *Eyes on the Prize* series I'd watched during my shifts in the campus media center. As I began to explore the history of the color line in Little Rock, I found I was missing much of the context for those events. I was ignorant of what preceded them and especially, of their aftermath, in which school segregation was reestablished and made more intractable than it ever had been, through seemingly mundane municipal development projects, with federal funds.

In the years leading up to Central High's desegregation, lawsuits had been filed across the country attacking segregation in public schools. School segregation meant that White children got access to classrooms in decent or good repair, reasonable class sizes and teaching resources, and bused transportation, while Black children made do with poor facilities, where they sometimes performed janitorial work themselves, studied in large classes with children of all ages and abilities, and walked long distances without busing, if they could walk to any school at all. In 1954, the Supreme Court decided the landmark *Brown v. Board of Education* case, marking the end of the "separate but equal" era that had been established under *Plessy v. Ferguson*. The Court found that in the context of schools, separate was inherently unequal, making all school segregation laws invalid.

Almost immediately, some scattered school boards in the South integrated schools by admitting Black students, which reduced the public cost of maintaining racially separate facilities and eliminated untenable commutes for Black students. This happened in Fayetteville, Charleston, and Hoxie, Arkansas, with relatively little conflict. However, the Arkansas governor, Orval Faubus, ran a successful campaign opposing "mandatory methods" of desegregation, invoking concerns about "communism" being imposed on the "Christian people" of the state, and "creating ill-will" between Black and White communities. At the national level, the Supreme Court decision in *Brown* was followed by another decision, known as *Brown II,* which softened the federal stance by presenting options for more gradual integration.

After Faubus's pronouncements and *Brown II,* the Little Rock school board announced a delayed plan of desegregating the city's public schools, to begin in 1957 with high school students and then eventually to include the city's middle and elementary schools. The Little Rock school board conditioned the desegregation of Central High on the completion of new high school buildings in the far western and the far eastern parts of the city. Each of these would serve areas for which segregationists and housing developers had plans. With aggressive new development, West Little Rock was to become an overwhelmingly White enclave. It would be built adjacent to White places of business, hospitals, the university, and City Hall, which stretched across the northern part of the city alongside the river, right into downtown. Black residents would be pushed to the south, out of the downtown core, and concentrated in the east end of the city. With schools in each of these areas, the board hoped to maintain school segregation as a function of municipal segregation, an intention they made clear by hiring an all-White teaching staff for Hall High School to the west and an all-Black teaching staff for Horace Mann High School in the east.

As a September 1957 deadline to integrate the schools approached, the Arkansas state legislature passed three bills to maintain segregation and to destroy further efforts at school integration in the state. These bills made attendance at integrated schools voluntary (which began the still hot debate around "school choice" as a means to maintain segregation), required registration of people and organizations involved in civil rights, and allowed school boards to use school funds to oppose integration lawsuits.

In the summer of 1957, the Little Rock school board subjected Black students who hoped to study at Central High to an application and vetting process, in which they were told that attendance at Central High would mean forgoing participation in any extracurricular activities, which would remain Whites-only. Nine Black students were ultimately approved, but segregationists continued to fight. In the final days leading up to the start of school, a local court granted an injunction to delay integration, which was then overturned in federal court by a judge named Ronald Davies, who had been appointed to the federal bench by President Eisenhower just two years before.

On the night before school was to begin, Governor Faubus announced that he'd gotten information about White supremacists from all over the state heading to Little Rock to cause trouble, and he'd had to call in 250 National Guardsmen, ostensibly to protect students and staff from the unrest they intended to create. Faubus went on to say that because of the threat, no Black children would be allowed to attend Central High School after all. This was widely understood as an attempt to again delay integration. A White mob gathered to enforce his directive. All but one of the nine Black children who had planned to attend Central that day got word about these announcements from their mentor and the head of the state NAACP, Daisy Bates. But Elizabeth Eckford's family did not have a phone. Worse still, prior to Faubus's announcement, the school superintendent had demanded that the nine students attend alone, without parents or trusted adults, saying that it would make it easier for the National Guard troops to protect the children.

So, when Elizabeth arrived, she walked toward the school by herself, thinking that she would find her eight brave Black classmates waiting to join her. Instead, Elizabeth was met with the threats and jeers of a crowd of White adults shouting, "Get her!" "Lynch her!" "Get a rope and drag her over to this tree!" Although she had forgone the support of her community in order to secure the protection of the Arkansas National Guard, the guardsmen made no effort to step in, instead blocking her entrance and raising their bayonets so she was at the mercy of the crowd. She escaped with the help of a *New York Times* reporter and the wife of a professor at the traditionally Black

Philander Smith College, who helped her to board a bus, and rode with her all the way to where her mother worked.

Unaware of what had happened to Elizabeth, Ms. Bates had organized ministers, two Black and two White, to chaperone the rest of the children into the building later in the morning, in spite of the governor's announcement. They approached the National Guard captain and were turned away on the order of Governor Faubus, but Faubus had miscalculated. Even under *Brown II,* the use of National Guardsmen to maintain segregation was too direct an assault on federal authority. The NAACP sought an injunction to prevent Governor Faubus and the National Guard from interfering with the integration of Central High.

By September 20, the matter was heard by Judge Davies, the same federal judge who had first ordered the school integrated by overturning a state injunction only weeks before. He granted the injunction, and the following Monday morning, September 23, the children and their parents gathered at Ms. Bates's house, where they prayed together, and then the nine entered Central High through a side entrance with a sizeable police escort. A violent White mob assembled outside became uncontrollable, shouting for shotguns and threatening to drag the children out of the building. The violence began to tumble through the neighborhood; White racists took two Black women from their car and beat them. Black men in a truck were also beaten and their windows smashed with a rock. Shortly after they escorted the nine children into the Central High School building, the police force realized they were unable to protect them from the escalating violence outside. They quickly led the children to escape through the rear delivery area of the school and back to their homes.

The fever pitch of the angry White crowd would not dissipate, and was instead vented violently on reporters and writers, and then any Black person in the city. Friends, journalists, and other activists took turns helping to guard Ms. Bates's home. Someone had thrown a rock through the Bateses' window, and they were getting regular telephone threats. A group of White people who had dynamite, guns, and clubs in their cars was stopped by the police.

On September 24, 1957, President Eisenhower stepped in to end the Whites-only blockade of Central High. He federalized more than ten thousand of the Arkansas National Guard troops, and the secretary of defense sent in a thousand paratroopers from the 101st Airborne Division of the 327th Army Infantry Regiment. Although this would be the decisive factor in those nine children gaining entry to Central High, Ms. Bates remarked, "Any time it takes eleven thousand five hundred soldiers to assure nine Negro children their constitutional right in a democratic society, I can't be happy."

The sentiment was prescient; Ms. Bates understood precisely what violent racist resistance meant for the children who would come to be known as the Little Rock Nine. Once within the school, they would be surrounded by many of the children whose parents had made up the racist mob outside. Their attendance at school would be a superhuman struggle of patience and fortitude every day. The children were subjected to ridicule and humiliation, physical attacks and threats. Their sacrifice tells the naked story of American bigotry and entitlement: Where education is the doorway to achievement, the powerful have insisted that it is theirs, and have worked to keep it exclusively for themselves, spending decades and untold resources to make it traumatic and unpalatable for others to get in and to stay in.

I retell this well-known history to set the scene for its less wellknown aftermath, which was *not* the successful integration of Little Rock. Black children in 1957 America were yet no more human in the eyes of White adults than were Native children in the era of Pratt or free Black children in the age of Harper. After the integration of Central High, the goal of the White power structure in the city remained to shut Black children away, at the greatest distance possible, extracting their parents' labor and eventually their labor while giving the very least in return. The governor, municipal officials, and White suburban families would successfully pursue this priority in the following decades. It would continue to shape the culture of Little Rock even in the late 1990s, so that my racially ambiguous body seemed to disrupt the carefully drawn Black-White divide in the city, wherever I went.

I needed an income fast after leaving ACORN. I started working at Little Rock's health food store, at the far west end of Highway 630 and across town from my apartment, which was on the eastern edge, right on the dividing line between the north and south sides. Driving Highway 630, the road that enabled White flight in the city, would be my personal introduction to the deep segregation of Little Rock and the struggle against it, which plainly did not end with the National Guard escorting nine Black children into Central High.

While still working full-time at the health food store, I also found the very best of Little Rock, entirely by accident. On the way to ACORN each morning, I had passed a beautiful old Victorian house, unmarked except for a sign out front that read THE WOMEN'S PROJECT. It didn't look like a shelter or a commune or a business from the outside, but neither did it seem like a private home. On a rare day off from work, I rode my bike over the bridge across the eastern end of Highway 630 to find out.

There was a single car in the driveway, but the building was otherwise quiet. After I knocked, the door finally opened, just a sliver, and then a few inches wider. Lynn, who was there working in the small library at the back of the building, was accustomed to getting all kinds of strange walk-up visitors. I explained that I was just curious about the sign out front, that I had come to the city to work for ACORN but was interested to learn what the other nonprofits and service organizations around town were. Lynn opened the door a little wider, but still cautiously, to check out the driveway.

"But how did you get here?"

"I rode my bike; it's right there, leaning against the building."

That seemed to reassure her that I was safe to let in. Stopping in that day turned out to be the very best thing I could have done. The Women's Project was a beacon in Arkansas for women who were, in one way or another, on the margins of an already deeply misogynistic culture. Its projects were straightforward, with direct impacts for the people they served, including undocumented farmworkers, incarcerated women, women with AIDS, and LGBTQ women.

In ways I have not seen in any organization since, the Women's Project was also the embodiment of its own ideals. When I was there, four of its small staff of six were women of color. Its founder was a powerhouse of a White woman named Suzanne Pharr, and its executive director was a powerhouse of a Black woman named Janet Perkins. Its staff was at least half LGBTQ and included two women with immigrant backgrounds; the community that showed up to browse the organization's library or to attend its events included women who were sex workers, women living with HIV, women who were differently abled, artists and activists. It paid each of its staff exactly the same salary, prorated for hourly workers, on the principle that women's time and work were equally valuable. That included the woman who came to clean the space after hours. For me, just out of college and painfully underpaid, this was the most humane policy I'd ever heard of. Long-term staff were compensated for their additional experience and contributions with paid sabbaticals and other nonmonetary but valuable benefits.

On my first visit, I told Lynn about my experiences at ACORN and she asked me to come back and meet Suzanne and Janet. She said to bring my résumé. I started working a handful of hours a week there, tracking violence against women as hate crimes in the state. More important, I was adopted into a network of the most beautiful women, who saw the work they did as an extension of who they were and what they believed. Once I was connected to the Women's Project, it felt possible that I could stay in Little Rock for a while. The awful anxiety of my first months in town eased up, just a little bit. Aaron and I relaxed into a new, wider circle of friends, with whom we found our way to Vino's, the local pizza place, on Friday nights, ending the week with comfort food and craft beer. Sunday mornings, we'd head over to the farmer's market on the riverfront to buy fruit and sometimes splurge on a tiny bouquet of wildflowers. One of my friends from college, Holly, came to stay for a couple of months, and

Aaron's new co-worker started hanging around the apartment. It wasn't home, but it was a place where I could catch my breath.

The woman who supervised me at the Women's Project, Judy Matsuoka, was the only other Asian woman I met in Little Rock that year. In fact, she was the only other person I met who was neither Black nor White, unless you counted the statue of a Native woman that stood outside the Arkansas Art Center as a sort of memorial. The Art Center was across a park from our apartment, and I'd started taking ceramics classes there in the evenings while Aaron worked late. I noticed the statue one day as I left for home, thinking I looked a little bit like her, reflecting on how people had responded to me when I was petitioning. They'd said, "What *are* you?" but I'd been terrified by the tone they used, which said something like "I thought you all were dead and gone."

As I went looking for a story of our country and a path forward for my family in it, I thought I knew how Little Rock would fit into the tapestry. But the story I found was far more complex, with a far more intentional, malevolent path to resegregation than I had anticipated.

During their first year at Central High, Daisy Bates continued to mentor the Little Rock Nine, recording and later publishing some of their experiences. The nine were routinely spat on, kicked, punched, threatened with acid attacks, knocked down stairs, ridiculed, humiliated, and beaten at school. Often, they were suspended or otherwise disciplined for defending themselves, while even the repeat offenders among White students were let off. They were told that any attack had to have an adult witness to be taken seriously and found that when there were adult witnesses, they were still punished as harshly as the White students who had attacked them. When the paratroopers from the 101st Airborne left in October, the Arkansas National Guardsmen tended to look the other way. Of the nine, Minnijean Brown was the only one expelled; this was in punishment for talking back to a White girl who physically attacked and verbally harassed her. When Ernest Green, who entered as a senior, walked across the stage to become the first Black student to graduate from Central High, 125 federalized National Guardsmen and several municipal police were on hand to protect him. Black journalists were barred from attendance.

By the end of the academic year, Governor Faubus had developed a plan to stop further integration. When he requested that the courts permit a delay of integration until 1961 and was denied, he oversaw passage of legislation that allowed him sweeping authority to simply shut down the schools at will. And then he used that authority to close *all* public high schools the following fall with the intention of leasing them as White, segregated private schools. He blamed Ms. Bates for this, saying, "If [she] would find an honest job and go to work, and if the U.S. Supreme Court would keep its cotton-picking hands off the Little Rock School Board's affairs, we could open the Little Rock schools!" In November 1958, his stance won him an unusual third term in office, after which he would serve an unprecedented additional three terms. Although the courts prevented him from privatizing the schools, the public high schools in the city remained closed for the entire 1958–59 school year.

At the start of that school year, segregationists had organized into a group called Save Our Schools and published arguments in the papers asserting that their desire to delay integration was justified and necessitated by Christianity, and that as "freedom-loving, God-fearing American people, [they would] not bow down by force from anyone." Still, the conflict and disruption had enough of an impact on White business leaders, worried about stagnant investment in the town, and White mothers, upset about their own children's lack of access to education, that over time the segregationists' hard-line position began to lose support. In this context, a more moderate school board was elected, and broke the standoff in the fall of 1959. The high schools reopened, but many of the stakeholders, even those who had pressed to reopen the schools, remained hostile to the NAACP and Black students, who they blamed for disruptions to local education and economy. The students continued to face violence and threats in Little Rock's newly desegregated schools. White power brokers in the city sought a more permanent solution to what they saw as the problem of having free, educated Black people among them. Strategically, they realized that the solution would not be had using the schools as the battleground.

Prior to "urban renewal" efforts, up until about 1940, housing in downtown Little Rock was reasonably integrated, with few completely Black residential districts despite broad segregation in stores and in schools. However, Black residents lacked access to municipal resources and had begun to argue, under the separate but equal doctrine of segregation, that they ought to have access to a city park, recreation facilities, and a pool, just as White residents did. Money was allocated for such a recreation center, but the land designated for it was far to the southeast of the city center, near a mining operation, difficult for builders to reach and inaccessible to most Black residents. There wasn't even a paved road that ran all the way to the site, which had been named Gillam Park.

During the 1940s, the Gillam Park project bled money through gross mismanagement and was haphazardly advanced. For example, a pavilion was built, but the roof was later removed with the approval of several city aldermen and placed on the hay barn at Fair Park Zoo, a Whites-only facility in the city. The unprotected wood pavilion rotted away. By 1950, the site had a completed swimming pool, which leaked within a year and was never fully staffed or utilized because of its location. In 1954, two months after the decision in *Brown v. Board of Education,* a twelve-year-old Black boy named Tommy Grigsby drowned in the pool, which had inadequate safety equipment and was a long ride from the city's hospitals. Gillam Park would languish in disrepair for the next fifty years. Money that had been earmarked for the continued development of Gillam Park was redirected in the late 1950s, used as a match to draw down newly available federal funding for "urban renewal" projects.

By the time the Central High standoff resulted in "the Lost Year" for the children of Little Rock, the city had already begun using federal urban renewal money intended for slum clearance and low-income housing development to concentrate Black residents in the southeastern part of the city, away from the downtown core on the Arkansas River to the north. Most of the homes slated for slum clearance were the property of Black homeowners and many of them were modern, fully functional, and on prime real estate in desirable parts of town. For example, the Dunbar neighborhood of the downtown core had been home to a substantial Black middle class before more than two hundred homes were torn down. Once the city targeted their homes for demolition, Black homeowners were forced to sell their property for very little under threat of eviction.

As it destroyed Black-owned homes in other parts of town, the city built public housing to the southeast, 99 percent of which would eventually be occupied by Black residents. Restrictive covenants and redlining were implemented to keep Black residents from getting mortgages and buying back into the downtown core and the western suburbs. Real estate agents steered Black home buyers away from White areas. And just as in Levittown, Pennsylvania, the effect was persistent segregation, locking would-be Black home buyers out of the opportunity to build wealth—or to maintain the wealth they'd already built—through investing in their homes. City officials understood that by using "urban renewal" as a pretext to segregate residential areas, they could create a situation in which most other city services and institutions remained segregated by default.

On top of all of that, in 1956, $25 billion in new federal money became available for highways across the country, intended to improve national security and support the postwar economy. Highways were an essential part of the vision of major suburban developers all over the country in the late 1950s and early 1960s because they could ensure that mostly White, middle-class suburban home buyers retained full access to business corridors and city jobs while efficiently returning them to segregated enclaves in the new suburbs.

There had been talk of a highway that would run from the easternmost edge of downtown Little Rock out to the not-yet-developed western suburbs as early as the 1930s. But it was in 1958, the first spring in which Black students attended Central High and the first fall in which the governor shut down the city's public schools in response, that city and state officials revisited the idea and began to plan in earnest. The 7.5-mile highway city officials envisioned was a wide concrete barrier between White people in the north and west of the city and Black people increasingly concentrated in the southeast. Over the next twenty-seven years, despite substantial community protest, Little Rock officials would build the highway, like a wall through the city.

During my year in Little Rock, I lived in an apartment tucked right up against the northeastern end of Highway 630, a short walk away from MacArthur Park. We had thought we'd chosen our apartment freely, but in retrospect it was right on the line, exactly where one might place a young, low-income, mixed White and South Asian couple in accordance with the prevailing segregation of the place. Our apartment was just a few blocks from the once thriving Black business district along West Ninth Street, which had been bisected by the highway. By 1996, West Ninth Street was a ghost town, not much more than a stretch of vacant lots and abandoned storefronts. But by the mid-1990s no one seemed to give the highway or the social landscape that it had created a second thought. It was as if the blight had always existed rather than having been engineered.

In fact, the city had worked for a decade to obtain land rights to complete just the first mile of Highway 630 in 1969. That was also the year that the National Environmental Policy Act was passed, requiring planners to provide an environmental impact statement (EIS) for the project, which included reporting the steps taken to minimize the loss of parks and addressing the isolation of "minority" neighborhoods. The EIS also allowed community groups and residents an opportunity to understand and take a position on the planned route in a regulated process. ACORN, for example, expressed the concern that the highway would be a "physical barrier between black and white neighborhoods." However, ACORN was neither able to successfully organize and partner with Black residents nor to gain the necessary support of journalists, businesspeople, or politicians to stop the project.

Since its completion, the highway has allowed White workers to come into a largely White downtown, avoiding local roads and predominantly Black neighborhoods to the south of the highway. It shaped the flow of goods, services, and workers in a way that encouraged developers to build vast suburban housing developments sprawling beyond the western edge of town. Eventually, those suburbs would make up their own separate part, almost 40 percent, of a redefined Little Rock, with its own, mostly White, schools.

Nearly two decades after the battle to integrate Central High, the city implemented a public school busing strategy to bring White children in from the west and Black kids out from the east, mitigating the new era of school segregation that had resulted from "urban renewal" and "highway development." The number of private schools in West Little Rock quickly doubled. Public schools were simply abandoned by large numbers of White families in favor of private schools, which were de facto segregated. Today, only 19 percent of students in Little Rock public schools are White, although just over half the city's residents are.

In Little Rock, as in many other American cities from the 1950s through the 1970s, the dislocation of largely Black neighborhoods and businesses was dismissed by White officials as a collateral effect of important infrastructure programs. Highways, public housing complexes, and private schools were effectively used to carve permanent racial disparity into the landscape. From the historical record, we know that this was often intentional. Alfred Johnson, executive director of the American Association of State Highway Officials at the time the National Interstate and Defense Highways Act was passed, recalled, "Some city officials expressed the view in the mid-1950s that the urban Interstates would give them a good opportunity to get rid of the local 'n****rtown.'"

More than fifty years later, the problem of school segregation in

Little Rock is still making headlines. In January 2015, the State of Arkansas took over the city's schools because of failed quality assessments in several of them that served a high proportion of students of color. Five years later, with the number of troubled schools climbing, the state proposed that it would retain control of most of the city's schools but relinquish the whiter, better-performing schools—all of the schools north of Highway 630 except one—to municipal control. The proposal caused an uproar, with residents feeling this would create yet another institutional barrier to integration by splitting the administration of the city's public schools along racial lines, leaving schools with more Black students governed by remote and inaccessible state officials. Subsequent proposals have left the balance of power murky, and the integration of Little Rock schools no closer to resolution.

In fact, because White municipal officials, city planners, and school board members have spent the past several decades using varied tools and plenty of federal money to make sure that the Black people of their town remain on the other side of a six-lane highway, the integration of Little Rock schools, and the town itself, is substantially more difficult today than it was in 1957.

A similar story about the racist function of federal urban renewal funding and highway planning can be found in most, if not all, of America's urban centers today. Predominantly Black West Oakland is contained by I-580, I-880, and I-980. State Route 40, the sunken six-lane artery also known as "the road to nowhere," was built through Baltimore's Black middle-class Ninth District neighborhood and divides the city's north and south sides. In Detroit, the historic "Black Bottom" neighborhood was cleared as a slum, replaced by freeways, hospitals, and universities. St. Paul, Pittsburgh, Flint, Orlando, Los Angeles, Charlotte, Miami, Birmingham, Atlanta—all of these cities and many more in America have a story about a highway built on the rubble of or to segregate a Black community.

A couple of months after arriving in Little Rock, I left the health food store to work full-time at Advocates for Battered Women, keeping my handful of hours at the Women's Project. The only residential women's shelter in Little Rock, it was housed in a boxy two-story brick building. My work there was meaningful, if sometimes painful. One woman at the shelter had walked with her three children from the mountains west of the city into Little Rock on bare feet because her abuser took her only pair of shoes with him whenever he left the house. Her youngest, a five-year-old little girl, tiny for her age, wouldn't speak at all. Once, I had to talk a seven-year-old boy off the third-floor stairwell railing post to keep him from jumping. He told me that his father trained their dogs to attack "n****rs." Living in the shelter's dormitories, which served both White and Black women and their children and provided integrated accommodations, the boy was beside himself with rage and confusion.

Before living in Little Rock, I would not have understood how such a child could exist. But segregation was so exact in the environment, so carefully institutionalized, socialized, and maintained, that in people's minds, it was integration and the free movement of people of different skin colors that seemed an unnatural state, something troublesome and forced. That child perched on the railing and threatening to jump was struggling to understand how he could possibly survive it.

The shelter itself was a prime example of the rigor of segregation in the town. Although the dormitories themselves were integrated, the staffing of the shelter was not. When I arrived, administrative staff worked at the front of the building with offices to themselves. These were Anne, the executive director, and Meredith, the volunteer coordinator, both White. The kitchen and the children's play space were at the back of the building, with an office shared by advocates who worked directly with women and children also at the back, up a flight of stairs. When I arrived, all of the advocates for women and children were Black except me.

Working half a day at the front of the building and half a day in the children's space, I was the only one who moved regularly between the segregated spaces to do her work. My office on the administrative side was furthest back, toward the shelter, and my workspace on the other side of the building was downstairs, nearest the administrative offices. Neither White nor Black, my in-between body landed physically on the line of racial demarcation, kind of like our apartment. It's not that Black advocates never came to the front of the building for staff meetings, or to use office equipment, or that White administrators wouldn't enter the back of the building to help out. In fact, midway through the year I was there, the head advocate, Alma, was provided a desk in a shared office with Meredith at the front of the building in addition to another at the back. Nonetheless, the premise of the building was the premise of the town; it hinged on people knowing and returning to their places, no matter who they might befriend or what status they might achieve.

The staff was silent about the reality of segregation within the shelter, as if it were too distasteful to discuss among generally liberal company, and too intractable to ever challenge. And there was silence about the long history that kept segregation in place. At a staff meeting early on, I came into the group where Anne, Meredith, and a court advocate were talking about vacationing in Eureka Springs, a beautiful and popular spot in the Ozarks northwest of the city. Still new to town, I asked about it, and noticed all of the shelter advocates go silent. I asked Alma about it later, and she explained that Eureka Springs was close to the town of Zinc, to the headquarters of a branch of the Ku Klux Klan. "Only White folks go up there."

I went looking for Judy Matsuoka, my supervisor at the Women's Project, twenty-five years later, when I returned to Little Rock in the fall of 2019. I wanted to know why a Japanese American woman in her thirties had chosen to live in Little Rock, as segregated as it was and as conspicuous as our Asian faces had been there. I wondered if her family had been taken there during the Japanese internment. No one I knew was still in touch with her, and I kept hitting walls.

After visiting with Suzanne and Lynn, I drove out to the Japanese American Internment Museum in McGehee, Arkansas. The woman staffing it recognized Judy's name immediately, saying, "her family was at Jerome, a few miles down the road." By Jerome, she meant one of the World War II concentration camps in which people of Japanese ancestry from the West Coast—two-thirds of them American citizens—were locked up between 1942 and 1946. After spending some time in the museum, I took a dusty drive out along two-lane Highway 165 to where the Jerome camp had been, eighteen miles away. I missed the spot at first, turning around on one of Jerome's three short residential streets, each with just a few houses. It was the kind of place where people stop to watch a car they don't recognize; I passed a sign that read JEROME, POPULATION 39.

On the land across the narrow highway from that cluster of homes, nearly every trace of the barracks that housed eight thousand prisoners is now gone. There is a lonely memorial off the driveway to a privately owned farm, and beyond it, a smokestack from what used to be the hospital incinerator rising straight out of an enormous flat field. Standing in that place, I saw immediately why the War Relocation Authority chose it as a site for internment. It was isolated, with land on which prisoners would be expected to grow their own food. It was close to the railroad but not near any station.

The Jerome and Rohwer war relocation centers, named for tiny towns just twenty-seven miles apart from each other in the southeastern corner of Arkansas, were the last two concentration camps to be built in America during World War II. In all, there were ten camps, most of them scattered west of the Rocky Mountains, and they would hold more than 110,000 ethnically Japanese prisoners. One of the camps was at Bosque Redondo, New Mexico, the same barren place in which thousands of Diné had died nearly eighty years before.

The Japanese Internment was a domestic response to the attack on Pearl Harbor on December 7, 1941, which also launched American military involvement in World War II. Along with Pearl Harbor, Japanese forces had attacked Singapore, Guam, Wake Island, British Hong Kong, and the Philippines. President Franklin Roosevelt was concerned about a strike on the West Coast and, on the later discredited advice of General John DeWitt, inferred that people of Japanese ancestry living in California, Oregon, and Washington, whether they were citizens or not, posed a threat to national security. Roosevelt issued an executive order on February 19, 1942, allowing the secretary of war to create military zones on the West Coast and granting him complete discretion to exclude people from those zones. Within weeks, the FBI was rounding up Japanese and Japanese American community leaders and had frozen the bank accounts of ethnically Japanese people not born in the United States.

Months after I traveled to Little Rock, an alum of the Women's Project called me to say she'd found Judy. I'd begun to think Judy didn't want to be found, but instead learned I'd gotten an email address wrong, and Judy had spent much of the previous three years caring for her bedridden partner of many years before her death in 2016, with little time to check social media messages. Over the phone, Judy and I caught up and then had a conversation about how strange it had been to be neither Black nor White in Arkansas. She'd moved there for a job, she said, but also to unearth her family's connection to the camps at Jerome and Rohwer.

Judy's father was born in California, where her paternal grandfather had migrated from Japan in 1905 to avoid the Russo-Japanese War. When he arrived, California was less than hospitable. Under the federal Naturalization Act of 1870, only "free White persons" and those of African descent were permitted to naturalize as American citizens, making first-generation Japanese immigrants like Judy's grandfather ineligible for citizenship. In 1905, the San Francisco Board of Education declared that it would send Japanese children to existing "Chinese schools" to avoid a situation where White children's "youthful impressions might be affected by association with pupils of the Mongolian race." By 1909, the California state legislature introduced approximately seventeen anti-Japanese measures, eventually narrowed to three bills aimed at preventing land ownership, enforcing school segregation, and enacting municipal segregation.

Many families who were transported to Jerome and the other camps had nonetheless owned their homes and been successful farmers, fishermen, and small business owners in California. In 1942, the California Farm Bureau reported that Japanese American farmers were responsible for growing 40 percent of the state's fruit and vegetable crops, including almost 100 percent of celery, tomatoes, strawberries, and peppers. Their growing wealth and importance in America's food economy had already made them a target of relentless attacks aimed at moving their land and their wealth back into the hands of White Californians. When the federal government announced the mandatory evacuation of all people of Japanese ancestry from the West Coast, the Japanese community was forced to sell land, equipment, retail or restaurant inventory, cars, and personal belongings for pennies on the dollar, even leaving behind family pets. The only alternatives were to leave possessions behind to be seized by the government or to store them at the risk that they would be looted. Those who were interned lost an estimated two to five billion dollars' worth of wealth in 2017 currency; their losses were a tremendous windfall in real estate and other assets to their White neighbors, who made up more than 95 percent of Californians at the time.

Judy's grandfather had made a living as a vegetable farmer until World War II. In 1942, he was forcibly removed with his wife and his citizen children to the Santa Anita racetrack, where they were housed in the stables for several months. After that, most of the family spent four days on board trains under armed guard, the journey extra long because their train would have given way to those carrying wartime military troops. Ultimately, they reached a shoddy government concentration camp on a swampy stretch of agricultural land in the Arkansas delta, where most of the family would remain for more than two years, behind barbed-wire fences broken by guard towers, until Jerome was closed and everyone was transferred to nearby Rohwer.

Judy's father, Yoji (Lewis) Matsuoka, avoided Jerome when he was drafted into the military, instead completing basic training in North Little Rock. He served in the Military Intelligence Service headquarters as an interpreter and translator during the war before getting a job as a house servant in Chicago, working his way through college classes to learn shorthand and court reporting. Outside of camp, he'd avoided completing the form on which the interned were asked to attest to their willingness to serve in armed combat for the United States, despite being held against their will by the government, and to foreswear allegiance or obedience to the emperor of Japan. The "loyalty oath" form caused panic for those in the camp: What would happen if those interned pledged these things in writing but then were deported by the government back to Japan? Would the first generation, who had been precluded from naturalization in the United States, like Judy's grandfather, become stateless if they renounced Japan? And could a Japanese American depend on the protection of a government that had already relegated them to a concentration camp? Although these questions were reasonable and were of existential importance to the people in the camps, they went unanswered. Those who refused to answer, answered incorrectly, or even wrote in qualifiers to their answers to the loyalty oath provisions were removed to the maximum-security concentration camp at Tule Lake, California, or to county jails.

By 1950, Lewis had met and married Judy's mother, Fusa Hirata, whose family had avoided internment by having immigrated from Japan to the East Coast rather than the West Coast. Still, their lives were shaped by an era in which their country had made them the enemy based on their ethnicity. They raised their children with Western names and no fluency in Japanese, in a mostly White suburb of Chicago. Judy explained that they were raised to be "200 percent American," and told to answer, if anyone asked where they were from, simply that they were American. After Jerome closed and then nearby Rohwer, Judy's grandparents returned to California with their daughter and her husband. Judy's grandfather died in 1951, surviving just a few years after his release from camp, like many first-generation, or Issei, Japanese immigrants. Many of those who avoided internment, like Judy's parents, were traumatized nonetheless, unable to explain the history of the camps to their children and grandchildren, and driven in their attempts to assimilate.

In my search for Judy, I'd crossed paths with a woman who would have been interned at Jerome during the same period as her family. Ninety-two-year-old Rinko Shimasaki was only fifteen years old when she boarded a bus from her hometown of Strathmore to the Fresno Assembly Center in California. Along with her mother, Hatsu Shimasaki, she and her seven siblings were responding to the flyers circulating in their neighborhood requiring "all persons of Japanese ancestry" to gather at Fresno, leaving behind everything except what they could carry. Her family would be detained there, sleeping on sacks they'd been told to stuff with straw, using shared latrines, just a row of six holes about fifty yards from where they slept, until they departed several weeks later for Jerome. Her eldest brother, Toshimi (Tom), who had a wife and a young child of his own, with one more on the way, had only recently reappeared after having been taken by the FBI for questioning. Like the families of many male community leaders and heads of household, the family had been given no information about where he had been taken, or even when and whether he would return. This was an effective way to circumvent any resistance to the Internment: Those most likely to lead such a resistance were or had recently been in FBI custody, which was enough to intimidate them and their family members into compliance.

The Shimasakis owned very little and piled all of what they did have into Tom's small bunkhouse, leaving the strawberry patch he owned in the care of a neighbor. The rest of the family had lived in a rented house on the farm that Rinko's parents had worked for the owner, Mr. Crawford, until Rinko's father passed away some years before the war. After his death, Hatsu continued to work the farm, and to prepare simple meals for the other workers, and for her children. They left Mr. Crawford's property with little idea of what would happen to their family next.

Rinko's brother Shizuo (Sam) was taken ahead to Jerome, to clear and prepare the site that would eventually be covered in rows of barracks, 20 by 120 feet long. These would be divided into rooms by walls that didn't quite reach the ceiling, furnished with only a stove for heat and cots for beds, and each family would be assigned a room to share. Sam and two of his brothers would eventually be permitted to leave camp to serve in the military. The desire to demonstrate one's loyalty during wartime was especially strong among Japanese Americans. Doing so could provide opportunities to get better jobs and training and to earn money as well as freedom from camps, including the threat of forced removal to the militarized prison camp at Tule Lake. It meant no longer being vulnerable to the routine abuses and humiliations one might endure as a camp prisoner. To leave camp during the war required government permission, and movements outside of the camp were monitored by the War Relocation Authority (WRA). Eventually, in response to advocacy by civil rights and Quaker activists, some Nisei, or second-generation, young people were able to secure leave from camp for college attendance, seasonal agricultural work, or other jobs. Those who successfully applied to leave camp were purposely scattered to areas with low or no Japanese settlement in an effort to force their assimilation outside of California.

There were two all–Japanese American military regiments that fought during World War II. These were largely made up of soldiers from Hawaii, where more than one-third of the peacetime population was ethnically Japanese, and where the internment was limited to a relatively small number of community leaders. When the two regiments trained at Camp Shelby and visited nearby Jerome, the Hawaiian troops were shocked to see that the families of their fellow Japanese servicemen from the mainland were imprisoned there. Japanese American troops were risking their lives fighting a war started by the racist machinations of the Third Reich while many of their own families were being held in American concentration camps based on their ethnicity. The racist rhetoric aimed at the Japanese internees was not so unlike that of the Third Reich. The U.S. representative from Mississippi John E. Rankin responded to wartime rumors that Japanese Americans incarcerated in Wyoming camps had access to unlimited rations of goods by calling Japanese Americans "brutal apes" who needed to be "wiped from the face of the earth."

Back in the camps, Rinko was looking for a way to leave as her brothers and an older sister had done. She was able to secure permission to live in Chicago with her older sister, who with the help of Quaker missionaries had been able to go to college. She was given twenty dollars and a one-way train ticket there, and she found a job in a Baby Ruth candy factory to pay for basic necessities. But she'd had to leave her mother with her two younger brothers in the camp and she was quickly called back when her mother was diagnosed with stomach cancer. Her mother needed more intensive care than could be found at Jerome, so Rinko secured permission and funding to take her mother and brothers to the U.S. Army post in Tooele, Utah, where her brother Tom was working. When they arrived by train, her mother was so ill that she was lifted out of the train's window on a stretcher and immediately admitted to the hospital in Salt Lake City, where she died several days later. Her body was transported back to Lindsay, near Strathmore, where she could be buried next to her husband.

The site of the Rohwer camp still contains a cemetery, where many interned families had no choice but to bury loved ones, far from the places they called home. The cemetery at Tule Lake was bulldozed, the remains of the deceased plowed into a landfill. In the aftermath of the incarceration, the Shimasaki family found itself scattered around the country. Rinko now makes her home in Virginia, next door to her daughter Eileen, while other members of the family are on the West Coast and in the Midwest.

After the war, the Shimasakis and the Matsuokas and Japanese families all over America who had been in the United States for three or more generations continued to battle the presumption that they were "enemy aliens," rhetoric that is remarkably similar to that which would later be used to target American Muslims after 9/11. In 1945, at the end of the war, the California legislature's Joint Committee on Un-American Activities issued a report in which it affirmed retroactively that Japanese people had posed a threat because they were "fanatical in their faith that they are destined to conquer the world" and believe "their cause is holy because it is divinely inspired." Divine inspiration, though considered praiseworthy in the context of Christianity and manifest destiny, was taken as a clear indication of loyalty to Japan rather than the United States in the context of Shintoism.

Perhaps because of the especially intense anti-Japanese sentiment in California, only about 40,000 of the nearly 94,000 who were forced to leave the state in 1942 made the journey back with the assistance of the War Relocation Authority in 1945. The return to California was fraught with painful memories and the threat of violence. Many returning Japanese families were attacked by night riders, modeled on similar anti-Black terror groups in the South, their property targeted by arsonists and vandals.

Aaron and I developed a ritual a few months into our time in Little Rock. "One year or two?" one of us would ask. And the other would always answer "one," meaning we'd leave after a little more than one year in Little Rock, not two. All the pizza and wildflowers in the world couldn't make Little Rock home. A few months in, I'd begun to realize how naïve it was to think I should be organizing in a place and among people where I had such limited relationships. The people I'd most grown to admire were those who were deeply rooted in the community, working to meet the basic needs of the people around them, and basing any broader advocacy on years of staying put, listening, and learning.

I still wasn't sure where my own community would be, and I also wasn't sure how I might be of use in the world. I *was* sure that I didn't want to live paycheck to paycheck for the rest of my life and that I was intellectually bored. I still wanted, as I had at college, to understand more clearly how our society was structured. I wanted to understand why the rich were rich and the poor were poor, how government priorities were set, and why the vulnerable had so little support. Even more than that, I wanted a set of technical skills to offer wherever I finally ended up. So, that winter in Little Rock, I applied to law schools, mostly in the Northeast, though also two in the Midwest. Aaron seemed offended, even a little angry, when I asked him to look at my essays and tell me what he thought, like I was asking him to do something wrong, or something he thought I couldn't manage on my own and that he didn't want to be pulled into. He stayed remote while I was writing applications, not interested even in discussing which schools I was going to apply to. In the end, I went through the process without any input from him and I wasn't sure if that was an indication of a larger intention to push me away.

Aaron and I went on a long hike at a place called Cedar Falls one spring weekend, and I talked about the admission offers I'd gotten. I'd quickly eliminated the law schools closer to my parents' home, not yet ready to return, and narrowed the contenders to the University of Wisconsin and Northeastern in Boston. I was sure I wanted to go to one of them, and the solidity of that intention made me feel strong enough to consider that Aaron might have other plans. We'd leaned on each other a lot over the year because we were in a strange town. His parents had come to visit for Thanksgiving and we'd gone to their place for Christmas. But in addition to his reticence during the application process, Aaron had been working long days and often on weekends, while I'd spent a lot of that time at the pottery studio and with Meredith from the shelter. I was relieved when, on that hike, Aaron said he wanted to go wherever I went. I asked him to choose where he'd rather be, Boston or Madison. He chose Boston, which meant I'd attend Northeastern. Late in the summer of 1997, we'd make our way there, with a month-long stop at his parents' home in Virginia.

CHAPTER NINE

STATES' RIGHTS

Charlottesville, Virginia

The destroyers will rarely be held accountable. Mostly, they will receive pensions.

—Ta-Nehisi Coates

In addition to recent holiday visits while we lived in Little Rock, I'd been to Aaron's parents' house several times during college. In my second year, when Aaron and I had first moved in together with our roommate, Laura, I'd spent a fall break there and maybe a spring or Thanksgiving break later on. That first fall break, after a late dinner, I unpacked in the basement guest room and then made my way back upstairs only to find Aaron closed away in his second-floor bedroom. Unsure of the rules of the house, and assuming that it would be inappropriate to go upstairs to Aaron's room, I waited around awkwardly for a while in the living room, where Aaron's mother, Susan, was reading.

Aaron's parents knew that we shared an apartment at school, and while they didn't approve, their disapproval did not overcome their desire to be supportive of Aaron and engaged in his life, or to meet me. When I interrupted Susan to ask if it would be safe for me to take a walk in the neighborhood, she seemed pleasantly surprised to realize that I was avoiding going up to Aaron's bedroom and maybe a little relieved that I wouldn't do so without permission. She told me, smiling, that while it was fine to walk in the neighborhood, it would also be fine to go up and knock on Aaron's bedroom door. From that interaction, there was a sort of softness in our relationship, a sort of mutual recognition that is often the foundation of lifelong friendship. I found that despite our differences in age, identity, and personality, I *liked* Susan, a lot. In his last year of study in Gainesville, when Aaron got a letter from a family friend telling him that he ought to call home once in a while, I suggested he invite his parents to visit, and I'd come up to join them. They did, and we all explored the town and the campus together.

The Schrocks had been so present in our lives when we lived in Little Rock that it had seemed reasonable to ask them if they'd put us up for the month of August 1997, between when our lease in Little Rock expired and our lease in Boston was set to begin. We packed our few belongings into a U-Haul once again and drove through the Appalachian Mountains to their house in Charlottesville, Virginia. Aaron's parents were, in many ways, a lighthouse for me after college. My own family, both my immediate family and also a broad web of aunts, uncles, and cousins, remained distant. All the way through college, much of my extended family had continued to immigrate in groups of two or three families at a time. Stunned by culture shock and the hard work of rebuilding their lives outside of Pakistan, they had no interest in or capacity for engaging my life and its adventures. Mostly, they didn't even know about them. Having straddled cultures for so long, I understood the reasons for this, but still felt the absence of my family acutely.

My search for a truer American history might have excluded my detour through Virginia in a different telling. After all, I spent only one month there, and that because of lease terms that didn't quite match up. But in the process of excavating my memories, I found that my time there was as pivotal in my life as it has been to my developing understanding of American history. The part of Virginia where I landed is surrounded by the sites of Civil War battles; it is where much of the war over slavery and its central role in the American economy was fought. This well-known history is the portal to a lesser-known history.

In 1807, Congress had voted to abolish the transatlantic slave trade in an act that would become effective in January 1808. But the way in which Americans generally understand that moment, as one of liberation and great success for abolitionists, is mostly wrong. When the transatlantic slave trade was abolished, it was at least as much a victory for Virginia's slavers as it was for abolitionists. Wealthy Virginia planters had amassed a lot of land, and much of it was already depleted from growing tobacco. They also had an extraordinarily large enslaved labor force, no longer fully employed at producing that large cash crop, who planters had begun to view as a crop in and of themselves. The Chesapeake planters in Virginia and Maryland hoped to become the primary suppliers of enslaved people to the newly emerging cotton- and sugar-producing states of the South. Abolition of the transatlantic slave trade actually accelerated one of the most horrifying aspects of American slavery: breeding humans for sale. This undertaking was incredibly lucrative. By 1860, just before the Civil War, Virginia was home to two-thirds of America's millionaires.

I am now about the same age as Aaron's parents would have been in that summer of 1997, and in retrospect, we were—and especially I was—probably a much greater disruption to their empty-nest peace than I realized at the time. At a very young twenty-one, I was not yet in the habit of considering my parents or my friends' parents as whole human beings with priorities and desires that had nothing to do with us. Susan was launching a new career at the time, and I imagine in that context might not have wanted to endure houseguests for a full month. It probably didn't help that for all of my concern and study of women's rights and conditions, I pitched in only when asked, to cook dinner once a week or so, to do dishes, and to help clean toward the end of our stay. As I vacuumed the spaces between each wooden rail upstairs in the two-story brick house, Susan commented that she might've asked for my help sooner had she known how thorough I would be. It was only then that I realized I should have been the one to offer.

I had left Little Rock less certain than I had ever been about my ability to organize myself and succeed in adult life, and so I was a sponge in the Schrocks' well-ordered and frugal home. The Schrocks come from long lines of ministers and farmers and their house was a place with a distinctly plain sensibility, part farmhouse, part study, not ornate, but beautiful in its simplicity. Objects that might be store-bought in other homes were instead homemade or had some senti-mental value. Every corner was clean, considered, organized. I studied how each thing had its place, how bills were collected neatly on the desk in the tidy mudroom, to be opened with a letter opener from the drawer underneath, paid, and their envelopes stored in a separate drawer to be recycled as scraps for grocery lists later. The furniture and floors were wooden, all in an unassuming medium oak stain. There were no crystal chandeliers, extra throw pillows, or glittery ob-jects. The television was wheeled out on a cart, rarely, when someone planned to watch something specific. The radio, if it was on, played quietly, and sometimes Aaron played guitar. Conversations were also quiet, not overly animated by either excitement or anger. The base-ment had a spare freezer for garden extras and a workbench; the yard had large rectangular garden beds with a square plot of corn, toma-toes, rows of lettuce, and plenty of flowers.

My life for that month took the shape of the Schrocks' lives and home, with dinner seated together at the table, and long, brisk walks afterward around the neighborhood. In fact, my life still bears some of the imprint of my time there. Living in their orderly home helped me learn how to organize the space around myself, and, when I arrived at law school, my studies. It gave me a lasting appreciation for the beauty of plainness. Years later, in Yardley, I built a compost system out of wooden pallets much like the one I'd seen in the Schrocks' yard, with sections for each stage of rotting before the stuff could be shoveled into the garden beds. Today, Nadeem, the children, and I tuck our cloth napkins into a bowl after dinner, with a different kind of napkin ring for each of us, just like I'd done at their home.

The truth is, I loved the calmness and regularity of the Schrocks' lives, the carefulness of their home and food and conversation, and I'd grown to love *them*. I also felt loved by the way that Susan would engage me, casually asking for my opinion and sometimes sharing her own, listening carefully, but without the feeling that either of us needed to influence the other. Her demeanor had a sort of easy confidence I'd found missing in my parents' home and community, in which the experience of postcolonial migration had stripped away any sureness that my parents and their friends and siblings might otherwise have felt. I absorbed the way Susan pressed at the boundaries of her own cultural and faith identity, but still resolutely claimed them as a woman and a scholar. This interested me, as I also felt myself caught between the often rigid gender expectations of the culture into which I was born and the opportunities that seemed so readily available in certain progressive pockets of American culture.

In that month with Aaron's parents, I was more intimate with a family other than my own than I ever had been before. But as much as I struggled against it, our closeness filled me with apprehension. My longing to belong was tangled up with the confusion and loss of migration, and the persistent desire to more fully understand the traditions from which I'd come. Although I was soaking in the quiet goodness of the Schrock household, I sometimes found its routines stifling, as if everything had already been worked out, organized, and decided. I learned that while there were many differences between the Schrock family and my own, there were also surprising parallels. On the surface, the story of how Aaron's parents met could not have been more different from my parents' story of arranged marriage, in which my mother technically could have declined but was always expected to marry and be dependent on a husband vetted by her family and community. But when Susan explained how she'd had to wait to be asked out (and not do the asking herself) and how Lloyd was, in the end, the man who asked her, therefore the one she married, I realized that she had been nearly as constrained as my own mother.

Both women's stories had the same effect on me. They made me want to continue making my own choices, without the constant fear of transgression. They made me want to succeed at law school and practice law in service to my ideals. They made me want to avoid what felt to me like misogyny and the needless limitation of women's lives. Aaron fit right into that vision; I saw our mutually chosen cross-cultural partnership based on shared politics as an alternative to both his parents' and my own parents' worlds.

Even if I'd wanted a life more rooted in my own family or culture, I wasn't sure how I'd ever build it. I knew Aaron and I could never have visited my parents' home unmarried. In fact, even if we were married, I wasn't sure that any ritual or commitment would ever be enough to make our relationship valid to my parents, constrained as they were by the fears and prejudices of their first-generation immigrant community. In that community, in the late nineties, children were expected to marry spouses as similar to themselves as possible, as an assurance that cultural and faith identities from "back home" would be preserved. As racial and religious minorities, my parents and their peers were defined by their own sense of precarity. They had not yet come to embrace the inevitable results of their own migrations—that their children had grown up in a society that is neither Muslim nor Pakistani and that we were already making concessions and adaptations as we went.

Perhaps collectively they could have navigated these second-generation changes more gracefully, but the families in my parents' community chose instead to struggle separately, afraid of one another's judgments and abandonment. Many young women in my generation often stayed away as they came of age, as I did. Our parents, in their longing for children they could fully understand and protect, did much to prolong our alienation, holding tightly to the idea that we ought to be younger versions of themselves. Most of them would not reckon with the assimilation that migration demands until yet another generation had been born and they were motivated by the less complicated love of grandchildren.

By the time Thomas Jefferson was born in 1743, on a Virginia plantation that is just a few miles from Charlottesville, the city of London had been importing massive quantities of tobacco from plantations like his across the Atlantic Ocean for a hundred years. The demand for tobacco encouraged plantation owners to keep massive labor forces to handle the several steps of its planting, cultivation, and harvest, as well as its preparation for shipping. Slavery, of course, allowed planters to keep the greatest profit from that work for themselves. So by then, the Chesapeake region was already a society of fixed, racialized classes, with the estimated 129,000 enslaved Africans who disembarked in Maryland and Virginia, and hundreds of thousands of their descendants, at the very bottom.

People captured and trafficked on the west coast of Africa were purchased at a premium from boats landing in Virginia, as it was dangerous and difficult to sail the ships that carried them, naked and packed as cargo, beyond more accessible destinations in the West Indies. Planters of seventeenth- and eighteenth-century Virginia paid anyway, knowing both that a lifetime of unpaid captive labor would maximize their agricultural profits, and more important, that their purchase would provide what they called an "increase." Enslaved people were expected to bear children who would be their owner's enslaved property, and who could be used as collateral, forced to labor, or sold as separate commodities.

By the late eighteenth century, more than a century of widespread tobacco farming had depleted nutrients from the topsoil and planters were beginning to grow wheat, a less labor-intensive crop. The value of the enslaved as a labor force fell in Virginia just as it rose sharply in the newly settled regions of the South. In addition, cotton and sugar planters in what would become Tennessee, Alabama, Mississippi, and

Louisiana preferred to purchase the children of those already enslaved in America rather than those arriving on transatlantic ships, because they spoke English, were immune to American diseases, knew plantation work, and had no military experience. In response to this demand, Virginia planters were breeding enslaved people for sale. Men, women, and children from Virginia were routinely chained or tied neck to neck and handcuffed in pairs in coffles, forced to walk across the rural South. Sometimes, after days of shackled trudging, they'd be forced onto oceangoing vessels, and then later onto steamboats and trains. Between 1790 and 1860, nearly one million enslaved Black people were transported into the cotton- and sugar-producing states of the Lower South. That's twice as many people as the highest estimate of trafficked African people ever to arrive in the ports of the continental United States. Among them, only about 15 percent had traveled with their slavers; the rest were sold in the domestic slave trade.

In 1757, a fourteen-year-old Thomas Jefferson inherited both land and the enslaved people from his father's estate. His father had been one of Virginia's elite, a wealthy planter and surveyor. At twenty-nine, Jefferson inherited even more enslaved people from his father-in-law after his marriage to Martha Skelton. In 1776, when Jefferson was only thirty-three, he drafted the Declaration of Independence, with its iconic prose:

> We hold these truths to be self-evident, that all men are created equal, that they are endowed by their Creator with certain unalienable Rights, that among these are Life, Liberty and the pursuit of Happiness.—That to secure these rights, Governments are instituted among Men, deriving their just powers from the consent of the governed,—That whenever any Form of Government becomes destructive of these ends, it is the Right of the People to alter or to abolish it, and to institute a new Government, laying its foundation on such principles and organizing its powers in such a form, as to them shall seem most likely to effect their Safety and Happiness.

He would spend most of the following thirty years in public office, as the governor of Virginia, Virginia's delegate to the Second Continental and Confederation congresses, minister negotiating treaties on behalf of the fledgling United States, minister to France, and secretary of state before becoming vice president in 1797 under John Adams, and finally president of the United States in 1801. During this period, despite all that he'd written about unalienable rights and the consent of the governed, Jefferson was personally engaged in all of the same ordinary brutalities as other slavers, who made up an estimated 14 percent of southern White people.

In 1794, he operated a nail factory on his property, which was worked by boys ages ten to sixteen whom he enslaved. The boys "spent their formative years in captivity, living together and making nails all day until they were sixteen, when they were transferred to field labor." Jefferson kept detailed logs of each boy's productivity and the amount of wasted scrap metal they produced. When one boy, Cary, injured another, he instructed his son-in-law:

> it will be necessary for me to make an example of [Cary] in terrorem to others, in order to maintain the police so rigorously necessary among the nailboys. there are generally negro purchasers from Georgia passing about the state. . . . if none such offers, if he could be sold in any other quarter so distant as never more to be heard of among us, it would to the others be as if he were put out of the way by death.

The southern railroad was, by then, a wretched tool of cruelty. It was built by enslaved men and boys, who could not hope to gain anything from their labors but to be sold off or forced to maintain the railroad after it was built. With southbound cars sometimes dedicated to trafficking enslaved people, it was a constant threat to those of the Chesapeake region. Children like Cary might be sold away to threaten others into compliance, and women could readily be sold away to the crushing sugar plantations if they failed to comply with demands that they be sexually available and reproduce on demand. If a mother managed to avoid that fate herself, she could be relatively certain that the interests of her Virginia slaver would eventually see her children sold away.

Children ages eight to fifteen made up a quarter of the enslaved people trafficked south, demand for their young bodies permanently destroying their families and further obscuring their lineages. Boys were more commonly sold than girls, except young, pubescent girls, ages twelve to fifteen, sought out as sexually available to their owners as well as available for breeding at slavers' direction. All of this was legal, as the fertility of the enslaved of both sexes was itself a commodity.

The systematic, terrorist sexual assault of enslaved women has been widely examined, but the systematic breeding of enslaved women for the express purpose of creating human commodities, less so. Both sellers and buyers were conscious of the fertility of the people they enslaved; they priced for it, and they purchased for it. Planters routinely planned for 25 percent more enslaved people every ten years, through reproduction that they had absolute authority to force or coerce. This was a core depravity of America's slave system, playing out in sexual predation by men and boys of the slave-owning class, and in the forced intercourse they imposed on both the men and women—often the boys and girls—they enslaved.

In 1787, when Jefferson was minister to France, he took the fourteen- or fifteen-year-old Sally Hemings to Paris as his daughter's nurse and sexually exploited her, as far as we know, for the rest of his life. She gave birth to six infants who have been shown to be Jefferson's biological children, and who were also enslaved by him. By the time Jefferson was elected president in 1801, the "concubinage" of Sally Hemings was a scandal, so he did not take Hemings, or, initially, any of the other girls he enslaved at his Monticello plantation, to the White House. However, during his time there, he did eventually send to Monticello for three other young women and girls, reportedly to apprentice them to the White House's French chef. Each of the three gave birth at the White House: Ursula Granger Hughes arrived at the White House in

1801 at the age of fourteen, gave birth to a baby boy by March of the following year, and had departed the White House by summer. Edith Hern Fossett arrived several months later at the age of fifteen and bore three children during her seven years at the White House, while Frances Gillette Hern was eighteen when she arrived in 1806 and bore one child while there. While the paternity of the children of these three girls has not been established, their ages and pregnancies demonstrate that Jefferson's female slaves were expected to spend their lives after puberty providing him an "increase" in human assets, in addition to whatever other work was required of them. What Jefferson wrote to his overseer, Joel Yancey, in 1819 confirms this:

> the loss of 5. little ones in a year induces me to fear that the overseers do not permit the women to devote as much time as is necessary to the care of their children: that they view their labor as the 1st object and the raising their child but as secondary. I consider the labor of a breeding woman as no object, and that a child raised every 2 years is of more profit than the crop of the best laboring man.

Children labored and were sold away, those of childbearing age were forced into both manual and reproductive servitude, and even old age did not provide a respite. Jefferson regularly reduced by half the rations of the people he enslaved who had grown too old to work.

Jefferson's preoccupation with protecting the wealth of slavers was personal, and it was one of his central aims as president. He owned more than six hundred enslaved people in his lifetime, and of those, freed only seven. Jefferson believed that to secure his wealth and the wealth of the Virginia elite, he had to accomplish two things: He had to eliminate the transatlantic slave trade, which brought cheaper, competing "goods" through South Carolina, enriching the traders of that state, and he had to encourage westward expansion, eliminating Native peoples so that land could be taken and settled by Europeans, creating expanding markets into which he could sell the children of the people he enslaved.

Jefferson presided over the Louisiana Purchase of 1803, and then pressed Congress to block the importation of enslaved people from Africa at the earliest possible date permitted under the Constitution, in 1808. This dramatically increased the value of his own holdings and the market for them. More important, it helped to establish the frame of an economy premised on the forced breeding of other human beings to maintain an endless supply of free labor, to enrich White Virginia planters, and to establish a new generation of White cotton and sugar planters in Mississippi, Louisiana, and beyond. Jefferson's greed reinforced his racism, and his racism justified his greed, to truly monstrous ends.

As we know from the earlier discussion of the American Colonization Society, Jefferson supported the deportation or "colonization" of free Black people out of America. In 1824, two years before his death, perhaps no longer so occupied with his personal wealth and increasingly concerned about an armed rebellion of the enslaved, Jefferson wrote a letter outlining a colonization scheme to rid the country of *all* Black people, including the enslaved. A key element of his scheme was to minimize *the cost to slavers* for the loss of their property, by "carry[ing] off the increase." He proposed that the government would purchase the infants of the enslaved cheaply, to pay only for their nourishment "while with the mother" and to then send them off to Haiti. Meanwhile, he wrote, in America, "the old stock would die off." His plan never came to fruition, as the ACS removal of free Black people to Liberia was already under way.

Aaron and I would continue to visit his parents regularly for the next three years, while I was in law school. I'd had, by then, enough distance from my parents' home and from the professor who mistook my interest in studying Islam for an interest in the Muslim Brotherhood that my yearning to understand Islam reemerged. I was not yet a person of faith, but I could be moved to tears by the call to prayer. I had so assiduously closed myself off from any Muslim community that I lacked the resources or the knowledge to find my way forward. In this context, I continued to be drawn to the cultural and religious cohesion of the Schrock household.

At the same time, I grew more convinced that it was not mine. I was always the only person of color in the room with the Schrocks. When Susan's sister showed up in shalwar kameez, sometimes called a Punjabi, but distorted each vowel so it was "pooonjahbeee," when food at the table was consecrated in Jesus' name (so that for a Muslim the food became impermissible, as is any food consecrated to someone other than God), when Aaron's grandmother expressed concern that my eternal soul was destined for hell because I had not accepted Jesus as part of a trinitarian theology—those were the hard stops in a series of pauses, places where the things I hadn't yet reconciled about existing in a segregated White, Christian space surfaced. Each of these also launched tense conversations between Aaron and me.

After I forced down several bites of the meal after the blessing "in Jesus' name," Aaron and I went up to our bedroom. I was close to tears and tried to explain to Aaron why.

"He didn't mean anything by it. It's a totally normal way to end grace; he's been doing it that way his whole life," Aaron responded.

"I know that—I'm not saying I was offended by it. But the thing is, I can't eat food that is consecrated in a name other than God's. I can't *do* things in any other name. It doesn't feel right." I tried to explain, my voice rising the way it does when I'm hurting but sound mad.

"There are so many other ways that you don't practice—and Muslims think of Jesus as a prophet anyway. Does this have to be such a big deal? I can't ask my father to stop believing what he believes."

"I get that—I do. It's really not about being capital *M* Muslim— it's about being me. I just can't eat the food, Aaron. Please talk to him." Aaron spoke to his father, who—I'm humbled now thinking of it—with such grace, adapted his blessing so that I could live and eat comfortably there for the rest of our stay and every stay thereafter.

The fact remained, though, that I was stretching myself over a divide rather than standing firmly in a deeply rooted or examined identity. And in such a vulnerable state, the missionary nature of the Schrocks' faith and culture felt frightening. Lloyd and Susan had been on a missionary trip in South America several years before, and ongoing missionary work was a central feature of their faith community. I knew, and could even understand, that the Schrocks felt called to provide service in the context of their faith. What I could not resolve was how they had to go all the way to South America to do that. Why not preach their faith while providing service to the people in their own neighborhood instead? Why not provide service in rural Appalachia (as some in their community had done) or in downtown Washington, D.C.? Why not preach to other White people?

I knew, even then, that Christian missionaries, like Thomas Riggs in South Dakota, have long been tools, wittingly or unwittingly, of colonial dispossession. Desmond Tutu, the Black South African Anglican cleric and anti-apartheid activist described what so many Brown and Black people around the world know and have experienced when he said, "When the missionaries came to Africa they had the Bible and we had the land. They said 'Let us pray.' We closed our eyes. When we opened them we had the Bible and they had the land." Missions and colonial projects have generally been premised on the powerful idea that the faiths, cultures, and resources of Black and Brown people are there to be converted to the needs and interests of White people, whatever they may be. They have a long, terrible history of spreading the twin ideas of White and Christian superiority, merging racial, cultural, and religious identity into one and presenting it as salvation. A convert, though, even one acculturated to European or American habits, cannot erase the color of their skin. Predictably then, in the missionary project, there remain tiered levels of access. And the vast majority of resources are afforded to the Whitest of the saved.

Although I was never proselytized to by any member of the Schrock family, I felt anxious, and, though it seems excessive now, endangered, as if my ancestry and identity would be so easily wiped away in the context of Christian certitude. Over the last twenty years, some missions have begun to focus less on traditional "church-planting" and driving acceptance of Jesus as "Lord and Savior." Newer approaches allow room for missionaries to consider the value and engage the faith traditions of host cultures, with a clearer emphasis on service provision. These approaches are still in the minority though, and more broadly, the premise of missionary Christianity remains. Missions began, and remain rooted in, the idea that non-Christians, often Brown and Black people, whether in North America or in the global south, are inherently in need of salvation through Christianity and the European cultures in which it is practiced. Meanwhile, the long-standing racist campaigns of slavery, Native dispossession, forced removal of free Black people, and even school segregation have all been explicitly justified in the name of or in relation to Christianity.

Aaron's parents described their own mission trip as an adventure. Although each participated in service work while there, their adventure was encapsulated in missionary identity, an opportunity to interact with people radically different from themselves without ever risking, or even considering, their own assimilation to or transformation by the host culture. They didn't learn the language, investigate the effects of colonization, or adopt the habits and perspectives of the people they worked with—it would not have occurred to them to think they ought to. Aaron himself tended to avoid the word *missionary* and its troublesome implications.

Missions like the Schrocks' have been so overwhelmingly successful at converting large numbers of Brown and Black people as to create a debate in their community over members' ethnic versus religious identity. There are now terms used to distinguish White European members of their community and their descendants, also identifiable by their family names, from the converted, who include an increasingly diverse array of people from countries and cultures around the world. Ironically, though not surprisingly, there appears to be widespread discomfort among those of European origin with the very result of their own missionary ventures—the inclusion of Black and Brown people in their faith communities. In truth, even as they proselytize their faith as universal, a great deal of their identity in North America is premised not on faith but on common ancestry and a common culture, an exclusive identity rooted in whiteness.

Despite the sweetness of their tradition, in spite of my appreciation of their history of pacifism and four-part harmony, in spite of the deep generosity and kindness of the Schrocks, I already knew, deep down, that I did not want to be absorbed by them. I did not want to pass as or pretend to be White. I did not want to *disappear into* America after all, but to find a way to be whole and myself in America, a blend of two valuable cultures, in my Brown body. And I knew, in a muddy and conflicted way, that if Aaron and I did continue together, if we got married, I didn't want to convert, as culturally and spiritually alienated as I yet felt from my own family, and I didn't want to blend in. When presented with an exceptionally attractive opportunity to do so, I did not want to be enveloped by even a softly spoken, peace-church Christianity. I did not want to be stuck in the anteroom of someone else's faith or cultural tradition. Even aside from my central theological rejection of the trinity, the thought of it made something in me feel broken.

Like any close-knit cultural or faith community, the Schrocks' community can have a strong sense that they are doing everything in *the* right way: food, music, ways of speaking, and, especially, social rules and organization. Like most religious communities in America over the last thirty years, they are struggling with new ideas about the constraints of women in church leadership and LGBTQ inclusion. In the end, witnessing those struggles helped me to find my own way home. I recognized the conservativism and struggles of their community because they are present, in many similar ways, in American Muslim communities. Over the years I knew the Schrocks, Susan returned to school and began a second career. I admired her drive to pursue an unorthodox, feminist leadership role. More than that, I was intrigued by her attempts to do so from *within* her community, with a sense that she was entitled to be there, and to take up space.

I wondered what it would be like to belong to such a cohesive community in America, and also to be recognizable in every way to the majority culture. To have one's name easily pronounced wherever one went, to have one's faith broadly recognized, to be culturally so familiar that there is room for one's most unorthodox ambitions. I knew that wouldn't be possible for an American Muslim, at least not foreseeably, in my lifetime. But I began to consider that, even as a racial and religious minority, it might be possible to carve out a place for *some* unorthodox ambitions within my own immigrant and faith communities. There might be resources and experiences I hadn't yet found that would help me design a composite identity; it might be possible to enjoy two cultures and to live a Muslim American life, to live out the progressive ideals I saw as resonant and compatible with Islam.

Had Aaron and I driven a bit further north, we might have come to Clover Hill Farm in Manassas, near the site of the first major land battle of the Civil War. Clover Hill Farm, also known as Johnson Farm, predated the war; Rutt Johnson purchased his one thousand acres there in 1770 from a tobacco planter. Thomas Jefferson would have been twenty-seven years old that year, absorbed in the building of his home at Monticello to the south. Johnson eventually gifted a parcel of 130 acres to his daughter, Sally, while his son, Joseph, ran the main farm until he died just before the Civil War. This left Joseph's wife, Emily Eliza Johnson, and their children behind as the war began. They fled south when the fighting started, along with the sixteen people they enslaved at the time. In the scheme of things, the Johnsons were average slavers; 88 percent of the enslaved in America were held captive in places with fewer than fifty other enslaved people. After the war and the abolition of slavery in 1865, the Johnson family returned. Their house was burned down but the slave quarters, where they lived as they rebuilt, remained. A photograph of their new home in 1883 shows a grand two-story Victorian house, with decorative railings along a wide front porch and balcony running the length of the building. The family had retained significant wealth even after the war.

Joseph senior's youngest son, Joseph Benjamin Johnson, took over Clover Hill Farm, putting in orchards and in 1900 setting up a dairy farm. In the 1970s Manassas swallowed the farm, breaking up the 382-acre island with traffic and surrounding it with new development. After more than two centuries, and six generations of Johnsons drawing security and livelihood from that particular parcel of land, Joseph Benjamin Johnson's great-grandchildren, among them yet another Joseph, would be the ones to finally sell the remaining farmland to residential builders for a $300 million development project in 1987.

News stories about Clover Hill Farm tend to heroize the Johnsons. They are the farmers of an earlier America, building and planting and hanging on to their land so that their wealth could pass through generations. One *Washington Post* article, from 1979, frames the imperiled modern Johnson dairy farm and adjacent family land this way:

"Together, their land forms a green island, its shores lapped by concrete. The Johnsons fix a stern eye on the rising tide. People living in the same place over time forge a loyalty to it—because that place, with its rhythms, is faithful to them."

In fact, this is how we Americans often tell the story of the early White farmer, the settler, or the cowboy, as if their relationship to the land is primal. We carefully excise the complexity of colonization, of what became of the land's original occupants, of who actually cleared and worked the land and under which circumstances. That particular article about the Johnsons emphasizes how they *belonged* to and in Manassas, how their persistence and labor on the land made them somehow more entitled to it, and so how their loss is a communal one. By contrast, this is rarely how we discuss or record the hundreds and sometimes thousands of years' long relationships of Native peoples to their homelands in North America. Even referencing that relationship is seen as sentimental, or irrelevant in the modern world. We know this by how few of us would recognize the names of the seven federally recognized tribes of Native people from what is now Virginia: Pamunkey, Chickahominy, Eastern Chickahominy, Upper Mattaponi, Rappahannock, Nansemond, and Monacan, though those peoples would have had an intimate relationship to the land on which they lived for many generations, long before the Johnsons arrived.

Neither do we cultivate empathy for the people who would have done the hardest labor on the Johnson land over several generations. The last generation of the Johnson family to own the Clover Hill property donated eight acres of land, including the original quarters of those their ancestors had enslaved, to the Grace United Methodist Church, which has commemorated nineteen people held captive by the Johnson family on a placard. It reads:

> The family's records provide the names of the slaves who worked on the farm: Ben "formerly called Gator," Richard "a blacksmith," Milly, Martha, "Old Frank," Sarah, Rachel, Eliza, Tony, Peter, John, Bill, Ann, Issac, Harriott, George Sally, Amos, "little Frank," and Matinoa.

This list is not exhaustive. Another historical marker at nearby historic Lucasville School, a segregated school for Black children in operation until 1926, contains a picture of Emma Chapman in adulthood, saying that she attended the school and "had been enslaved at Clover Hill." The placard also says that many Chapmans attended the segregated school, and that many still live in the community around it. Yet another woman, enslaved in childhood by the Johnson family, shows up in the Johnson family papers held by the Manassas Museum. Malinda Robinson sent this plea to Mrs. Emily Eliza Johnson just over a year after the Civil War:

New Orleans, Oct. 18, 1866

Mrs. Joseph Johnson: Dear Mistress:

My family and myself once belonged to your deceased husband and were raised on the farm on which you now live. Having been gone so long, I had lost, until lately, all knowledge of my relative and friends. For that purpose I engaged a man and he wrote a letter for

me to the Commissioner of Freedman and a like one to the sheriff
of your county.

Ms. Robinson goes on to beg that Mrs. Johnson pass the letter, containing her contact details, to any one of her four siblings. Ms. Robinson is clearly concerned that a letter sent back directly to her, as a
Black woman, would not reach her: "Please be careful to direct your
letters thus, or I will never get them: Malinda Robinson (colored),
Care of Reverend Scott Chinn."

Malinda Robinson's ancestors, perhaps even her parents, had been
stripped of their ancestral homeland and cultural identities across the
ocean. She was deprived of her family and, as an enslaved woman, any
bodily autonomy. These invaluable things are lost forever. But Malinda Robinson and her descendants were also denied the wealth they
and their ancestors generated through their labor on the Johnson
Farm. That generational wealth instead accrued to the Johnsons. Even
the sale of their own bodies did not enrich the enslaved or their descendants, but the slaver class.

Just as the men, women, and children enslaved by the Johnsons are
mostly absent from the historical record, disappearing into the anonymous brutality of postslavery sharecropping Virginia no wealthier for
their labors, so are millions of others. As a nation, we offer widespread
poverty in place of reparations for the generational losses they suffered, and to add insult, pretend that America is a meritocracy and
Black poverty is the result of Black failure. In reality, the genocidal
nature of the transatlantic slave trade continued unabated in the machinations of Jefferson and other Virginia slavers, through those of the
American Colonization Society to deport free Black people, and has
persisted in modern segregation, racialized mass incarceration, and
police brutality today. America has never stopped behaving as if Black
lives are expendable unless they are producing sufficient value for
White America.

In October 2020, the Virginia state senator Richard Stuart was walking on the farm he'd just purchased not far south of Manassas, along the Potomac River, when he saw what he thought looked like gravestones. Exploring with his wife, Lisa, he determined that they were indeed headstones, and there were lots of them. When he went looking for their origin, he learned that they were from Columbian Harmony Cemetery, the first burial ground in Washington, D.C., for free Black people. The cemetery was supposed to have been dug up and relocated in 1960, making room for commercial development, but the headstones were "discarded like scrap," bought by the Stuart farm's previous owner to provide erosion control on his riverfront. More recent development has unearthed human remains at the cemetery site, suggesting that little was done to properly relocate or protect the resting places of the nearly 37,000 people buried there. Even in death, not deemed worthy of the very land they were buried in, they were forced out.

Black cemeteries like Columbian Harmony continue to be unearthed all around the country. Four have been discovered from 2019 to 2020 in the Tampa Bay area of Florida alone. Others have been found in Portsmouth, New Hampshire; in Philadelphia; in Fort Bend County, Texas; in Durham, North Carolina; and in Crownsville, Maryland. Black cemeteries across the country have been abandoned, bulldozed, or looted, suggesting that only certain Americans have ever been entitled to rest in peace. Some have been paved or built over, some had always been obscured for protection from overseers. The discovery of these defiled or obscured cemeteries has become so frequent as to inspire a bill to establish an African American Burial Grounds Network as part of the National Park Service introduced in Congress in 2019, which would provide education and training to state and local governments to identify and preserve Black burial grounds and associated artifacts and landscapes. That bill has yet to become law. In a notable contrast, Senator Stuart was able to identify and purchase the same farm owned by his family in previous generations, in a place where his family first settled almost four hundred years ago, and where there remains an intact Stuart family cemetery.

In driving from Charlottesville to Boston, Aaron and I would pass within ten minutes of my parents' home. And though it was hard to pass such familiar landmarks without stopping, I knew that I wasn't yet ready to return. What I did not yet know was that during this period, when I felt so deeply estranged from my parents, they were as embattled in their own home as they ever had been. A local teenager who had targeted my younger brother with racial harassment at school had begun to target my family outside of school as well. That fall, he set a fire against my family's front door, which fortunately didn't catch, and on New Year's Eve, he returned to deliver a dead cat in a box to their front drive. After the police intervened, the vandalism of their home stopped, but the harassment my brother faced at school continued until he graduated early to escape it.

Every time I've heard my parents talk about these events, they've made light of them: It was just a stupid kid. The fire didn't catch. The silly police officer seemed to think hitting the box with his stick would be a good way to determine what was inside, though the reason my father had called the police in the first place was to check for explosives! My parents tell these events laughing, as if to ease the horror of a neighbor trying to set their house on fire because my brother was visibly Asian at school. This last time they told these stories, I listened more carefully, hearing hurt and pain, and their sense that they were powerless to shield my brother from what he endured at school. I told my parents about the history of racist violence in their region of Pennsylvania—about the racist mob outside the Myerses' house in Levittown and the threats against the Swann family when they moved into Warrington. I watched them put their own experiences into that larger, harder-to-laugh-off context of racist violence. This larger context is essential. It makes sense of our deeply segregated landscape so that its design becomes clear: the enduring, normative intention to minimize or erase Black and Brown people.

CHAPTER TEN

NATION OF IMMIGRANTS

Boston, Massachusetts

> *But the belief in the preeminence of hue and hair, the notion*
> *that these factors can correctly organize a society and that they*
> *signify deeper attributes, which are indelible—this is the new*
> *idea at the heart of these new people who have been brought up*
> *hopelessly, tragically, deceitfully, to believe that they are white.*
> —Ta-Nehisi Coates

When I'd made the decision to attend Northeastern University School of Law rather than Wisconsin, I discounted admission to Rutgers, which today would have been my top choice among the three. It's close to home, has a large Muslim Students' Association, and employs one of the most diverse faculties in the country. But I wasn't yet ready to go home, and I did not yet understand how much I needed the community and mentorship of people who looked like me. I left the final decision between Madison and Boston to Aaron, who preferred Boston and quickly found work with a nonprofit in the city.

I arrived shaken in my identity. I had spent a little more than a year standing directly on the color line in Little Rock, and then a month in the Schrocks' home, steeped in their identity and culture. I had visited Northeastern's campus from Little Rock at the start of summer, making my way across the street to a realtor's office. I told them I was looking for a one-bedroom in the $600 range. They just laughed; the going rate was nearly twice that in the late nineties. I'd arrived in yet another place where I did not know the rules or the expectations. This only drove my intention to study law—to understand the place where I was born, and to undo some of my persistent sense of being on the outside of my own life in it.

Our first year in Boston, Aaron and I lived in an apartment several blocks from Northeastern in a not-yet-gentrified part of town. We unloaded the same boards and bricks we had taken to Little Rock and carried them up to our crumbly third-floor walk-up on Massachusetts Avenue. Aaron helped me haul a large solid wooden slab home from the hardware store to make a desk for the nook in the bedroom. I had struggled in high school and at college to organize my thoughts and my writing, and was terrified that law school required a degree of discipline and precision that would be challenging for me. I may have been too preoccupied to notice that the reticence Aaron showed about my applications to law school had resurfaced. He carefully avoided conversations about what I was studying or how things were going at school. When I bought my first suit for court appearances, he responded by saying, "Beware endeavors that require new clothes." At the time, I was relieved to escape my studies for a while when we'd eat or grocery shop or hang out on weekends.

By then, Aaron and I had been together for five years. If there was one thing in my life that felt stable as I began law school, it was our relationship. We began to plan a wedding for the summer of 1998. I waffled about whether to tell my parents, who I knew would view our wedding, at best, as a problem to be solved. After explaining that I would love for them to be involved, but that the wedding date had already been set, my parents insisted on and then grudgingly prepared a gender-segregated ceremony and a reception at my childhood mosque, ISCJ. That would be followed by the ceremony Aaron and I had originally planned, to be held outdoors near the Schrocks' house.

In the end, the mosque ceremony felt haphazard and chaotic, not a reflection of either Aaron or me, except one small element. At my request, the imam who officiated the ceremony recited a repeating verse of the Qur'an that means "So truly, with hardship there is also ease; truly with hardship there is also ease." I imagined the wedding itself to be the hardship I had to endure in order to return to the ease of the life Aaron and I had made together. The ceremony we'd planned—the one *I'd* planned, really, with help from Susan—around Sindhi wedding rituals, also fell flat. It was not accompanied by the usual elation, the singing and dancing that are the real fun of a Pakistani wedding. It was so funereally quiet for my side of the family that two of my mother's sisters and their husbands stood to sing, kindly and off-key, in Sindhi. Afterward, a line of five or six of my father's brothers lined up to shake hands with several of Lloyd's brothers; my aunties and cousins in headscarves, or dupattas, around their necks, decked out in the silks and gold of wedding wear, greeted Aaron's aunts and cousins, all in cotton dresses.

In spite of the hardship of the wedding and its awkwardness, it softened my parents toward Aaron and especially toward his parents. They were comforted, I think, by how much they had in common; they were alike in their introversion, frugality, and shared focus on gardening. For Aaron and me, however, the wedding marked a beginning where there ought to have been an ending.

Northeastern's curriculum, which was focused on social justice, felt like a good fit for my interests. Its co-op program allowed me to spend a full academic year, or four quarters, as a legal intern in four different organizations. The co-ops helped ground what I was learning, and I found that working as an advocate in low-income communities of color was meaningful to me in a way that nothing else had been. They offered opportunities to work in communities I identified with, which I'd been missing at SJDI and at ACORN, and also to develop skills I'd lacked when I worked at the domestic violence shelter and at the

Women's Project. Most important, the work was in direct service to clients, their needs and conflicts, rather than in service to an ideological agenda. I'd come to see the latter as dangerous. Whether theological or political, work that began with an ideology rather than with meeting people's basic needs had begun to feel misguided to me, lacking in humility, somehow *missionary*.

First-year legal education is standardized across American law schools, and law schools are notoriously competitive. One of the most unusual things about Northeastern, besides its co-ops and lack of grades in favor of narrative evaluations, was its brand-new mandatory first-year course called Law, Culture & Difference (LCD). My LCD class was divided into cohorts and I was paired with a White student named Matt and a Latino student, Victor. Victor showed up to exactly two classes that whole semester, and then, during exam week, called to beg Matt and me to let him do a piece of the final project so that he could pass the class. Of course we said yes. At our meeting the following week, he proceeded to hand us a single sheet of notebook paper with a single line of text on it the day before the project was due. Pacing, and sweating, he grew agitated when I explained that we couldn't spend the time to tutor him through his part of the project during exam week. We'd just have to pull together his portion ourselves.

Matt was passive. Victor decided I was the enemy. I got a voicemail late that night after a day of studying for exams, asking me to meet one of the faculty organizers of the LCD program, also a woman of color, in her office the next morning, before my first practice exam review of the day. Victor was there, having complained that I was not nurturing enough in his time of need. Our professor, to my great bewilderment, took his complaint to heart. I had been through a grueling first semester, I had worked harder than I'd ever worked in my life, and I wasn't having it. I explained my position, asked what they needed from me, and when they had no answer, I left.

I learned a week or so later that our professor had used the scenario, which she described as a conflict between a White woman and a student of color, as a lesson for her teaching assistants. When a TA who knew me and knew the situation pointed out that, actually, two students of color were involved in her scenario, our professor responded, "I'm talking about *real* students of color." Being rejected in that way by another woman of color was more than I could bear; her explicit erasure was more painful than any of the racism I'd encountered up to that point in my life. The experience would shape me, push me to finally assert my own identity and to refuse the isolation of passing.

Asian American identities can be hard to get a handle on in America. We make up less than 6 percent of the population, and there are significant differences in language, culture, migration history, and appearance among us. These differences are big enough that we don't typically organize ourselves across them, so that, for example, Korean Americans occupy different spaces than Indian Americans, Indians from Pakistani Americans, Pakistanis from Chinese Americans, and so on. My law school was one exception; at Northeastern we organized ourselves into the Asian Law Students Association. There weren't enough of us for anything else to make sense and having some way to organize around our mutual interests felt important. As I'd learned in that first LCD course, it was essential that I assert my own identity if I wanted to avoid having one assigned to me.

Chinese Americans make up the largest and oldest segment of the Asian American population, and in many ways, have been the bellwether of how other Asian American groups would be viewed and treated in America. Asian Americans have often been and still often are assessed as if we are a transitional workforce, available to fill holes, but otherwise invisible. We are sometimes railroad workers and laundry workers, sometimes doctors and cab drivers, we fill STEM doctoral programs and run convenience stores, gas stations, and ethnic restaurants. We are sometimes the model minority and sometimes the underclass; almost always, we are associated with an economic niche, a specific labor value. And often, the things about us that are at first ridiculed or denigrated—the way we dress, our pungent food, even our faith traditions and rituals—become valued and then quickly appropriated.

In many ways, the story of Boston's Chinatown and so many other American Chinatowns is illustrative of the experience of being Asian in America. Urban Chinatowns have been viewed as marginal spaces, available for urban development even when they are densely inhabited centers of social and cultural life. Just as ostensibly race-neutral initiatives became tools of segregation in Little Rock, similar initiatives have been implemented in ways that "box in" and carve away at Boston's Chinatown and Chinatowns across the country.

Boston's Chinatown was, for many decades, a narrow site of specialized businesses: restaurants, ethnic grocery stores, and laundries. Its residents were mostly male because of a combination of cultural and economic factors and then, later, an immigration law that made the entry of women or whole families nearly impossible until the middle of the twentieth century. In the post–World War II era, that law had been repealed and an elevated train that had hemmed in Chinatown's growth and made the area noisy was removed, changing Boston's Chinatown dramatically. Chinatown grew, swallowing up the streets around it with more diversified businesses, attracting both established and new Chinese residents as well as non-Chinese customers from the downtown theater and shopping districts.

In the 1950s and 1960s, however, Boston's Chinatown became vulnerable to the concerted, well-funded efforts of "urban renewal" and "highway development." By a similar process as the destruction and dislocation of Little Rock's Black homeowners and Black business district, the city of Boston drew down federal dollars and employed them in ways that left Chinese residents and business owners with a narrower, less desirable space within the downtown core.

Interstate 93, which runs north and south along coastal New England, was built in the mid-1950s; the Massachusetts Turnpike, built between 1962 and 1965, runs west from Boston across the state. Together, these two main arteries carry traffic into and out of the city, converging in a swirl of access ramps in its historic Chinatown, taking up one-third of its land and boxing it in on two sides. The construction of these highways eliminated an estimated 1,200 units of low- and moderate-income housing from the neighborhood, mostly row homes and storefronts with apartments above. Half a century later, the effects of the highways that limit the small neighborhood are still pronounced. The highways created hard boundaries, curtailing Chinatown's growth and the potential for retaining green or community spaces, making the neighborhood noisier and more polluted due to traffic, and creating increased health concerns for residents.

On a third side, Chinatown is now encroached upon by the expansion of Tufts Medical Center. Since the 1930s, the neighborhood was already home to the institution that became the New England Medical Center; the addition of Tufts University School of Medicine and Tufts Dental School of Medicine in 1950 launched an era of institutional expansion that would continue to gobble up land, affordable housing, and storefront businesses right in the center of Chinatown for the next seventy years. A generally top-down approach to urban renewal that privileges infrastructure and institutional development over residents, particularly low-income residents with little social and political power, has resulted in a serious challenge to Chinatown as an ethnic enclave. It has compromised the neighborhood's historic function as a commercial center as well as a transitional cultural and linguistic space for immigrants.

Today, Boston's Chinatown is home to 12,000 residents in a footprint of a quarter square mile. They continue to battle the encroachment of Tufts Medical Center and School of Medicine, as well as land speculation and development driven by Greater Boston's exorbitant real estate values. Chinatown's proximity to downtown makes it an attractive site for high-end developers to build luxury high-rises. They incur only minimal obligations to provide the low- and moderate-income housing that Chinatown's traditional residents need. As of

2020, more than 50 percent of households in two of three Chinatown census tracks earned less than $30,000 per year, making them "extremely low income" for a family of four under the U.S. Department of Housing and Urban Development's guidelines for the city, a deep level of poverty by comparison with other Boston neighborhoods. Traditionally low- and moderate-income Chinese residents tend to be pushed out by new developments, so that today, fewer than 50 percent of Boston's Chinatown residents are Asian.

This is, broadly, the same situation as in the Chinatowns of New York, San Francisco, Los Angeles, and Philadelphia. These Chinatowns all evolved in the United States as social, cultural, and economic enclaves. They made the reproduction of culture and familiar comforts accessible to their residents and to people of Chinese origin living nearby. They also offered some sanctuary from the waves of anti-Asian racism that are perennial in America and an alternative narrative about Chinese Americans through a collective presentation of arts and culture. Though urban Chinatowns have consistently provided this essential set of services by and for Asian, especially Chinese, immigrants, the space they occupy is quickly disappearing, targeted for development, taken through eminent domain, or subjected to environmental hazards.

As far back as the 1950s, Boston's Chinatown residents worked collectively to defend their community and resist dislocation, forming the Chinatown Merchants Association to oppose the routing of I-93 and to remake Chinatown as a community center and commercial destination within the city. In the 1960s, Chinatown residents secured two thousand low-income residential units in a negotiation with Tufts Medical Center. Several more recent battles beginning in the 1990s have given rise to a new generation of experienced organizers, activists, scholars, and attorneys, who are working together to study, advocate for, and regain control over land use in Boston's Chinatown. Since its inception in 1987, the Asian Community Development Corporation has worked to create at least five mixed-income housing developments, as well as projects to create green space, secure pedestrian pathways, and support homeowners and youth.

Lydia Lowe is the director of the Chinatown Community Land Trust, an agency that was incorporated in 2015 to increase community control over property in Chinatown. She credits a growing strategy of broad political education, voter registration, and engagement among Chinatown's residents, small business owners, and allies for their more recent successes. In 1990, a section of Chinatown's row homes won residential zoning status, with greater protections than the previous industrial zoning designation allowed. The city has a long track record of permitting zoning variances to override zoning codes meant to protect the viability of Chinatown as a place where new immigrants, the elderly, and small business owners can survive. More recently, as a result of persistent organizing, Lowe says that she sees new commitments from the city toward stabilizing the neighborhood. The city's mayor has helped create a temporary Chinatown branch of the Boston Public Library and promised a permanent branch. In addition, the community won passage of an ordinance that would slow the growth of short-term, hotel-style rentals, reducing land speculation that drives up the cost of living. Activists have won bilingual ballots for Chinatown and organized support for mayoral and city candidates who prioritize their community's interests. The president of the Chinatown Community Land Trust even ran for city council twice, and though she did not win those campaigns, the visibility elevated Chinatown's priorities. Chinatown continues to be at risk, with longtime residents remaining vulnerable to eviction and large corporations proposing high-density luxury housing in their place. But now, Lowe says, political candidates "see Chinatown as a place they need to campaign."

Northeastern offered a number of opportunities beyond LCD for me to explore what the rule of law provided for immigrants, and for

Black and Brown people in America. In addition to enjoying the critical approaches of my professors in courses like Criminal Justice and Property, I took Battered Women and the Law, International Human Rights, Disability Law, Welfare Law, Labor and Employment, Immigration, and Critical Legal Theory. I studied the legal legacy of White America's attempts to rid itself of Black America, first by withholding liberty, then by withholding mobility, property, and education, a framework that made sense of the social reality I saw all around me in Boston, still one of the most segregated cities in the country today. I observed the Supreme Court's persistent struggle over racial categories in America through its interpretation of immigration and naturalization statutes, in which it developed the definition of "free white person" under the law.

Asian Americans played a critical role in the court's developing ideas about race. As SCOTUS interpreted the law, it acknowledged the categories of White and Black, and delineated Native peoples, the ethnically Chinese, then the ethnically Japanese outside of these categories. Still, Asianness presented enough complexity to challenge the court and expose the arbitrariness of racial categories. Bhagat Singh Thind came to the United States from India at the age of twenty-one, seeking higher education. He enlisted to fight in World War I, was promoted to the rank of acting sergeant, and then was honorably discharged. When the Bureau of Naturalization declined his application for citizenship on the basis that he was not a "free white person," a requirement of naturalization since Congress passed the first Naturalization Act in 1790, he sued the government.

In the 1923 Supreme Court decision that followed, *United States v. Bhagat Singh Thind,* Justice Sutherland wrote for the majority, explaining that whiteness is neither a synonym for Aryan, which he said indicated linguistic origin or compatibility, nor for Caucasian, which he said was an unreasonably overbroad category, in which scientists had included "the Hindu" and "Polynesians." The court found that Mr. Thind's appearance did not indicate the correct parentage, nor allow for the assimilation which would allow a finding of whiteness.

Justice Sutherland ultimately decided Thind could not be White because "the average well informed white American would learn with some degree of astonishment that the race to which he belongs is made up of such heterogeneous elements."

In other words, the court created a legal standard for racial classification *based entirely on the imagined, subjective experience and assertions of the average White American, for whom the court then presumed to speak.* After passage of the Immigration and Nationality Act of 1965, racial classification no longer governed eligibility for naturalization and much has changed in American immigration law since *United States v. Thind,* but a central element of its finding holds firm in American society. We still employ an average White American standard to impose racial classifications on one another.

The early predecessors of modern Chinatowns emerged in California, formed by Chinese men who came to America to work in mines or on the transcontinental railroads. Both mining and railroad industries required large amounts of manual labor for dangerous and hard work. Unlike the southern railroads, the transcontinental railroads, which mostly ran through free states, were not built by enslaved Black people. In addition, the many free Black and White men who might have laid railroad track were taken up in battle across the country. The Union army was engaged both in the Civil War and in attacks on the Native peoples of the Southwest and the Great Plains, partly to take land for railroad construction. New Irish immigrants to the East Coast *were* drawn into railroad work, but typically were employed on the Union Pacific Railroad starting in Omaha, Nebraska, and heading west.

Despite the ongoing Civil War, the California coast remained the compelling goal of westward expansion. Before the railroad was completed, traveling between the coasts was an arduous journey of at least four months overland, or a journey of five to eight months around the tip of South America by sea, presenting an enormous obstacle to trade, communication, and transportation of goods. The western stretch of the Central Pacific Railroad (CPRR) was to run from Sacramento to meet the eastern stretch of Union Pacific Railroad at Promontory Summit, Utah. It promised to make the continental United States cohesive and the agricultural and natural resources of California accessible, if only there were a cheap, effective labor force to do the deadly work of blasting through the Sierra Nevada mountains and laying endless miles of track through the desert. Work on the Central Pacific Railroad began in 1863 with a small, mostly White group of workers. Within months and with only fifty miles of the railway completed, workers were abandoning the railroad in droves, heading to silver mines in California. After work stalled, CPRR director Charles Crocker recruited a few dozen Chinese workers from mining communities on the West Coast. These first workers were part of a stream of migration spurred by rumors in the coastal province of Guangdong, China, that there was gold to be found in the hills on the West Coast of North America.

With demand for Chinese railroad workers, the stream became a wave, and by 1865, Chinese men made up the vast majority of CPRR labor, with perhaps as many as twenty thousand Chinese migrants working on the railway over the next twenty years. In 1866, eight thousand of the more than ten thousand men working on the CPRR were Chinese. Chinese men had become the preferred workers of the four owners of the CPRR, who actively recruited labor both from among those already in California and directly from China through Chinese contract labor companies.

Although Chinese men working on the CPRR were free, not indentured, labor, they were seen and treated as a lesser, racialized labor force, occupying a place between enslaved and free White labor. The term "coolie," referring to a class of Chinese indentured worker that had arrived in South America and the Caribbean in earlier decades, did not properly apply to those arriving in California, but the term showed up—and still shows up—in textbooks, newspapers, and speeches. This persistent mischaracterization tells us something about the margin that Chinese migrant workers occupied in postslavery America. They had lower wages, fewer benefits, and longer hours, and had no pathway to citizenship.

Anti-Chinese discrimination, the cost of supporting and sheltering a family during travel for work, cultural education, and the cultural obligations of married women to care for their in-laws were all factors that kept the numbers of Chinese migrant women and girls low during the early period of mining and railroad migration. Chinese women who did manage to migrate to America during the railroad period were, by contrast to their male counterparts, often kidnapped, enslaved, and sex trafficked by Chinese merchants to service both White and Chinese men. Their exploitation would shape an ongoing modern stereotype of the hypersexualized, available Asian woman. The Page Act of 1875 barred the entry of those "held to a term of service" as well as those "imported . . . for the purposes of prostitution." Because the presumption of the time was that Chinese women would *only* be entering America if they were being sexually trafficked, the number of Chinese women entering America dropped precipitously after passage of the act, leaving Chinese women at only 4.6 percent of the entire Chinese population residing in America by 1880.

Despite their marginalization and isolation from wives and families, Chinese railway workers made a profound contribution at great personal risk to the construction of modern America as we know it. Paid half to a third of the wages of White workers, at about twenty-six dollars per month without meals, compared to the forty dollars per month with meals included paid to their White counterparts, they worked more effectively and efficiently, so that "without them [building the railroad] would be impossible," as the CPRR president Leland Stanford reported to President Andrew Johnson. Overcoming the presumption of their employers that they were not strong or skilled enough for the strenuous labor required in railroad work, they proved consistently to be able to lay more track, more quickly, than other groups of workers and also to maintain peaceful and sober work camps. In a brutal exercise, Charles Crocker set up a competition between groups of Chinese miners and Cornish miners in the Sierra Nevadas to see who could cut through more rock in a given time; the Chinese workers always won. Most migrants, excluding merchants, were from poor, rural families, deeply motivated by a need to earn money to send home in remittances, and to return home with savings for themselves. Still, the archaeological record indicates that the work they did took a terrible toll. Recovered remains from railway worker camps show frequent physical injury from hard manual labor.

Railway work on the CPRR route in the Sierra Nevadas entailed chipping, carving, and blasting away through expanses of granite, without power tools of any kind, in snowdrifts of up to forty feet. Blasting required workers to manually lower one of their own in a basket down into a tunnel to install and light explosives by hand, and then hurriedly raise the worker back out before the impact of the explosives injured him. Although this is the most graphic example of the dangers of railroad work, all of the work was brutal and often at high elevations—up to seven thousand feet, requiring grading for level ground, tunneling through mountains, and building bridges and retaining walls. In the winter, workers lived and worked in burrows beneath the snow, with the constant threat of avalanche. In the summer, as the track stretched into the desert beyond the Sierra Nevada, workers withstood 120-degree heat, with limited access to water.

In 1867, two years after the end of the Civil War, the Chinese CPRR workers went on strike in what was the largest mass labor action in American history up to that point. Mark Hopkins, who along with Leland, Crocker, and Collis Huntington, made up the "big four" owners of the CPRR, contemplated breaking the strike by employing newly freed Black labor, driving one racialized workforce against another. The strike was instead broken when Crocker cut off food and supplies to the work camps along the rail line. Still, the workers were not entirely defeated: Wages were raised and the big four came to understand that the CPRR workers were as strategic and disciplined in collective action as they were in laying rail.

Nonetheless, the efforts of the Chinese CPRR workers went mostly unmarked. They were excluded from photographs and celebrations marking the completion of the first transcontinental railroad on May 10, 1869. On that day, when the CPRR met the Union Pacific line at Promontory Summit, Utah, the two were connected by a ceremonial golden spike. That spike was not driven by the Chinese railroad workers who had blasted through the Sierra Nevadas. Instead, Chinese workers were dismissed beforehand, or sent back along the line to make repairs, and were erased in the remarks given on that day by transportation secretary John Volpe. "Who else but Americans could build 10 tunnels in mountains 30 feet deep in snow? Who else but Americans could chisel through miles of solid granite? Who else but Americans could have laid 10 miles of track in 12 hours?" he said, knowing that the Chinese workers who had done *all of those things* in the service of America were nevertheless prevented by law from becoming American.

Early Chinese migrants were uniquely able to maintain a connection to their common language, culture, and even food and items for personal use. A well-developed economy of trade and network of merchants supplied Chinese work camps with familiar items and services. When CPRR workers were dismissed, many moved on to other work opportunities on the West Coast, partly to stay connected to the distinct supply chains that allowed them to maintain their cultural identities.

They would find the West Coast first inhospitable and then violently hostile. By the time the CPRR was completed in 1869, California was already in the midst of a campaign to exterminate its Native peoples. State and federal governments would spend a combined $1,700,000 between 1846 and 1873 on the slaughter and enslavement of Native peoples. The efforts of U.S. military, state militia, and vigilante campaigns along with disease, dislocation, and starvation would reduce the Native population of the state from 150,000 people to about 30,000 by the end of that period, in campaigns described by dozens of American historians as a genocide. By 1880, the Native population of California would be further decimated, leaving just over 16,000 survivors.

It was in this larger racial context that Chinese railroad workers sought work in mines, in manufacturing, as farmers and fishermen, and in domestic work or laundries in California's cities. There they were often limited to low-quality, overcrowded rental housing and lacked city services. While Chinese migrants made up only about 10 percent of the workforce in 1860, they made up 12 to 23 percent of mining communities and were the largest visible non-Native minority in California.

Unsurprisingly, White workers perceived Chinese men as undesirable competition for jobs. This sentiment drove an era of prolific state and local anti-Chinese legislation, as well as widespread racist violence against Chinese communities and individuals. In 1850, California passed the so-called Foreign Miner's Tax, and though it was repealed in 1851, it was modified and re-passed. Several individual counties passed their own legislation prohibiting or impeding Chinese miners from working. In 1854 the California Supreme Court held that a California statute preventing Black, mixed-race, and Indigenous people from testifying in court against White people also applied to Chinese people, which made the prosecution of hate crimes and racial violence against Asians nearly impossible. A year before that, California imposed a "commutation tax" requiring ship captains to post a $500 bond for each foreign passenger that disembarked, and a year after, it imposed a $50 tax on anyone not eligible for naturalization and on board a ship docking in that state. At that time, only White people were eligible for naturalization. In 1860, a state tax was levied on Chinese fishermen, who had founded California's saltwater fishing industry only ten years earlier. They had, in the interim, built up dozens of fishing villages mostly around Monterey, the San Francisco Bay, the Sacramento and San Joaquin rivers, and San Diego.

There were also Chinese fishing camps at Humboldt Bay, Santa Cruz, and Santa Rosa, among other scattered locations.

In 1859, San Francisco's school board opened a segregated Chinese school in response to demand by Chinese parents for access to education. The school was established in a room of a church in San Francisco's Chinatown, one of the state's largest Chinese communities. Lack of funding, curriculum, and teaching staff; repeated closings and re-openings driven by lack of political commitment; and relocation of the school outside of Chinatown compromised its quality and attendance over the next several years. Although a subsequent treaty with China, meant to offer protection to Chinese migrants in America, affirmed the right of Chinese children to attend public schools, California later amended its laws so that it no longer acknowledged an obligation to provide even segregated education to Chinese children. During that time, some Chinese parents created private options while others took up the political battle for equal access to public education. In an 1885 case filed on behalf of "Mamie Tape, the 8-year-old American born daughter of an 'Americanized' Chinese immigrant, who had lived in San Francisco for fifteen years," the Supreme Court of California finally established that Chinese children must be afforded access to White public schools in the absence of specific legislation to the contrary. Rather than admitting Chinese children, the state legislature obliged by immediately passing a law explicitly mandating the segregation of Chinese students.

During the same period, there was a flurry of additional anti-Chinese legislation in San Francisco, making work, housing, and cultural practices inaccessible. Chinese people were barred from San Francisco city hospitals and the city banned hiring Chinese workers on municipal projects, banned the use of carrying poles for selling vegetables, created prohibitions meant to close Chinese overnight laundries, barred the use of firecrackers or ceremonial gongs, and required five hundred cubic feet of air in boardinghouses (which was meant to reduce available housing in Chinatowns). A piece of municipal legislation was passed that required Chinese prisoners to cut off ponytails, called queues, in which many wore their hair. This racist trend in California state and municipal legislation continued into the twentieth century.

The number of Chinese residents in the United States tripled from 1860 to 1890, growing from 30,000 to over 100,000, heavily concentrated on the West Coast. During this period, anti-Chinese sentiment only grew. Leland Stanford, the founder of Stanford University, was elected governor of California in 1861, having run on a platform opposing Asian immigration to the state. The California state constitution of 1879 provided that no "native person of China, no idiot, insane person, or person convicted of any infamous crime" would ever vote in that state. But the state did not act alone in pushing out Chinese migrants. There were at least two private racially motivated attacks on Chinatowns during this period. One in Los Angeles in 1871 resulted in the lynching of seventeen Chinese men, and another in San Francisco in 1877 resulted in the deaths of at least four Chinese people and an estimated $100,000 in damage to Chinese-owned property when the neighborhood's stores and homes were burned.

In this context of growing violence, Chinese residents of the West Coast began to seek safe harbor elsewhere in America, driving Chinese migration to urban areas across the country, where they would eventually establish the nation's Chinatowns. In 1870, Calvin Sampson, the owner of a shoe factory three hours west of Boston in North Adams, Massachusetts, contracted seventy-five Chinese workers from San Francisco to come work for him for three years. They would be strike breakers in his factory, where Sampson's previous employees had walked out when he announced a 10 percent pay decrease during the slow season, demanding an end to the ten-hour workday and access to the company records to align worker wages with profits.

The Chinese shoemakers' arrival sparked tens of thousands of news articles and editorials, evidencing a dramatic national debate on the role of Asian migrants in America, and the issue of naturalization. Although some articles portrayed the Chinese shoemakers as dangerously alien, others described a "model minority." White America had begun a discussion among themselves about whether Chinese people would be acceptable neighbors for the average White American. In addition to competition between White and Chinese workers, White manufacturers had become wary of increasing competition from Chinese manufacturers. Ultimately, the anti-Chinese sentiment that had engulfed the West Coast for decades paired with the economic and social anxieties of East Coast White communities and became national immigration policy in the Chinese Exclusion Act of 1882, which barred entry of almost all Chinese migrants to the United States. This restriction would remain the law until 1943.

Emboldened by congressional support for anti-Chinese sentiment, White people in the West began to violently expel their Chinese neighbors. More than two hundred communities, spread throughout California, into Oregon and Washington, and as far east as New Mexico and Wyoming, forced Chinese residents out in 1885 and 1886. Expulsions were sometimes preceded by boycotts and deadlines for departure but were themselves violent and often deadly. White men herded and beat, and sometimes shot or lynched, their Chinese neighbors; they looted, bombed, and burned their homes, belongings, tools, and businesses. Arson was particularly effective at destroying the historical record of early Chinese residents on the West Coast, so we have little idea how they understood and responded to the racism that was directed against them. In a period called "the Shasta Wars," vigilante White miners took it upon themselves to travel from one Chinese mining camp to another, attacking and ordering Chinese men at gunpoint to leave and not return. And although there were some efforts by the local sheriff and at least one judge to impose order, the vigilantes were ultimately released before trial or found not guilty. By 1913, Chinese people, in legislation broadly aimed at those not eligible for citizenship, were barred from land ownership in California.

In periods of instability or economic scarcity, access to land and capital is more likely to be viewed as a problem of racial competition, and old tropes about Chinatowns or Chinese businesses as alien sites of disease or vice re-emerge. In 2020, President Trump weaponized the Covid-19 outbreak against China and Chinese Americans, exciting old prejudices by persistently calling Covid-19 "the China virus." Human Rights Watch issued a global call to governments to prevent and prosecute hate crimes amid increased accounts of anti-Asian harassment, violence, and vandalism. Stop AAPI Hate, an Asian American advocacy group, catalogued 2,800 hate incidents directed against Asian Americans across America in 2020, including verbal abuse, physical assault, and murder. Chinatown businesses on both coasts have struggled under the weight of the economic impacts of pandemic response measures compounded by racist stigma.

Two of my eight first-year courses were taught by Black women, one by a first-generation Chinese American woman, and another by a Jewish man from Cuba, all representative of Northeastern's broadly diverse faculty. In my first and second years, Northeastern had a Black dean, David Hall, who had featured prominently on the school's promotional materials. Though I spent little time with him, Dean Hall would have an outsized impact on me. Specifically, he gave a speech in which he exhorted each of us, *"Know where you stand!"* His words echoed in my approach to law school, and my life after law school.

There were Black, Hispanic, Asian, and LGBTQ law students' associations at Northeastern, and each of those demographics was reasonably well represented in the student body. Being surrounded by strong, successful people of color, with a shared commitment to social justice and emboldened by the study of law, was transformative. Over the next three years I entered a new reality in which acknowledging my identity, my family, culture, and faith of origin felt not only possible, but valuable. This was the resolution of a twenty-year fissure in my identity, caused by the realities of being a sometimes White-passing Pakistani Muslim in overwhelmingly White, Christian, or post-Christian environments. It was like exhaling for the first time, although it also meant the slow, painful work of undoing all the protections, performances, and even some of the relationships in my life up to that point.

Early on, I visited mosques in Boston and Cambridge and sat quietly through Asian Law Students Association meetings, trying to find something that could help me better define myself. In 1999, during my second year of law school, I followed some Indian friends from the law school to a local conference on socialism, activism, and South Asian identity. During a panel on South Asian faith traditions, the Muslim-identified speaker, someone I had not ever heard of, nor have I ever since, began by calling Islam irrelevant and obsolete, and I found myself outraged, standing up with the one other Muslim (who was then a complete stranger) in the room, each of us moved to say how integral Islam was to our commitment to social justice. We were right, or at least consistent: Faisal Alam went on to a career of social justice and queer rights activism. I went on to a career in public interest law. Both of us continue to identify strongly as Muslim, vocal in our sometimes unorthodox views.

At a local conference on Islamic law and jurisprudence the same year, I heard the then Harvard Law doctoral candidate, now University of Wisconsin professor of law Asifa Quraishi-Landes detail the history of Islamic marriage contracts. They were intended, she said, and certainly still had the potential to be, true contracts, with notably liberating effects for women. She provided several historical examples where contracts were not formulaic, but were negotiated by and protected the specific interests of each party to a marriage. She provided others that suggested women had contracted for the protection of their economic, social, and scholarly rights within marriage, divorcing when the terms of those contracts were violated.

That winter, Aaron and I traveled to Hyderabad, Pakistan, to attend my older brother's wedding. Beautiful and exuberant as it was, it remained in stark contrast to what Asifa described, the contract a standard form, discussed neither before nor after the wedding by my brother and sister-in-law. I began to realize that my interests and my identity were aligned with the Islam that Asifa had spoken to, and not the cultural expectations of my parents' generation. Maybe more important, Asifa was the first Muslim woman I had ever encountered in person who seemed to me both entirely American and entirely Muslim, outspoken, and secure in a feminist, religious, and racialized identity. Although I had been reading the Muslim, progressive, and feminist works of Amina Wadud and Fatima Mernissi, Asma Jahangir and Leila Ahmed, those women felt remote to me. Meeting Asifa cemented what I was beginning to believe possible: I could be entirely myself, a Brown Muslim woman, a social justice lawyer and advocate, an American. I could inhabit an identity with integrity and honesty, based on where I had actually come from and what I had experienced, without ever allowing myself to pass for White again. In fact, I was suddenly aware that I had no other choice.

In this new realization, I was no longer threatened by other traditions or identities, and the world seemed to open up. I began to bring my identity and experience into the papers I wrote for my Critical Legal Theory class, arguing more decidedly and passionately. Academically, my evaluations crested; I achieved the coveted "outstanding," Northeastern's version of the highest marks, both for coursework and for the final three of my four co-op placements. At the same time, my relationship with Aaron seemed to develop a new sweetness. After exam week in my last year just before winter break, Aaron came home from work with a surprise. He had a blindfold for me and told me to dress warmly. He'd never done anything like this before, and I had no idea what to expect. By then, we'd moved to an apartment in Allston, so he steered me toward the Green Line headed toward downtown. When he finally had me take off my blindfold, we were at Boston Common's Frog Pond, which I'd never been to in the wintertime, all lit up and turned into an ice-skating rink, a magical light snow falling.

I had, in many ways, always been more committed to Aaron and to our marriage than he was to me, both because I adored and respected him and also perhaps because I had so little else to hold on to when we'd met. At law school, as my sense of self deepened and I learned to investigate rather than hide my insecurities, I became more whole. Aaron, I think, grew more in love and in admiration as I became a fuller, more contented version of myself. Susan would remark later that she was the happiest she'd ever been about our relationship in that final year I was in law school. She'd noticed Aaron's warmer affection, and how he'd started calling me "honey" rather than my nickname, Sof. Perhaps moved to unburden himself in our new, closer relationship, Aaron broke down one day. We were at his parents' house for a week at Christmas. His younger brother was visiting as well, excited to tell us about his first serious relationship. He was so enthralled with this new thing he was experiencing that he'd bought a book about relationships and he wanted Aaron and me to look at it.

It was our turn to cook dinner, so we took it with us to the grocery store. Aaron was driving and I was reading bits out loud. I don't remember what exactly it was, but there was a question in the book, a conversation starter, for couples about sexual fantasies. I asked him it, thinking it was innocuous, even fun. He went silent for the rest of the ride home, unresponsive to me in every way, and was impassive all evening.

I told Aaron that his reaction scared me a little, and that I didn't think it was fair. I told him that I'd be sleeping in the guest room until he could explain what was going on. Late that evening, after everyone else had gone up to bed, Aaron led me into the den, which was next to the main family room and had a door. It was a large room, lined with bookshelves, that his mother used for an office. We sat on the sofa, me with my legs tucked under me, facing him, and Aaron leaning forward with his elbows on his knees.

"Aaron, *what* is going on?" I prodded after a long silence.

"I don't know where to start."

"Well, the question was about fantasies—why don't you start there? How bad could it be if it's imaginary?"

And then he started to explain, in pained brevity, how he was turned on by images of violence and degradation of women. I had a friend in law school whose partner was addicted to porn; he'd been confiding in me about their struggle for several months, and I thought maybe Aaron was struggling with something similar. No, he told me, it wasn't that. He would turn to the back page of *Ms.* magazine, to which I had a subscription, where they printed examples of misogyny in advertising. *That* was what he was getting off on.

I could tell there was more, but he wouldn't say anything else. He said that was it. He was ashamed and upset, and I was not thrilled, but also not devastated. I was mostly exhausted and confused. How did this fit with the Aaron I knew? The next day we'd planned to drive up to my parents' house for their annual extended family gathering on New Year's Eve. On the way up, I asked Aaron what he wasn't telling me, but he put me off. When we arrived, my parents were out running an errand. We unloaded our duffel out of the hatchback and walked to a nearby playground, where we could talk in private. There, Aaron told me that when we were in Little Rock, he'd take breaks from long afternoons of "field organizing," mostly door-knocking and petitioning, and park outside Central High. He'd wait and watch schoolgirls, who would have been in their teens, come out at lunch or at the end of school.

"Central High, Aaron? *Central High?* And so, what . . . you just watched them?

Silence.

"Aaron, were you watching for specific girls or just checking out random girls?"

"There were specific ones." His voice was barely audible.

"And when you saw them? What were you doing? Saving them to fantasize about? Jerking off?" I felt like I was in someone else's body, in someone else's life. This was my husband. We'd not yet been married for two years.

It was too much for me. What he'd done, but also, overwhelmingly, the sense that I had *no idea* who he was. I quietly slid off my simple white gold wedding ring. Aaron saw and looked devastated.

"Sof. No."

"I don't know who you are. I need to know everything. I need to understand what is happening. What the *fuck*, Aaron. We went there to be *organizers,* to *help* the people in that community, not *stalk their fucking daughters.*"

I don't know how we got through the next two days at my parents' house, except that in a big extended family, it's fairly easy to not really engage anyone. I plastered on a smile, wore the right clothes, and Aaron did the same. Then we drove home, mostly in silence. Over the next ten days, back in our one-bedroom apartment in Allston, I learned more each day. My winter co-op had not yet started, and Aaron had a few days before he went back to work. Unable to sleep, unable to eat, I asked Aaron every day if that was all, if there was anything more. Aaron said he had watched daughters in houses where he had door-knocked for work. He said he didn't do anything, just fixated on them, fantasized about them, returned to their houses unnecessarily. He revealed that on a training trip to New York, he'd followed a woman through a subway station, so immersed, he said, that he hadn't been fully aware of what he was doing.

"But why would you do that? What were you hoping would happen?"

"I was watching her, and when she looked up, I felt like she recognized me."

"Was she someone you knew?" I was so, so confused. Whose life was this?

"No. No, it's just like I was in a fantasy and couldn't stop."

"What does that mean, you couldn't stop?"

"It's like, I mostly feel like I'm not quite here in my life, in my body. It's like I'm living it through a wet suit, like nothing is ever real. Nothing ever *really* happens and I can't *really* feel it. Like it's all a dream and I'm separate from it."

He said he stopped when she ran, but I couldn't tell anymore what was true. There were other stories, stories that were less terrifying but that betrayed Aaron's deep disregard for women and resentment of me. Things he'd chosen to do or not do to make me feel smaller, to withhold affection and attention from me that he'd then focus on *this*.

Although I had no way to gauge reality anymore, I pressed for every detail. Not just what he'd done and not done—although certainly that. It had begun to dawn on me that while I'd been working out our budget, making pottery, sewing curtains for our apartment, growing tomatoes on the fire escape, studying in the evenings, *planning our wedding,* Aaron had been occupied with *this.* I collected it all in my mind, going over it, madly trying to make sense of who he was. This is a man I'd slept next to, and *with,* for years, someone who I had believed to be consistently and profoundly committed to making a better world, someone who drove down from Gainesville to run the Take Back the Night event with me on campus. There was no making sense of it. It just didn't make sense.

I was wrecked and I hated myself and Aaron both. I was devastated and exhausted at the unfairness of having fought so hard to make a life with someone who did not actually exist. Underneath that, I was crushed because I had twisted myself up to be worthy of love, and still found my life broken in a way that seemed like it couldn't be fixed. I unrolled my prayer rug in a corner of the apartment, wrapping my head in a long cotton scarf, rolling through the motions of prayer. Unable to get up when my prayers were done, I just lay there and went to sleep. Even if I did get up, what could be done? What was to be done now?

I asked Aaron to choose a friend or a family member to tell, someone who could be inside this new reality with me that we could both trust. I wanted to stop feeling so alone but was still concerned about keeping his confidence. He was a fairly private person. So, I was stunned when he instead wrote an email to his entire extended family, hitting send before showing it to me. Then I read it. He'd *excluded* all of what he'd been doing except for a brief reference to fantasy, saying he felt ashamed, that I was distraught, and that he hoped they'd be supportive of me. Not surprisingly, his note triggered a lot of confusion in the family, and some general disdain for me. *The story he'd told was so incomplete as to be untrue.* One cousin, in particular, told him I was being unreasonable and a prude. I don't know that Aaron ever corrected the picture he'd created, though I asked him to, especially with his parents.

I suspect he did not, because when I spoke to Susan a few weeks later, she told me she had asked colleagues and friends who had been through rough patches in their marriages what kept them with their spouses. She told me a story I think she viewed as compelling, about a woman who stayed with her unfaithful husband because she found it so comforting to know that he was just there in the house with her, even if he was in the other room. I did not find that story relevant, nor did I find it compelling. I found it sad and confusing and terrible. At the age of twenty-five there was—and still now at forty-seven there is—nothing comforting about the idea of living my life alongside someone who stalked schoolgirls and followed a terrified woman through a subway station, someone who was aroused by his transgression and their fear. I also felt that underneath it all, Aaron resented me. He'd lived with me, and spoken softly to me, and slept with me all while actually *loathing me*.

I moved in with Ashley, a friend from law school, briefly. Unable to find my footing, I told my family and asked the advice of shocked friends. Strangely, I found myself interrogated. Were we even married at the time? Was Aaron just "sowing his wild oats"? Maybe Aaron should just not have told me. Was there any actual intercourse involved? Both friends and family, like Susan, seemed to confuse stalking women and children with a consensual affair. Some wanted to know exactly how old the children were, as if that *mattered,* and as if what the children themselves wanted or could even grasp about Aaron's predation mattered *not at all*. I called a therapist I'd seen during my second year of law school. I'd gone to her hoping she could help me deal with a persistent sense of anxiety, which I had thought was from the stress of law school, and to help me understand recurrent nightmares I'd been having, of being chased and of doors and windows that wouldn't stay locked. The sessions hadn't really gone anywhere, and I hadn't seen her for weeks or months when I called to tell her I thought my marriage was ending.

When I began to recount what was going on, starting with the violent fantasies, my therapist rolled her eyes. I could read her impatience: Fantasies? Your marriage is ending over fantasies? By the time I told her about the woman in the subway station, she seemed somewhat less apathetic. I wondered if I was insane, wondered if there was something wrong with me instead of Aaron. I asked if she could recommend a marriage counselor. Aaron and I went to see the woman she recommended the next week. That therapist ended our first session, in which we'd spent an hour laying out Aaron's stalking behavior and the crisis it had created in our marriage, by asking Aaron *if he was satisfied with our sex life*—as if Aaron's sexual satisfaction was the critical piece, and as if ending the session that way would be anything other than catastrophic for my mental health.

I found that very few people wanted to contemplate the facts of what Aaron had been doing, the terror he'd inflicted, and no one at all wanted to pass judgment. Not a single person wanted to be in the position of counseling an end to the marriage, no matter how violative Aaron's behavior was of the law, of social norms, of anything he'd ever represented himself to be. Certainly no one seemed prepared to confront what all of this meant for me, or how I could possibly reconcile this person with the man I married without losing my mind, not to mention my self-respect. And no one seemed to grasp the danger I might be in. This was an important lesson for me in the propensity of well-meaning people to step away from, cover over, or reinterpret terrible acts.

Aaron himself, after a couple of weeks of contrition, though not really reflection, seemed ready to be over it, as if inside of him, a door that had opened briefly in a vulnerable moment was swinging shut. I had not yet put my wedding ring back on. There was a door inside me, too, I discovered. He wanted to move past it, wanted to know why I couldn't. We were in the car when I explained to him, "Imagine if one day you learned that instead of swerving to avoid squirrels in the road when I drive, I liked to swerve toward them. Maybe I don't usually hit them, maybe I never hit them at all, but I get off on—I'm *aroused* by—scaring animals, even, that are smaller and more vulnerable than me. Would you think that was an attractive quality? Or would you think I was a psychopath?" When I finally told her what was going on, a law school friend remarked, "Better that you find out now than in ten years, by walking in on him in the basement messing with your nine-year-old daughter." That's an image that sticks with you.

I could see the door closing in Aaron as clearly as if it were real. Jamming my foot into it, I asked him one last question. During our year in Little Rock, one of my tasks at the Women's Project had been to archive news stories about misogynist violence, violence aimed at women because they were women. In one of those news stories a man who'd been married for decades shot his wife in the head as she slept. I asked Aaron, "Is that me? I'm terrified that's me, that you have a rage inside of you that's aimed, at least partly, at me. Is that something that could happen with us?" In one final shred of honesty, he said, "I think it could." He seemed not to register how monstrous his words were, seemed still to expect my response to be to comfort him and not to recoil.

Although I was crushed by the reactions of friends and family, who seemed not to grasp the tremendous mind-fuck of my situation, and although I still sometimes desperately imagined Aaron and I could remain in each other's lives—because I could not imagine anything else—I knew that I could not stay. Later, I'd tell friends that it was like I had been on a train moving thousands of miles an hour on a track in one direction, and without warning, I'd been plucked out from above and dropped into a different train, going not just in another direction, but into a new reality. In March of my final year of law school, with only two months left to go and not quite two years after Aaron and I were married, I moved out.

I found a postcard from Aaron, all these years later, addressed to the apartment I moved into that month. It's an image and a quote from Che Guevara in English and in Spanish: "Let me say, at the risk of seeming ridiculous, that the true revolutionary is guided by great feelings of love." On the back, Aaron wrote, "Hola, compeñera! I think of you when I see this card. Maybe when you get this you won't be sick anymore. A haiku from my ride this morning . . ." It was the last piece I have of the old Aaron, the one I thought I'd known. He left town, I heard, with the mass action activists who'd come to Boston to protest BIO 2000, a big biotechnology exhibition at Boston's Hynes Convention Center that spring, and never resurfaced.

I still wonder when I read it: How was it that I'd believed I was the one with a split identity all of those years? How does one person inhabit such idealism and such darkness at once? How did I miss all of the small resentments and rejections I now see so clearly in that relationship? Who was I that I needed to accept them? I had, for so long, felt that I had value because of my proximity to Aaron. I had picked up from my experiences in Fallsington and Levittown and later, in high school and college, that my perceptions were not valuable or even credible in the mostly White contexts of my life. When I finally grew to understand that I might have independent value of my own, the mirage I thought was Aaron evaporated.

Shortly after I left Aaron, a friend from college named Sylvia settled in town, dragging me out of my law school circle and the trauma of my imploded marriage to explore Boston and Cambridge. These forays included several visits to Memorial Church in Harvard Yard to hear a celebrated reverend and scholar, the late Peter Gomes, preach. I'd actually heard him once before when the attendees at that earlier Islamic Legal Studies conference, a racially and religiously diverse group, took a break from Sunday-morning sessions to attend his sermon. Back then, and again in my visits with Sylvia, I felt that Reverend Gomes spoke directly to me, even as I perched on the margins of my own identity, trying to imagine where I belonged. Now that I know more about who he was, his ability to make everyone feel seen and witnessed is not so surprising. A Black theologian and preacher at Harvard from 1971, who came out as gay twenty years later in response to right-wing, homophobic student attacks, he had every possible insight on what it meant to live in a racialized body in a White context, and also to proclaim one's faith in a religious tradition that might prefer to erase him. The light of his integrity was a beacon for me.

One Sunday just before I graduated, I attended Memorial Church one last time. That morning, Reverend Gomes preached the parable of the Prodigal Son, punctuated with the refrain "Go home!" Even as we break the molds our families set out for us, he explained, home has a special function in self-realization. Home is where the lessons of the world are integrated, where our coming-of-age is consummated, where the primordial mirror of self-knowledge is kept. My life was not as I expected it to be as I finished law school. Many of my law school friends were leaving for jobs in other cities. I'd applied for and accepted a one-year clerkship with the state courts in Massachusetts.

Most days, I was alone in that manic, devastated place that often follows the end of a marriage. I survived largely because a half dozen friends showed up that year, one by one, like angels to help distract me from my grief. None came too close—as if what had happened to me, the implosion of my life, might be contagious—but they loved me from the outside of the turmoil, played with me, checked in on me, sometimes dragged me out into the world. Somehow, that spring, one year after everything fell apart, I was offered my dream job in Philadelphia, at Community Legal Services. Stripped of everything I thought I knew, I was heading home.

CHAPTER ELEVEN

LAW AND ORDER

Philadelphia, Pennyslvania

> *[Prison] relieves us of the responsibility of seriously engaging
> with the problems of our society, especially those produced by
> racism and, increasingly, global capitalism.*
> —Angela Davis

B ack in the Delaware Valley, I was coping with the aftermath of divorce. In their pain and shame over it, my parents were materially supportive but emotionally absent. I stayed with them for a month, in July of 2000, clearing the Pennsylvania bar to begin work at the North Philadelphia office of Community Legal Services (CLS). I was eager to start, but the adrenaline that had carried me through the end of law school and most of my clerkship had worn off, and I was left open and raw.

I moved into the basement room of a shared house in the Spring Garden neighborhood on the other side of City Hall from Philadelphia's Chinatown. My childhood friend Allison, the one I made trouble with in Old Fallsington, was already living there with two progressive lawyers. The two lawyers had served with the Jesuit Volunteer Corps (JVC), an organization that focuses on exemplifying faith through service in poor communities (though not on proselytizing or "church-planting" in those communities), and had stayed on in

Philly. Our house was just across the street from the city's historically all-White boys' preparatory school, Girard College. I had thought about sharing a place farther out in Upper Darby with a friend I had met more recently, a Palestinian American woman, and friends of hers—a Somali refugee and a first-generation woman from India, all Muslim. I was not ready to do battle with their more conservative, and sometimes culturally rigid, ideas of Muslim womanhood, and so I chose Allison's house, happy to reconnect after many years, and happy for a shorter commute.

Community Legal Services was and still is, in many ways, my dream job. It paid very little, which was not ideal given my law school debt, but the work and the opportunity for advocacy on behalf of low-income communities was everything I wanted. Several years before, Congress had passed a law to restrict federal funding, limiting the kinds of advocacy that legal services organizations could pursue and which clients they could represent if they received that funding. CLS had chosen to decline that funding in order to continue serving clients of every immigration status (including no immigration status), to bring class-action lawsuits, and to, where necessary, sue the government. I was excited to join lawyers who were unsung national heroes, defending and protecting parental rights, consumer rights, language access, welfare rights, access to healthcare, and small businesses in low-income communities, often communities of color. By then, some of my own relatives on the edges of Philadelphia were a part of those communities. It was the right place to begin again; it was in every way a homecoming.

Two days into work, I walked through the waiting room and around the corner to my office. I had a window into the conference room next door, which was full of co-workers huddled around a ten-inch black-and-white television. It was the morning of September 11, 2001, and the first World Trade Center tower had fallen.

In those days, Muslims had not yet been so thoroughly demonized by the American public. I did not even stop to consider that the events of September 11 could be attributed to an international terrorist group that claimed to speak for Muslims. But I watched my country reel from the terror attack, and then, in the very next breath, turn their rage toward Muslims. Not the hijackers who flew planes into the World Trade Center towers, not the extremist groups that spawned them, but all of us. The thin scab I had grown in the wake of my divorce was torn away in the post-9/11 furor. The U.S. attack on Afghanistan followed barely a month after 9/11, the entire country still caught in a confused haze, and then, a year and a half later, America attacked Iraq. When only one other colleague in my progressive office headed downtown with me for the first anti-war rally, and a different colleague suggested that the widely reported U.S. "carpet bombing" of Taliban targets in Afghanistan was justified, I was crushed.

My concern was directed at the ordinary people of those places. In the United States, my job was to represent low-income people; I saw the precarity of their lives, their lack of influence on and protection from the world events around them. Reading the news, I imagined what American attacks would mean for Afghan civilians with similar constraints and was repulsed by my country's misdirected vengeance and bloodthirst. The crassness with which the Bush administration manipulated the devastation of 9/11 to achieve neoconservative aims did not seem to register in the post-9/11 American public consciousness. Few were willing to question their government or to appear unpatriotic in a time of war. This was unsurprisingly also true among those who felt themselves to be suddenly vulnerable to ostracism, discrimination, deportation, or even extrajudicial persecution and torture at offshore sites. Even progressive and Muslim American communities seemed cowed into silence.

September 11 and its cynical, destructive aftermath compounded my sense that the world around me had gone mad. The United States had opened the torture camp at Guantanamo, filled with men turned in for bounties to U.S. authorities, many of them held without charge, without access to counsel, and subjected to torture. In my extended family and larger Muslim community, men became especially wary of flying, and when they had no choice but to fly, they were often turned away from flights without explanation or detained for long hours on departure and arrival.

These events prolonged and intensified the despair I already felt. I still hadn't fully made sense of how opposite Aaron was from who I'd believed him to be, nor the many bizarre responses of family members and friends to his revelations. I was still, in my personal life, a mess. I was confused, in pain most of the time, terrified of being alone. I was alternately manic, like a spinning top, and overcome by the adrenal exhaustion that followed the prolonged stress of the previous year. Then after 9/11, while our nation laid waste to large Muslim civilian populations in Afghanistan and Iraq, President Bush gave several speeches saying that "our Muslim friends" were not the enemy. I could not reconcile the two, and neither could I excuse the discrepancy. I saw plainly that my country was no longer a safe place for people like me. Though I had committed myself to its service as a legal aid lawyer, I could no longer assume its commitment to me, because I was Muslim.

My first real experience of trying to understand news reports of current events was on May 13, 1985, when I was ten years old. That day, the City of Philadelphia bombed a residential row home thirty minutes away from Fallsington, where I lived. As a result, sixty-one row homes on three city blocks were burned to the ground. The MOVE bombing, as it has come to be known, exposed such an egregious and inexplicable disregard for human life that it penetrated the idealistic childhood filter through which I then viewed my country.

More than two decades before the bombing, Frank Rizzo was working his way up in city government. He served as deputy police commissioner from 1963 to 1967 before becoming police commissioner and staying in that role for five years, until 1972. During that time, he gained a reputation for brutality and anti-Black racism. When, in 1968, Black Philadelphians protested for entry to the all-

White Girard College, Rizzo ordered police onto their motorcycles to ride into and over protestors. Later, at the same site, he ordered police cars to leave their engines running so that overnight protestors in sleeping bags would be overcome with their fumes and carbon monoxide. In another example of Rizzo's tactics, Black Philadelphians who protested discriminatory hiring practices while Rizzo was police commissioner were cuffed between their legs, forcing them to hop, hunched down, to police vans. They were then led into the station between two rows of police, beaten as they walked in, "like running a gauntlet."

More than a decade before the MOVE bombing, in 1972, Frank Rizzo was elected mayor of Philadelphia. The new role did little to curb Rizzo's overt racism: He championed segregation in the city. Back then, Jon Stein, an attorney at the legal services organization I'd eventually join, sued Rizzo in federal court on behalf of Black families seeking affordable housing. Rizzo had taken action to block the construction of 120 single-family, subsidized row homes, taking the position that he

considered public housing to be the same as Black housing in that most tenants of public housing are Black. Mayor Rizzo therefore felt that there should not be any public housing placed in White neighborhoods because people in White neighborhoods did not want Black people moving in with them. Furthermore, Mayor Rizzo stated that he did not intend to allow PHA [the Public Housing Authority] to ruin nice neighborhoods.

As mayor, Rizzo was notorious for allowing the police to act with impunity. On average, between 1970 and 1978, the Philadelphia police killed one person per week; those killed were disproportionately Black Philadelphians. In 1979, Rizzo ordered a raid of the Black Panthers' Philadelphia headquarters, during which members were handcuffed and stripped naked. Rizzo later boasted, "They were humiliated. We took their pants off them, to search them." At the same time, he railed against journalists who questioned violent police tactics, saying they encouraged disrespect for authority. However, the Rizzo administration's excesses attracted the attention of the U.S. Department of Justice, which filed a civil rights complaint against the Philadelphia Police Department, the first such complaint ever filed by the Department of Justice against a municipality.

By the late 1970s the MOVE organization had become a target for Mayor Rizzo. MOVE was a small organization that never had more than 150 members, created in the early 1970s by a man named Vincent Leaphart, known to his followers as John Africa. Black MOVE members wore their hair in natural dreadlocks and often took the last name Africa; several members lived together at a single home in West Philadelphia. Some of what MOVE stood for was a precursor to later environmental movement priorities and trends: animal rights, vegetarianism and a raw food diet, attempts at composting food waste, and a rejection of lives centered on technology. Other aspects of MOVE were in line with Black Power organizations of the time: protests against police brutality and institutional racism in law, government, and industry.

MOVE itself might have rejected these characterizations, seeing their organization as religious as well as political, not centered on either environmentalism or Black Power so much as on the teachings and leadership of John Africa, which contained elements of each. Prior to 1978, MOVE was headquartered in a single home in Powelton Village, a predominantly Black neighborhood just a twenty-minute walk from the University of Pennsylvania. Neighbors first seemed to view the group with tolerance and even interest, describing MOVE men selling watermelons from handcarts and children playing at the park. MOVE members operated a carwash, shoveled sidewalks, and did repair work for elderly neighbors to make money. Eventually, though, MOVE's less orthodox activities began to draw complaints from neighbors. They built a wooden barricade across the front of their row home, boarded up the first- and second-floor windows, took in stray dogs that wandered as a large pack—forty-eight dogs by one count—and drew rats and insects with their haphazard efforts at composting. Neighbors also expressed concern about MOVE children frequently seen naked in the neighborhood, sometimes asking to be fed or going through the trash.

Members of MOVE were repeatedly arrested and beaten in confrontations with police, and they believed that they were targets of persecution. Their animal rights and other political protests—and even their use of profanity—led to 142 arrests, with substantial bail and court fees. In 1976, police were called to investigate a disturbance in the Powelton Village MOVE house, and their presence resulted in a deadly physical confrontation. When police arrived, Janine Africa was standing outside her home holding her infant son, who police allegedly knocked out of her arms. According to statements by MOVE members, his skull was crushed when an officer stepped on him. When confronted, city officials denied the incident and questioned whether the baby even existed. In response, MOVE invited journalists and city officials to come to their house, where they were permitted to view and record the infant's lifeless body.

The following year, on May 20, city health inspectors responded to neighbors' complaints by trying to enter the house in Powelton Village. Armed MOVE members blocked their entry and the city inspectors withdrew. Afterward, MOVE members barricaded the home to prevent future intrusion. The following spring, Mayor Rizzo initiated a fifty-eight-day blockade of the home, cutting off the water supply. The blockade was intended to "starve them out," by preventing MOVE members from getting food and supplies into the house. The standoff eventually resulted in a compromise: Mayor Rizzo agreed to expedite the trials of any jailed MOVE members and to refrain from arresting members with no outstanding warrants, and MOVE agreed to surrender its weapons and vacate their house in Powelton Village by August 1.

By August 8, MOVE members had not vacated the house, citing the city's failure to make good on its promises to expedite trials. In response, police drove a bulldozer through the wooden barricade in front of the house and blasted it with high-pressure water hoses. What happened next remains in dispute. The city maintains that someone fired a shot from within the MOVE house; bystanders and journalists have said that the shot was fired from behind the crowd amassed on the street, perhaps by a police officer. Both groups agree that the initial shot sparked a flurry of gunfire, which killed a police officer named James Ramp. Eight other police officers and firefighters were wounded; MOVE members huddled in the basement were showered with debris. The city ultimately used tear gas to drive MOVE out, arresting twelve adults and removing eleven children aged eighteen months to twelve years. Within hours of the conflict, Mayor Rizzo ordered the house razed, destroying all evidence of the crime scene. Ed Rendell, then district attorney of Philadelphia, spoke at a press conference that afternoon, saying, "The police probably would have been legally within their rights, subsequent to the shooting of Officer Ramp, [to have] stormed the house and killed all of the people in that basement." Police officers did attack at least one MOVE member that day, as well as several uninvolved Black neighbors.

A *Philadelphia Inquirer* reporter captured footage of three officers repeatedly kicking, stomping, and beating the MOVE member Delbert Africa after he came out of the house unarmed, bare chested, with his hands spread out to his sides. The attack continued even as Africa lay on the pavement, curled into a fetal position. Police Commissioner Joseph O'Neill would testify at the trial of the three officers that Africa "was not a man, but a savage." The officers charged with Africa's assault were acquitted when the judge interrupted proceedings and curtailed jury deliberation, finding that the prosecution failed to demonstrate that the police officers were not acting in self-defense. Delbert Africa would ultimately serve *forty-one years* in prison, dying just six months after his release in January 2020.

A total of nine MOVE members were convicted of killing officer Ramp and were sentenced to *thirty to one hundred years* in prison each, though police testimony at their trials was that only one of those charged was armed and that the single bullet that killed officer Ramp and the bullets that injured three other officers were all fired from the same gun. Parole of each member of the MOVE Nine was conditioned on their repudiation of MOVE. Their refusal has meant that each of them has served most or all of their decades-long prison terms, separated from their children and families. Debbie Africa gave birth to her son, Mike Africa, Jr., in prison and waited forty years to reunite with him in 2018. Mike Africa, Sr., was released the same year and reunited with them both at their son's house outside of Philadelphia.

By 1982, the MOVE members who were not imprisoned had relocated their headquarters to 6221 Osage Avenue, in the middle of a long block of row homes in the historic Cobbs Creek neighborhood on the far western edge of Philadelphia. Cobbs Creek was, at that time, a Black neighborhood with one of the city's highest proportions of owner-occupied homes, a cohesive, tight-knit community with its own shopping district. In other words, most if not all of MOVE's neighbors were deeply invested in their neighborhood. In a country that had spent the previous hundred years passing legislation and devising policies to make Black home ownership difficult to achieve, they had overcome. And despite a general sense of tolerance among neighbors, MOVE disturbed their peace.

Wilson Goode, elected the city's first Black mayor in 1983, seemed intent on avoiding a confrontation with MOVE. But when MOVE's initial efforts failed to win the release of the incarcerated MOVE Nine, they began to employ more confrontational methods. They built what they called a bunker on the flat roof of their row home, with high, narrow openings in place of windows, and a five-gallon gas tank. Neighbors reported seeing an armed MOVE member up there. They installed a bullhorn, from which they would announce the directives of John Africa and make profane complaints, broadcasting continuously for a thirty-six-hour stretch over Christmas of 1983. MOVE members continued to collect animals and refuse as they had at their Powelton Village home. The residents of Osage Avenue complained to and met with the city at least three times between May and July 1984 about the escalating threat they felt MOVE represented. In 1985,

John Africa's sister, Louise Africa, who was also a member of MOVE, would testify about the increasing militarization of MOVE:

> When MOVE first surfaced in the early 1970s we were armed only with the truth. The system says that we are entitled to freedom of speech . . . (but) every time we opened our mouths we were beaten, bludgeoned, kicked, stomped, babies killed. . . . Finally MOVE decided we weren't going to get beat anymore.

In May 1984, the U.S. Attorney, the FBI, and the Secret Service took the position that there were no grounds for federal action against MOVE and warned Philadelphia officials against violating the civil rights of residents of the MOVE house on Osage Avenue. Mayor Goode had little of the institutional support from the federal government that might have ensured an organized, peaceful negotiation with MOVE and its neighbors on Osage Avenue. Inexplicably, the city also rebuffed the offers of local third-party activists, journalists, and community members to negotiate a workable relationship between MOVE and its neighbors in Cobbs Creek.

Instead, on Goode's order, police evacuated MOVE's neighbors on May 12 in preparation for a raid of the house to evict MOVE. They provided the homeowners of Osage Avenue little reason to believe that they should pack anything but overnight supplies. In addition, there was no plan at all to safely remove the children present in the MOVE home that day. In a single thoughtful move, Goode ordered that the raid not include police officers involved in the 1978 conflict, wary that old grudges and policing precedents from the Rizzo administration could only escalate matters.

Mayor Goode watched events on television across town, where he lacked the ability to communicate directly with anyone but the city's chief of operations at the scene. By 4 A.M. on May 13, electricity and gas were cut off to the MOVE home. At 5:35 A.M., the police commissioner used a bullhorn to demand the surrender of four MOVE members for whom arrest warrants had been issued. MOVE members used their own bullhorn to announce their refusal. Over the next two hours, police trained a water cannon on the Cobbs Creek property as they had in Powelton Village, but also used tear gas and smoke projectiles to breach barricades, fired ten thousand rounds in the space of ninety minutes, and set off explosives to enter the property from adjacent row homes without notice to or consent from their owners. There were six children living in the MOVE house at the time. Michael "Birdie" Africa, thirteen years old and the only child to survive the attack, would later explain that the children in the house were afraid and confused, huddled under wet blankets in the basement, when they heard the explosions.

By that afternoon, there had been substantial damage to homes both across the street and adjacent to 6221 Osage Avenue. Although the entire front of the house itself had been blown off, police officers still did not enter. Instead, the police commissioner gave the order to begin constructing a bomb to be dropped on the roof of the building. Goode approved the use of the explosive device at five P.M. and it was dropped within thirty minutes. As the building began to burn from the top down, several men, women, and children attempted to flee, but were driven back by gunfire. Officers would take only two survivors into custody, Ramona Africa and thirteen-year-old Michael. Five children and six adults died in the blaze.

"Let the fire burn," Goode ordered, so that by the time firefighters began to work in earnest and had the fire contained near midnight, sixty-one homes on three city blocks were lost, leaving 250 people homeless. Those whose homes were destroyed were temporarily housed at the wildlife preserve at Tinicum National Environmental Center. In the immediate aftermath of the bombing of Osage Avenue, the mayor created an eleven-member citizen special commission to find facts and make recommendations. Its report would find fault with each party to the events of May 13. The commission ultimately lacked the authority to hold anyone accountable, so no city official paid a price for the tragic assault that left eleven people dead and hundreds of others dispossessed and displaced. Still, it would provide an authoritative citizen voice on the politics of race in the City of Philadelphia:

> The Commission believes that the decisions of various city officials to permit construction of the bunker, to allow the use of high explosives and, in a 90-minute period, the firing of at least 10,000 rounds of ammunition at the house, to sanction the dropping of a bomb on an occupied row house, and to let a fire burn in a row house occupied by children, would not likely have been made had the MOVE house and its occupants been situated in a comparable white neighborhood.

In November 2020, local lawmakers issued an apology, acknowledging the "fundamental injustice, cruelty, brutality and inhumanity of the MOVE bombing." The following spring, papers reported on the mishandling of MOVE remains taken after the bombing on Osage Avenue. One set of remains was allegedly released by the city's medical examiner to an anthropologist named Alan Mann at the University of Pennsylvania for further analysis. There, the remains of Katricia "Tree" Africa, fourteen at the time of the bombing, were carelessly stored and passed between faculty for twenty-eight years. In 2014, Dr. Janet Monge, the Penn Museum's associate curator, who had custody of the remains, attempted to contact Consuewella Africa. When communications were rebuffed, she continued to display and handle the remains in museum demonstrations at least ten times before 2019. Amid public protest, the University of Pennsylvania, Penn Museum, and Princeton University scrambled to locate and identify the remains that had been used in Dr. Monge's demonstrations. Consuewella died in June 2021 at the age of sixty-seven. The remains of her daughters, returned by the museum after her death, were buried in July 2021 under the tree where her ashes had been scattered one month earlier.

Another set of remains held by the city had been ordered cremated and discarded in 2017 by Philadelphia's health commissioner, Thomas Farley, without regard for the family's wishes. Farley, who was asked to resign when this issue came to light, expressed "profound regret" for having made such a decision without consulting the family members of the bombing victims. The remains in question were later found in a refrigerated storage area, in a box simply marked MOVE.

Within a week of 9/11, after consulting my housemates, I put a sign in our front window that read OUR GRIEF IS NOT A CRY FOR WAR. It was, I thought, the perfect message for the moment: expressing shared pain over the loss of innocent life in the 9/11 attacks, but also dissent from the Bush administration's even greater threat to innocent life in Afghanistan. However small the gesture was, it felt essential to me, a way to cope with my fellow Americans' calls to bomb an entire society "back to the Stone Age."

A week after I taped the sign in our window, I got a call at my office from Allison.

"Hey, Sof," she said.

"Hey! Is everything okay?" I responded. Her brother had been in the second of the World Trade Center towers to fall, and although he had made it out without physical injury, her family was still shaken.

"Yeah. I have a favor to ask."

"Sure, what is it?"

"My parents are coming to visit this weekend and I was wondering if it'd be okay with you if I took the sign out of the window?"

I was silent for a moment, my lunch rising in my throat. "But that sign just says our grief is not a cry for war. Why would your parents be offended by that?"

"I know, but they're upset; I just need to know if it's okay with you to take it down, Sof."

"Allison, they were at Woodstock; I thought they were anti-war?"

"Is it okay with you?"

"No, it's not okay with me."

"Sof."

"No. It's your house, too, and if you need to take it down, take it down, but it's not okay with me."

The sign stayed up, but I never viewed Allison or her family in the same way. She explained her parents' sudden pro-war stance by saying they were working-class and had been the first in their families to go to college, and her father had been laid off from jobs that didn't pay well enough to begin with and he blamed that on the influx of immigrants. Her once-hippie father was now angry at the people who he imagined took his jobs, which merged with anger at those who nearly killed his only son and became a broadly pro-war stance. By that time, more than a dozen of my own aunts and uncles had immigrated, relying on factory jobs in the early years of their resettlement. My family were the new immigrants competing for jobs traditionally filled by Levittown's working class.

Allison still didn't understand, and perhaps she didn't want to understand, that my father was also the first in his family to go to college, and that my mother had not had the opportunity. The circumstances from which they had come were many times yet removed from American prosperity than her family's native English-speaking, working-class backgrounds. My parents were the first in their families to purchase actual toys for their children, to have hot running water—even potable running water—reliable electricity, a stove rather than coal or a fuel canister, and a refrigerator. They could shed neither their accents nor their skin colors to achieve the opportunities and dignity afforded White people in America. Allison seemed to accept her parents' sense of entitlement to available working-class jobs and even that their class status justified their growing racism and pro-war sentiments. More surprisingly, in that conversation, she seemed to believe that I should too.

I was late in arriving to this understanding. For years before and even after the conversation about the sign, I had treated Allison like family: lending her my car when hers was in the shop, traveling to see her when she was at graduate school, sharing my bed with her when she visited me after law school. But that was not reciprocal, and it never had been. When she told me, years later, that her mom had been diagnosed with breast cancer, I'd immediately offered my parents as a resource, saying that since they lived close by, they would be happy to help with drives to doctor's appointments or whatever might be needed. Our parents had, after all, known each other for more than fifteen years. She looked at me as if I were insane. That was the kind of offer that family makes, and I was not her family. I found that realization especially crushing in the wake of divorce and in the broader context of post-9/11 anti-Muslim sentiment.

During the same period, Dana, that friend of mine in the house of Muslim women I almost lived with, called, asking me to join her at a local zikr group. I was uncertain. I still experienced Islam as a social or cultural identity, and until Aaron's revelation, when I didn't know where else to turn, I had not even prayed regularly. Zikr is the Muslim meditation practice I mentioned earlier in which the divine attributes of God are remembered, often accompanied by a halaqa, or discussion on a religious topic. For me, it was a salve. The wound Aaron had left, then 9/11 and the loss of a childhood friend in Allison, had all left me feeling as though I had no skin, as if I were a burn survivor, susceptible to every passing slur or slight as if it were a deadly infection. Meanwhile, I was trying to launch a legal career in an adversarial system. In my professional life I needed not just a skin, but a thick one, to properly represent my clients. Weekly zikr and regular prayer, or salat, neither of which had been features of my childhood, were unexpectedly fortifying. They were the spiritual equivalent of wrapping myself in a cloak, a personal, invisible shield from the antagonism of the world around me, one that was reset with each of the five daily prayers. In prayer, my body relaxed, with my shoulders down and chin even, as if a weight had been lifted from me. My prayer rug was the one place where I felt whole. So began a several-year immersion in a Sufi Muslim community, organized loosely around a mosque in the racially diverse neighborhood of Overbrook in Philadelphia.

About a year after I arrived in Philadelphia and several months after I began attending the weekly zikr, I also began wearing hijab, or a headscarf, in a further effort to contain and repair all of the parts of me still hurting from the personal and political challenges of the previous years. With it on, I carried the feeling of being whole throughout the day, even off the prayer rug. It was like a cocoon, protective but also transformative. It became the container for a rich internal life, so that I was less driven by and hungry for the acknowledgment and appreciation of others. With the space that it allowed, I studied my responses and reactions to the world around me. I could see clearly my own desperation, my desire, my excesses. I was intrigued to find that in hijab, maintaining a sense of myself within White contexts became virtually effortless. With it on, I no longer passed in White spaces and easily avoided relationships with people who had contempt for Muslims or immigrants; or rather, they easily avoided me. As an unanticipated bonus, men and women in the overwhelmingly Black Muslim business district along Germantown Avenue, just one block from my office at CLS, acknowledged me as one of theirs whenever I walked down the street, calling out, "Asalaamu alaikum, sister!" It was one more homecoming.

The Muslim community in Philadelphia is fantastically beautiful. It is layered, diverse, and active, and it is deeply integrated with other faith communities in the city. As one in a small network of Muslim lawyers practicing in Philadelphia in 2004, I was invited to join the founding board of directors of the Philadelphia chapter of the Council on American-Islamic Relations (CAIR-Philadelphia). We started out sitting in a circle on the carpet of a tiny office downtown, not yet able to afford furniture. We grew by providing volunteer services, like referrals and broad community education on Islam and Muslims. A large part of my work was with Iftekhar (who would eventually open the Sunday school that my kids would go to when we lived in Yardley) to develop trainings on Islam and Muslims for CAIR-Philadelphia, presenting them all over the Delaware Valley. Then, after we'd raised enough to hire a full-time staff person, I supervised her, helping her to set up intake protocols and workflows. CAIR-Philadelphia emerged quickly as a first point of contact for Muslims in the city and across the state dealing with now commonplace anti-Muslim speech, discrimination, and attacks.

In the same year, Adab Ibrahim, an activist and friend from the Al-Aqsa Mosque community, organized with other progressive faith leaders to create the annual Interfaith Peace Walk. The Peace Walk continues to draw between five hundred and a thousand attendees each year, creating new routes for the interfaith group to walk between mosques, synagogues, churches, and parks in the city, and has grown to include Sikh, Hindu, and Buddhist communities. A team of activists and artists from Al-Aqsa, the Philadelphia Mural Arts Philadelphia, and the Arts and Spirituality Center came together to redesign the exterior of the Al-Aqsa Mosque in a project called Doorways to Peace. The mosque sits in the middle of what had long been an economically impoverished, predominantly Black neighborhood with a large contingent of first- or second-generation Palestinian and other immigrants. Housed in the old Dubin furniture warehouse, it *looked* like an old furniture warehouse in 2004. Doorways to Peace transformed the massive building and in doing so, transformed the neighborhood. Like so many other artists, activists, and youth, I got drawn into the massive project, which took over a year of planning and the same in implementation.

By then, I'd moved out of the house I'd shared with Allison and the others to a tiny apartment with gleaming wood floors and deep windowsills over a violin shop in Germantown. I'd return home from long days at CLS to my new home, in a neighborhood on the same land where early Mennonites had written their anti-slavery letter. There, I'd spend my evenings perched on a stool at an old wooden drafting table, carving the ninety-nine names for God into clay tiles that would become part of the mural. They were the same names I repeated in zikr every week, and as I carved, I whispered them aloud: As-Salaam, the Giver of Peace. Al-Mu'Min, the Giver of Faith. Ar-Razzaq, the Sustainer. Al-Halim, the Enduring. Al-Lateef, the Gentle. Al-Hafiz, the Guardian. Al-Mujib, the Responsive. Al-Wadud, the Loving. Al-Haqq, the Truth. An-Nur, the Light. As I carved my heartfelt prayers into the tiles, I hoped to inculcate these traits in myself, but I was also calling out in absolute need: *Oh, my Guardian! Oh, my Loving, Responsive, most Gentle of Sustainers. Provide me Peace, endow me with Faith, help me to distinguish what is True and carry Light.* When I was done, I delivered the tiles to the mosque to be fired, glazed, and installed on the building, and then I stuck around to help paint the doors a brilliant gold.

At the zikr group, I was introduced to the spiritual practice of asking plainly for divine permission and guidance in my life, with the intention to act accordingly. I asked all kinds of things. I asked for help waking for the pre-dawn prayer and laughed out loud when I was awoken by the sound of a mousetrap going off, empty, the next morning. For weeks I had charley horses, a sort of intense muscle spasm, in my legs at precisely the time of prayers—something I'd not experienced before and have not since. I asked what to do with my perennial sense of wanderlust and dreamed vividly that night of being led through my apartment's back garden gate, where my landlord and friend had allowed me (in real life) to plant zucchini and basil that spring. In the dream, my garden patch was covered instead in a lush green ground cover and I felt more than heard that this was not the time to plant for harvest, but the time to nourish the soil. The intimacy of these moments rushed in to fill places I hadn't realized were empty. I felt as I had upon hearing the azaan in Egypt, that these moments were tiny, private gifts intended for me, in the specific language of my life and experience. It was like an inside joke with my oldest friend, but somehow more joyful and the friendship eternal. It was as in this translated verse from the Qur'an: "Surely, we created the human being and know what their souls whisper to themselves; we are closer to them than their jugular veins." I felt both that I was precisely loved and seen in my modest life, and that *I always had been.*

Philadelphia's faith communities were blooming, in spite of, and maybe in some ways because of, the wars raging in our names overseas. Driven by a desire to develop enough social and political power to challenge what was happening, abroad and at home, Muslims had begun to teach ourselves how to protect and defend our communities in America. We were reaching out to allies in other faith communities in new ways. I was, for the first time, reading Christian theology alongside the Qur'an with interest, able to observe the places where the two diverged and converged. In hijab, I reclaimed my identity in public and restored the privacy I needed to mend what felt fragile. My anxiety dissolved in a new ability to surrender the politics and pressures that felt so beyond my control while still remaining engaged. Hijab, salat, and zikr were ultimately tools to do the work that two Black men of faith, Dean Hall and Reverend Gomes, had set out for me: to reflect until I knew where I stood, and to find my way home.

When I started at CLS, I had hung a small scrap of paper with the translation of a single line from a poem written by the Muslim mystic Shams Uddin Muhammad Hafez above my desk. It said: "I see in you the wounds that have not yet healed. They exist because God and Love have not yet become real enough to you to allow you to forgive the dream." I'd pinned it there not because it reflected my reality, but because I hoped someday it could. As I developed a consistent spiritual practice, I found myself in an intimate, daily negotiation with God, with an unshakable feeling of being seen and nurtured. The constant flutter of anxiety in my chest quieted. I no longer felt like I was living at the edge of a cliff, but in a constant embrace. I still felt and thought passionately, but also more evenly and more precisely. I was no longer embattled, even in the middle of advocating for a client or in my outreach work for CAIR.

When I first encountered the poetry of Hafez, I had not yet been able to imagine what it meant for God to be real, for love to be something abundant rather than coveted. And then finally, I could not imagine anything else.

More than forty years after he left office, Frank Rizzo remained a symbol of White violence in the City of Brotherly Love. The ten-foot-high, two-hundred-pound bronze statue of Rizzo that stood outside of the Municipal Services Building for twenty-one years was often the target of citizen vandalism and even officials' protestations. It was finally removed in June 2020, amid nationwide protests of police brutality and the alarming resurgence of White supremacist organizations throughout the country. But the city's problem with anti-Black racism and brutality did not begin with Frank Rizzo, and it did not end when he died.

Within twenty years of Pennsylvania's inception, the colony already had a separate, more punitive and deadly set of laws governing punishments for crimes committed by Black people, and far more restrictive laws governing the lives and assembly of Black people. Two hundred years later, when W.E.B. Du Bois wrote *The Philadelphia Negro,* he provided an account of how and where Black people lived in the segregated city. He also recorded their overwhelming criminalization. Prior to emancipation and the enactment of the postslavery laws known as Jim Crow, Philadelphia had one of the largest Black populations in the North, making up about 5 to 8 percent of the total population of the city from 1829 to 1854. And yet, Black people accounted for between 16 and 40 percent of total commitments (largely, though not exclusively, from Philadelphia) to Eastern State Penitentiary during the same period.

In December 2020, *The Philadelphia Inquirer* published a two-hundred-year timeline of anti-Black policing. Theirs was an incomplete list, and, truly, a complete list would require more space than is available here. Still, I've filled in the timeline they created with additional events and detail to more accurately convey the relentlessness of anti-blackness in urban America. The *Inquirer* timeline begins in 1838, when the Philadelphia police patrol stood by while a newly built abolitionist meeting hall was attacked by White protestors and burned to the ground. Though firefighters worked to prevent the spread of the fire to adjacent buildings, they did nothing to save the hall. Months after Black people won the right to vote with passage of the Fifteenth Amendment in 1870, police attacked a long line of Black men waiting to vote at a poll at Fifth and Lombard. A year later, in 1871, Black voters were beaten while trying to cast their ballots in South Philadelphia; that night, the Black political educator and activist Octavius Catto was shot, and his killer found not guilty, despite the testimony of six eyewitnesses.

In 1915, a group of a thousand Black men protesting the opening of the racist film *The Birth of a Nation* at the Forrest Theatre was assaulted by a mob that included police officers. An article in the *Harrisburg Telegraph* reported that police officers guarding the theater were "forced to use their clubs." Ongoing police brutality led Black Philadelphians to form the Association for the Protection of Colored People; members were given cards to show during police stops indicating they had legal representation.

During World War I, Black workers migrated to Philadelphia; the population of the community rose by 58 percent, to 134,229 people. As they moved into White areas, they were met with increasing hostility. G. Grant Williams, a journalist for *The Philadelphia Tribune,* a Black newspaper, wrote in June 1918 about White supremacist attacks:

> They have ever been a menace to the peace and the decency of the district and many of the police either feared or worked in collusion with them . . .
>
> But knowing as we do the facts, that our people are driven from pillar to post looking for houses to rent and that they pay more rent than whites for the same shacks, our patience runs out.

His article was followed by weeks of violence; in those weeks, sixty Black people and three White people would be arrested.

A 1924 study by the city found that Black people continued to be disproportionately arrested in Philadelphia, making up 9 percent of the population but a quarter of all arrests, with 20 percent of arrests for vague or subjective offenses such as vagrancy, disorderly conduct, concealed weapons, and "suspicious behavior."

In 1946, with the nation embroiled in conflicts over school segregation, students from a White school and a Black school in Southwest Philadelphia fought, their adjacent neighborhoods a battleground of segregation. Police arrested fourteen Black students, but no White students, until the complaints of parents and clergy forced police to arrest the White students involved in the conflict. A survey of Philadelphia police conducted the same year found substantial support for the belief that Black Philadelphians were more given to crime, with officers saying, "Negro crime is the result of housing, employment, and heredity" and "You don't have too much trouble with Negros if you keep them in their place."

In 1957, the mayor approved patrols by "shotgun squads" in predominantly Black North and Center City Philadelphia. Unsurprisingly, the following year, Black residents testified before a city council committee about illegal police home raids, street frisks, and verbal harassment. When the mayor responded by creating the nation's first civilian review board, the Fraternal Order of Police sought an injunction that shut it down.

In 1963, a landmark study on police shootings showed that while Black Philadelphians were 22 percent of the city's residents, they accounted for 90 percent of those killed in police shootings. The same year, Frank Rizzo became deputy police commissioner, launching the era marked by police violence and impunity discussed earlier in this chapter; in 1969, the mayor abolished the Police Advisory Board, which handled citizen complaints against the police. During the Rizzo administration, a federal court found that police department hiring practices violated the Civil Rights Act of 1964 and it mandated quotas that would result in hiring Black and Hispanic officers, as well as women. In 1984, a *Philadelphia Inquirer* investigation uncovered the Philadelphia police force's out-of-control police K-9 unit, which initiated 350 dog attacks over thirty-three months, without justification.

The ACLU filed a class-action suit against the city for conducting 1,500 warrantless police stop-and-search encounters without reasonable suspicion that a crime had been or was about to be committed.

After an FBI investigation, a grand jury found that between the late 1980s and mid-1990s, officers from the thirty-ninth police district had engaged in a scheme of shaking down mostly Black residents of North Philadelphia, "beating, robbing, lying, and planting phony evidence." The officers pleaded guilty to violating the rights of hundreds of defendants, whose convictions were overturned. A police internal affairs investigation showed that police who were fired were often "quietly reinstated."

In 2011, the city settled a lawsuit alleging that its police were conducting unlawful stop-and-frisks, disproportionately targeting Black and Latino residents. In the same year, the state's prison population peaked. Half of the inmates were Black, although only 12 percent of Pennsylvania's residents were Black. In 2012, despite a drop in crime rates, Philadelphia police shot fifty-two people in a single year.

A 2015 review by the U.S. Department of Justice found that 80 percent of people shot by Philadelphia police between 2007 and 2014 were Black. In 2017, for the first time in twenty years, a Philadelphia police officer was charged with homicide for having shot David Jones in the back for riding a dirt bike on a city street. The same officer had previously paralyzed a Black man named Carnell Williams-Carney by shooting him in the back.

In the spring of 2020, following the police killing of George Floyd in St. Paul, Philadelphians joined nationwide protests. Downtown stores were looted, protestors were met with pepper spray and tear gas, and a curfew was imposed. Meanwhile, on the third night of protests, a group of a hundred White men armed with baseball bats walked the Fishtown neighborhood, reportedly assaulting two people, including a journalist. Photos circulated on social media of police officers taking selfies with the group and standing by while they roamed for more than two hours after curfew.

The MOVE bombing is best understood in this context of racist police persecution. In fact, the city's institutions, arteries, and neighborhoods are a record of its efforts to maintain segregation and to protect White prosperity, while eroding or preventing Black prosperity.

The North Philadelphia office of CLS sits at the corner of Broad Street and Erie Avenue, an overwhelmingly Black neighborhood in obvious distress. Some brick row homes on the main boulevards have plywood in the windows. The water and electricity are sometimes shut off in cramped row homes along side streets; sidewalks are patched haphazardly with uneven asphalt. Citizens Bank is in good repair, with the sort of historic marble façade you would expect on a building near Independence Hall, but just across the street is a high-rise with its windows knocked out and covered in graffiti, including an enormous, vertical, mystifying message, FOREVER BONER. Around the high-rise and above the sidewalks there is a green awning to protect pedestrians from debris the building might shed.

CLS maintains its office in North Philadelphia because so many of its clients live there. The area is a miles-wide food desert and its public schools are in obvious disrepair, with playgrounds made of fenced-in patches of plain asphalt, leaky ceilings, and poor ventilation. Philadelphia has a poverty rate of over 25 percent, the highest among America's ten largest cities. CLS attorneys advocate for the poorest communities, which are disproportionately communities of color, within it. The only people guaranteed a lawyer in America are those charged with a crime. Even then, public defenders are burdened with overwhelming caseloads in a system designed to press poor people into pleading guilty and incurring a criminal record, rather than receiving fair trials. For civil disputes and concerns like divorce and parental rights, employment issues and unemployment benefits, welfare benefits, consumer protection, civil rights, public utilities, public housing and tenants' issues, immigration, zoning and licensing, there is no right to counsel. Millions of low-income Americans are left on their own to wade through an adversarial system with impossibly confusing bureaucracies and rules. In our legal system, their poverty, and the lack of representation that comes with poverty in America, defeats them.

At CLS, I started out representing clients whose food stamps, welfare, and Medicaid were unlawfully terminated. Clinton-era welfare reforms were just being implemented, and my clients were often forced to leave their children with subsidized daycare providers on one side of town and go to work themselves as daycare providers on the other side of town to meet nonsensical welfare-to-work requirements. They were frequently caught in the bureaucratic grind, with basic food and medical benefits cut off because a form went missing or an appointment was missed and the process to fix these problems was too much of a bureaucratic mess to navigate. Appeals required access to a computer, fax machine, and registered mail, as well as documentation of all communications, each step a nightmare for people already in distress. All these years later I remember one of my first clients at CLS. In her nineties, she was frail and lived alone in what was once a row home before the block crumbled around it. Inside, the furnishings and décor were a time capsule from the 1950s. It was all immaculately clean. My client had been rationing her food supply since she got a routine food stamp termination notice, which she did not understand how to appeal. She came to me just before Thanksgiving of 2001, only when every crumb was gone; she had no car, no internet, and no way of locating, let alone transporting groceries from, one of the city's food pantries. I filed her appeal, called around to find a pantry still open before the holiday weekend across town, and then drove her there and back home with the groceries. I remember her for her dignity and independence, for her perfectly preserved home in the midst of chaos and decay, but she was representative of every one of my clients: human and deserving of respect, starving in a country with plenty.

Later, through a makeshift clinic, I represented undocumented clients with medical emergencies, whose lack of English proficiency made hospital emergency rooms and the Emergency Medicaid for which they should have been eligible inaccessible to them. I saw a client who had been catheterized and discharged repeatedly, a client whose epilepsy had been misdiagnosed as "a pimple on her brain" by a pseudo doctor preying on the uninsured, a client with a cancerous growth the size of an orange on his throat, and dozens of others, all of whom had been working in area factories as day laborers, part of an underground and marginalized economy. But when I met with the state's secretary of public health, to advocate for better pathways to apply for Emergency Medicaid, I was careful to emphasize that my clients included people on student visas and visitor visas, all of those noncitizens who could not access regular Medicaid but could also not be called "illegal." Strategically, advocating for the undocumented was a nonstarter, even though the Emergency Medicaid to which they are entitled is a federally mandated program, a time-limited benefit meant to be afforded regardless of immigration status. In America, some people occupy social margins that are so politically distasteful to power brokers as to make them unmentionable. When I saw this disdain, I recognized it, because increasingly, American Muslims occupied the same margins.

Eventually, I was burned out by the miserliness and brutality of our nation's welfare, food, and medical assistance programs for the poor. I began representing women who were trying to start businesses, often daycares, in their homes, helping them to navigate the opaque zoning and licensing regulations required to stay open. Each business owner was required to appear before the municipal zoning board at Broad Street and Spring Garden, to provide scale drawings of their business spaces and proof of compliance with the applicable laws. Without representation, none of my clients knew where to begin, and the zoning and licensing bureaucracies were effective barriers to them building capital in low-income neighborhoods.

Although CLS serves clients who meet their financial eligibility requirements regardless of race, the vast majority of my clients were

Black and a large minority were Hispanic or Asian. Immigration status, limited English proficiency, lack of access to quality education, severe generational poverty, and the constant struggle to achieve stable food, shelter, clothing, and personal hygiene were chronic barriers to their employment and entrepreneurship, as well as to their health and survival. I won just about every appeal, every application for Emergency Medicaid, all but one zoning application, and even the criminal record expungement case I took on, and not because I'm unusually skilled. Rather, it was because I learned to navigate the bureaucracies that governed my clients' lives and their access to healthcare, safety net benefits, or even work. These systems are deeply dysfunctional and set up to deny access, but they cannot bear the weight of any reasonable challenge.

While painting the Al-Aqsa Mosque's doors gold, I met Aisha, who became a beloved friend. One day in the spring of 2005, months after the Doorways to Peace project was finished, Aisha invited me to lunch. As we were eating our meal, she told me that she needed to introduce me to a man she'd met at a lecture given by a mutual friend on the Penn campus the week before.

"But if he's so great, why do you want *me* to meet him?" I wanted to know.

"He's not my type," she said.

I was not at all sure that I was ready to give up my, by then, years of equanimity for romance. "What's not your type about him?"

"Just trust me; meet him. He's tall. Tall is sexy."

"Aisha, I'm only five-two." But then I relented. "Okay, what does he do?"

"He's a biochemist."

"Snooze. Like every other good Pakistani boy. What's his name?"

"No, no, he does breast cancer research. His name is Nadeem." She took out his business card.

"Okay, but . . . Nadeem? That's my brother's name, so . . . gross."
Except that I had had a dream just two weeks before. In it, I wandered
around the Overbrook mosque and its grounds, wondering why the
people in the mosque were dressed up and carrying steaming trays of
biryani. In the dream, I finally encountered the host of my real-life
zikr group and asked her what was going on. It turned out that we
were all there to celebrate my engagement—to a man named *Nadeem,*
which means "companion." As soon as I said the name out loud to
Aisha that day, the dream came back to me. I agreed to meet Aisha's
Nadeem.

In the years after my return to Philadelphia, I'd rebuilt a relationship with my parents and with my extended family. My younger
brother had moved to Philadelphia after college, and the two of us
often met up at my parents' house on weekends, playing Frisbee in
their backyard and doing laundry. My older brother, my sister-in-law,
and my niece had moved to a house just an hour away. We had survived the overwhelming anti-Muslim torrent after 9/11 together, and
those things in me that were culturally alien to them were now bridged
in faith. My family recognized my dedication to work at CLS as an
expression of that shared faith, and they recognized my work with
CAIR as a valuable contribution to our mutual community. I had a
new appreciation for the struggle of my parents' migration, and they
seemed to have a new willingness to recognize the implications of
it—that they might have to accept amalgamations of new and old cultures in their children.

This meant I'd told them about Nadeem when I'd met him back in
April, and they knew I'd continued to see him regularly since then. In
an unprecedented gesture of openness, my parents had invited
Nadeem to their huge annual picnic of extended family and friends,
and then again to a large family gathering at their place. An unrelated
auntie, the sister of a family friend, had shown up to the picnic, interested in me as a potential bride for her son until she saw Nadeem and
me in the three-legged race, our arms wrapped around each other's
waists. When she asked my mother, pointedly, whether Nadeem was

my brother, my mother answered, smiling, that he was my "friend." Although it was just as scandalous for an unmarried woman to have her arm around the waist of a male friend as it ever had been in that community, the sky did not fall. My parents and I had come to enjoy being present in each other's lives and honest with one another.

So when, eighteen months after having met, Nadeem and I were married, the ceremony contained all of the richness of our lives in Philadelphia. Colleagues from work and activist endeavors, old friends from all over, family and family friends, all gathered for a beautiful ceremony led by Imam Razzaq, also known as Richard Miller, the imam from our mosque in Overbrook. My parents hosted a reception the night before in their home, to which out-of-town guests could be welcomed, and overrode our initially modest plans for an outdoor venue by choosing, and springing for, a fancy downtown hotel for the wedding itself. My younger brother and cousins, in Sindhi tradition, held Nadeem hostage as he made his way up the aisle, demanding payment for the right to proceed. Nadeem had come prepared, with a thick wad of ones in his pocket.

After Imam Razzaq gave his wedding sermon, or khutbah, my mother's younger sister presided over several ritual exchanges between us, a shared glass of spiced milk, dry rice poured from Nadeem's hands into mine and then mine into his, and our heads bowed gently together by a succession of elders, siblings, and friends in a gesture of blessing. These parts of the wedding didn't need to be scripted; they were, as they have been for countless generations, customary. Nadeem and I had designed the rest together, working on the details of invitations and art, of the reception playlist and our exit in a horse-drawn carriage. It was a wedding full of grace, more elaborate and celebratory than I could ever have anticipated, the ease with hardship promised by that verse from the Qur'an I'd selected for my first wedding, years before.

For the first time in my life, I was walking down the street with someone who had a life parallel to my own. He was Pakistani, but born and raised in London, with a British latitude for good-natured profanity. He was progressive, which he explained was merely centrist in British politics. I didn't have to edit anything about my worldview or my politics with him.

Both because I am unusually pale for a Pakistani, and because Nadeem is darker, with a kink in his coarse black hair, we were regularly perceived as a biracial couple in Philadelphia. In our Germantown neighborhood, and all over Philadelphia, Nadeem would typically get what he called "the Black nod" from other people of color, while I was studiously ignored. That would likely have been different had I continued to wear hijab, but by the time I met Nadeem, I hadn't worn hijab in months. I had taken it off with the relief one feels at removing a bandage that has done its job. I'd never believed it was a religious requirement, but an essential spiritual tool for my healing. And that healing, in turn, was necessary for me to serve my clients at CLS and my larger community through CAIR-Philadelphia. Over several years, the skin I'd felt was torn away in the divorce from Aaron and in the aftermath of 9/11 had regrown. I found myself able to be present in my work and in my faith without hijab, and unable to justify the potential for prejudice to my clients because of it. The experience of wearing hijab revealed I was raced differently depending on what I wore, which neighborhood, school, or workplace I was in, who I happened to be standing next to, and whether someone knew my last name. As confusing as this was, it offered a flexibility my husband clearly did not have. Although he identifies as a British Pakistani child of immigrants, Nadeem is always racialized by White America's fickle response to the skin he's in.

My relationship to Nadeem would force me into several new realizations about race in America. No matter which identity I assert or Nadeem asserts, racialization is largely something that continues to be done *to* me or *to* him. The default designator of race is sometimes an individual, but more often a system, in which whiteness is unquestionably central and desirable. Racialization is a gatekeeping exercise within that system, and, like most gatekeeping exercises, it is always subjective, serving and preserving White supremacy. At its core, racialization is still premised on the "average White person standard" established in *United States v. Bhagat Singh Thind* in 1923, and deeply embedded since then in American culture and practice.

Having struggled through the politics of mostly passing, I was now faced with the politics of mostly *not* passing by proximity to Nadeem. Sometimes my paleness and the folksy demeanor I had learned to employ for such occasions could still soften the aggression of White Americans toward my Black-passing husband (who had what seemed to them a mighty uppity British accent). I worried most about when it couldn't. I used to make fun of Nadeem for driving like an old lady, until one day he explained that he was pretty sure getting pulled over would not be in his best interests—he knew that much from having lived in America for eight years.

CHAPTER TWELVE

THE HEARTLAND

Chicago, Illinois

Apartheid does not happen spontaneously, like bad weather conditions.

—Jonathan Kozol

Nadeem and I both wanted children. If I was ever going to pay off my law school debt *and also* take some time off work when my children were babies, I'd need to earn more than a legal services salary. But it wasn't easy to leave CLS. I felt like I had hit my stride there; it was good work and it challenged me. But the work was also demanding and time sensitive. It would leave me little margin after a couple of months of maternity leave, which felt like an inadequate start for my children, who would be racial and religious minorities. This worried me acutely after 9/11, an era of increased animus toward American Muslims. If I continued to work full-time, would I have to leave my babies with people who saw our family and our faith as dangerous, foreign, and inferior? The roots of my own cultural and religious identity had been in a household where my mother was present, even if she was struggling with her own identity in North America. That was an important, if slippery foundation. It gave me enough of a glimpse of where I had come from that I could, in the end, resist the idea that my worth was in rejecting my Muslim Pakistani American identity and culture in favor of a European American one.

If I did keep working in legal services, the cost of childcare for two would eat up much of my salary, leaving us Nadeem's research science salary, just a bit higher than what he'd earned as a postdoctoral student. We went looking for alternatives and each managed to land jobs in Chicago, Nadeem at the British consulate, where his accent would raise no eyebrows and he could transition from research to a broader application for his science background, and me at the America Bar Association (ABA), helping to safeguard legal services funding.

We found a small rental apartment on the very outer edge of the Chicago suburbs, in Naperville, which had caught our attention by being named one of the best places to raise a family in some magazine or other. And then we went house hunting. We wanted to be outside of the city, with lots of green space, but we also found that we needed to be closer to our downtown jobs than Naperville, so we started with Oak Park. We quickly stumbled over Austin Boulevard, which marks the color line at the edge of Oak Park, Black people living on one side of it and White people living on the other. We drove around a bit to make sure—there it was, Black on one side, cross to White on the other. We thought maybe Evanston, a college town, would offer something different, more of a mix of people. Nope—there it was again—Ridge Avenue. A single street, one side mostly Black people, the other side mostly White.

We looked farther out at suburbs like Glen Ellyn and Wheaton, where there were great schools and no discernible color line. But there was no such line only because barely any people of color at all lived there. We finally settled on Lombard, more modest than both Glen Ellyn and Wheaton, and still predominantly White, but with a more visible mix of people, including significantly bigger Black and even Asian populations, some first generation, and others like us.

I thought that I was reasonably aware of how race worked in America and the impacts it had around me. But a couple of years into being married to Nadeem, I realized how much the straightness of my hair and paleness of my skin had shielded me from some of the most overt and the most dangerous forms of White supremacy. We flew down one weekend to visit Nora, who'd become one of my closest friends in the years since college, along with her family on their farm in a tiny rural community outside of Nashville, meeting up there with our mutual college friend Sylvia and her then-husband, Marco. Marco was similar to my husband in that his thick Mexican accent made him confusing and foreign to White Americans, but dissimilar in that he, so long as he isn't speaking, passes for White. Despite my experience in Little Rock, and that conversation at the shelter about White people vacationing near a town known as Klan headquarters, I didn't think twice about suggesting we visit Nora in an all-White area of middle Tennessee. I'd been there before, more than once, and I thought nothing of it.

Nora's farmhouse would not accommodate us all, so we stayed nearby in what might have been a nice place in the 1920s, when the area attracted visitors to its mineral waters. In the summer of 2009, it was a somewhat mildewed bed-and-breakfast, run by a friendly gray-haired woman, who explained that her previous job had been with the police department. She said she had been assigned to Black areas outside of Macon County, so it was a wonder she hadn't been killed. I didn't know it then, but her comment was terribly ironic. The White residents of Macon County had violently expelled their Black neighbors about one hundred years before.

Nadeem's presence elicited casual racism everywhere we went on that trip. He and I went for a walk on the grassy roadside in the town of Cookeville, where we were visiting for the day, happy to be alone for a bit in a pretty place. We stepped farther onto the grass to make room for a pickup speeding past, unconcerned until we heard someone yell "Go home!" from inside. It was an entirely different exhortation than Reverend Gomes's had been six years before. It was not a call to self-awareness; but it didn't sound angry, either. It was a casual, almost offhand, threat, the kind that is just unpleasant enough to keep White places White. We watched to see if the truck would swing around to pass again and were relieved when it didn't. I thought about how when I stood next to Nadeem, White people often saw me as several shades darker. I thought about how he had never experienced life in any other shade of skin.

Nora and her husband took us to the home of her friend Tom for dinner one night; I'd met Tom before, an organic farmer with a long beard and about every other earmark of a counterculture White guy in America you can imagine. Nora, Sylvia, and I were happy to be there and settled easily into the social standard that felt familiar from college.

Nadeem and Marco, on the other hand, had just begun to enjoy the beauty of Nora's farm earlier that day when she explained to them that sitting in the grass would likely result in chiggers, a type of skin-burrowing insect that would create itchy welts. They'd run for the creek, until Nora elaborated that chiggers liked crevices and they'd have to get naked. They switched direction immediately, heading to the cars for showers at the bed-and-breakfast. So, they were a little on edge by the time we got to dinner. Tom and his friend Joe got up early in the meal and went outside, probably for a drink and a smoke, and came back less inhibited. Somewhere in the muddied conversation, Joe cracked a joke about "shooting Mexicans" as if for sport. It was so out of context and bizarre for us but clearly a common way of talking for them. Having found himself unexpectedly breaking bread with Brown people, Joe seemed to feel the need to assert that he was still White, and still in a White place. His words were violent, but his tone was almost jovial.

Sylvia broke the stunned silence that followed by telling the table that Marco was Mexican, and that she was an Iranian Jew, which Joe had no idea what to do with. Still, half the table ate the rest of the meal uncomfortably, the taste of dirt in our mouths. Joe was buzzed.

We made him nervous and maybe, underneath that, angry. He had expressed his discomfort by saying something that meant Brown people were worthless. In his world, this was so patently true, and violence aimed at Brown and Black people so ordinary, that he felt safe to say so out loud. Joe's casual comment, which didn't merit a mention or an apology from Tom, stuck to us. Our host's comments at the bed-and-breakfast, being told to "go home" from out of the pickup truck, and the subtle threat at Tom's table were enough to do their job on us a hundred years after Macon County went all-White: None of the four of us visitors would ever go back, certainly not with our kids.

But there, at the dinner table that night, none of us made a stink, either. Not Marco, not Sylvia, not Nadeem or I, though any of us could have passed for Mexican. Not Nora or her husband. Not Tom, or Joe's family, who were also at the table. Over a decade later, I'm not quite sure why. Having brought Nadeem to that table and not left in that moment of clear personal degradation remains a powerful regret. When I think of how well trained we all are to betray ourselves and each other, to accept the violence directed at Brown and Black people in America, I think of that moment, of finishing that meal, and saying thank you for it.

Southern Macon County was home to several slavers before the Civil War and maintained an armed "patroller" unit meant to capture and terrorize the enslaved. Still, the county had been divided in its support for the Confederacy, and Confederate fury at local unionists was slow to die. That fury against unionists returning from military service to the mostly rural state found expression in the creation of the Ku Klux Klan in Pulaski, Tennessee, and a similar terrorist group within Macon County, perhaps successors of the original patrollers, called Night Riders. Once established, the Night Riders attacked Union soldiers, but soon found Black residents to be easier targets, especially given their limited economic and political power.

About a quarter of wartime Macon's 1,049 Black residents, the vast majority of whom were formerly enslaved, had already left the county in search of paid work in the immediate aftermath of the war. Many of those who remained worked as day laborers, sharecroppers, and servants, although some owned farms and businesses. In short order, the state legislature created poll taxes and literacy tests to prevent them from voting.

That had been the status quo for nearly fifty years when, in 1911, a White man in a community four miles west of Macon's county seat found his elderly White neighbor, Frank Baker, dead in the Bakers' pigpen on a June day. Other neighbors and the sheriff in Lafayette quickly concluded, without evidence, that a Black man named Dave Winston, who worked locally as a day laborer, had killed him. Though they asserted that Winston's motive was to rob Baker, Baker's widow was found at home undisturbed. Nonetheless, the sheriff arrested Winston, and upon his release a few days later, a White mob of more than a dozen shot him thirteen times.

Night Riders in Lafayette turned Baker's death into a rallying cry, calling for the expulsion of all the Black residents of Macon County. That summer, they expelled all twenty-six of the town of Lafayette's Black families, who lived in a small cluster of homes, throwing a half-stick of dynamite onto each of their front lawns, and threatening violence against any White neighbor who might dare to intervene. Each of the few homeowners among them was forced to sell at a fraction of their home's value, and all left behind what they could not quickly pack. The Night Riders targeted Dave Winston's relatives just outside of Lafayette next, maiming his brother, who was forced to flee with his family. Between 1905 and 1920, the several modest Black schools in the county, including trade schools, were burned to the ground. Another third of Macon County's Black residents would be chased out before 1920. By the 1970s, when Nora's parents and their back-to-the-land friends moved to Macon County, the Klan commonly held "roadblock fundraisers," stopping cars to greet their White neighbors and solicit donations, as casually as the Girl Scouts might sell cookies in front of a grocery store.

Today, Macon County is nearly 95 percent White, with the remaining 5 percent largely Hispanic. It is far Whiter than the state as a whole, which is about 75 percent White, and far more exclusive of Black people specifically, who make up more than 15 percent of the state's population. James Loewen, the nation's premier scholar of "sundown towns," describes Macon County as a "probable" example of the phenomenon in his book by that name.

Interestingly, Loewen describes sundown towns, places where Black people were prohibited from remaining overnight in a place, as most prevalent *outside* the American South, a response to the Great Migration. In the first several years after the Civil War, a period known as Reconstruction, the new federal Freedmen's Bureau created thousands of Black schools and three universities in the South, provided food and medical aid, built hospitals, negotiated labor contracts, and helped reunite families. Black people served in the U.S. House of Representatives from South Carolina, Florida, Georgia, Alabama, Mississippi, North Carolina, and Louisiana, and dozens more served in state legislatures throughout the South.

However, the liberatory advances of Reconstruction were deeply compromised from the beginning. After the war, President Johnson reversed the order of General William T. Sherman to seize Confederate landholdings in coastal Georgia and South Carolina and distribute "forty acres and a mule" to those formerly enslaved. Instead, Johnson gathered back the already-distributed land, on which forty thousand free Black people were already living, and returned it to Confederate landowners. His actions foretold a regressive post-Reconstruction era in which formerly enslaved Black southerners would be returned to poverty, brutality, and servitude. Southern states quickly passed Black Codes, which forced most Black southerners into similar working conditions as they had known during slavery. Those who resisted risked being forced to labor in convict leasing schemes that proliferated in the South, and being beaten, raped, or lynched. "Someone was lynched," Dr. Ibram X. Kendi writes in his landmark book *Stamped from the Beginning,* "on average, every four days from 1889 to 1929."

So, the Great Migration of six million free Black people out of the South beginning in 1916 was a forced migration, a flight away from decades of racist terrorism in the Jim Crow–era South and toward wartime industries and the jobs they promised in the North. Sundown towns were meant to turn them back, or at least away. They were sometimes created with one great attack or massacre on Black families and sometimes with several smaller, unrecorded instances of racial threats, harassment, or violence. These acts sometimes chased Black people out of smaller communities, towns, or entire counties. All-White places were often maintained by local ordinance, police and private harassment, threatening signs, and the public presence of racist terror organizations like the Ku Klux Klan. Federal, state, and local governments, Loewen writes, "openly favored White supremacy and helped to create and maintain all-White communities. So did most of our banks, realtors, and police chiefs." By 1908, the famed historian and journalist Ray Stannard Baker wrote about the reemerging color line in the North, where employers, public shops, and accommodations increasingly refused Black workers and customers. The discrimination and exclusion only worsened during the Great Depression, so that by 1930 the number of counties outside of the South without a single Black resident had doubled.

Illinois, where Nadeem and I had landed, was no exception. As we searched for the right place to settle, we were mostly ignorant of the impact of what Loewen calls "The Great Retreat," the era during which Black residents were systematically driven out of towns and counties throughout Illinois, as well as much of the Midwest, the West, and northern parts of the country. By 1970, 70 percent of Illinois towns with more than one thousand residents were entirely White. Out of 424 towns in our new home state, Loewen confirmed official racist policies in 145. One of these, a town in the southern part of the state called Villa Grove, was known for the ritual of sounding a whistle or a siren at six P.M. every evening, warning Black people present in the town that they needed to get out for the night. Loewen asserts that almost all the remaining towns in the state had also been sundown towns at some point, with policies and practices that kept Black residents out long after the policies stopped being explicitly or officially enforced.

In 1950, a man named Percy Julian tried to move to Oak Park, where Nadeem and I first went looking for a house. In response, White residents bombed and set fire to his home. Although Oak Park has not officially been a sundown town since the 1970s and is now sometimes called an integrated suburb, it retains the easily discernible color line that Nadeem and I tripped over along Austin Boulevard, which is the narrow boundary that separates it from the mostly Black neighboring town of Austin. In stark contrast to Oak Park, Austin has a poverty rate of well over 25 percent, and fewer than 25 percent of its residents have a high school education. Before 1930, Austin was an Irish and Italian middle-class neighborhood; by the late 1960s, it had become a food desert and undergone massive White flight, produced in part by realtors and lenders engaged in "blockbusting." Blockbusting is the practice that often precedes redlining. When Black people move into a mostly White neighborhood, realtors incite racist fear of the new Black neighbors, creating a sudden, community-wide panic sale and a large volume of business for the realtor. The former White residents of Austin moved farther out to communities like Glen Ellyn and Wheaton, Illinois, which remain disproportionately White compared to the rest of the state.

Cicero, closer to the city, was a notorious sundown town. In 1951, a Black Chicago bus driver named Harvey Clark was prevented from moving into a Cicero apartment by police. When he tried to move his family in a month later, having enlisted the legal support of the National Association for the Advancement of Colored People (NAACP), a White mob gathered across the street, much like the mob that would gather outside the Myerses' house in Levittown, Pennsylvania, six years later, yelling slurs and throwing stones through their windows.

When the family did not stay the night, the mob broke into the apartment, looting what they wanted and burning the rest in the courtyard outside. When a larger iteration of the mob swelled to 3,500 people the next night, the governor called in 450 National Guardsmen to stop the violence. In fact, the town of Cicero's history is a litany of racial violence, in which activists and ordinary Black citizens have been stoned, lynched, and terrorized to maintain its whiteness. In a twist that belies America's complexity, Cicero's White residents have not resisted the in-migration of Mexican Americans in the same way, although they may have ultimately left Cicero because of its changing demographics; today, Cicero is 80 percent Hispanic.

When Nadeem and I moved to Lombard, we were unwittingly buying into a town still recovering from several decades as a sundown town. In fact, all of DuPage County, in which both Naperville and Lombard, as well as Glen Ellyn and Wheaton, are located, was a sundown county, part of a ring of sundown suburbs around Chicago. While we lived in Illinois, we made several trips to Louisville, Kentucky, where Sylvia lived, and to which Nora and her family could easily drive. In traveling from DuPage County south through Indiana, Nadeem and I unknowingly left one sundown county to drive through dozens more sundown towns along the way, towns that used to have signs posted at their entries, warning N*****, DON'T LET THE SUN SET ON YOU HERE. Loewen has never yet failed to confirm an all-White Indiana town as a sundown town with an explicit law or a documented practice that made it so.

Upon discovering this, I spent some time looking up various towns I've lived or vacationed or worked in, finding several known sundown towns among them. Rehoboth Beach, Delaware, where Nadeem and I and our preschool-aged children would vacation when we moved to Yardley, had long banned Black residents, Jews, and so-called Moors, biracial people who probably looked a lot like Nadeem, my children, and perhaps even me. Beautiful Longboat Key, where I visited a friend after college graduation, still had not a single Black resident as of the 2010 Census. Eureka Springs, that vacation town I learned about when I lived in Arkansas, has remained overwhelmingly White, home to only thirteen Black, nine Hispanic, and twenty-six Asian people among its almost two thousand residents.

Nadeem and I now joke that you can tell how well you pass for White by how willing you are to live in or even explore its rural places, especially if your people aren't from there. This is also true of how welcome we feel in America's leisure spaces, its islands and beaches, and many of its suburbs, so often created in an era of racially restrictive covenants violently enforced by both state and private actors. The demographic map of our country shows communities of color overwhelmingly pressed into urban centers, with vast stretches of land, which is both capital and the basis for human subsistence, in the exclusive hands of White landowners. This is not accidental. Brown and Black people do not simply prefer cities to the country; we are not incapable of seeing the great benefit of having our wealth invested in the land. We've consistently been the targets of violent or discriminatory campaigns to prevent such investment. Simultaneously, we've been the targets of discriminatory government policy. Successful Japanese American farmers were dispossessed during World War II, Native land was allotted in such a way as to encourage its sale to non-Native buyers, and discrimination in government farm subsidies and systemic racism resulted in a 90 percent decrease in Black-owned farmland between 1910 and 2000, so that by 2017, only 1.4 percent of American farmers identified as Black.

Nor are urban enclaves safe havens for Brown and Black communities, as evidenced by the bombing of Osage Avenue in Philadelphia, the encroachment of Chinatown in Boston, and the many similar attacks on and campaigns against urban communities of color. Our narrow confinement is not a choice, but is instead the consequence of a widespread public and private alliance that has been in place for over a hundred years, policing Black and Brown people out of sundown towns and into the narrow margins and urban labor markets of America.

Nadeem and I were nesting in Lombard. The summer before Jahan was conceived, the first summer after we moved into the house in Lombard, we spent long hot evenings watching Urdu film marathons and sharing entire watermelons. We were exhausted from daily commutes into the city that took over an hour each way and involved a drive, a walk to the train platform, several stops, and then either a bus or, more often, a mile-long walk. But it was summer, and all of it felt so much lighter than it had through the brutally cold winter.

We had settled into a nearly one-hundred-year-old house set back from a main road. It would require massive renovation and might otherwise have drifted into foreclosure. It still had its original wood floors, though, and a spectacular sunroom in which the children, when we had them, would learn to roll over, and crawl, then walk, and, eventually, hold tiny dance parties. We found a skilled craftsman, who spoke only Polish and charged something we could just about afford, through one of my colleagues at the ABA. He took a hammer to the wall the day we closed and didn't stop until it was beautiful.

Lombard felt different from Glen Ellyn and Wheaton, each of which were nearly 90 percent White at the 2010 Census. Partly, it was because Lombard is significantly more diverse, and partly because our particular neighbors were welcoming. I'm sure that renovating the house back from foreclosure helped, but John and Nancy and Tana and Jason, the neighbors on our street, became friends, helping us to dig out of a massive snowbank at the bottom of our drive just months after our daughter was born, and lending me a car to pick up my daughter from preschool when I was locked out of the house. They were the sort of neighbors who come to a kid's birthday party in the backyard with some spare lawn chairs and then invite you to their own for a barbecue.

Still, sometimes Lombard felt like a town that was trying to stay White in a changing country. One winter early evening, after sundown, I was home with both our two-year-old and our baby. Nadeem drove to the nearest convenience store for something we were out of. It was at the center of town, just a few blocks away, extremely well lit, next to the commuter train that we both used to get to work each day. One or the other of us had been there a thousand times in the past thousand days, at least.

But Nadeem made the mistake of neglecting to turn on his headlights as he pulled out of the lot. He was immediately pulled over, within fifty feet of where he'd started. The officer came to his window and demanded, "What are you doing?" Nadeem, confused by the question and, in the puddle of a streetlamp, completely unaware that his headlights were off, replied, "What do you mean?" Despite my earlier warnings and all he'd gathered about policing in America, he did not call the officer "sir," because growing up in England, he had learned to expect officers to address citizens that way, not the other way around.

The officer was visibly pissed off at the question, or perhaps at Nadeem's failure to immediately apologize, or his accent, and Nadeem was shaken. The officer kept him there for a good while, badgering him about why he was out, why his lights were off, where he was going, and where he lived, although our nearby home address was listed plainly on his driver's license and his registration. Eventually, having found nothing to hold him on, the officer ticketed Nadeem and let him go—for driving less than fifty feet at dusk without his lights on, on his way out of a well-lit parking lot. Nadeem had been gone far longer than he should have been and I was worried. So when he walked in the door and told me all of this, I was overwhelmed with relief. I was glad for the ticket because it meant he made it home alive, and that I didn't spend the rest of the night—or the rest of my life— alone with the babies, wondering what had happened to the love of my life.

⸻

We were unprepared for Chicago: the endless commute times, the long, hard cold season, the near absence of Black faces on specific sides of specific lines. Philadelphia is nearly half Black, and the more integrated Germantown/Mount Airy neighborhoods, especially, reflected that. But in Chicago, as in Little Rock, the color lines were stark, dividing races by neighborhood and by seating charts in the workplace.

At CLS in Philadelphia, where I'd worked alongside other attorneys of color and where people of color filled nearly every level in the organizational hierarchy, there was an active organizational mission to identify and utilize the strengths of employees. Within a week of being hired there, a colleague pulled out a map of Philadelphia and asked about the immigrant communities I was connected to, where in the city they lived, and what their legal needs might be. Every staff person self-assessed their language capacity in languages other than English to strengthen the organization's emergency response to clients unable to communicate effectively in English. Race and identity were on the table and in the room, by which I mean to say, there was space to raise them and to value them in our work.

By contrast, the color line at the ABA was relentless, and no one ever discussed it. I arrived on the nineteenth floor to a private office with a view of the Chicago River. All but two of the three or four dozen private offices with windows that formed the outer ring of the floor were occupied by White men and women. I was one of the two South Asian women in the private offices. Every other person of color worked in a cubicle toward the windowless center of the floor. When I arrived, the ABA followed a tired pattern of nonprofit leadership organization: White men in charge of most of the sections, as well as organizational leadership and of the board of directors, with several White women reporting to them, and a mix of younger White women and Brown and Black people (of all ages) beneath them in the hierarchy. With ten years of extensive legal experience in which I managed a full caseload, led policy campaigns, and ran an offsite clinic, I was one of three women of color reporting to Deb, a White woman leading a narrow project on legal aid funding within our section; my colleagues, a meeting planner and an administrative assistant, were Black women.

In my role as staff counsel, which required a law degree, I found myself being micromanaged in the task of downloading and printing out hard copies of legal funding rules from every state to file in a physical cabinet, even though the year was 2009 and the internet was ubiquitous, certainly accessible to anyone who might be looking for their state legal services funding regulations. Another of my tasks was to take minutes at very expensive meetings in nice locations to which predominantly White lawyers and judges would be flown, with daily spending allowances, to discuss issues on an agenda already hammered out and developed by staff. And finally, I was to edit articles written for a newsletter. I was bored out of my skull, spending hours at a time watching the window cleaners on adjacent skyscrapers, and for this I was paid nearly twice what I'd earned as a practicing lawyer.

Through soul-sucking meetings, I endured Deb doling out the smallest slivers of autonomy to me while curtailing my Black colleagues' prerogative to even pick the color of paper on which to photocopy a flyer. I had unknowingly been incorporated into a toxic and egregiously racist power structure. In retrospect, I see that I probably had just enough status to call Deb out on how she maintained—even policed—our autonomy. I should have challenged or even ridiculed her for stepping in to tell my colleague what color paper she was required to use on a project. I still regret that I didn't.

Social cliques seemed no better at the ABA: Black staff and White staff remained segregated, even over lunch. Within months of isolated existence at the ABA, and after several failing attempts to bridge racial divides, I introduced myself to the one other South Asian woman with an office on my floor, finding that by some strange coincidence she was a long-lost family friend. Yasmeen and I had both changed our names when we were married, and I only understood who she was from a photograph of her sister in her office.

Contemplating her name change, I realized that my own married name, which I'd had for just over a year, raced me. My maiden name had never identified me clearly as Muslim, and had often allowed me to pass as White. Meanwhile Ali-Khan made me identifiably Muslim and so, in the American paradigm of whiteness, definitively not

White. I was open to that change; I was tired of the internal chaos and suffering caused by passing in a racist society, and I remembered how liberating wearing hijab had been in that it solved that problem entirely. I knew by then that the confusion and isolation of not always being claimed by my people in public spaces, as well as the pain and degradation of being racialized according to the whims of the people around me, had taken a deep toll. I also knew that asserting my identity would take a different toll.

Yasmeen and I lunched together from the time we met, although we belonged to two entirely different units and had no work in common. The precision of segregation at the ABA was just as it had been in Little Rock, Arkansas, and the relief of our colleagues that we had finally put ourselves in our correct place was an almost audible sigh. And although everyone was very polite and collegial, no one else was really vying for our social attentions in the organization. All of the social rules, all of the awkward silences, all of the invitations within that organization operated to quietly guard the color lines.

In the end, the rigid racial hierarchy and, on our team, Deb's dogged micromanagement would drive me out. A little over a year into working at the ABA, the head of our section, Kevin, gave me some actual responsibility related to my experience. The single member of color on our division's advisory team, an Asian man, had taken an interest in language access. There was an internal, competitive process at the ABA to fund special projects, and I was tasked with writing a grant for the creation of ABA standards for language access in the courts. For the rest of the division, it seemed to be a throwaway project. For me, the project was interesting and exciting, requiring the sort of systems planning and language access expertise I brought from CLS. I was left alone to develop a plan for the project itself and then write the grant. To Kevin's evident shock, the elaborate grant I wrote won us funding for the project, and he celebrated by congratulating me and asking me to take the lead on making the project a reality.

Within hours, Deb stopped me in the hall, having heard from

Kevin that I was being delegated some real responsibility—and with it a path to demonstrate my expertise and leadership capacity.

"I heard the good news!" she said. "Congratulations!"

"Thanks, I'm really excited about it."

And then the other shoe dropped. "Listen, I spoke to Kevin just now and explained to him that you couldn't really take that project on and keep up your other responsibilities. I just think it's going to be too much. Kevin agreed to give it to someone else."

I clenched my teeth and invited Deb into my office. I was deeply aware of the privilege that I *had* an office to invite her into and didn't have to have the rest of our conversation in the hallway. In addition, I had already interviewed at a legal services organization where I'd be doing work similar to what I'd done at CLS, with an office just a few miles from my house. They had already made an offer. Deb just made the decision easy, and Kevin said nothing to challenge her or to protect my professional interests. Deb's extreme approach was perhaps unique to her, but its effect was to maintain the power structure of a decidedly White organization, led by White people, with no advancement opportunities for qualified, intelligent, capable Black and Brown people. Unsurprisingly, more than ten years later, the ABA seems much the same. While the old guard, including both Kevin and Deb, have retired, the rigid racial hierarchy of the organization appears to have remained.

If the Midwest is the heartland of the country, then Chicago is the heart of the heartland. It was the last of the cities that I would examine, and I had a sense of what I might find. As a legal services lawyer, I'd already seen that there were groups of people who were generationally, categorically excluded from America's prosperity and promise; I knew the conditions of my clients' lives. I'd already understood that the rhetorical promises of equality and liberty were not a reality, that they were, at best, aspirational. But my research in eleven of my twelve towns had uncovered a relentlessness, a consistency of law, policy, and government and private action with a remarkably unified purpose and outcome: to create or maintain a White America. It suggested that America's liberatory, visionary rhetoric is not and has never been representative of White America's aspiration for itself. There is a rhetorical America—an America of equality and freedom, liberty, and justice—and then there is an actual America, in which the forced migrations of Brown and Black people are a consistent, integral feature of an ongoing American colonial project.

Chicago's rigid color lines were brutally drawn in the summer of 1919, also known as "the Red Summer." The weeks-long battle that would forever define Chicago's racial landscape are often traced back to a single, casual assault that killed a seventeen-year-old Black boy named Eugene Williams while he swam at the beach with his friends. Williams and four of his friends were swimming at the Twenty-fifth Street beach on Lake Michigan one hot Sunday, July 27, 1919, four blocks from the exclusively White beach at Twenty-ninth Street. The boys were using a homemade wooden raft, trying to paddle to a post in the direction of, but still one thousand feet away from, the Twenty-ninth Street beach. Somewhere near Twenty-sixth Street, the boys floated past what one twenty-three-year-old White man named George Stauber deemed to be the invisible line of racial segregation in the water.

Stauber began to throw stones at the boys, though from seventy-five feet away, so that the boys remained unpanicked. This fact alone is, in hindsight, stunning: A grown White man attempting to stone Black teenagers as they swam was, in 1919 Chicago, not an event that provoked much of a reaction, on the beach or in the water. The boys believed they could dodge the stones, but one landed, hitting Eugene Williams with enough force that he lost hold of the raft. His friend, John Harris, saw Williams and grabbed him. Quickly pulled under by Williams's grasp, he got free to save himself and swam back to the

Black beach to find a lifeguard. Eugene Williams drowned before help arrived and his body was recovered by divers half an hour later.

A Black police officer named William Middleton accompanied Williams's friends to the Twenty-ninth Street beach to search for Stauber, and though they were able to identify him there, a White police officer named Daniel Callahan refused to arrest him and prevented Middleton from making the arrest. Unsatisfied, the boys returned to the Twenty-fifth Street beach, where beachgoers were still upset from a rock fight earlier that day, beginning when a group of Black beachgoers had entered at Twenty-ninth Street beach, intending to swim there. When Officer Callahan arrested a Black man for that earlier unrest, but not Stauber in the death of Eugene Williams, it unleashed the anguish of Black beachgoers. Their sense of injustice first inspired a hail of rocks directed at an arriving police wagon, and eventually a gunfight leading to events that would be remembered as a citywide "race riot."

Chicago's weeks of acute violence in 1919 were actually the culmination of several months of escalating violent assaults against Black people in the city. By 1919, a small group of Black elites had coalesced in America. The number of Black landowners in the South had grown against all odds, and a new vanguard of Black artists and thinkers had given rise to the Harlem Renaissance, as well as a broader movement that championed "the New Negro" in the North. In addition, still segregated and under-resourced Black schools had nonetheless given rise to newly literate generations, and dozens of Black newspapers and publications had begun to create a national Black consciousness. The effects of this progress were staggering; there were new platforms in the country for Black voices and visible examples of Black creativity and prosperity, as well as new opportunities for organized and effective Black resistance to America's deep-seated racial animus.

Black Chicago, like so many other Black communities at the turn of the twentieth century, was made up of the hopeful and the persistent. It was made up of those solicited by northern factories for work, people who had traveled far and spent what they had to avail themselves of the free exercise of citizenship and mobility. It was also made up of some of the 370,000 returning World War I veterans from at least two well-regarded Black regiments. In the spring of 1917, the United States had joined allies in World War I and initiated a selective draft. White southerners who continued to resist emancipation opposed the arming and training of Black Americans, feeling that these measures would permanently compromise White supremacy.

The War Department had created Services of Supply (SOS) to maintain segregation and exploit Black labor while keeping arms out of Black men's hands. SOS were labor battalions, seen as an inferior posting for inferior people, in which Black enlistees were abused or even hired out to private contractors as they could expect to be under convict leasing schemes in the post–Civil War South. But Black leaders had spent the years after the Civil War organizing. They pressed for Black engagement in combat, believing that combat service would be the death knell of widespread discrimination against Black Americans. Combat was dangerous, but for Black enlistees so was SOS service and that came without training or status. Eventually, two segregated Black combat units were created, the Ninety-second and Ninety-third divisions. To curb the racism of White troops against Black troops, the Ninety-third Division was forced to serve under French command for the duration of the war, and the Ninety-second Division's commanding officer issued a bulletin ordering his men to accept racist treatment. Still, both divisions performed well in combat and the Ninety-third distinguished themselves in battle. Black women had played their part in the war effort as well, rolling bandages for the Red Cross and providing literacy classes to those Black enlistees who could not yet read or write.

The result of Black service in combat was as many White Americans had long feared: An unprecedented number of Black Americans had guns and knew how to use them effectively. Both during and after the war, Black leaders and veterans publicly espoused the view that postwar America ought to be different, ought to repay loyalty with loyalty and to show Black Americans the respect they had earned. But rising expectations built on service were instead met with diminished accommodations and opportunities in cities like Chicago. In the years before the Red Summer, from 1910 to 1920, nearly half a million Black people had migrated north. In that period, the Black population in Chicago increased by 150 percent, to 109,000 people. Black Chicagoans readily found jobs in wartime factories and stockyards. With more than two million White servicemen returning from the war in the spring of 1919, competition for work became fierce, and the demand for better wages high. Some large employers used this as an opportunity to replace Black workers with White workers, and others exploited racial barriers to unions by hiring Black workers to replace White strikers. Because of this, Black workers were then broadly seen as strikebreakers when in truth they were frequently left out of labor organizing campaigns or were barred from joining White unions.

At the same time, 90 percent of Black Chicagoans were concentrated in Chicago's "Black Belt," a narrow strip of neighborhoods stretching from Twelfth to Thirty-ninth streets north and south, and from Wentworth Street to Lake Michigan in the east. There, they lived in overcrowded, run-down housing, often lacking electricity and heat. Supply was limited by racially restrictive rental and lending practices, as well as violent resistance from the mostly Irish neighborhoods to the west, so Black residents were forced to pay 15 to 25 percent more than their White neighbors. As demand for more and better housing grew, White neighbors to the south and to the east also began to organize violent attacks to keep Black Americans out.

In the months before Eugene Williams was killed, the offices of Black and White realtors who did not steer customers along established lines of segregation to constrain the overflowing Black neighborhoods were bombed, as were the homes of twenty-five Black residents who lived beyond Thirty-ninth Street to the south. One bomb blew out the windows and ceilings of an apartment building and killed a six-year-old girl. Surrounding White neighborhoods guarded the segregation boundaries with gangs made up partly of the sons and relatives of police officers in local precincts and euphemistically called "athletic clubs," beating Black neighbors they saw as trespassers.

While Black Chicagoans were increasingly frustrated in their claims to finally be fully American, many White Chicagoans remained determined to make things as they were before World War I, with clear racial hierarchies that persisted despite emancipation, citizenship, Reconstruction, and Black military service. When the Eighth Illinois National Guard, part of the all-Black Ninety-third Division, marched with White soldiers upon their return in February 1919, they were cheered by Chicagoans. But several months later, after Eugene Williams was stoned to death in the water for being a Black child rather than a White one *and nothing was done about it,* the city erupted. In the immediate aftermath of the Twenty-ninth Street beach gunfight, outraged Black Chicagoans attacked several White men—two were taken from a streetcar and beaten, and some were pulled from cars and beaten or stabbed. The "athletic club" gangs that had violently policed the borders of the Black Belt were quick to respond and began attacking Black people, beating, stabbing, and shooting those they encountered. The following day, Black workers were assaulted in or near their jobs at the stockyard and beaten on streetcars. Police failed to intervene, perhaps because of their associations with the gangs. By the middle of the week, the gangs were targeting Black homes, breaking windows, firing shots, looting, and setting fires.

Returning Black soldiers identified the violence as an attempt to maintain a racist social order. One asserted, "The Germans weren't the enemy—the enemy was right here at home." On Monday evening, a week after Eugene Williams's death, Black veterans and civilians stood armed on the streets of the Black Belt. Chicago's police force had been sent to patrol the same area, and when rumors circulated that a Black woman had been killed and that further attacks on the Black Belt's residents were imminent, a gunfight ensued in which four men, three Black and one White, were killed. When White veterans were not prevented from joining with White gangs in racist violence, and neither group was stopped by the police force, more Black Chicagoans felt justified in taking up arms and coordinating their defense.

In the following week, 38 people died (23 Black and 15 White), 537 people were injured (about twice as many Black people as White people), and about 1,000 Black families had lost their homes. A governor's commission would release a report three years later, finding that racial inequality was a leading cause of the summer's violence. Red Summer violence echoed all around the country from late 1918 through 1919, sometimes sparked by casual White brutality as in Chicago, sometimes sparked by the studied resistance of an individual Black person to official or unofficial Black codes. Major clashes took place in Washington, D.C.; Charleston, South Carolina; Longview, Texas; Bisbee, Arizona; Knoxville, Tennessee; Omaha, Nebraska; Gary, Indiana; Phillips County, Arkansas; and Bogalusa, Louisiana, with dozens more clashes in other cities. Nevertheless, the hopefulness and persistence of Black America would continue to grow, coalescing into Black Power and civil rights movements, and reawakening movements for Native rights and autonomy by the 1950s. As in the Red Summer, the White backlash to those movements would be fierce, so that even the seemingly mundane institutions and functions of our society—school funding, highway construction, energy production—would be weaponized to cement the segregation and marginalization of Black and Brown people into the landscape.

Both of my children were born in or near Chicago; both spent their first few years of soft, sleepy babyhood and had nearly all of their toddler firsts in our house in Lombard with its wide front porch and enormous windows. There was a lot of sweetness for Nadeem and me in that time with them, memories of nighttime feedings in the rocker, of drooly grins, of family visits, of each of their first wobbly steps. But they had both arrived prematurely, after an earlier ectopic pregnancy. Our experiences in a healthcare system that was at best indifferent and at worst incompetent left us feeling desperately vulnerable. This sense of precarity would drive our desire to return to friends and family in the Delaware Valley.

When I was pregnant for the first time, I was elated to have my first ultrasound. We had been in our Chicago jobs for only six months, and the ultrasound was scheduled for an inconvenient time, on a Friday early in the morning before a long weekend. Nadeem had a full day and so I went alone, planning to rush to work just after. When I arrived, I was told that the doctor was unavailable but that the technician would forward her the report. At least I'd have the printouts, I thought, to share with Nadeem. But the technician didn't turn any monitors around, print any images for me, or say anything at all, really, except that the doctor would be in touch. As it turned out, what she'd seen on the monitors suggested a life-threatening ectopic pregnancy. But I was sent home for the long weekend with no explanation of what an ectopic pregnancy was, of its risks, or what to watch for.

Two days later, I was bleeding heavily and cramping, concerned and then more certain I was miscarrying. We were just about to move to the house on Lombard, and when I stopped packing to lie down between boxes, Nadeem decided to override my protests and get me to the emergency room in Naperville. I was triaged immediately and given methotrexate and morphine for the pain and released within forty-eight hours. I had little idea of what to expect and returned to work, only to pass the ectopic tissue, tearfully, in the stall of a communal bathroom. My doctor's office had received a report from the emergency room but made no effort to follow up.

A year later, we were finished with the renovations in our house and I was pregnant with my daughter. I had, overnight, developed excruciating pain in my arms every time I lay down and then got back up again. I have a fairly high pain threshold, so when the pain left me distraught, something even the ectopic pregnancy had not done, Nadeem took me to the ER again. It was midsummer at about midnight, and we came into an empty ER with hoodies over our pajamas. I was visibly pregnant. The doctor, a young resident, took one look at us, noted that the complaint was only pain, and only in my arms, and then disappeared for three hours. When he finally came back it was to tell us that my blood test results looked fine, and since my pain had abated during the time I was there (I was sitting up), he didn't see anything else to do. No consult with maternity, no consult with an attending. I went home terrified to recline or to sleep, dreading the pain that would follow and concerned for the baby I was carrying. As the sun rose, I thought to call my midwifery practice, which diagnosed pregnancy-related carpal tunnel over the phone and prescribed effective treatment with a snug Ace bandage. When I wrote an angry letter to Elmhurst Hospital, signed with "JD," several weeks later, the director of emergency services apologized profusely, reprimanded the resident and returned my fifty-dollar copay.

I had managed the carpal tunnel and was otherwise in good health when I inexplicably went into labor at thirty-one weeks. I arrived at the nearby community hospital, where the midwife on call, a new hire who I'd never worked with or even seen before, met me. Nadeem and I were, again, in pajamas. Nadeem had come home from work feeling like he was getting a cold, and I called him out of bed when my water broke. We hadn't been thinking about looking our best. I explained in the hall outside an exam room to the midwife that I thought I was in labor. She replied, coldly, "I hope not. For your sake." And then she went quiet.

Later, after I was transferred to a downtown hospital, I was given medications to accelerate my daughter's lung development and to delay labor. But by dawn, I was ready to push. When Nadeem asked what we should do, the nurse who was in the room with us looked up, shrugged, and walked out. It was an hour before the end of the shift. No one was interested in delivering my baby. Someone must have looked at a monitor somewhere and seen me on my hands and knees and Nadeem standing ready to catch the baby, who, at that gestational age, would be in need of immediate medical assessment and care. Several moments later, the labor and delivery team rushed in. One of them, a resident who was heavily pregnant herself, stayed past her shift to deliver Jahan, who weighed just under three pounds.

Nadeem and I advocated to have Jahan transferred to a level-three NICU much nearer our home, a couple of weeks later, once she was big enough to make the journey. Within days of arriving, she had had several blood draws; doctors were concerned about her elevated temperature. I was spending every day with her on my chest, in between milk-pumping sessions, and I knew that she was maintaining a steady, normal temperature. I told both nurses assigned to her as well as the doctor on duty, but they continued to look for an infection that didn't exist. Finally, I pulled aside the one with the least abrasive ego, pressed down my sense of urgency, and spoke deferentially.

"Doctor, can I ask you something?"

"Sure."

"You've seen me here, holding Jahan every day. It feels to me like she's holding her body temperature steady. Do you think *the incubator itself* could be elevating her body temperature?"

He thought about it for a moment. "We generally don't see infants hold their temperature at her body weight."

"There's no other evidence of infection. Can we try taking her out of a heated environment and see if it helps?"

He thought again, and then made eye contact for a bit. "We can try it, but if her temperature becomes unsteady, she'll have to go back into an incubator."

"Yes! Yes, definitely. Okay." Her temperature was no longer elevated outside the heated environment. She was regulating it herself. They stopped poking and prodding her.

By the time I was pregnant with Isa, I had gone several more rounds with healthcare providers and I was better able to make choices that would help us avoid being at the mercy of the healthcare system. Still, Isa was also born early and I spent two weeks in a different NICU with him before coming home to Jahan and Nadeem. More than once in the previous few years, we'd wondered if our repeated awful experiences with healthcare providers were the result of racism, reactions to us as a young Brown couple in hoodies, me pregnant or with a baby in my arms. There was no way to know, but the incompetence and sometimes disdain we'd experienced left us feeling that we needed to be vigilant and it was exhausting. Tired already from all the fighting we'd needed to do, we were now home with two babies under three. Premature babies extend the period of infancy, and the sleeplessness and fragility that come with it. Nadeem and I had begun to feel, acutely, the need for a village in which we could feel nourished and safe, so we could help our children to feel that way, too.

After Jahan turned three and Isa turned one, I'd returned to work part-time. By some miracle we found a babysitter that felt like family, a woman about my age, with an older daughter of her own. I couldn't have afforded to pay her what she was worth. I'd been right when I left CLS that after paying for childcare, I barely made anything at all. Going back to work was my effort to be engaged, to build more of a life for us in the Midwest. But not long after I returned, Nadeem began looking for jobs back East. Our village was in the Delaware Valley.

While we were busy having babies, in the decade after the 9/11 attacks, the machine of war was still raging. The United States continued bombing seven different countries, all with Muslim majorities, in North Africa, the Middle East, and South Asia. Almost eight hundred Muslim men and boys had passed through or were still being held at Guantanamo Bay, twenty-two of them minors, mostly without charge. In addition to Guantanamo, reports of extrajudicial CIA "black sites" in other countries had surfaced.

Government officials were still careful to distinguish between those terrible foreign Muslim men and *American* Muslims in their speeches and press statements, saying that *we* were not the enemy. But we had begun to understand that our Americanness could not protect us; our Muslimness made us suspect, even at home. Many of us had a passport stamp from travel abroad, maybe to Iran or Pakistan; many of us stopped to pray five times a day, even when we were in public; many of us had common, identifiably Muslim names. We knew that any of these might be seen as damning evidence that we, too, were terrorists. This wasn't a figment of our collective imagination. My earlier work with CAIR has been rewarded with my appearance on a list of "Prominent Islamists" on the website of Daniel Pipes's Middle East Forum, which bills itself as a right-wing "think tank." The material on the site says Islamists "seek hegemonic control via a worldwide caliphate that applies strict Islamic law in full." Pretty lofty ambitions for a union legal services lawyer sharing stale cookies and coffee while explaining my faith to community organizations and adult education classes. It is also, of course, entirely and dangerously false in a broadly anti-Muslim environment.

Pipes is plainly anti-Muslim, but was not a marginalized figure because of it. He's now seventy-two, but his career helped shape the modern American sensibility that Muslims are, like Native and Black and Asian people before them, savage. He was, through projects like his "Islamist Watch," firing warning shots at those of us who worked in community leadership. These attacks on us, whether they are rhetorical or physical, drive enormous fear and anxiety in Muslim communities. Even though we are an incredibly diverse multiracial group, and not recognized as a protected racial class under American law, we are now a racialized group. To be Muslim is to be non-White, regardless of your skin color or national origin. And to be non-White in America has always been dangerous.

Through CAIR and the National Association of Muslim Lawyers (NAML), I knew about men being detained at length in transit or persecuted for community activism and human rights work. In one example, Dr. Sami Al-Arian, a professor of computer engineering at the University of South Florida, was swept up in what has been called "a post 9/11 campaign by the US government to criminalize aid and support to Palestinians." At the time, Dr. Al-Arian was a prominent Palestinian civil rights activist, with both a career and a family. In 2003, the U.S. Department of Justice targeted him, along with eight other men, bringing seventeen terrorism-related charges alleging material support for a specific organization that worked in the Israeli-occupied Palestinian territories. Dr. Al-Arian was kept in solitary confinement for nearly all of the three years of his pre-trial detention, subjected to strip searches and denied visitation with family. Amnesty International said that the conditions of his incarceration were "gratuitously punitive."

At trial, a jury acquitted Dr. Al-Arian of the most serious charges against him and deadlocked on the rest of the charges. Al-Arian accepted a guilty plea on one of the remaining charges. Instead of being released, Al-Arian was then subjected to civil and criminal contempt charges for his refusal to participate in the unrelated prosecution of Muslim-run charities based in Virginia, serving an additional eighteen months in prison and several more years under house arrest. In 2014, when the U.S. government dropped all charges against Al-Arian, he was nonetheless forced into exile under the terms of his original plea deal. Widely understood to have been the subject of racist profiling and persecution in the United States, Dr. Al-Arian is now the director of the Center for Islam and Global Affairs and a public affairs professor at Istanbul Sabahattin Zaim University in Turkey. Looking on at the relentless persecution and criminalization of their community leaders, a great many Muslim Americans were too frightened to send money to family members overseas, to donate to their own mosques, or to give charitably to humanitarian organizations for fear that any Muslim-sounding recipient of funds would be construed as a terrorist threat by a racist and xenophobic American public.

Nadeem was, during our time in Illinois, consistently being pulled aside for extra questioning when he flew for work. He'd get home and report conversations like this with TSA agents:

"Nadeem Ali-Khan?"

"Yes."

"Where are you from?"

"The UK; you're holding my passport."

"No, but where are your parents from?"

"The UK; they also hold UK passports."

"What languages do you speak?"

"French, English, Urdu, Hindi . . . and a little—"

"Okay, wait. Uuuur, can you spell that?"

Or he'd report that the flight attendant read out a list of Black and Brown passenger names before takeoff and made them put their hands up to identify themselves. Or that he'd been monitored by security at the gate and patted down before boarding.

One fall, I'd spent a week home with the babies while Nadeem traveled to the UK for work. I was relieved to get a call from him, saying he had landed in Chicago. And then I grew worried when I didn't hear from him again for two and a half long hours. He had been stuck in a room without permission to use a phone and hadn't known why he was being held or how long it might be. When the security official there questioned him about his position at UKTI at the British consulate, he had been inept:

"So, you're a con-sul-ate?"

"No, I'm a vice consul. At the British consulate; it's a place, like an embassy."

"So you're an ambassador?"

He smothered a sigh. The sigh is always silent if you want to make it home.

CONCLUSION: HOME

Every empire, however, tells itself and the world that it is un-like all other empires, that its mission is not to plunder and control but to educate and liberate.

—Edward Said

O ur return to the Delaware Valley, to family and friends and home, was as comforting and expansive as we had hoped. But as the 2016 election cycle ramped up and I witnessed the rising terror in Muslim communities and in other Black and Brown communities, even that sense of home was not enough. After all that had happened with Aaron and after 9/11, all that I'd seen in America's poorest neighborhoods and shiny glass skyscrapers, and all that I'd come to expect from healthcare providers and kindergarten teachers, I'd had enough of pretending to find good where there was something deeply, insidiously wrong. People—even my own parents—wondered how we could leave America. After my daughter was asked to hide that she was Muslim at kindergarten, how could we stay? Given the choice, how could we allow our kids to live with such a terrible erasure, all the while being forced to consume and repeat a narrative of freedom and justice for all, each morning? How could we do that to them and expect them to survive it? I had no honest answer to that question, so at the first opportunity, we left.

In America, we are taught history as if in daguerreotype photography, a kind of early black-and-white portraiture, capturing a precise likeness but of a limited and usually manicured subject. We are taught out of order, out of context, rarely with local or personal connections, and generally so partially that what we learn is mythology rather than history. The purpose of that mythology is to establish and maintain the narrative of a good country. For example, when we are introduced to the portrait of Thomas Jefferson, we are taught a certain catechism about him: He was a founding father, the author of the Declaration of Independence, the third of our nation's presidents between John Adams and James Madison, a property owner, and, when he was secretary of state, champion of Eli Whitney's cotton gin.

We are not taught, though, that he was a serial rapist of the child Sally Hemings, whom he enslaved all the way into her adulthood, keeping her in a basement room that adjoined his own bedroom, and eventually having at least six children by her, but never freeing her. We are not taught that Sally was the half sister of Jefferson's wife, Martha, and that she was the daughter of a woman who had been enslaved, and raped, by Martha's father.

We are not taught that Jefferson was born to wealth as the son of a Virginia planter and slaver and then accumulated exponentially more wealth when he married another Virginia slaver's daughter, thereby inheriting more people whom he also enslaved. We are not taught that his interest in the Louisiana Purchase was rooted in his intention to profit by breeding Black children for sale to the new cotton and sugar plantations there. We are not taught how, as president of the United States, he aimed to abolish the transatlantic slave trade only because it promised to increase his wealth in the domestic slave trade.

We are not taught that Jefferson was committed to the forced removal of Native peoples from east of the Mississippi. Or that he established a national policy of trapping Native people in debt in order to rob them of vast quantities of land, but also to eliminate any challenge they might pose to colonial rule. Or that his vision for Native peoples comprised only two options: complete assimilation to White (or post-European) American identity and culture, or extermination.

We are not, in effect, *taught anything about who Jefferson actually was, what drove him personally and politically, or the America he envisioned and helped create.* This erasure is critical because Jefferson's ideas about and aspirations for the nation haunt us today. Even without a clear understanding of where these ideas originated, and the European colonialism in which they are rooted, Americans continue to be divided by them. Some of us argue that "all men are created equal, that they are endowed by their Creator with certain unalienable Rights, that among these are Life, Liberty and the pursuit of Happiness" ought to be interpreted to allow killing and starving Native peoples to take their land, while pressing Black and Brown people to the margins. A great many Americans assert this tradition with pride, carry the Confederate flag to declare it, call it their heritage. Some of them declared it by storming the U.S. Capitol on January 6, 2021, at the urging of President Trump, whose politics in office were arguably not so far removed from those of the actual, historic Jefferson.

Others of us have instead reimagined the Declaration of Independence in accordance with evolving ideas about human rights and about who, in fact, constitutes humanity. We have been changed and challenged as the world grows smaller; we have migrated willingly and unwillingly, interacting with people outside of our racial, religious, and cultural identities, crossing traditional lines of socioeconomic class and gender to understand each other in new ways. Our ideals, premised on a belief in shared humanity across race, fly in the face of the settler colonial project in which Jefferson and his fellow founders were engaged. The 2007 United Nations Declaration on the Rights of Indigenous Peoples affirms, for example, "Indigenous peoples have the right to self-determination. By virtue of that right they freely determine their political status and freely pursue their economic, social and cultural development." In 1948, the United States and most of the world's nations signed the Universal Declaration of

Human Rights, Article 4 of which establishes, "No one shall be held in slavery or servitude; slavery and the slave trade shall be prohibited in all their forms." We have long since understood the need, given these principles, for land and monetary reparations, economic and social restitution, fact-finding, public truth telling, and reconciliation for historic and ongoing gross violations of human rights.

Why do we then fail to overcome and reform the regressive, ardently racist elements in our society? Why is America, as a nation, so slow to remedy egregious racial disparities that persist today, much less provide reparations for what has been and what continues to be done, particularly to Black and Native communities? Why would a wealthy country, *a good country,* fail to address the most basic of injustices: the lack of clean drinking water, environmental racism, police brutality, mass incarceration? Certainly the resources exist. Yet these injustices are left without repair and each modern administration introduces a slew of regressive policies that further the disproportional incarceration, impoverishment, and dispossession of Black and Brown communities: the war on drugs, mandatory minimum sentencing guidelines, draconian welfare-to-work policies that offer no avenue out of minimum wage jobs. We act surprised every time, especially when these policies are enacted by supposedly liberal administrations, but the failure to right the wrongs and to legislate for remediation of past injustices should not surprise us. The injustices are design features, not flaws of the settler colonial state. *We find versions of them in the legal and social landscape of every one of the world's settler colonial societies.*

When I went to law school, I understood myself to be an outsider in my country of birth, but I thought I could do something, learn something, contribute something to justify my place within America. By going to law school, and especially by practicing law, I committed myself to what I saw as a good, if imperfect, set of institutions through which a better country could be made. I believed that the American Revolution had already happened, and that improvement depended on the daily march through ordinary bureaucracies, civil challenges in courts of law, forms filled and taxes filed. And certainly, there is much to be said for stability and for modern liberal democracy.

When Nadeem and I decided to come to Canada, and not to go to Pakistan, we talked about the relentless suffering that postcolonial *instability* has caused in Pakistan, where even upper-middle-class homes are often surrounded by solid concrete walls topped with barbed wire and protected by the military, while the rest of the population lives in abject poverty. We *want* stability because we understand what instability means for quality of life—how instability makes getting clean drinking water, going to school, and holding a job so much less possible.

But in writing this book, in understanding the human cost of America's settler colonial vision, I've begun to see that stability of my country's institutions as they exist today *is also* the stability of American racism. It is the stability of the "average White person standard" established by the Supreme Court in 1923 to adjudicate every American's race and status, and it is the stability of the settler colonial project. This project *requires* the ongoing subjugation of Native peoples and the maintenance of an indebted Black and Brown working class. In other words, a commitment to the stability of America without an active repudiation of the settler colonial project *is also* a commitment to the *persistent destabilization* of Black and Brown communities. As we have seen, this destabilization is not subjective or imagined, but has been a continuous, linear pursuit of paired state and private interests. It is a cornerstone of the entire American project; the subjugation of Black and Brown Americans is *the* seminal and persistent policy objective of the settler colonial state. It has been written into our law, enforced by our police, reinforced in our schools, cemented into the landscape. And it is enforced by Americans who behave *as if they are still embattled settlers,* grabbing up resources as though they are pursuing manifest destiny, or from free Black people run out of town, or in the name of urban renewal from torched Chinatowns, or from interned Japanese families. In fact, we reenact the enrichment of White settlers through the confiscation of land and resources from Black and Brown

Americans, both the living and the dead in their cemeteries, regularly in this country. American political and thought leaders often encourage a sense of scarcity which results in the ongoing degradation of Black and Brown Americans and a broad cultural impoverishment, stymieing both democratic and egalitarian progress as well as celebrations of culture and faith, lest these threaten the apartheid we have so carefully built up.

Our society is still premised, like Israeli, South African, Australian, Canadian, and New Zealand societies have been (though each of these is distinct in other ways), on the obliteration and erasure of the primary and most legitimate claims to the territory on which it lies. America's historical and economic achievements are largely based on the violent extraction of labor from a racially defined slave or servant class, and on underpaid, marginalized immigrant workers.

And yet, I might never have thought to leave America if my parents hadn't already made the migration from Pakistan one generation before. Maybe my parents' migration made our smaller one, only an eight-hour drive away, though across an international border, easier for me to imagine. Maybe their migration instilled a sense of agency in me, a sense that I should, if I could, free myself from a government that would so deeply betray my community, my family, and my children. Maybe my aspirations stood on the shoulders of theirs, so that where they had hoped for peace and stability, I hoped to live a life engaged with, not in spite of, my own government.

I wonder also if I'd have thought to leave if I hadn't first experienced such profound gaslighting and betrayal as I had with Aaron, and then of Muslims in the wake of 9/11. I was primed by these personal and political experiences to recognize that the most convenient or prevalent telling of a story is often *not* what is true or real or good. Instead, that telling is often designed to elide or justify terrible things. In the months before my divorce, the prevailing view of each element of my diverse community was that my marriage must be saved at all costs, despite Aaron's habit of stalking young women and girls. The prevailing view of my countrymen after 9/11 was that more than a billion Muslims worldwide were collectively culpable for the egregious acts of nineteen men. Most seemed to feel that America's attacks on sovereign nations were justifiable, even when stories about Iraq's weapons of mass destruction proved false, even when other credible reasons for our military occupation of Iraq and Afghanistan surfaced. By the time Trump began his presidential campaign in 2015, I had spent a decade and a half trying to unpack these contradictions. What was it that made the people in each of these examples so willing to excuse the excesses of the powerful and the privileged, while accepting the persistent suffering or collective punishment of others?

In 2015, my mind and heart immediately rebelled against the particularly twisted nature of Trump's rhetoric and character. The headlines said he was something new, an "outsider" and a "successful businessman" who would "drain the swamp." He campaigned as a populist and an unrepentant racist. The smaller, quieter headlines warned of nepotism, cronyism, misogyny, and a litany of unscrupulous business practices. Before he was ever elected, Trump drove a surge in hate crimes against Brown and Black Americans, and against Jews and Muslims. Maybe it was my hard-won, heartfelt faith that made Trumpism so impossible to endure.

But when we moved our family to Canada in 2017, it wasn't Trump that finally drove me out. It was that I had confronted the mythology of American exceptionalism, of America as a good, if imperfect, country. I knew that Trump was only a middle chapter in a long American tradition. Our country, my home, *is* exceptionally good—at so radically misrepresenting its own story that it can avoid making amends, doing what's right, and striving for better. It is exceptionally good at manufacturing euphemisms like "manifest destiny," "free enterprise," and "urban renewal" to make some of our greatest failings seem like victories. It is exceptionally good at segregating its people, adjudicating each new group as either civilized or savage, to maintain a White and a Christian national identity. *America wastes its great potential in these central pursuits.*

By 2017, I had spent more than fifteen years watching Muslims be increasingly designated as disposable from the average White person vantage point. As a newly practicing lawyer, I had watched the law remade in spurious ways to legitimate indefinite detention and extraordinary rendition of Muslim men, as well as the military and corporate colonization of Iraq. Doing outreach for CAIR-Philadelphia, I interacted with hundreds, if not thousands, of conservative and liberal Americans alike who made plain to me that they felt Muslims were to be mistrusted, were deserving of abuse, or were appropriate subjects for stereotyping and generalizing. In so many daily, small ways, I had already begun to understand the trajectory of how Muslimness was being reconstructed in America.

Once the Republican campaign rhetoric of the 2016 presidential election took open aim at Muslim Americans and our civil liberties, I understood that the state had begun to define us as people no longer entitled to the benefit of the doubt. We had become a people on the other side of the line from whiteness, so that we would always be presumptively criminalized. And I realized that this reality was not the one my parents would ever have knowingly chosen for their grandchildren. Not only was my country not willing to face and reform its settler colonial premise, but it was doubling down, reinforcing the walls of White Christian America so that they came together more tightly, more precisely. That imaginary line of whiteness, which had been expanded to include Poles and Italians and Hungarians, *would not* be pushed into the Muslim Middle East and South Asia.

It is unacceptable that any American's security in their country is dependent on whether they land on the White side of the line. It is unacceptable that this is and has always been the premise of America. To escape our horrific history, America must acknowledge and remake its design as an embattled settler colonial state, for which the primary goal is to maintain power at the expense of its colonized peoples, as well as Black and immigrant workforce populations.

Our daughter is healthy now. After three long years of misdiagnosis and ineffective treatment in America, nine months after moving to Canada we had both a diagnosis and an effective treatment plan. Now, if you met her, you'd never guess how seriously and chronically ill she'd been. This is what Nadeem and I remind ourselves when we wonder at what we've done, transplanting ourselves here, away from home. Then we soothe ourselves with observations about the society around us. We don't worry that the children will face anti-Muslim bigotry at school anymore. Despite the anti-Muslim sentiment that washes over the border and simmers in some pockets of Canadian society, we've been able to count on surprising diversity and inclusion in the curriculum and the social life of their public schools here. There are far fewer guns and there is far less money in politics. Canadians *are,* actually, as *nice* as everyone makes them out to be. Our neighborhood is extraordinarily diverse by race, by religion, and even by income level in ways you wouldn't think possible if you've grown up with the redlining and segregation so pervasive in America.

One early fall day in 2017, just after we'd moved to Ontario, Nadeem and I took the kids to a nearby cul-de-sac to practice on their scooters. We chose the place for the grassy circle at its center, thinking the kids would enjoy going round and round and collapsing in the grass when they got tired. That little spot happened to be surrounded by houses easily worth two million dollars, something that became clear only when we got to the end of the street. This is a feature of Canadian housing developments so rare in American ones—mixed-income housing, so that the same development, and often the same street, contains apartments, condos, townhomes, duplexes, and detached homes of various values.

What happened next was even more unusual from an American perspective. I was slightly nervous about being in this posh cul-de-sac, a Brown family who didn't live there with their kids laughing and playing. I had assumed, without realizing it, that a wealthy environment would also be an exclusively and perhaps aggressively White one. That assumption would have served me well in every American town I can think of. But this time, as individuals and entire families came and went from several houses on the circle, my assumptions fell apart. First it was an Asian family, then a South Asian man, then a

mixed-race family, then a Black family. My immediate, American response was "What are they doing in this neighborhood?" In my experience, rich neighborhoods with lots of Black and Brown people in
them don't happen without extraordinary persistence and planning
in the United States. Brown and Black wealth and unity is not part of
the design, so these things have to be organized and strategized. For the
first time, I was experiencing what was possible—what was *inevitable*—
in a multicultural community where redlining and racially restrictive
covenants had not been widespread. I saw that my children were there
with me and realized that they could have lives in which they experienced diverse, mixed-income spaces and their right to be anywhere in
them as completely normal.

In our years here, my two elementary-aged children have both had
lengthy public school lessons on what settler colonialism is, the injustices of colonization, and the First Nations lives, cultures, and livelihoods that were lost in the making of Canada. They've visited the
sites of re-created First Nations villages, and hear modern First Nations viewpoints at school, on the radio, and in the news directly from
First Nations thought leaders and public officials. Their school events
and announcements include land acknowledgments, and hallways are
lined with maps showing what was guaranteed to First Nations peoples in treaties. They understand themselves as settlers who owe a debt
to First Nations, Metis, and Inuit people in Canada, because it is the
valid cost of the bounty we share in as immigrants. This has not made
them sad, scared, or small. On the contrary, they show up at the dinner table bursting to tell what they think is fair or unfair, considering
how to treat others as they would like to be treated, asking questions
and making assertions about how best to right wrongs and grow from
mistakes. Learning Canada's history has given them an early introduction to the complexity of being human and of having a place in a history that began long before they were born and will continue long
after they are gone. This sense of belonging to something larger than
themselves seems to give them purpose and hope. It gives them pride,
but it also gives them humility. We hope this portends a newer, better

society, one where everyone recognizes the need for a substantial re-distribution of land and resources.

The Canadian government has begun the work of reconciliation in notable ways. Canada's Department of Justice website contains this remarkable acknowledgment and commitment:

> The Government recognizes that Indigenous self-government and laws are critical to Canada's future, and that Indigenous perspectives and rights must be incorporated in all aspects of this relationship. In doing so, we will continue the *process of decolonization* [emphasis added] and hasten the end of its legacy wherever it remains in our laws and policies . . .

> The implementation of the *United Nations Declaration on the Rights of Indigenous Peoples* requires transformative change in the Government's relationship with Indigenous peoples. The UN Declaration is a statement of the collective and individual rights that are necessary for the survival, dignity, and well-being of Indigenous peoples around the world, and the Government must take an active role in enabling these rights to be exercised.

This statement of the intention to "decolonize" and the need for an active transformation of the government's relationship with Indigenous people is an elemental shift on the path to creating an equitable, pluralistic society. It openly acknowledges that the modern nation of Canada originated in racist ideology and apartheid and then commits to the project of reversing the structures that maintain those founding principles and ongoing practices.

Canada is not there yet. It has its own long path before it as a society with a history quite similar to America's of destroying and displacing its indigenous peoples, as well as a shorter and less pronounced history of slavery. As I write, the Canadian government has deployed both police and military forces to Wet'suwet'en First Nation territory to ensure the construction of the Coastal GasLink pipeline across it.

Advocates of the pipeline argue the sovereignty, and supremacy, of Canada's parliament and legislation over First Nations—of the supremacy of the settler colonial state. Words are not enough. Canada's progress thus far is the result of tremendous activism and organizing by First Nations, Metis, and Inuit communities and their allies, and sometimes good-faith allyship by non-Native private and government actors. For example, Canada's Truth and Reconciliation Commission was created and funded under a settlement agreement reached when victims of residential schools sued churches and the Canadian government. The agreement included financial compensation for children who attended these facilities, and a separate compensation process for those who allege to have suffered specific forms of abuse within them. The Canadian Truth and Reconciliation Commission has completed a seven-year-long set of studies that document the extent and the abuses of Canada's 139 federally run residential schools, resulting in nearly a dozen published reports analyzing the roles of perpetrators, the impact on victims, and the potential for reconciliation. The history and significance of the residential school era, more than 160 years long, has made its way beyond the official reports onto public radio platforms and into the Canadian consciousness. The commission has issued ninety-four calls to action, and has become a permanent working endeavor, housed at the University of Manitoba.

The Canadian government now maintains public documentation of its progress on all ninety-four calls to action on its website. As a result of these calls to action, the Canadian government completed an independent national inquiry on Missing and Murdered Indigenous Women and Girls. More recently, it has made international headlines for providing funding and for supporting the work of identifying the graves of children who died at residential facilities. Three facilities' grounds have been examined as of July 2021, and approximately 1,100 graves identified already; there are yet 136 more sites to search. It is hard to convey the effect this has had on the Canadian national consciousness. The recovery of these children's remains is discussed in the news, on the radio, and in schools. On Canada's National Day for

Truth and Reconciliation, suburban children write the slogan EVERY CHILD MATTERS in chalk on their steps in my neighborhood. Schoolchildren, teachers, people out and about in my neighborhood wear orange shirts with the same poignant phrase. These sights are not at all uncommon.

In September 2021, a tenth grader named Skyla Hart got reprimanded in her Winnipeg public school for refusing to stand for the national anthem, in honor of her Cree and Ojibwe ancestors. Her school offers language instruction in English, French, German, Spanish, Ukrainian, and Japanese, but not in any of Canada's Aboriginal languages. The two national languages of Canada are French and English; most labels and signs throughout the country are bilingual in these two languages, but labels and signs in Aboriginal languages are absent or scarce. When interviewed, Hart's mother explained, "When a child walks into a school and sees nothing that reflects them, it's like . . . looking into a mirror and seeing no reflection." I know that to be true from my own experience. Hart's statement points further down the road of reconciliation for settler colonial societies, toward, for example, the path New Zealand has taken.

Since the 1980s, New Zealand has pursued a national policy of "biculturalism," a national commitment to combined Maori and settler European culture. This path attempts to turn the old, standard colonial paradigm, with its policies of segregation and forced assimilation, on its head, so that both Maori and settler cultures can be recognized as standard, each accommodating the other. Ideally, identities and traditions might evolve toward and alongside each other, but neither would dominate, and neither would be lost or destroyed. This policy comes closer to modern human rights standards, which recognize and repudiate the trauma of forced assimilation and colonization. It has the potential to become the foundation for a credible, cohesive culture. A similar path may still be available to America, but it requires telling the facts of our history as they have occurred. It requires exploring what drove and still drives the forced migrations of Black and Brown people to the edges of our society, and acknowledging the brutality many of us face there. *It requires the hard work of reversing these things, destabilizing them, taking down walls and highways and designing for pluralism and integration. It requires land and monetary reparations to Black and Native people, especially.* Because America needs a common story—a true one—that we are not ashamed to tell, one that we are not frantically trying to erase. A culture premised on *the eradication* of its own story is not a culture at all.

Maybe, one day, I'll stop dreaming of a house on the Delaware River and maybe I'll stop dreaming of a home in the Indus Valley. What claim do I have to those places, after all? It doesn't seem to matter how complicated it is, or even whether I can ever return, the *homeness* of these places remain in me. For me, home in the Delaware Valley is made up of so many moments, so many small ways I fell in love over time with a turn in the road or the breadth of an oak leaf, every small thing bound in layers of memory. It wasn't all good, and some of it was painful, but that complexity required me to reckon with my whole self, through the eyes of people who have seen me at my best and at my worst. I suspect Reverend Gomes, who presided at Memorial Church when I was in Boston, knew about this complexity when he preached the story of the Prodigal Son with an exhortation to all of us to "Go home!" He was telling us to make a pilgrimage to that place, wherever it might be, to reckon with and make amends for whatever we might find there. I imagine that as a gay Black man in America, Reverend Gomes appreciated that to go home at all, and certainly to live there in peace and security, is a privilege. That for so many Black and Brown people who find themselves in the ongoing colonial project of America, it is a dream not yet realized.

ACKNOWLEDGMENTS

I am indebted to the many people who contributed to this book and to my story as it is rendered here. Mark Warren and Chayenne Skeete at Penguin Random House spent countless hours spelunking in my memories, helping me find the deeply personal threads that hold it all together. Somehow, given all the demands on Mark's time, he made every conversation intimate, important, as rambling as it needed to be to find the heart of the matter. Mark, you asked all the right questions of me, and I know that it is because you do the great work of asking the questions in your own life. Thank you so much for guiding me through and sharing in this process. It has been transformative and I'm so glad grace chased you into my path. What a gift to be able to work with such talented, insightful, *lovely* people as you both are.

I want to thank those that contributed to *A Good Country* at Random House: legal counsel Yuki Hirose, production editor Ada Yonenaka, copy editor Alison Kerr Miller, cover designer Robin Schiff, and interior designer Elizabeth Rendfleisch. You all have done brilliant work on this project.

I had no idea in 2015 that I was writing a post that would become this book. It would not have had it not been for the people who dropped into my life to propel me forward. Priscilla Warner, co-author of *The Faith Club* and author of *Learning to Breathe,* reached out after having read that post and introduced me to Leslie Meredith, who represented me first at Mary Evans Inc., and now at Dystel, Goderich & Bourret. Leslie helped steward this project from an idea to a proposal, carving and framing and challenging me as I learned what a project of this size would require. Without you both, this could never have happened. Thank you will never be enough.

I owe a special debt of creativity and diligence to Michelle Fogiel for developing the website and cover concept for this book.

Dr. Kate McDowell and Nora Edwards, this book is as much a testament to your friendship and generosity as anything; I am forever indebted to you for these years of countless drafts, comments, edits, consultations, and conversations about the state of the country, the world, and our hearts and spirits. I love you and am so grateful for you, every day, all the time. Several dear friends and family members read partial drafts, commented, and provided the mental health support required to face this material every day: Amy Andre, Brandi Askin, Sylvia Benito, Maggie Cino, Kerry Lobel, Nadeem Memon, and Asma T. Uddin. Thank you, my writers-in-arms, Jennifer Lunden and Jen Dornan-Fish. You both have been sudden, dear friends of the best kind, willing to read drafts as well as talk me through the maze that is publishing, and the anxiety that is bringing a finished book to the world. Dr. Kameelah Mu'min Rashad, your response to paper clips as a liberal protest was the sharp edge that began to tear open the narrative for me. I only regret that it took so very long, despite all that I saw around me.

Suzanne Pharr and Lynn Frost, thank you for letting me walk with you and break bread with you all day long in Little Rock. I am humbled to call you friends. Acadia Roher and Dr. Whit Barringer, thank you for pointing me in all of the right directions, for feeding me, for all of your work to record and continue the tradition of justice, equity, and community in Little Rock. Thank you, Dr. Uzi Baram, for being my host, my teacher, and ultimately my friend in this project. Fellow legal services warrior and mentor, Cyndi Mark, thank you for fielding my not-yet-refined questions about Boston's Chinatown and the many layers of history behind its modern struggles. Katherine Mallory, thanks for setting me up to talk to Steve Meacham, who was also so generous about fielding my open-ended, exploratory questions about Boston's history. Professor Andrew Leong and Lydia Lowe, thank you for making time to tell me about your scholarship and activism on and in Boston's Chinatown, making real to me streets I hadn't seen for twenty years.

Professor Linn Washington, thank you for a lifetime of journalism on the most important issues of our time. I'm grateful that you could make time to speak with me about your coverage of MOVE and Philadelphia. Professors David Love and Sarah Katz, your willingness to share contacts and your network with me made this work possible; I'm really humbled to be working alongside friends like you. Thanks to Professor Jason Osder, director of *Let the Fire Burn,* for letting me pick your brain, especially right up against the holidays. Leo Demski, thank you for being willing to have a wandering conversation with an old friend that unexpectedly led to my interest in the town of Truckee, California, and the anti-Chinese pogroms. And thank you for hunting down those articles in the middle of a pandemic. I sincerely hope that one day we can break bread.

Holly T. Bird, Dr. Jon Conway, and George Stonefish, thank you for speaking with me about your work in service to Native communities; it is an inspiration and a light. Kate Hawke and Mark Sorensen, thank you for allowing me to present some of the story of your lifelong work and commitment to the Diné. Rachel Tso and Camille Manybeads Tso, Eileen and Rinko Shimasaki, thank you for entrusting me with some of your family's precious oral history and your own journeys. Kimiko Marr, thank you for connecting me to Eileen and to Rinko, and for your profound work hosting pilgrimages back to the sites of the camps. Judy Matsuoka, it was a pleasure to work alongside you and an even greater pleasure to find you again. I am humbled by your willingness to let me tell part of your family's story. Lauren Swann, thank you for keeping the memory of Concord Park and its vision alive, and for being willing to share them with me. I am also indebted to the late Sam Snipes of Morrisville, and his family in the lower Delaware Valley. I spoke to Sam only shortly before he passed and I am so grateful that he and his family were so generous with that precious time. I won't ever forget it.

I want to thank my favorite research librarian, Mitch Silverman, for answering all of my most ridiculous questions about how to find things without always having an academic library at hand. You always fielded my questions about citations and statutes with grace and insight. I also want to thank the brilliant reference staff at Princeton University Library, particularly the Special Collections staff, as well as the staff at the Butler Center for Arkansas Studies in Little Rock, at Ca' d'Zan Museum, and at the Pennsylvania Historical Society. Mary Helen Dellinger at the Manassas Museum contributed the letter and story of Malinda Robinson, without which that remarkable portrait of what was lost would have been left to the readers' imagination. Mary Ellyn Kunz at Pennsbury Manor generously shared her and her colleagues' most recent research on the history of the enslaved at Pennsbury.

Thanks to Dave and Emily Goldberg, Tahija Vikalo, Yasser and Mariam Mahmud, and Jessica DeRose for your early encouragement; you have no idea how important it has been. And thank you, Menjit Dhillon, for your willingness to walk with me, listen to me ramble, and let me become more friend than neighbor while I obsessed over each new research topic. Thanks to Dr. Jennifer Carnahan, Nureed Saeed, Asha Ramachandran, Leslie Morgan, Cheryl Zalenski, Atiya Aftab, Greg Williams, Mitchell Gomez, and John Waters for helping check my memory on the details and answering my oddly specific questions. Thanks to Mohamed Ismail Hussein Ali at Waraqa for acting as my translation consultant for the verses of the Qur'an that appear in this text. English translations have yet to catch up with modern English gender pronouns and I hope to have correctly conveyed the meaning of the original Arabic here. Any mistakes are mine alone. Thanks, Cynthia Harrington Ficenec, for asking me how you could help all those years ago, inspiring that first post that became this whole project, and thank you, Rabea Murtaza, for making time to think through titles with me.

I'm blessed by the love and encouragement of my parents, Nazir and Shahnaz, who have taken such care of us despite the trials of migration and continue to be our rock on this shore. Nadeem, Shazi, Aisha, and Ameera, I'm grateful for your love, and Nadeem, thank you for offering fact checks and edits in the first chapters, as well as your memories.

Without the brilliant support, edits of a million drafts, constant reading, and loving partnership of my best friend and husband, (also named) Nadeem, I would have stopped before I started. This final, full manuscript is what it is because you marked it up. You are this book's true patron and my biggest champion. Everything is because I come home to you. Despite our children's often loud presence in these pandemic stay-at-home days, the two of them always want to know what I'm studying, what I'm writing, and when there will be an elementary or middle grade version for them. For Jahan and Isa, I will always work for better.

In memory of my dear friend Justin Willie.
May he be at rest in the arms of the Beloved.

NOTES

Sources upon which this book relies include original interviews, historical documents such as letters, recorded speeches and papers, deeds and maps available in research libraries, historical society and museum collections, news articles, case law, statutes, census data, and countless academic journal articles, books, and theses. For ease of use, the full endnotes, along with related photos and other materials, appear online at SofiaAlikhan.com.

In writing my personal experiences, I have relied on memory and wherever possible, consultations with others who appear or were present. So many of these moments were mine alone, or alongside people who are not available to consult. In these passages, I have tried to recount truthfully what happened from my own perspective, with a focus on how that affected me, not what others meant or felt. There were certainly moments or scenes for which I could not definitively recall the order of events or the words that were said, and I have done my best to render them as accurately as possible, focusing on the meaning conveyed and how it moved the larger story forward.

Writing about race and identity is tricky because, in the era of European colonization and White supremacy, our very language, even the names we use for our own dispossession, tend to minimize the harm done to us.

In this text, I avoid the use of "internment" where it tends to minimize or obscure incarceration in concentration camps. I also struggle with the use of the term "residential schools," a euphemism for the incarceration, family separation, and abuse enacted on hundreds of thousands of Native children for about 150 years from 1819. I have not yet seen an alternative term used to refer to these institutions in the United States or in Canada, so I use the generic "facilities" in several places. Black and Brown people have been disproportionately deprived of their liberty in America, whether by mass incarceration, in concentration camps, in "residential schools," on reservations, or in racially segregated institutions and housing. Wherever this history is told, one should consider how the brutality of that experience is being sanitized by nomenclature.

I avoid the use of "ethnic cleansing," even though it is the phrase most often used to mean racist forced migration, because it suggests White supremacist notions of "cleaning up" or "cleaning out" Black and Brown people from an area or institution. We are not dirty, and our elimination and dispossession is not cleansing. If anything, these things belie the soiled state of White supremacist thought and history. In a few places, I instead use the term *genocide* to refer to the history of removing Native peoples, in the Delaware Valley and in America in general. The historic record supports both the intention and the elements of the act of genocide as it is defined in international law, and other historians have argued these claims in depth elsewhere.

I sometimes use "deportation" in place of "removal," or try to describe the specific methods of forced migration, which are often themselves brutal. I also reclaim the word *colonial* in its full pejorative context, in an attempt to strip away the new American usage of the term, in which it means "quaint" or "historic."

I avoid using epithets wherever they are not absolutely necessary to describe racist thought because of the painful and damaging effect their gratuitous use may have on readers; when it is unavoidable and not part of a quotation from another source, I use the convention of a first letter and asterisks to signify an epithet.

I use the terms *Black* and *Brown* to describe people of color. This is an imperfect choice. I prefer the use of BIPOC for its emphasis, in the American racial landscape, on Black and Native people as the targets of original and monumental dispossession and brutality. I hope it is clear from the narrative itself that the weight Black and Native communities carry in the struggle against American White supremacy is overwhelming, and that all of us who came after owe these groups, especially, both reparation and solidarity for what has been taken from them for generations. But BIPOC felt inaccessible to readers unfamiliar with the term, and the persistent use of an acronym felt like it disrupted the narrative. I also avoided the use of *African-, Asian-* and *Native-American,* for example, because those terms can make for clumsy writing, but also because the pathology of racism remains so plainly obsessed with the shade of one's skin, which is different from one's geographical origins. I do use the terms *Black* and *Native* to designate these groups separately from other Brown people when writing about them specifically.

I use *Native* with the understanding *Indigenous* and *Aboriginal* are not terms that Native communities in the United States use widely and *First Nations* has specific legal implications in Canada. I use the names that Native peoples use for themselves whenever possible, because the meanings embedded in the names assigned to them by the government or settlers are often pejorative, and because the right to name and identify oneself is fundamental. I have done my best to ascertain and confirm correct usage of these names and offer my deepest apologies if I have made any errors or missteps in this or in any of the above choices.

I have used actual names whenever possible, but when individual people have voiced concerns about security or where individuals appear at some length and I have not gotten their consent, I have purposely obscured their names and, sometimes, identifying details in the text. I also obscure the names of one or more organizations. It's been my aim to tell my story, not anyone else's, in a way that illuminates the persistent and evolving battle for a White America. I have done my best to preserve the privacy of people who may not want to be known through my telling.

The character of Aaron is a composite, as is the timeline I have created for him. He is not a true and accurate representation of any one real person. However, the composite character of Aaron and my interactions with him allow for a true and accurate representation of my own state of mind and experiences.

BIBLIOGRAPHY

For readers who would like more depth on broad subject areas covered, I am providing a bibliography of the several books and dissertations that helped frame my understandings here. For specific and thorough citations, please see the complete endnotes at SofiaAlikhan.com.

Ball, Eve, Nora Henn, and Lynda Sanchez, editors. *Indeh: An Apache Odyssey.* Normal: University of Oklahoma Press, 1988.

Bates, Daisy. *The Long Shadow of Little Rock: A Memoir.* Fayetteville: University of Arkansas Press, 1986.

Blackmon, Douglas A. *Slavery by Another Name: The Re-enslavement of Black Americans from the Civil War to World War II.* New York: Anchor Books, 2008.

Brown, Dee. *Bury My Heart at Wounded Knee: An Indian History of the American West.* New York: Henry Holt and Company, 1970.

Brown, Isaac Van Arsdale. *Biography of Robert Finley, of Basking Ridge, New Jersey.* Philadelphia: John W. Moore, 1857.

Cameron, Catherine, Paul Kelton, and Alan Swedlund. *Beyond Germs.* New Haven, Conn.: Yale University Press, 2012.

Carleton, James Henry. *To the People of New Mexico: This Paper Sets Forth Some of the Principal Reasons Why the Navajo Indians Have Been Located upon a Reservation at the Bosque Redondo.* Warsaw, Poland: Andesite Press, 2015.

Carley, Kenneth. *The Sioux Uprising of 1862*. St. Paul, Minn.: Minnesota Historical Society, 1961.

Chang, Gordon H., and Shelley Fisher Fishkin, editors. *The Chinese and the Iron Road: Building the Transcontinental Railroad*. Palo Alto, Calif.: Stanford University Press, 2019.

Chen, Thomas C. "Remaking Boston's Chinatown: Race, Place, and Community in the Postwar Metropolis." Thesis, Brown University, 2014.

Child, Brenda J. *Boarding School Seasons: American Indian Families, 1900–1940*. Lincoln: University of Nebraska, 1998.

Churchill, Ward. *From a Native Son: Selected Essays on Indigenism, 1985–1995*. Boston: South End Press, 1996.

Cooper, Helene. *Madame President: The Extraordinary Journey of Ellen Johnson*. New York: Simon & Schuster, 2017.

Du Bois, W.E.B. *The Philadelphia Negro*. Philadelphia: University of Pennsylvania, 1899.

Dunaway, Wilma A. *The African-American Family in Slavery and Emancipation*. Cambridge, UK: Cambridge University Press, 2003.

Fitzpatrick, Laurie. "'As Is His Right,' Seventeenth-Century Scandinavian Colonists as Agents of Empire in the Delaware Valley." Thesis, Temple University, 2018.

Gagnon, Gregory O. *Culture and Customs of the Sioux Indians*. Winnipeg, MB: Bison Books, 2012, p. 26.

Gammon, C. L. *The Macon County Race War*. CreateSpace Independent Publishing Platform, 2016.

Gigantino, James J. *The Ragged Road to Abolition: Slavery and Freedom in New Jersey, 1775–1865*. Philadelphia: University of Pennsylvania Press, 2015.

Glenn, E., et al., editors. *The Hopi Nation: Essays on Indigenous Art, Culture, History and Law*. Lincoln: University of Nebraska, 2008.

Hamalainen, Pekka. *Lakota America: A New History of Indigenous Power*. New Haven, Conn.: Yale University Press, 2019.

Harris, Dianne, editor. *Second Suburb: Levittown, Pennsylvania*. Pittsburgh: University of Pittsburgh Press, 2010.

Hawke, Ethan, and Greg Ruth. *Indeh: A Story of the Apache Wars*. New York: Grand Central Publishing, 2017.

Hill, Marc Lamont. *Nobody: Casualties of America's War on the Vulnerable, from Ferguson to Flint and Beyond*. New York: Atria Books, 2016.

Inniss, Lolita Buckner. *The Princeton Fugitive Slave: The Trials of James Collins Johnson*. New York: Fordham University Press, 2019.

Kendi, Ibram X. *Stamped from the Beginning: The Definitive History of Racist Ideas in America*. New York: Bold Type Books, 2016.

Lancaster, Jane F. *Removal Aftershock: The Seminoles' Struggles to Survive in the West, 1836–1866*. Knoxville: University of Tennessee Press, 1994.

Lawson, Michael L. *Reservoir and Reservation: The Oahe Dam and the Standing Rock Sioux*. Pierre: South Dakota State Historical Society, 1976.

Liu, Michael. *Forever Struggle: Activist Identity and Survival in Boston's Chinatown, 1880–2018*. Amherst: University of Massachusetts Press, 2020.

Loewen, James W. *Sundown Towns: A Hidden Dimension of American Racism*. New York: New Press, 2005.

Lopez, Ian Haney. *White by Law: The Legal Construction of Race*. New York: New York University Press, 2006.

Macy, Beth. *Truevine: Two Brothers, a Kidnapping and a Mother's Quest: A True Story of the Jim Crow South*. New York: Little, Brown, 2016.

Madley, Benjamin. *An American Genocide: The United States and the California Indian Catastrophe, 1846–1873*. The Lamar Series in Western History. New Haven, Conn.: Yale University Press, 2016.

Marsh, Dawn G. *A Lenape Among the Quakers: The Life of Hannah Freeman*. Lincoln: University of Nebraska Press, 2014.

Meyer, Stephen Grant. *As Long as They Don't Move in Next Door: Segregation and Racial Conflict in American Neighborhoods*. New York: Rowman & Littlefield Publishers, 2000.

Minderhout, David J., and Andrea T. Franz. *Invisible Indians: Native Americans in Pennsylvania*. Amherst, N.Y.: Cambria Press, 2008.

Oberg, Barbara B., editor. *Papers of Thomas Jefferson*. Princeton: Princeton University Press, 2013.

Ostler, Jeffrey. *The Lakotas and the Black Hills: The Struggle for Sacred Ground*. New York: Viking Books, 2012.

Pacifici, Robin Wagner. *Discourse and Destruction: The City of Philadelphia Versus MOVE*. Chicago: University of Chicago Press, 1994.

Papenfuse, Eric Robert. *The Evils of Necessity: Robert Goodloe Harper and the Moral Dilemma of Slavery*. Philadelphia: American Philosophical Society, 1997.

Penn, William. *The Political Writings of William Penn, Introduction and Annotations by Andrew R. Murphy.* Indianapolis, Ind.: Liberty Fund, 2002.

Pfaelzer, Jean. *Driven Out: The Forgotten War Against Chinese Americans.* New York: Random House, 2008.

Pumphrey, Darcy. "An Interstate Runs Through It: The Construction of Little Rock's Interstate 630 and the Fight to Stop It." Thesis, Utah State University, 2013.

Riggs, Thomas Lawrence. *Sunset to Sunset.* Pierre: South Dakota State Historical Society, 1997.

Roberts, David. *Once They Moved Like the Wind: Cochise, Geronimo, and the Apache Wars.* New York: Touchstone Press, 1993.

Rothstein, Richard. *The Color of Law: A Forgotten History of How Our Government Segregated America.* New York: Liveright Publishing, 2017.

Snipes, Samuel Moon. *The History of Falls Township.* Doylestown, Pa.: Bucks County Historical Society, 2001.

Soderlund, Jean. *Quakers and Slavery: A Divided Spirit.* Princeton: Princeton University Press, 1985.

Soennichsen, John. *The Chinese Exclusion Act of 1882.* Westport, Conn.: Greenwood Press, 2011.

Staudenraus, P. J. *The African Colonization Movement, 1816–1865.* New York: Columbia University Press, 1961.

Stebbins, G. B. *Facts and Opinions Touching the Real Origin, Character, and Influence of the American Colonization Society: Views of Wilburforce, Clarkson, and Others and Opinions of the Free People of Color of the United States.* Boston: John P. Jewett and Co., 1853.

Sublette, Ned and Constance. *The American Slave Coast: A History of the Slave Breeding Industry.* Chicago: Lawrence Hill Books, 2017.

Voyles, Traci Brynne. *Wastelanding: Legacies of Uranium Mining in Navajo Country.* Minneapolis: University of Minnesota Press, 2015.

Washington, Harriet A. *Medical Apartheid: The Dark History of Medical Experimentation on Black Americans from Colonial Times to the Present.* New York: Harlem Moon Broadway Books, 2007.

Wasserman, Adam. *A People's History of Florida, 1513–1876: How Africans, Seminoles, Women and Lower Class Whites Shaped the Sunshine State,* 4th edition. CreateSpace Independent Publishing Platform, 2009.

INDEX

ABOUT THE AUTHOR

Sofia Ali-Khan is a writer and an accomplished social justice lawyer. She became a national leader on the right to language access while also practicing in the areas of welfare law, Medicaid access, immigration, housing, and community economic development. She was a founding board member and activist with the Pennsylvania chapter of the Council on American-Islamic Relations in the years after 9/11. A second-generation Pakistani American born and raised in the United States, Ali-Khan now lives in Ontario, Canada, with her family.

ABOUT THE TYPE

This book was set in Bembo, a typeface based on an old-style Roman face that was used for Cardinal Pietro Bembo's tract *De Aetna* in 1495. Bembo was cut by Francesco Griffo (1450–1518) in the early sixteenth century for Italian Renaissance printer and publisher Aldus Manutius (1449–1515). The Lanston Monotype Company of Philadelphia brought the well-proportioned letterforms of Bembo to the United States in the 1930s.